Spanish Texas, 1519–1821

DONALD E. CHIPMAN

University of Texas Press
Austin

Copyright © 1992 by the University of Texas Press
All rights reserved
Printed in the United States of America
First edition, 1992

Requests for permission to reproduce material from this work should be sent to Permissions, University of Texas Press, Box 7819, Austin, TX 78713-7819.

∞ The paper used in this publication meets the minimum requirements of American National Standard for Information Sciences—Permanence of Paper for Printed Library Materials, ANSI Z39.48-1984.

Publication of this work has been made possible in part by a grant from the Program for Cultural Cooperation between Spain's Ministry of Culture and United States Universities.

Portions of chapter 2 were published previously in *Southwestern Historical Quarterly* 91 (October 1987): 127–148. Reprinted with the permission of the Texas State Historical Association.

LIBRARY OF CONGRESS CATALOGING-IN-PUBLICATION DATA

Chipman, Donald E.
    Spanish Texas, 1519–1821 / Donald E. Chipman. — 1st ed.
        p.   cm.
    Includes bibliographical references and index.
    ISBN 0-292-77656-X (alk. paper). — ISBN 0-292-77659-4 (pbk. : alk. paper)
        1. Texas—History—To 1846.   2. Spaniards—Texas—History.
    I. Title.
    F389.C44   1992
    976.4'02—dc20   92-6116
                                                                          CIP

For my sons, Zachary and Jason

Contents

ILLUSTRATIONS

Acknowledgments

IN THE FALL OF 1984, RANDOLPH B. ("MIKE") CAMPBELL, MY colleague at the University of North Texas, urged me to take an active role in writing entries on Spanish colonial Texas for the new *Handbook of Texas,* targeted for publication in the mid-1990s. It was a propitious suggestion. My involvement with the *Handbook* and special interest in Texas history grew steadily from that moment. Trained and educated more years ago than I like to remember by France V. Scholes at the University of New Mexico, I approached the early history of the Lone Star State from the perspective of a colonial Mexicanist, and I soon saw the need for a one-volume synthesis of the Spanish experience, which I hope to fulfill with this work. Initially, I wish to express appreciation to Mike for opening the vistas of Texas history; to the legacy of France Scholes for serving as my mentor and professional role model; and also to my students at North Texas for having refined my approach to history over one and a half generations of teaching.

Since 1984 I have received assistance and encouragement from many individuals and institutions. Remembering them and expressing my gratitude is one of the more pleasant parts of writing a book. Over the years, several colleagues in the Department of History at the University of North Texas have offered advice and constructive criticism. I am indebted to our history faculty seminar, NT-LASH (National Topics—Local and State History), especially to William H. Wilson, who "lashed" three of the chapters into better shape. Apart from NT-LASH, Randolph Campbell read every word of the manuscript, and I have profited enormously from his advice and sympathetic encouragement. I am grateful also to my department chairman, Robert S. La Forte, who has been invariably supportive of my work; to Betty S. Burch, administrative assistant in the Department of History, for assistance in copying computer disks and photocopying materials; and to student secretary Jamie Sue Robinson, who performed careful and much appreciated proofreading. Diana S. Campbell, senior secretary in the Dean's Office, College of Arts and Sciences, helped teach me the miracles of Macintosh Microsoft Word and optical scanning from Kaypro-generated hard copy. Typing, alas, was my responsibility.

In the spring of 1990, I received a Faculty Development Leave from the University of North Texas, which exempted me from classroom responsibilities and permitted research in Spain. I also received grants from the Faculty Research Committee to cover the expenses of airfare, map preparation, and photo duplication. Melody Kelly, Ken Lavender, and Martin Sarvis of the North Texas libraries have been invariably helpful, despite other demands on their time. Doris I. Chipman, also of the North Texas libraries, ably prepared the index.

Off campus I was assisted by a grant from the Ottis Lock Foundation, which helped underwrite the expenses of research at the Barker Texas History Center in Austin. In Spain, Doña Rosario Parra Cala of the Archivo General de Indias and Doña Esperanza Salán Paniagua of the Archivo Central y Biblioteca del Ministerio de Economía y Hacienda and their staffs provided courteous and vital assistance. Professor Joseph W. McKnight of the Southern Methodist University School of Law and Professor Emeritus Thomas N. Campbell of the Department of Anthropology at the University of Texas at Austin read parts of my manuscript relating, respectively, to the legacy of Spanish law and Texas Indians. As manuscript referees for the University of Texas Press, excellent suggestions for improvement of this work came from Donald C. Cutter, Professor Emeritus of the University of New Mexico and St. Mary's University, and David J. Weber, Robert and Nancy Dedman Professor of History at Southern Methodist University. Special appreciation is likewise extended to Theresa May, Carolyn Cates Wylie, and Nancy Warrington of the University of Texas Press and to my copy editor, Barbara Cummings.

My greatest debt is to my friend and former doctoral student, Dr. Harriett Denise Joseph of the University of Texas at Brownsville. Denise labored over each word and punctuation mark with the care and attention one reserves for special people in one's life. In doing so, I am afraid that Denise slighted her own work.

Those who have read parts or all of the manuscript have spared me a number of factual errors and challenged my interpretations. I, of course, accept full responsibility for the final product.

Introduction

SPAIN'S PRESENCE OFF THE TEXAS GULF COAST BEGAN WITH
the voyage of Alonso Alvarez de Pineda in 1519. Its direct influence over
significant parts of the present Lone Star State, sporadic until 1716,
lasted until 1821, when the flag of Castile and León was lowered for the
last time at San Antonio. At varying times, modern Texas was part of
four provinces within the vast kingdom of New Spain: the El Paso area
was under the jurisdiction of New Mexico; missions founded near the
confluence of the Río Conchos and Río Grande (La Junta de los Ríos)
were under Nueva Vizcaya; the coastal region from the Nueces River to
the Río Grande and thence upstream to Laredo fell under Nuevo Santander after 1749; and Tejas, initially known as the New Kingdom of the
Philippines, was briefly (1694–1715) under joint jurisdiction with Coahuila. All of these regions receive treatment in this work. Emphasis,
however, is on the area that formally constituted the Spanish province
of Tejas.

An adequate one-volume synthesis of the Spanish experience in Texas
and a treatment of Hispanic legacies enduring beyond 1821 does not
exist in any language. Furthermore, throughout the state, college and
university courses devoted to Texas history are typically structured as
one-semester surveys, with little attention directed to the Spanish colonial era. Apart from the University of Texas at Austin, where Texas history is divided into a three-semester sequence, no institution of higher
learning structures its courses in a manner that directs substantial attention to the Spanish period. In writing this book, I would like to help
challenge the misguided notion that the colonial period—aside from six
restored missions, one reconstructed presidio, and a few other old buildings—is a colorful but largely irrelevant chapter in Texas's past.

That there is a significant history of the Lone Star State beginning three
centuries before the coming of Anglo-Americans is an article of faith with

many contemporary scholars. Without their contributions, my work would not have been possible. I did not wish to devote ten or fifteen years to writing the history of Spanish Texas solely from manuscript materials. Fortunately, this was neither necessary nor advisable. Keeping in mind that historians, myself included, all too often fail to read what our colleagues have written, I set out to weave a blend of published works and selected archival materials into a readable, balanced, and accurate narrative of present-day Texas in the Spanish colonial era. If I have succeeded, this book will make an important contribution to the historiography of Texas. At some juncture my efforts will undoubtedly be superseded by a new one-volume synthesis. I do hope, however, that such a project is not launched immediately!

The published literature on colonial Texas, some good and some not so good, is quite extensive. Early volumes of the *Southwestern Historical Quarterly* and its ancestor, the *Quarterly of the Texas State Historical Association,* contain, for example, seminal articles by Herbert E. Bolton, William E. Dunn, and Charles W. Hackett. Not surprisingly, because of the archival grubbing that went into those works, they have stood the test of time. More recently, the contributions of scholars such as Félix D. Almaráz, Jr., Nettie Lee Benson, Odie Faulk, Jack Jackson, Elizabeth A. H. John, David J. Weber, and Robert S. Weddle made my task much easier. I am especially indebted to Weddle's books, written by the "dean" of Texas colonial historians. My use of archival materials in the text is intended to add vitality and authenticity to the narrative and to satisfy a conviction instilled in me by France V. Scholes that one should not attempt the writing of colonial history without dirtying one's hands on old paper.

It is common practice in an introduction to summarize the contents of the various chapters that follow, but I will depart from custom. Each chapter begins with a brief synopsis of the contents, and the narrative is arranged chronologically except for Chapters 1 and 12. After the era of La Salle in Texas, the subsequent history of the province receives treatment in segments of approximately fifteen to twenty years. Only in Chapters 3 and 4 will the reader find a substantial overlap of years under consideration.

The rendering of Spanish names in the text, appendixes, and bibliography deserves more than casual mention, especially to those not familiar with that language. In most instances, I have tried to use the most commonly recognized names in the English-speaking world. For example, Francisco Vázquez de Coronado was never referred to by his associates as Coronado. He was instead known to them as Francisco Vázquez, the latter part of his name being patronymic. Accuracy aside, herein he is often referred to as Coronado. On the other hand, it is not proper to shorten Alvar Núñez Cabeza de Vaca into Alvar Núñez because he preferred and consistently used the more prestigious matrilineal name of Cabeza de Vaca. Similarly, I have used Fernando for the first name of Cortés, rather than Hernán or Hernando, for that is how he spelled his own name.

Throughout the book, I have made a determined effort to be accurate but sensible in the placement of diacritical markings. On occasion it may appear that I have been inconsistent. For example, I have not used an acute accent mark on the final *a* in San Saba when the name refers to the river of the same name or the present county in Texas. This representation reflects a conscious attempt to be in agreement with contemporary Texas usage. On all other occasions, the spelling will be San Sabá. By contrast, Río Grande commonly bears no accent in English context. For reasons of consistency, such as a sentence containing both Río Sabinas and Río Grande, I have chosen to place an accent on the *i* on all occasions. It seems, however, pedantic to accent the *e* in Mexico, and I have not done so. On the other hand, Yucatán and Michoacán are accented. Some Spanish names such as Ruiz may or may not bear an accent. In those instances, I have endeavored to follow current scholarship in rendering those names.

Finally, I believe the history of Spanish Texas deserves far more attention than that traditionally accorded to it. By and large, the few thousand subjects of Spanish monarchs who made their lives in the province known as Tejas demonstrated extraordinary loyalty to king and cross. Cabeza de Vaca, my favorite Spaniard in Texas, displayed remarkable growth of character during an incredible ordeal that spanned nearly eight years. He entered Texas in 1528 with the pride and arrogance of a Spanish don. He departed having learned a fundamental truth. Stripped of all worldly trappings, traveling naked as the day he was born, he came to accept the brotherhood of man. Today, Texas is an Anglo-dominated state and is likely to remain that way in the future, but its history has been greatly enriched by Spaniards such as Cabeza de Vaca and by a Hispanic past that unfolds in the following pages.

ONE

Texas: The Land and the People

TO WALK THE BOUNDARIES OF MODERN TEXAS WOULD require a trek of more than 3,800 miles. Circumscribed would be a remarkably diverse land encompassing 267,338 square miles of rivers, beaches, plains, woodlands, basins, deserts, and mountains. The physical dimensions of contemporary Texas have led scholars such as D. W. Meinig to use the word "imperial" in describing the size and importance of the Lone Star State. Even when writing about only the eastern two-fifths of Texas, where black slavery thrived in the antebellum period, Randolph B. Campbell called that region *An Empire for Slavery*, for it equaled in size the combined states of Alabama and Mississippi.[1]

To be sure, Hispanic Texas as a physical unit comprised far less than the totality of the present state of Texas, but the province—known to the Spanish as Tejas or the New Kingdom of the Philippines—was nevertheless imperial in size. It lay north of the Medina River and east of its headwaters, extending into present Louisiana. However, throughout the three centuries that Spain laid claim to Texas, her soldiers, missionaries, settlers, and pathfinders traversed every major physiographic region of the modern state. In carrying out land and sea explorations, military campaigns, and missionary enterprises, Spaniards came into contact with the "first Texans," Native Americans who had hunted and farmed the land; fished the creeks, rivers, and shorelines; and gathered the fruits of nature for hundreds of years. The Indian cultures of Texas, many of which no longer existed by the time Europeans permanently settled the province, were perhaps as varied in their patterns as the landscape itself. This chapter describes the physical, environmental, and human dimensions of Texas when its modern history began in the first decades of the sixteenth century. Texas Indians are addressed as they entered the recorded annals of the state's history through contacts with European explorers and conquistadors.

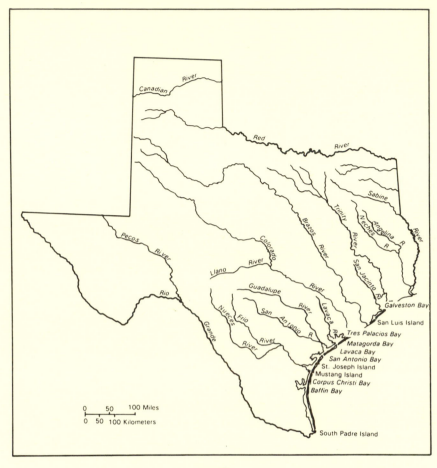

FIGURE I

*Major rivers and bays in Texas. This map locates the major rivers and bays that
are mentioned in the text. (Cartography by William M. Holmes.)*

GEOGRAPHERS HAVE LONG DEBATED THE QUESTION OF
whether Texas is a single entity or many, just as historians have questioned whether the state is essentially southern or western. To Spaniards
entering Texas, the land must have seemed astonishingly diverse, as indeed it was. Accordingly, I have elected to follow the approach taken by
Terry G. Jordan and his associates, John L. Bean, Jr., and William M.
Holmes, in a recent book on the geography of Texas. The authors of
Texas: A Geography chose to emphasize the "formal plurality of Texas
rather than its functional unity."[2] Generally, it can be said that the land-

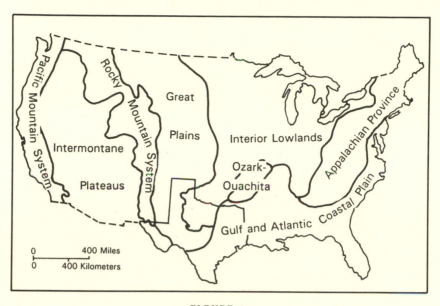

FIGURE 2
*Physiographic regions of the United States. This map depicts
the extension into Texas of four physiographic regions of the United States.
(Cartography by William M. Holmes.)*

scape of Texas decreases in elevation from north to south, while rainfall increases from west to east; and the overall land configuration tilts
gently to the southeast as evidenced by the course of all major rivers as
they make their way to the Gulf of Mexico (see Figure 1). Aside from
these broad statements, Texas requires analysis by particulars rather than
by generalizations.

Four physiographic provinces of the United States are found in Texas.
They include Gulf and Atlantic Coastal Plain, Interior Lowlands, Great
Plains, and Basin and Range or Intermontane Plateaus (see Figure 2).
One of the largest of those provinces in Texas is the Gulf Coast Plain,
wherein lay the heartland of Hispanic settlement. It makes up the eastern
and southern regions of the state, and until recent geologic times much
of it was inundated by the Gulf of Mexico. The western and southern
boundary of this province is the Balcones Escarpment, running roughly
eastward from Val Verde County on the Río Grande to San Antonio and
Austin, where it bends northward. Because the entire Texas coast has
only recently been uplifted from the Gulf of Mexico, the shoreline is characterized by poorly drained marshlands, shallow bays, and offshore barrier islands like Galveston and Padre.[3]

In colonial times the Río Grande, or Río del Norte as the Spaniards often called it, carried a formidable volume of water with swift and dangerous currents. At certain times of the year, it was navigable from its mouth by shallow-draft vessels for a distance of more than one hundred miles. But Spanish settlements at San Antonio, La Bahía (after 1726), and Nacogdoches all had to be supplied by land. The general absence of navigable rivers to the interior, especially from Matagorda Bay, must be viewed as a significant impediment to Hispanic colonization of Texas.

The southern limits of the Interior Lowlands, which extend southwestward from the Great Lakes and constitute one of the largest physiographic features in the United States, lie entirely within Texas. In North Central Texas, the terminus of the Interior Lowlands is commonly called the Rolling Plains, Osage Plains, or North Central Plains. The western portion of the province is defined by the Cap Rock Escarpment, which roughly divides the southern Texas Panhandle along a north-south axis.

A third physiographic province of the United States also encompasses a sizable portion of the Lone Star State. Lying immediately east of the Rocky Mountains, the Great Plains occupies all of the northern and western portion of the Texas Panhandle. Here it is also known as the High Plains, or Llano Estacado, with its eastern border formed by the Cap Rock Escarpment. Many Texans insist upon "Staked Plain" as a translation for Llano Estacado, but because of the Cap Rock's appearance to Spaniards as they approached it from the west, it should be rendered as "Stockaded" or "Palisaded Plain."[4] The Cap Rock represents one of the most striking land forms in all of Texas. Its spectacular canyons and sheer cliffs of colorful rock, especially at Palo Duro Canyon in Randall County, have been a source of amazement for viewers from Francisco Vázquez de Coronado to the present. By contrast, the High Plains themselves are noted for the absence of identifiable land features. This phenomenon, too, was a source of wonderment and anxiety for Coronado, who navigated an apparent sea of grass by magnetic compass and at times logged his progress by ordering a poor foot soldier to count every step taken by his horse![5]

The Great Plains broadens like an anchor as it extends into southwest Texas. Commonly known as the Edwards Plateau, this portion of the physiographic province as it protrudes into extreme northern Mexico is bordered on the east by the Gulf Coast Plain and on the west by the Intermontane Plateaus. The Edwards Plateau itself ranges in elevation from about 850 feet along its eastern border to approximately 4,000 feet at the base of mountains to the west. Much of the plateau appears as level or gently rolling land, but its southern and eastern limits in the uplands of the Balcones fault zone are extremely rugged. Springs, creeks, and rivers have eroded and dissolved limestone strata, and the plateau loses its identity in the Hill Country of Central Texas.[6] The Llano Basin, lying to the east of the Edwards Plateau and north of the Balcones Escarpment, has been eroded by the Colorado River and its tributaries. It is characterized by outcroppings of ancient rock from the Paleozoic and pre-Cambrian eras as well as hilly terrain in the southwestern portion. This erosional basin in present San Saba County represents the geographic center of Texas.[7]

To the west of the Edwards Plateau is the Basin and Range Province. Lying mostly to the west of the Pecos River, this major physiographic province represents the extreme southern portion of the Rocky Mountain System, and it constitutes the western extremity of Texas. Herein are found the true mountains and deserts of Texas. If, however, one excludes this region from the Rocky Mountain complex, as some geomorphologists do, then Texas possesses the highest landform in the United States to the east of the Rocky Mountains. Rising to 8,751 feet, Guadalupe Peak is just one of many mountain clusters found in the trans-Pecos region. The mountains there vary in geologic age from Lower Paleozoic to Permian and Cretaceous. All of them, however, share a common landscape feature. They are surrounded by extensive desert flatlands that encroach the mountain slopes to an elevation of approximately 5,000 feet.[8]

Of the four major physiographic provinces of the United States that are found in Texas, the Basin and Range region was least known to Spanish settlers. Alvar Núñez Cabeza de Vaca and his three companions skirted part of its western extremities in the 1530s; travelers to and from New Mexico regularly traveled the course of the Río Grande from La Junta de los Ríos to El Paso del Norte; and on occasion expeditions returning from New Mexico followed the upper Pecos River into the Toyah Basin country; but overall this area did not attract Spanish settlements except in the environs of El Paso del Norte. Even today, with the exception of El Paso, the huge counties of extreme southwest Texas—some of which are individually larger than either of the two smallest states in the United States—are among the least populated of the 254 political units that make up the Lone Star State.[9]

With its immense physical size, Texas presented a formidable challenge to Spanish colonization. It seems certain that nowhere else on the North American continent did the king's subjects encounter a land of greater contrasts in soil, biota, climate, and human inhabitants. For example, recent studies of soil surveys in Texas counties have identified more than eight hundred series. Spanish settlers themselves recognized that they had entered a diverse and fertile land with great potential for agriculture, especially when compared to the northern regions of Mexico. In areas of Texas where annual rainfall and seasonal distribution were adequate, crops of corn, wheat, potatoes, cotton, and beans prospered. Unfortunately, dependable farming at San Antonio required irrigation. However, even in East Texas, where average annual precipitation exceeded forty inches and irrigation was unnecessary, farming did not develop to its fullest potential (see Figure 3). In the latter locale, such circumstances as remoteness from other Spanish settlements, lack of developed roads, and the absence of trade with New Spain proper kept agriculture at roughly subsistence level.[10]

Geographers Jordan, Bean, and Holmes have argued that Spaniards and later Mexicans coped well with semiarid conditions in Texas—better in fact than did more recent Anglo-American and other European settlers—but not so well in the piney woods of East Texas.[11] There is much merit in their contention, for Spaniards by virtue of long experience had learned to deal effectively with drought conditions. One finds little evidence in colonial records of Spaniards noting anything unusual about the landscape of northern Mexico or, for that matter, about the countryside near San Antonio. Both regions reminded them of Spain and therefore evoked little by way of unfavorable comments.[12] Quite the opposite was the case when they entered East Texas.

As the Spanish quickly discovered, the countryside around Nacogdoches "was a very different sort of place." It lay within the forests of East Texas, and there were no open prairies within one hundred miles. Accordingly, ranching in the manner to which Spaniards were accustomed was not possible. There the population typically accrued rather than resulted from a deliberate policy of colonization. The motley and heterogeneous settlement of French and other foreigners that made up the population of East Texas in the Hispanic period came about because most Spaniards preferred not to live in woods full of swamps, snakes, and insects.[13]

Ironically, early travelers had reported favorably on the landscape of East Texas. This apparent anomaly may perhaps be explained by remembering that the observers were simply passing through the region, rather than intending to live there. In diaries and letters, Hispanic observers often commented on the dense and varied vegetation. The profusion of trees, for example, left them pondering species, for they recognized few of them. As early as 1690, Alonso de León commented favorably on the lush greenery of that portion of the province. He also noted an abundance of bison and other kinds of game while observing that the fields of

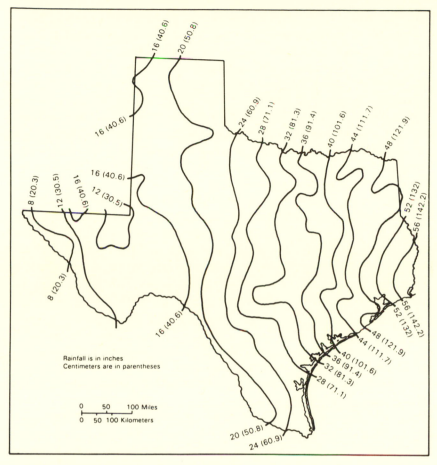

FIGURE 3

*Average annual precipitation in Texas. This map depicts average precipitation
in contemporary Texas. (Cartography by William M. Holmes.)*

the Indians contained bounteous crops of corn, beans, squash, watermelons, and cantaloupes.[14]

Later, after the reoccupation of East Texas in the 1720s, an anonymous diarist entered Texas from Coahuila and also set down his impressions of the region. Prior to his arrival at a mission site in East Texas, the
diarist's remarks about the environment were limited to his complaints
of being attacked by "an intolerable plague of mosquitoes of enormous
numbers" as he passed puddles of water to the north of the Río Grande.
But on reaching his destination in East Texas, he marveled at the variety
of trees, none of which he could identify other than oaks, pines, and

medlars. He also commented on the profusion of bison and deer. There were bear, much valued by the Indians for their fat, and rats the size of young rabbits that the Indians regarded as food. The profusion of birds likewise drew the anonymous chronicler's attention, and he recorded hearing a "nocturnal bird"—probably a mourning dove—with a cry so sad it produced melancholia. Finally, the diarist commented on rivers and creeks that teemed with fish of unfamiliar species.[15] Still later and in a different region of the province, Spaniards found alligators as far north as the San Gabriel River—an observation recorded by José de Ecay Múzquiz in 1750.

Reports of unusual fauna encountered in northern Mexico and Texas apparently intrigued King Charles III (1759–1788), who is known to have possessed a broad range of interests. In the late 1770s, one of his most capable officials in America, Teodoro de Croix, tried on at least two occasions to send domesticated buffalo to Spain at Charles's request and expense. A male and a female, presumably calves, died in transit in 1778. In the following year, Croix tried again. Male and female buffalo, each about six months in age, were captured in Texas, and the commandant general ordered Governor Domingo Cabello to search for additional animals, which were to be dispatched to Chihuahua as soon as possible. Croix also had deer shipped southward from New Mexico, again as unusual examples of New World species intended for the king's pleasure.[16]

Aside from the king's interest and more important, to what extent did soil conditions, unfamiliar biota, and varying climate influence Spanish settlement patterns in Texas? Those factors, it seems, were far less important than in the Anglo experience. Perceptions of terrain, climate, and prospects of making a living from the land have long played an important role in the settlement patterns of Anglo-Americans. For the most part, after 1783 Anglo-Americans were free to go where they wished in claiming lands between the Appalachian Mountains and Spain's colonies. Spanish settlement in Texas, however, was planned by the king and his agents, usually with the intent of achieving specific military, political, and spiritual objectives. This is not to suggest that squatters and itinerant drifters were absent in Spanish Texas, for they were not. Persons of that nature were more common than uncommon in East Texas, and they were present in small numbers at San Antonio. For the most part, however, Spanish entries into Texas were executed under royal license or with the formal approval of civilian enterprises. Those restrictions applied to the early land expeditions led by Alonso de León, Domingo Ramón, Martín de Alarcón, and the Marqués de San Miguel de Aguayo, as well as to sea expeditions captained by Andrés de Pez and Martín de Rivas. Even the formation of the first official civil government at San Antonio was the product of crown planning. Therefore, with few exceptions, Spanish subjects went where they were directed to go. They could also be told where not to live, as evidenced by the forced evacuation of civilians from East Texas in the 1770s. Again, perceptions of land and fauna figured far less importantly in the Spanish experience.

In Hispanic Texas, climate likewise seems not to have had a major influence on settlement patterns, although Spaniards were not so stoic that weather conditions escaped their attention. Average temperatures, perhaps significantly cooler in the sixteenth and seventeenth centuries than they are today, occasioned many comments. For example, Cabeza de Vaca and his companions remarked on the bitter cold of the Galveston Bay area during the winter of 1528–1529. He was the first person to record a "norther" in Texas, a weather phenomenon known from Dalhart to Brownsville, and also complained about the cold fronts that sweep down in winter from western Canada and the northern plains, often bringing sharp drops in temperature and freezing precipitation in their wake. During his attempts to reach Mexico in the 1530s, he saved his life during a siege of cold weather in South Texas by finding burning embers—probably from a lightning strike—that he stoked into a fire that he fed for warmth. Similarly, the Coronado expedition, while camped in the Cap Rock canyons of West Texas, experienced a terrible hail storm with stones "as big as bowls and even bigger and as thick as raindrops." Weather phenomena such as this are still all too common, especially in the high plains region of Texas.[17]

Despite the extremes noted by Cabeza de Vaca and Coronado, Spaniards generally perceived much of Texas as having a climate similar to their native land. One observer in 1730 saw little difference in the two regions, except in the southern part of Texas where the land approached the Tropic of Cancer. There, in the words of Juan Alvarez Barreiro, when the sun reaches its apex "the heat is insupportable," especially along the coastal regions where physical discomfort was greatly worsened by plagues of mosquitoes.[18] To be sure, Spaniards complained of dust, drought, heat, cold, flies, mosquitoes, wind, rain, and snow. Texans today continue those same grumblings about the weather, but at least they have greater control over their choice of residence than did the king's subjects. The remoteness of settlements in Spanish Texas, the nature of soil and terrain, the biological makeup of a region, and the extremes of climate all influenced the quality of life. But the sum total of those circumstances, even under the most dire conditions, paled in significance when compared with the actual and perceived dangers of sharing a land with potentially hostile natives and contesting them for its control.

The sprawling and varied landscape of Texas had attracted a wide range of Indian groups, tribes, and nations in both prehistoric and historic times. As a general observation, it should be noted that Indian Texas was far more complex than historians and ethnohistorians have presented it. Because many Texas Indians left few if any artifacts to interpret, it is not possible, based solely on archaeology, to present a "snapshot" or "satellite" photograph of the native population at any one time in history. Accordingly, early ethnographic information flows by necessity from the contacts and observations of various European pioneers in Texas. These descriptive data, however, have often been melded into composite portraits without clear indication that they constitute impressions formed over a considerable span of time. Scholarly sins have likewise resulted by equating, linguistically and culturally, groups that occupied the same geographic area but at different times. There has also been a tendency to give equal weight to all observers, even though some were not as reliable as others. As a further cautionary, it should be noted that even the most dependable eyewitness accounts of Texas Indians were filtered through a European frame of reference. As anthropologists remind us, all present populations are the descendants of hunters and gatherers. However, Europeans who first contacted Native Americans in Texas, especially those along the southern Gulf Coast, had had no previous experience with people who depended on hunting and gathering, for that mode of livelihood had long since disappeared in the Old World. Those firsthand accounts often reflected a certain disdain for natives who appeared to live like animals of the land. Until very recent years, that notion has served to disparage such cultures "and by implication to deny its people their essential humanity." Contemporary scholars who have presented more impartial assessments face the enormous task of "loosening the cold, dead grasp that traditional ignorance and misinterpretation have frozen onto the image of those native Americans."[19]

In presenting an overview of Texas Indians, I have tried to avoid ethnocentric judgments. The reader should also be aware that I have "glossed over" many Indian groups, especially those encountered by the earliest observers, that cannot be related to the major groups that are described. All too often, historians and anthropologists who work with manuscript materials have come across nothing more than a name for Indian groups—as heard by a Spaniard or a Frenchman and rendered in his native tongue.

The first recorded contact between Europeans and Indians in Texas came in November 1528 as two small craft bearing members of the Pánfilo de Narváez expedition landed to the west of Galveston Island. The makeshift barges came ashore on a small island, which Cabeza de Vaca named Malhado, or Isle of Misfortune. Indians on Malhado and along the mainline shore to the environs of Corpus Christi Bay were Karankawas. Our earliest knowledge of those Indians, who were "not a political or possibly even a homogeneous cultural entity," rests entirely on the observations of Cabeza de Vaca. The Spanish chronicler described Karankawa men as generally tall and muscular. They adorned their bodies with pieces of cane thrust through the breast nipples and lower lip, and in some bands they wore no clothing at all. Karankawa women, however, regularly dressed in skirts of Spanish moss or deerskin.[20]

Collectively, Karankawas of the early sixteenth century appear to have had no organization other than chieftains who exercised authority as elders within small bands of kinspeople. Their livelihood depended on food items such as cactus fruit, roots, fish, shellfish, and small game. Living as they did on strips of islands and the mainland, and given their meager material possessions, Karankawas were often at the mercy of the coastal environment. In winter they were able to kindle fires for warmth, and in other seasons they covered their bodies with alligator and shark grease to ward off plagues of mosquitoes. The popularly repeated assertions of cannibalism among the Karankawas rest on unreliable evidence. Indeed, Cabeza de Vaca recorded the shock and revulsion of these Indians when they learned that five Spaniards, in desperate straits on the mainland during the winter of 1528–1529, had partaken of human flesh.[21] This reaction, however, may well have been prompted by their horror that Spaniards would show such disrespect for their own dead. If Karankawas did consume the flesh of their enemies, a practice not substantiated by eyewitness accounts, this kind of cannibalism appears to have a function of revenge or religious belief rather than of sustenance. Their less than favorable reputation in Texas history appears to have been the product of journalistic sensationalism that has done much "to malign a rather inoffensive, poorly known, much put upon, extinct, coastal people."[22] Although often defamed in Texas literature, Karankawas were survivors. With reduced numbers, they remained along the Texas coast throughout the Spanish period. The last mission in Texas, Nuestra Señora del Refugio, was founded for them in 1793.[23]

Associated with the most southwestern Karankawa groups were far more numerous hunting and gathering people, often identified collectively as Coahuiltecans. Unfortunately, the dearth of recorded vocabularies makes it very difficult to determine which ethnic units spoke a dialect of Coahuilteco and which did not. It must be frankly admitted that the Coahuiltecan concept—commonplace in literature on Texas Indians—is useful only if reduced in scope, and even then it has severe limitations.

Characteristic of all hunting and gathering groups, these people divided and then subdivided into a large number of bands. In the 1950s anthropologist John R. Swanton identified more than two hundred groupings.[24] Coahuiltecans, once thought to be related to the Hokan group of California, have been the object of recent research in primary documents, especially by Thomas N. Campbell and his student, Martín Salinas. As Salinas has noted, the scarcity of recorded information about Indian languages once spoken in northeastern Mexico and southern Texas leads to the regrettable conclusion that the total number of those tongues and dialects "spoken in the area will probably never be known." What seems certain is that the few recorded samples of languages are not "truly representative of an entire language." For the lower Río Grande area, only two recorded languages have been assigned formal names.[25]

As in the case of the Karankawas, much of what is known about Indians traditionally labeled as Coahuiltecans comes from the observations of Cabeza de Vaca, who spent several years among them as merchant, slave, and medicine man. In recent decades anthropologists, especially W. W. Newcomb, Jr., Campbell, and Alex D. Krieger, have made extensive use of his narrative. Newcomb credited Cabeza de Vaca with knowing more about these hunting and gathering groups "than any other European or American ever did afterward." Similarly, Campbell noted that Cabeza de Vaca "looms large as an ethnographer" and that the cultural information in his *Relación* is superior to all other sources combined.[26]

Cabeza de Vaca did not leave Malhado until late 1532, when he traveled down the Gulf Coast and at a "river of nuts" encountered three of his former companions. It was also at this juncture that Cabeza de Vaca gained extensive firsthand experience with hunting and gathering bands of that locale and beyond. He named seventeen Indian groups that were apparently located from the lower Guadalupe River southwestward to the Río Grande.[27] Four of the seventeen, the Guaycones, Quitoles, Camoles, and Fig People, were shoreline Indians located between the Guadalupe River and San Antonio Bay. Inland from the lower Guadalupe and the lower Nueces were an additional eleven groups. Arranged roughly in the order of their locations along a northeast-southwest axis, they were the Mariames, Yguazes, Atayos, Acubadaos, Avavares, Anegados, Cutalchuches, Maliacones, Susolas, Comos, and Coayos. The remaining two groups mentioned by Cabeza de Vaca, the Arbadaos and Cuchendados, appear to have lived west of the sand plain of contemporary Brooks and Kenedy counties.[28]

Cabeza de Vaca spent slightly more than two years among the Mariames and Avavares, and through this experience he later recorded unique ethnographic information. He specifically mentioned the fare of the Yguazes, who ate spiders, ant eggs, worms, lizards, snakes, rotten wood, and deer dung. These foods and others, which Cabeza de Vaca could not bring himself to mention, obviously offended his sensibilities, but they were the kinds of things eaten at one time by ancestors of everyone on this planet. From the Spanish perspective, some Indians who probably spoke a dialect of Coahuilteco did consume more appealing foods, which included cacti, mesquite beans, seeds, nuts, and berries.[29] Like other hunters and gatherers, these Indians did not eat balanced meals, but they had balanced diets because they received nutrients on a seasonal basis.

Cabeza de Vaca recorded annual migrations of hunting and gathering groups to feast on the fruit of the prickly pear cactus or consume pecans. They also participated in communal animal drives or "surrounds" to kill rabbits and other small game, as well as coordinated marches that forced deer into Gulf waters, where they weakened or drowned. More commonly, the physical endurance of the men was such that they could actually run down deer on foot.[30] Except during brief periods of catastrophic weather, such as floods, high winds, or extreme cold, food sources for these hunting and gathering people were certainly adequate. Otherwise, there would not be names recorded for so many groups. The arrival of Spaniards, competition for food sources with domestic livestock, and pressure from other Indian groups, especially the Apaches, who were themselves under duress, resulted in persistent displacement, fragmentation, and population decline.

Coahuiltecans, or more likely Indians from diverse areas whose native language was not Coahuilteco but who had learned to use it as a lingua franca, would eventually make up most of the neophytes in the five missions at San Antonio, but by the latter part of the 1770s they had virtually disappeared from the Texas landscape. Their demise, in part the result of assimilation into the emerging Tejano community, does much to explain the sharp decline of mission activity at San Antonio in the 1790s.

After crossing the lower Río Grande, Cabeza de Vaca and his three companions traversed northern Mexico and reentered Texas at the confluence of the Río Grande and Río Conchos. There at La Junta de los Ríos, near present Presidio, Texas, the travelers contacted the first Indians, identified as Jumanos, who lived in fixed houses. Because of their seasonal migrations to the north to kill buffalo, Cabeza de Vaca referred to the Jumanos as Cow People.[31] It seems certain that the Jumanos will never be more than superficially understood. Neither Cabeza de Vaca nor subsequent Spanish explorers in the region described them in a manner that approached completeness. Even their linguistic affiliation is obscure, although some evidence suggests that they may have spoken the Uto-Aztecan tongue. And the meaning of the word "Jumano" in its Hispani-cized form remains unknown.[32]

Spaniards added to the confusion by being unable to settle on a stan-dardized Hispanic rendering of the Indians' name in colonial documenta-tion, using variant forms such as "Xumana," "Humana," or "Sumana." Worse, there was a tendency on the part of Spanish observers to label as Jumanos all Indians who painted or tattooed their bodies. Since this was a common, if not universal, custom among Texas Indians, the Jumanos sometimes appear to have been virtually ubiquitous.[33] This impression has likewise been furthered by the absence of a concerted effort to iden-tify many Indian groups that were recorded as contemporaries of the Jumanos and who ranged over parts of the same lands in western Texas. Unfortunately, no one can say with certainty which of these Indians are classifiable as Jumanos and which are not. Given the absence of system-atic and innovative research on the Jumano problem over the past half century, we are left with the assumption that a large part of western Texas was once exclusively occupied by an Indian population called Jumano. It is presently standard practice to label Jumanos as transitional people who were settled gardeners in the Puebloan tradition and occasional buf-falo hunters in the manner of Plains cultures, although the latter's liveli-hood depended almost exclusively on killing bison.

By the late seventeenth century, the Jumanos had become the Vene-tians of Texas. From their winter headquarters at La Junta de los Ríos, they dispersed Spanish goods among other tribes as far away as the Gulf Coast and East Texas. Among the Hasinai Confederation, they held an-nual trade fairs where they offered for sale Spanish horses from distant Chihuahua. Juan Sabeata, the most famous Jumano chieftain, not only played a crucial role in influencing missionary efforts at La Junta de los Ríos in the early 1680s but also impressed Spaniards with tales of the great kingdom of the Tejas.[34]

Following the initial failure of missionary activity at La Junta de los Ríos and the abandonment of East Texas in 1693, Spaniards lost contact with the Jumanos for several years. The latter, who had long served as a southern barrier to the Lipan Apaches, began accommodation with their

ancient enemies in the early 1700s. The subsequent bond was so complete that they became known as the Jumano Apaches. After 1771 there
are no further references to Jumanos by name. By that date it may be
assumed that the absorption process had been completed.[35]

Spanish contact with other prehorse Plains cultures came within five
years after Cabeza de Vaca and his companions reached Mexico City.
Francisco Vázquez de Coronado set out to explore the north country in
1540, and in the following year he led an expedition from New Mexico
to Gran Quivira in present Kansas. In crossing eastern New Mexico and
the Texas Panhandle, Coronado came upon one or two bands of Indians
that he called Querechos.

The Querechos were members of the eastern Apaches, an Athapaskan
language group that included Jicarillas, Lipans, Mescaleros, and Kiowa
Apaches. Until the arrival of the Comanches in the early 1700s, the eastern Apaches were the dominant Indians of the southern plains. Given
their linguistic ties to Indians of Canada and Alaska in the Pacific Northwest, the presence of Athapaskan speakers on the southern plains has led
to considerable conjecture and speculation. How did they become separated from their northern neighbors? One hypothesis holds that the
southern Athapaskans were relative newcomers to the Southwest. Their
progenitors were possibly small nomadic bands that worked their way
south along the eastern flank of the Rocky Mountains. En route they
likely fought and overcame some of the natives they encountered while
borrowing material culture from others. The first arrivals in New Mexico
are often credited with being raiders who forced abandonment of outlying Pueblo villages prior to the arrival of the Spanish.[36]

The Querechos encountered by Coronado appear to have been peaceful folk whose encampments were partially determined by the slow movements of buffalo herds. When obliged to relocate, they transported their
meager possessions by means of travois pulled by large domesticated
dogs.[37] At this juncture, the Querechos in spring and summer probably
lived in small rancherías, where their women scratched out gardens and
small fields. They remained sedentary long enough to harvest those crops
before buffalo arrived on their fall migrations to the South Plains. Like
some hunting and gathering groups, the Apaches used communal hunts
and "surrounds" to capture and kill game.

In the late 1600s, the eastern Apaches irreversibly altered their semi-
agricultural and seminomadic life by adaptation to a horse culture.[38]
Their mounts came from strays that had wandered northward from Mexico or from successful raids on Spanish settlements in New Mexico. Once
the Apaches acquired sufficient numbers of horses, they were able to fol-

low the buffalo herds with greater facility, and the resultant nomadic lifestyle essentially spelled an end to all attempts at farming. Despite their dependence on horses, the Apaches never developed the use of these animals to the fullest extent. At times they kept horses primarily as a source of food, a custom that appalled both Spaniards and Comanches.

Of all Indians in Texas, the Spanish came to regard the Apaches as the lowest and most dangerous form of human life. Despite the pleadings of missionary friars, in the 1770s Spanish authorities targeted the eastern Apaches for extermination or even exile to an overseas region.[39] That this decision did not result in genocide may, in large part, be explained by Spain's inability to enact the necessary measures for its implementation. In many respects, the untenable position in which the Apaches found themselves is one of the sadder developments in Texas history. Once-proud warriors of the plains were driven from their traditional hunting grounds and reduced to thievery and scavenging.

Near the farthest extent of his march to Gran Quivira, Coronado encountered people known today as Wichitas. In the summer of 1541, he traveled some sixty-five miles through Wichita villages that extended beyond the great bend of the Arkansas River. Two subsequent expeditions in the late sixteenth and early seventeenth centuries renewed contact with the Wichitas, but they generally remained isolated in the heart of the Great Plains.[40] Living on lands that were remote from Santa Fe, the Wichitas were nevertheless affected by the consequences of European settlement in New Mexico. Before the end of the 1600s, Native Americans had learned to ride and care for horses. Because the Wichitas were blessed with an abundance of corn, beans, and squash, cultivated by the women, these wondrous animals were less essential to them than to other plains people.

Wichita men, however, had traditionally hunted game to supplement their diet. They quickly perceived the advantages of becoming mounted hunters and the absolute necessity of becoming mounted warriors. As Newcomb has remarked, "To hunt afoot one might go hungry; to fight cavalry afoot was to court certain disaster."[41] The chances of carrying out a safe and productive hunt were also greatly enhanced by the spread of European firearms to native peoples. Spaniards, however, refused to supply Indians with guns, powder, and shot, and they held to that policy throughout most of the colonial period. French traders, on the other hand, did not operate under such restraints.

Unfortunately for the Wichitas, the Osages, their mortal enemies, lived in closer proximity to the English and French and acquired firearms before the Wichitas were able to do so. Pressure from Osages to the north and east and attacks from Comanches to the north and west prompted a southward migration by the Wichitas toward the Red River and Texas. Near the end of the second decade of the eighteenth century, Wichita villages were scattered from the environs of the Kansas-Oklahoma border into Texas. As the Wichitas entered new lands to the south, they trespassed on locales traditionally occupied by the Apaches, who possessed a plentiful supply of horses.[42]

The appearance of the Frenchman Bénard La Harpe and the establishment of his trading post near modern Texarkana in 1719 was especially welcome news to the Wichitas. La Harpe and other Frenchmen began supplying the Wichitas with crucially needed firearms. Ultimately, the southward expansion of the Wichitas extended well beyond the Red River to the Brazos in Central Texas, where the modern city of Waco took its name from a subtribe.[43]

Almost simultaneous with Coronado's introduction to the Querechos and Wichitas, members of another Spanish expedition approached Texas from the east. Initially, some six hundred Spaniards under the command of Hernando de Soto had landed in Florida in May 1539. Over the course of three years, de Soto explored portions of perhaps nine southeastern states in the present United States. Shortly before his death (May 1542) on the banks of the Mississippi River, de Soto had released his command to Luis de Moscoso Alvarado. Moscoso, in the following month, set out at the head of the army in search of an overland route to Mexico. In late summer he contacted the most important and culturally advanced Indians in Texas.[44] Along the course of the Red, Angelina, and Neches rivers, Moscoso encountered Caddo-speaking Indians, whose language stock was common to much of the central and southern Great Plains. Only minor dialectical differences separated all Caddo tribes in East Texas, Arkansas, and Louisiana. However, to the west, Pawnee, Wichita, and Kichai Indians shared linguistically related tongues that were unintelligible to each other or to the Caddoes to the east.[45]

By the late 1680s, Caddoes with mutually intelligible languages had organized themselves into three confederacies, two of which were located in Texas. Between the Red and Sulphur rivers in extreme northeast Texas, extending into present Arkansas, was the domain of the Kadohadacho. Four tribes, the Kadohadacho proper, the Nanatsoho, the Nazoni, and the upper Natchitoches, made up this political alliance. The largest confederation was the Hasinai, situated along the upper and middle reaches of the Neches and Angelina rivers in East Texas. This southern group was composed of eight tribes: Hainai, Neches, Nacogdoche, Nacono, Namidish, Nazoni, Anadarko, and Nabedache.[46]

As a form of greeting among its members, the Hasinai Confederation used a word that the Spanish heard as "Tejas." Roughly translated, it meant "friend" or "our own people." Spaniards, on the other hand, employed "Tejas" or "Hasinai" interchangeably in referring to tribes of that confederacy. In Castilian Spanish, "Texas" was the phonetic equivalent of "Tejas" and eventually became the preferred spelling.

Although the Caddoes had well-established customs and legal procedures for keeping conflicts among themselves at a manageable level, they were no strangers to warfare. In October 1541 they had clashed with de Soto's soldiers in present Arkansas and had given a good account of themselves. The Caddoes also joined to wage war against a host of enemies that nearly surrounded them. To the northeast, they faced dreaded foes in the Choctaws, as well as occasional conflicts with the Chickasaws; to the north, raiders from the Osage nations threatened the very existence of the Kadohadacho tribes along the Red River; to the northwest, the Caddoes fought with the Wichitas and Kichais; and to the west, they clashed with hostile bands of roving Tonkawas. Only in the south did they maintain consistently peaceful relations with the more primitive Atakapans.[47] Despite their well-deserved reputation as warriors, the Caddoes were not an aggressive people. Their society did not hinge on war as did that of some Texas Indians, and they customarily avoided armed conflict except for defensive or retaliatory motives. If permitted to follow their natural inclinations, their lives would have revolved primarily around farming and hunting.[48]

While they never possessed the legendary "great kingdom of the Tejas," the Caddoes did develop a well-ordered society that was much admired by European observers. The essence of their polity was a theocracy, wherein there were clear-cut lines of authority. A *grand xinesi* served as high priest of each major grouping. With duties that were primarily religious, "he tended the eternal fire in the temple and served as an intermediary between the people and the gods. As the interpreter of divine will, he exercised virtually unassailable power." The office of *grand xinesi* was hereditary in the male line, and it brought great prestige to the family of the exalted high priest.[49]

The conduct of temporal affairs was the responsibility of a *caddi* (chief of each political subunit), and that position was also hereditary in the male line. Where the component group was large enough to require additional officials, the *caddices* were assisted by three to eight subchiefs (*canahas*) and their assistants (*chayas*). All political units contained law enforcement officers, known as *tammas*.[50] A hereditary and hierarchical polity of this nature was easy for Europeans to understand, and the same was true of Caddo religion. Caddoan theology accepted a creator and omnipotent deity who punished evil and rewarded good. This similarity to Christian belief, as well as the cultural attainments of the Caddoes, excited the missionaries in Texas and led them to believe that they could easily convert the Caddoes to Christianity. Experience, however, would demonstrate quite the contrary.[51]

The economic accomplishments of the Caddoes, which from the Spanish point of view made them the most desirable Indians in Texas, included a highly productive system of agriculture. Farming was a communal undertaking, with initial planting performed by men and women of all rank, except for the *grand xinesi,* who was exempt from labor. The tilled fields of East Texas were sowed with corn, several varieties of beans, sunflower seeds, squash, and tobacco. Once the crops were in place, tending them became the primary responsibility of women, thereby releasing the men to hunt or serve as warriors.[52]

Game such as buffalo, deer, and bear was available as well as a wide variety of fish. The Caddoes further supplemented their diet with fruits, nuts, and berries, which women gathered in the wilderness and processed for storage. Discipline was such that the Caddoes, except in years of severe drought, seldom faced food shortages, and even under the most dire conditions they never consumed the seeds reserved in sufficient quantities for two successive spring plantings.[53]

The sophistication of the Caddoes' political and economic arrangements as well as the appearance of the Indians themselves impressed Europeans. Cranial deformation among these Indians appears not to have been a universal practice, but the custom was nonetheless commonplace. On the other hand, tattooing and body painting for special occasions were invariably used by men and women. Both sexes were fond of adornments such as shells, bones, feathers, and colorful stones, which were worn as necklaces, wristlets, and armlets.[54] The clothing of Caddo men and women was also remarked upon favorably by European observers. Tanned and processed deerskin of lustrous black color was used for moccasins, shirts, leggings, and breechclouts. Dress-up clothing was richly adorned with shiny seeds and decorative paintings.[55]

Marriage customs among the Caddoes, however, were the object of scorn among the Spanish and French who contacted them. On the slightest pretext, a couple could divorce and seek new partners. Caddo marital practices, which scandalized the missionary clergy, can perhaps be described as "serial monogamy."[56] Another aspect of Caddoan culture, although not unique to it, was the custom of weeping and wailing by both sexes when they encountered unfamiliar persons. Such conduct was extremely disquieting to more reserved Spaniards and Frenchmen, and they noted that Caddo women were especially prone to profuse crying in the face of an impending death. In time the Spanish and French warily noted that the shedding of tears might presage danger to their own lives.[57] Taken as a whole, especially when compared to the Karankawa, Coahuiltecan, and Plains Indians, it is little wonder that the Caddoes made a lasting imprint on the minds of outside observers. In the words of Elizabeth A. H. John, both Indian and European "carried away from the Caddo world impressions of great power, beauty, and wealth."[58]

To the west of the Caddoes in Central Texas lived roving bands of Indians traditionally identified as Tonkawas. The first verifiable contact with these natives has customarily been associated with the Alonso de León expedition of 1690. More recent scholarship, however, suggests that the Tonkawas, like the Wichitas, were relative latecomers to Texas. Current research by anthropologists Campbell and Newcomb has postulated that the Tonkawas were associated with the High Plains at the time of the Juan de Oñate expedition (1601) to Gran Quivira. As Campbell has suggested, this radical revisionism profoundly alters traditional views of the Tonkawas. They are commonly regarded as very old Texas Indians, who had long been associated with the region of north-central Texas.[59] Specifically, it may well be proved by subsequent research that "the Tonkawa tribe of the nineteenth century represents the coalescence or consolidation . . . of a number of fragments of diverse tribes (or bands) from a wide geographic area." Furthermore, the Tonkawa proper may have been just one of the components that made up the tribe of that name and "were not necessarily the most numerous or influential."[60] By implication, it seems probable that a considerable number of Indian groups, long regarded as Tonkawa in speech and culture, have been misclassified. Controversy over the origins and composition of the Tonkawas is likely to continue for some time, and the matter will not be resolved until scholars have painstakingly studied all of the pertinent documents.[61]

Immediately to the east of bands traditionally identified as Tonkawas and along the lower reaches of the Trinity and San Jacinto rivers lay the Texas domain of poorly known Atakapan-speaking Indians. The name of one of the tribes, the Atakapa proper, means "man-eaters" or "cannibals" in the Choctaw language. Cabeza de Vaca in contacting an Indian group he called the Hans may have encountered Atakapans in the late 1520s. Aside from this possible encounter, Europeans knew nothing of the Atakapans until the 1700s. By then the most important tribes were the Orcoquizas, Bidais, and Deadoses.[62]

The Atakapans who lived along the marshy coast to the northeast of Galveston Bay occupied land that was subject to salt-water flooding. There agriculture was impossible, forcing those Indians to depend almost entirely on fish and shellfish as sources of food. To the interior the possibilities for farming improved, but even in those locales the livelihood of the natives largely depended on killing deer, bear, and occasional bison.[63] However, the Bidais and Deadoses, located nearer the Caddoes, did rely in part on agriculture. Like other Texas Indians, the Atakapans tattooed their faces and bodies. Eighteenth-century drawings of their warriors depict them as barefooted and dressed in breechclouts. They also show them using a calumet, or ceremonial pipe, and armed with bow and arrows. Their women apparently went about scantily clad, dressed in skin skirts fastened about the waist with thongs. The houses of these Indians appear never to have been more than semipermanent and at times probably consisted of simple, movable shelters.[64]

Since firsthand accounts of the Atakapans are generally lacking, distressingly little is known about them. Those living along the coast probably continued a beachcombing, scavenger existence, although by the late 1740s some of the Deadose tribes had ranged far enough inland that they were included in missions founded along the San Gabriel River.

THE WORLD OF TEXAS INDIANS WAS IRREVERSIBLY ALTERED when Spaniards stepped into it in the first decades of the sixteenth century. Europeans and indigenous cultures began three centuries of sporadic cooperation and conflict. The outcome on a day-by-day, year-by-year basis was not always clear-cut. It was not a contest between right and wrong or heroic Christians against pagan Indians. It was instead the story of human beings struggling for survival on a distant frontier.

Despite the rich human tapestry that was pre-Spanish Texas, the Indians were ultimately doomed. They succumbed because of lost ancestral lands, fatal diseases, limited numbers, destruction of the buffalo, and superior European technology. The record is inexorable, for not one original native culture remains in the state.[65] Apart from the important ethnic roots of Tejanos, one must search hard to find other significant Indian legacies in the Lone Star State. To make the record complete, even the Tejas, who gave Texas its name, were banished to Indian Territory in the 1850s.

TWO

Explorers and Conquistadors, 1519–1543

THE EARLIEST EUROPEAN CONTACTS WITH TEXAS AND ITS inhabitants were both accidental and sporadic. Explorers first approached from the east by sea along the Gulf Coast, then overland almost simultaneously from New Mexico and Louisiana. Those initial contacts were the result of historical processes generated within the West Indies and the vast Kingdom of New Spain, a viceroyalty that ultimately stretched from the northern limits of Panama to the Spanish Borderlands in the American Southwest. This chapter chronicles events in New Spain that related to Texas, and it focuses on the pioneering accomplishments of Alonso Alvarez de Pineda, Cabeza de Vaca, Coronado, de Soto, and Moscoso.

AFTER THE INITIAL COLUMBIAN VOYAGE OF DISCOVERY, THE Spanish empire in America began amid the major islands of the Caribbean Sea. The first explorers and conquistadors, most of whom were young men who hailed from proud but poor families in Extremadura in western Spain or Andalucia in the south, sought new opportunity in a New World, and they usually did so with the blessings of their monarchs. While jealous of their absolute powers, Spanish sovereigns lacked sufficient resources to meet the obligations of a nation that would soon claim the dominant role in Europe and America.

Until the discovery of rich silver mines in Mexico and Peru in the 1540s, the most important source of wealth on the continental land masses was gold and silver already in the possession of high Amerindian cultures. Consequently, in the first half of the sixteenth century, the crown not only favored expansion into unexplored areas but also endorsed free-enterprise ventures by granting contracts to private individuals. By this arrangement, the Spanish monarchs risked not a single peso, although they stood to profit from the actions of explorers and conquistadors who increased the Spanish empire in America while spreading the faith to pagan Indians. In the process these sons of Spain forcibly relieved the natives of their "excess" wealth, and the crown profited directly by claiming its share, the *quinto* (fifth), of all bullion and precious stones. The royal appetite for New World income was such that even conquistadors who successfully conquered regions without royal approval or sanction of contract could expect titles and rewards—after the fact. All salaries, however, must spring from revenues generated within those new lands.

Española, or Santo Domingo, as it is better known, was permanently settled by Christopher Columbus in 1493. By 1508 Puerto Rico and Jamaica had fallen, respectively, under the control of Juan Ponce de León and Juan de Esquivel. And in 1511 Diego de Velásquez initiated the conquest of Cuba, the largest island in the Antillean chain. From Puerto Rico, Ponce de León first touched Florida in 1513, formally opening the history of Spain on the North American continent. From Cuba, the Velásquez-sponsored voyages of Francisco Hernández de Córdoba (1517) and Juan de Grijalva (1518) to Yucatán and the southern Gulf Coast served also to heighten interest in the mainland.[1]

Governor Velásquez's choice as commander of a third expedition fell on Fernando Cortés, who had served him as secretary in the conquest of Cuba. Cortés, however, soon aroused suspicions in his patron. As preparations got under way, expenses mounted. Worse, Cortés displayed pretentious airs and an alarming independence, causing the governor to doubt whether he could control such a headstrong captain. At the last minute, Velásquez attempted to remove his commander, but it was too late. Cortés departed Cuba before his sponsor could replace him with a more compliant leader. While Cortés himself had invested in the expedition, he nevertheless left Cuba in February 1519 as a renegade conquistador.[2] After coasting the Yucatán Peninsula, Cortés founded Villa Rica de la Veracruz (today La Antigua), where he began preparations for the conquest of Mexico.

At the very time Cortés founded the first settlement in Mexico, Francisco de Garay, Esquivel's successor as governor of Jamaica, was likewise pursuing his interests in Gulf Coast exploration. Garay was an experienced colonist who had sailed with Columbus in 1493. He and his business partner, Miguel Díaz de Aux, won fame by finding an enormous gold nugget on Española valued at thirty-six thousand *pesos de oro*. Garay apparently used his share of good fortune to launch extensive livestock enterprises. At one time he employed some five thousand Indians just to tend his farms and livestock. Garay's interest in exploration and settlement of the mainland was piqued by news that Grijalva had col-

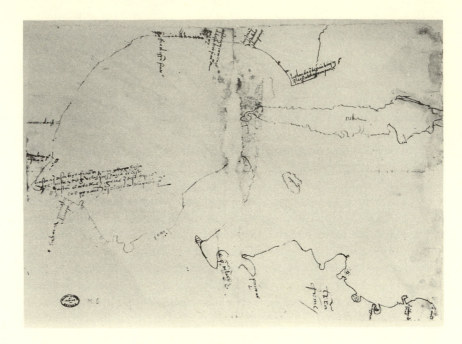

FIGURE 4
Sketch map of the Gulf of Mexico. This is the earliest known map that depicts the Texas coast. It was drawn by pilots of the Alonso Alvarez de Pineda expedition of 1519. (With the permission of the Archivo General de Indias, Seville, Spain; Mapas y Planos, México 5.)

lected twenty thousand pesos of gold in Yucatán. By early 1519 Garay had outfitted Alonso Alvarez de Pineda with supplies, four ships, and a crew of 270 men.[3] Pineda set sail from Jamaica and proceeded through the Yucatán Channel to the western tip of south Florida. From there he attempted to sail eastward, but a contrary wind forced him to turn about. He then ran the Gulf Coast from the Florida Keys to Veracruz. En route Pineda constructed the first map of the region, which he named Amichel, taking note of rivers and inlets (see Figure 4). On June 2, 1519, he recorded the immense discharge of the Mississippi River and named it the Río del Espíritu Santo for the feast day on which it was discovered. Later, Pineda and his crew were the first Europeans to view the entire coast of Texas, but there is no reliable evidence that they disembarked on Texas soil (see Figure 5).[4]

After several months at sea, Pineda's ships arrived off Villa Rica de la Veracruz shortly after Cortés had departed from there for the conquest

FIGURE 5
"Pineda Stone." This photograph depicts a carved stone tablet unearthed in 1974 near the mouth of the Río Grande. Its authenticity is highly questionable. (Courtesy of Eleanor Galt.)

of Mexico. Advised of a potential challenge to his supply lines and base of operations, Cortés returned to the coast where he rebuffed efforts by Pineda to establish a boundary between lands explored for Garay and those already claimed by Cortés. Thereafter, Pineda retraced his route northward and sailed six leagues up a river where he remained for forty days before returning to Jamaica. This river has often been misidentified as the Río Grande, the Río de las Palmas, or even the Mississippi, but it can be said with certainty that it was the Pánuco.[5] Having temporarily forestalled the claims of Garay through his agent Pineda, Cortés again directed his attention to the interior of Mexico. His defeat of the Aztec Empire is too familiar to repeat here, but an incident during the conquest of Mexico bears importantly on subsequent developments in Texas. Angered by the loss of his expedition to an upstart captain, in 1520 Diego de Velásquez outfitted an expedition to pursue and arrest Cortés. He placed an army of perhaps one thousand foot soldiers and eighty horses under the command of Pánfilo de Narváez, who had also served him in the conquest of Cuba. Narváez made port at Veracruz and later marched a short distance to the Indian town of Cempoala, where he headquartered his army. Confident that he held the whip hand because of superior numbers, Narváez scorned all conciliatory overtures from Cortés. Dividing his small army, which at the time occupied the Aztec capital, Cortés placed about 140 men in Tenochtitlán under the command of his trusted but impetuous lieutenant, Pedro de Alvarado, while he force marched a larger contingent back to the coast. Although outnumbered four or five to one, Cortés scored a dramatic victory over his challenger. In the brief melee, Narváez took a spear or pike thrust in the face, which gouged out his left eye.[6]

The outcome of this uneven clash between Spanish captains underscores the leadership qualities of Cortés and the ineptitude of Narváez. Still chafing over his treatment by Cortés, in the early 1520s Narváez returned to Spain, where he sought vindication before the emperor Charles V and his court. Instead of revenge for his injury, the red-bearded Narváez had to stomach full approval of Cortés's actions. On October 15, 1522, Cortés received an impressive array of titles and powers in New Spain, including the right to expel from the colony persons whose presence he deemed prejudicial to the best interests of the crown.[7] The fact that Velásquez's investment in the conquest of Mexico went unrecognized and unrewarded was clear evidence that the crown valued success above all other considerations. As for Narváez, there was no consolation until several years later when he received a royal patent to settle "Flor-

ida," a term then applied to the Gulf Coast stretching from the Río Pánuco to the Florida peninsula.

While Cortés had effectively parried Narváez, he had not discouraged
the governor of Jamaica. Through his agents in Spain, Garay in June
1521 won the right to colonize the region explored by Pineda. Cortés
probably learned of Garay's patent in late 1521 or early 1522. In any
event, by the autumn of 1522 he had formalized plans to occupy Pánuco
in his own right. After a month of hard fighting, Cortés overcame Indian
resistance and in early 1523 founded a *villa* (village), Santiesteban del
Puerto, on the south bank of the Río Pánuco.[8] For many years this poor,
mosquito-infested village would represent hope and salvation for Spaniards who struggled to escape the dangers and disappointments of lands
to the north.

Garay, meanwhile, had dallied and did not take action on his patent
until June 1523. By that time news of the conquest of Pánuco and the
founding of a *villa* there had filtered into the West Indies. This intelligence prompted Garay to sail for the Río de las Palmas, some ninety
miles north of the Río Pánuco. Exploration of the river and its banks
revealed a poor and virtually depopulated land. The few primitive Indians living there, however, were quick to suggest that a much richer land
lay *más allá* to the south.[9] Garay had little choice but to march overland
to a region already conquered and claimed by Fernando Cortés. Once
there, he was forced to capitulate, for news of the royal decree awarding
control of New Spain to Cortés arrived shortly after Garay had reached
Pánuco. Garay then journeyed to Mexico City, where he was graciously
received by Cortés. After dining with Cortés, however, Garay fell vio-
lently ill and died within two days. Even though suspiciously linked to
Cortés, this death was meaningless for the Pánuco region. Cortés was in
command there, a position he would maintain for the next four years.[10]

Having thwarted the ambitions of Garay, Cortés turned his attention
to Michoacán, the ancient Tarascan kingdom in western Mexico. With
the exception of the Aztec Empire, Michoacán was the wealthiest and
most powerful Indian realm in pre-Spanish Mexico, and its importance
to the unexplored north country was unsurpassed. Once conquered, it
would serve as the forward staging area for the conquest of New Galicia
by Nuño de Guzmán in the early 1530s. In turn, New Galicia's most
northern settlement, San Miguel de Culiacán, would become the departure point for several expeditions to the north and the refuge unknow-
ingly sought by four survivors of a second, even more ill-fated expedition
led by Pánfilo de Narváez.[11]

In 1526 Charles V finally awarded the "one-eyed casualty" of Cempoala a patent to settle Florida. The peninsula had already claimed the life of Juan Ponce de León in the early 1520s, but the region continued to attract the attention of treasure-seeking Spaniards for more than two decades.[12]

Narváez's ships cleared the mouth of the Río Guadalquivir on June 17, 1527. On board five vessels were some 600 men. Serving as treasurer and second in command was Alvar Núñez Cabeza de Vaca. The three-month Atlantic crossing to Santo Domingo was uneventful, and upon arrival Narváez remained in port for about forty-five days. During that time he gathered provisions and horses but lost 140 men due to desertion. From Santo Domingo, Narváez sailed to Cuba, where he intended to spend the fall and winter months. Arriving there in the early autumn, his expedition was battered and partially destroyed by the full brunt of a hurricane.[13]

Narváez re-outfitted, and in April 1528 five ships carried about 400 men to a bay, perhaps Sarasota, on the west coast of Florida. Shortly after the landing, Narváez, over the vigorous protests of Cabeza de Vaca, decided to separate 300 men from his support vessels and to reconnoiter the land on foot. He mistakenly believed that he was only a short distance from the Río Pánuco, when the actual distance was more than fifteen hundred miles via the coast.[14] The overland expedition in search of riches and an ideal site for a colony headed up the interior coast of the peninsula and was soon permanently detached from the ships.

By mid-June 1528 the expedition had arrived in northwestern Florida, where it remained for approximately three months. Faced with unfriendly natives and food shortages, Narváez decided that he must leave Florida by sea. Lacking boats, he and his men were forced to improvise. They jerryrigged bellows of deerskin and wooden pipes; they forged saws and axes from scraps of metal and used the tools to hew timber into planks; they killed their horses, lived on the meat, and used the tails and manes for rigging; they turned flayed and tanned horsehide into water bags; they used pine resins and palmetto fibers to caulk their crude barges; and they fashioned their shirts and trousers into sails.[15]

Five boats bearing less than 250 men left the Bay of Horses, so named because their mounts were slaughtered there, on September 22, 1528. The first month at sea went well. Hugging the coast, the small flotilla approached the mouth of the Mississippi River. On the thirty-first day, troubles began when a storm caught the barges and tossed them like driftwood. Several days after passing the mouth of the great river, Narváez released his command with the advice that "each must do as he thought best to save himself." His own efforts, however, were insufficient.

Later, his poorly anchored boat was blown into deep water off Matagorda Bay and presumably sunk. On November 6, 1528, the barge bearing Cabeza de Vaca and an undetermined number of men landed on an island near the western extremity of Galveston Island. A second boat containing Andrés Dorantes de Carranza, his African-born slave, Estevanico, Alonso Castillo Maldonado, and perhaps forty-five others apparently had landed nearby on the previous day, making them the first non-Indians in Texas. Those named, later known as the Four Ragged Castaways, were the only ones to survive the Texas portion of the Narváez expedition.[16] All others succumbed to exposure, disease, injuries, drowning, or violence at the hands of coastal tribes.

The initial landfall island, probably San Luis, was soon named Malhado. The approximately eighty Spaniards who were stranded there believed their location to be very near Pánuco. In hope of rescue, they selected four robust men, all good swimmers, and sent them down the coast with an Indian guide.[17] These men disappeared from history.

By the spring of 1529, hunger and dysentery had taken their toll. Only fourteen or fifteen Spaniards remained alive on Malhado. Believing Cabeza de Vaca had died on a trip to the mainland, all but two of them proceeded down the coast toward Pánuco. Cabeza de Vaca, however, recovered from a near-fatal illness and later became the first European merchant in Texas. He ranged inland, as well as along the present coastal counties of Texas, carrying conch shells and mesquite beans to the interior and returning with skins and red ochre. Cabeza de Vaca also gained stature among the Indians as a medicine man. At this juncture, his treatment of Indians consisted of blessing the afflicted, breathing on injuries, and reciting prayers.[18] The overall efficacy of his ministrations certainly suggests that some coastal Indians suffered from psychoneurotic disorders.

Cabeza de Vaca remained in the Galveston area because a lone surviving countryman, Lope de Oviedo, refused to leave Malhado. Finally, in late 1532 Cabeza de Vaca convinced the reluctant Spaniard to accompany him along the coast toward Pánuco, following the course the other survivors had taken nearly four years earlier. En route, Lope de Oviedo, frightened by unfriendly Indians and his inability to swim, turned back and also disappeared from history. All entreaties by Cabeza de Vaca, who "argued my utmost against such a craven course," were useless.[19] At the time the two parted company, they had already heard of other Christians nearby. Cabeza de Vaca continued on and within a few days rendezvoused with three astonished colleagues at a "river of nuts," probably the Guadalupe. At the river Cabeza de Vaca, Castillo, Dorantes, and Estevanico plotted their escape to Mexico, but they were delayed until 1534 by their circumstances as slaves of the Mariame and Yguaze Indians.[20]

Cabeza de Vaca spent some eighteen months as a captive of the Mariames. His descriptions of them and of the Avavares, with whom he later spent eight months, make both groups the best described Indians native to southern Texas. His narrative contains cultural information that "quantitatively exceeds that of all his successors combined."[21] Cabeza de Vaca lived among the Indians of the region and survived to write about them. No other Spaniard was able to do this. Accordingly, Cabeza de Vaca also deserves recognition as the first ethnologist in Texas. In his narrative he named a total of twenty-three Indian groups and located some of them relative to each other. All of the named tribes can be associated with the outer coastal plain extending from Galveston Island to the environs of present Falcon Reservoir.[22]

The ethnographic data alone strongly suggest that the four men followed this same inner coast toward Mexico. Controversy, however, over the Texas portion of the trek from the vicinity of Galveston Island to San Miguel de Culiacán has been particularly heated, and it has gone on for more than a century. Differences over route interpretations continue, for no one can prove with absolute certainty the precise course followed on any part of the journey.[23]

The starting point for all route studies must be Cabeza de Vaca's *Relación* and the Joint Report, a cooperative account written by the three surviving Spaniards. Both were composed shortly after the trek ended in 1536, and both are important as the first literature about Texas. In reconstructing the most likely route on the basis of these narratives, one should be sensitive to the biotic and physiographic information contained within them. This undertaking is worthwhile, for if it can be determined with reasonable confidence *where* the four men spent nearly seven years in Texas and *what* they saw, their experiences provide valuable data on Texas Indians, land forms, flora, and fauna.[24]

The crucial pieces of evidence in the narratives are the dimensions of the island where the initial landing occurred, the distance between and the crossing of four successive streams on the mainland, the description of a series of inlets along the coast toward Pánuco, the mention of a river of nuts and extensive stands of prickly pear cactus, the crossing of a large river comparable in width to the Guadalquivir in Spain, and the subsequent appearance of mountains near the coast that ran from the direction of the "North Sea." Those considerations coupled with the established goal of reaching Pánuco again suggest an inner coastal route for the Cast-

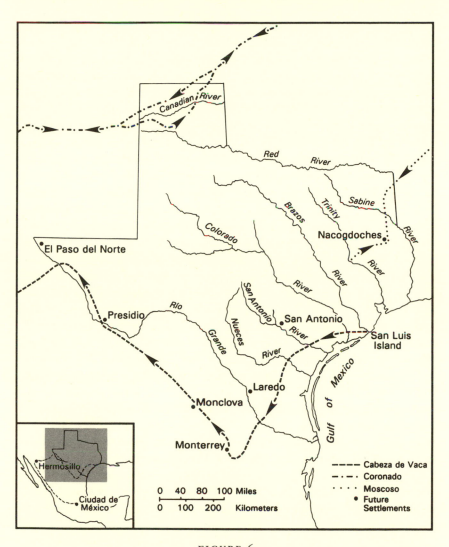

FIGURE 6
*Probable routes of Cabeza de Vaca, Coronado, and Moscoso. This map
indicates the most likely routes in Texas of three sixteenth-century pathfinders.
(Cartography by Caroline Castillo Crimm.)*

aways and point to a crossing of the lower Río Grande into Mexico near present Falcon Reservoir (see Figure 6).[25]

Within a day after they forded the Río Grande, Cabeza de Vaca and his companions sighted the Sierra de Cerralvo mountains in present northern Nuevo León, Mexico. On reaching the mountains, they decided to turn inland rather than head eastward toward the Gulf Coast. That decision, which contradicted their original intent to travel toward Pánuco, was based on several considerations. Friendly Indians reminded them that the shoreline groups were "very bad," while those in the interior were better disposed and possessed more food. The men's ignorance of the geography of the northwest coast of Mexico probably led them to believe that the Pacific Ocean lay no great distance westward. Finally, as Cabeza de Vaca admitted, by traveling inland they also had an opportunity to discover new lands and collect important information. In his words, "We concluded that our destiny lay toward the sunset and so took the trail to the north as far as we had to in order to reach the westward one and then swung down until eventually we came out at the South Sea."[26] The Castaways' journey across northern Mexico eventually brought them back to Texas at the junction of the Río Grande and Río Conchos near present Presidio. On that portion of the trek, Cabeza de Vaca removed an arrowhead from the chest of an Indian. The operation, a sagittectomy, has earned him remembrance as the "patron saint" of the Texas Surgical Society.[27]

At La Junta de los Ríos, the Castaways encountered agricultural people who lived in fixed houses. Cabeza de Vaca called these Indians, apparently Jumanos, the Cow People, because they left their settlements once a year to hunt bison to the north. After ascending the Río Grande on the east or Texas bank for some seventeen days, the four men recrossed the Río Grande about seventy-five miles down river from El Paso and turned westward toward the Pacific Coast of Mexico.[28] The path across northwestern Chihuahua and into northeastern Sonora brought the Castaways into contact with the "Maize People," generally believed to have been the Opata. These natives gave Cabeza de Vaca five green arrowheads that they used in their ceremonial dances. When he asked where they had come from, the Indians told him of a land to the north with populous towns and great houses set among lofty mountains. Later, Cabeza de Vaca lost the arrowheads, but it is reasonable to assume that they were of malachite or turquoise and from New Mexico.[29] Later in western Sonora, the four men came to a village where friendly Indians offered them six hundred opened deer hearts as food. Appropriately named Corazones by Cabeza de Vaca, the village was probably situated about forty-five miles from the coast near present Hermosillo, Sonora.[30] From Corazones to the completion of the odyssey in Mexico City, there is little controversy about the path followed by the Castaways. They arrived at the Río Yaqui around Christmas 1535, about seven months after they had departed from the Avavares in South Texas. South of the Río Yaqui, Castillo spotted an amulet tied to the neck of an Indian. It was a small sword belt buckle with a horseshoe nail stitched to it, unmistakable evidence that it had come from a Spaniard. In Cabeza de Vaca's words, "We could hardly restrain our excitement."[31]

As they hurried on, the four men saw more evidence of their countrymen's presence, such as tracks and traces of camps. Finally, Cabeza de Vaca and Estevanico, who had forged ahead of the other two, came upon a slave-raiding party to the north of Culiacán. The slave catchers, adherents of Nuño de Guzmán in New Galicia, were so astonished by the appearance of Cabeza de Vaca that "they just stood staring for a long time." The confrontation was equally a shock to Indians who had traveled with the Castaways. They refused to believe that Cabeza de Vaca could be a fellow Spaniard of Guzmán's hated soldiers.[32]

The Indians' perception of Cabeza de Vaca and his companions, in comparison to the reputation of Guzmán's adherents, underscores an important transition that had occurred in the Castaways. Despite years of privation and occasional harsh treatment from Indians when they themselves were slaves, the four survivors of the Narváez expedition had come to respect Indians as fellow human beings and to treat them accordingly. In Cabeza de Vaca's words, their native friends protested that "we had come from the sunrise, they from the sunset; we healed the sick, they killed the sound; we came naked and barefoot, they clothed, horsed, and lanced; we coveted nothing but gave whatever we had, while they robbed whomever they found and bestowed nothing on anyone."[33]

After the slave raiders had recovered their speech, Cabeza de Vaca, Castillo, Dorantes, and Estevanico were taken to Culiacán, where they were welcomed by the *alcalde mayor*, Melchor Díaz. They rested there for several days before traveling under heavy escort to Compostela for a meeting with the governor, Nuño de Guzmán. Guzmán was a gracious host, providing the wayfarers with clothing from his own wardrobe. Soon they were on their way again to Mexico City for an audience with the new viceroy, Antonio de Mendoza. The Four Ragged Castaways arrived in the capital on July 24, 1536, eve of the vespers of St. James. On the following day, they must have felt at home as they attended a fiesta and bullfight.[34]

In the following days and weeks, the four men told and retold stories of their astonishing odyssey to eager audiences. Against tremendous odds, they had survived nearly eight years of danger and exposure. In the last twenty-two months alone (September 1534–July 1536), they had covered an estimated twenty-five hundred miles, with most of that on foot. Their knowledge of the nature and extent of the north country revived interest in the legendary Seven Cities. In particular, Cabeza de Vaca's insistence that in the mountains of northwestern Mexico they had seen "undeniable indications of gold, antimony, iron, and other metals" created a fever of excitement from New Galicia to Mexico City. It also touched off a scramble among powerful men in New Spain who were anxious to sponsor a follow-up expedition.[35]

Among those who entertained hopes of exploring the north country was Nuño de Guzmán, but his star was rapidly fading. In the spring of 1536, the crown had selected his successor, Diego Pérez de la Torre, as governor of New Galicia. When word of the appointment arrived in New Spain, Viceroy Mendoza invited Guzmán to the capital to await the arrival of his replacement. Guzmán complied and was effectively removed from power in late 1536.[36] In 1537 Pérez de la Torre assumed his post in New Galicia, but his tenure was brief. He died in 1538 from injuries sustained in an accident while pursuing hostile Indians. On his deathbed, Pérez de la Torre named Cristóbal de Oñate, an able associate of Nuño de Guzmán, as his successor. However, when news of the governor's fate reached the viceroy, he moved quickly to secure control of New Galicia by appointing his own man, Francisco Vázquez de Coronado, as provisional governor.[37]

At this juncture, Antonio de Mendoza faced only Fernando Cortés as a serious rival to his plans for northern exploration. As viceroy, Mendoza held the upper hand, especially since Cortés's authority was limited to coastal exploration. But Mendoza did not have a free rein either, for his powers permitted only the sponsorship of peaceful penetrations by missionary friars. These limitations, plus the unwillingness of Cabeza de Vaca, Castillo, or Dorantes to serve as his agents, caused a year and a half to pass before the viceroy could formalize plans for an expedition.[38] Mendoza was finally spurred into action by information that Hernando de Soto was organizing a huge expedition in Spain that would approach the north country from the east and by knowledge that Cortés planned to explore the west coast toward the Gulf of California. To help ensure success, the viceroy acquired the services of Estevanico from Andrés Dorantes and assigned leadership of the enterprise to Fray Marcos de Niza.[39]

Fray Marcos had been introduced to the viceroy in the spring of 1537 by a fellow Franciscan, Bishop Juan de Zumárraga. De Niza was widely experienced in Santo Domingo, Central America, and Peru and had come to New Spain at the invitation of Zumárraga. He, a Franciscan brother, and Estevanico were conducted to Culiacán by the newly appointed provisional governor.[40] In early March 1539, a small party led by Fray Marcos de Niza left Culiacán and headed up the Camino Real, as the road to the north was then known. The brother, Fray Onorato, soon fell ill and turned back at the Río Sinaloa. At the Río Mayo on March 21, a fateful decision was made. Estevanico, restless over the slow pace of the friar and his support party, would push ahead as a scout. The agreed-upon means of communication would be crosses of varying sizes, which Estevanico would send back to indicate the magnitude of wealth discovered by him. In the days ahead, he proceeded to return crosses that were progressively larger and larger. Separated by several days' travel from Fray Marcos, Estevanico apparently made excessive demands on the Indians he contacted, and he violated orders by entering towns without waiting for his Franciscan companion. Estevanico was killed at Háwikuh, the southernmost of the Zuñi pueblos known collectively as Cíbola.

Distraught over news of Estevanico's death, Fray Marcos later claimed to have viewed Cíbola from a distance before turning back to the south— a contention that is widely disputed by historians. The padre reported his findings and the demise of the unfortunate Estevanico to Coronado and then officially to the viceroy in Mexico City on September 2, 1539. He asserted that Háwikuh alone was a settlement larger than Mexico City and that it was rumored to be the least of seven cities.[41]

The excitement created by de Niza's report again piqued the interests of Cortés and also of Pedro de Alvarado. Alvarado, conqueror of Guatemala, had recently returned from Spain armed with royal authority to explore the Pacific Coast toward the north. In 1539 he began building ships at the harbor of Iztapa in Guatemala. As for Cortés, he had begun preparations for a new sea expedition to the north even before the return of Fray Marcos. Cortés's commander, a relative named Francisco de Ulloa, departed from Acapulco with three small ships in the summer of 1539. Ulloa's voyage was notable for its discovery of the mouth of the western Colorado River, the Sea of Cortés as the Gulf of California came to be known, and the fact that Baja California was a peninsula. Unfortunately for Cortés, the effort yielded no returns from the land of Cíbola. It remained for Mendoza to organize and equip an overland expedition to retrace the route of Fray Marcos.[42]

Through a series of complicated negotiations, first between Pedro de Alvarado and the crown, and then between Alvarado and Mendoza, the two men formed a partnership in November 1540. The terms of the agreement called for each to share equally the expenses and rewards of land and sea enterprises that would be directed toward Cíbola. It was clear, however, that Alvarado would continue his efforts toward maritime exploration, while Mendoza would direct his own toward overland ventures. In fact, at the time the accord was formalized, Coronado was already in the field.[43] The viceroy's sense of urgency had been dictated by the plans of Cortés and by what he perceived as a more serious threat posed by royal concessions to Hernando de Soto.

De Soto's ambitions in Florida had triumphed over those of Cabeza de Vaca. The latter returned to Spain in the summer of 1537, seeking a royal patent to colonize the region he had explored, but he was too late. In April of the same year, the crown had appointed de Soto as governor of Cuba and adelantado of Florida. De Soto was at the peak of a brilliant career, carved out primarily in the land of the Inca. He was a wealthy nobleman, a skilled horseman, and a constant captain experienced in Indian wars. Affairs in Cuba delayed final preparations for the Florida enterprise, but de Soto was under way on May 18, 1539, two months after the departure of Fray Marcos de Niza from Culiacán. It was obvious that de Soto had a head start in the race for Cíbola. Furthermore, existing maps placed the Atlantic and Pacific oceans close together in the northern Gulf latitudes, and the presumed proximity of Florida and Cíbola made it all the more imperative that Mendoza proceed without delay.[44]

Mendoza did not receive crown approval for a military undertaking to the north country or confirmation of his appointment of Coronado as governor of New Galicia until January 6, 1540. He was, however, so confident of royal approval on both counts that he had gone ahead with preparations in New Galicia for an expedition to Cíbola. In late February 1540, the viceroy reviewed an assembled army at Compostela under the command of Coronado. The force then marched to Culiacán, where it attended to last-minute details.[45]

Finally, with Fray Marcos indicating the way, Coronado's command marched up the Camino Real toward Cíbola. On July 7 it arrived at Háwikuh. The bitter disappointment of viewing the small Zuñi pueblo with its adobe walls was a harbinger of things to come. To make matters worse, Háwikuh's natives were unfriendly, forcing Coronado to fight his way into the town. After overcoming resistance at Háwikuh and exploring the other equally unimpressive towns, Coronado established temporary headquarters at Cíbola. From there a reconnoitering expedition discovered the Hopi towns of northeastern Arizona. Another force led by García López de Cárdenas was the first to view the majesty of the Grand

Canyon. But neither of these efforts brought back evidence of wealth. A third entrada, however, was momentous for Spanish Texas.[46]

While Coronado camped among the Zuñi pueblos, a small band of natives from the pueblo of Pecos arrived at Cíbola. The chief of the delegation, a handsome mustachioed Indian dubbed Bigotes by the Spaniards, informed Coronado of other settled regions in New Mexico and of "cattle" beyond the mountains to the east. Coronado's choice to investigate the story fell on Captain Hernando de Alvarado. The officer was equipped with twenty soldiers and given a commission to explore for eighty days.

Alvarado was the first Spaniard to view the Sky City of Acoma, built atop a formidable rock outcropping. It was described by one of his party as "the greatest stronghold ever seen in the world." From there, the Spanish captain traveled to the heart of Pueblo country and arrived at the province of Tiguex, situated on the Río Grande near present Bernalillo, New Mexico. Continuing on, Alvarado reached Pecos, the terminus for barter and war between the Pueblos and Plains Indians. At Pecos two captive Indians from the plains, Sopete from Quivira and "the Turk" from beyond Quivira, fell under the control of Alvarado. Both were instrumental in Spanish exploration toward Texas.[47]

Using Sopete and the Turk as guides, Alvarado descended the Pecos River for some distance and then headed eastward along the Canadian River. After a few days' travel, he encountered bison, first described by Cabeza de Vaca in his *Relación*. The animals were so numerous that they were compared with fish in the sea. Near the Texas Panhandle, the Turk spun out a tale of Quivira, a land to the north with abundant gold and silver. It was, of course, a bald-faced lie, but it struck a responsive chord in the hearts of disappointed Spaniards. News of Quivira also prompted Alvarado to cut short his commission and return to Háwikuh with an exciting report for his commander.[48] Coronado had intended to winter at Cíbola, but Alvarado's favorable report about the country to the east changed his plans. The army instead moved to Tiguex, where it suffered through a bitterly cold season made worse by the growing resentment and then open hostility of the Pueblo Indians. Only the lure of Quivira and tales of the Turk softened the stay on the Río Grande.[49]

In the spring of 1541, Coronado and his entire army left Tiguex and set out for the land of Quivira. With the Turk as his guide, Coronado passed through Pecos en route to the Buffalo Plains. His army was the first to view the Llano Estacado, literally the "Stockaded" or "Palisaded Plain."[50] Near the western edge of the Llano Estacado, Coronado encountered one or two Querecho Indian encampments. The Querechos were prototypical Plains Indians whose subsistence depended almost entirely on buffalo. Bison provided meat for food and hides for tepees, while much of the Querechos' equipment came from the animal's carcass. These people of the plains drank the digestive fluids and blood from freshly killed buffalo, storing the excess in gut containers; and their migrations were determined by the herd's movements.[51]

Coronado probably approached Texas near the route of old Highway 66, and it was he who applied the name La Vega to the region adjoining New Mexico. Misled by the Turk, Coronado traveled southeastward and encountered several branches of Palo Duro and Tule creeks. The first sizable barranca he came to was Tule Canyon to the east of present Tulia, Texas, near the line between contemporary Swisher and Briscoe counties. While camped in the canyon, Coronado's army experienced the extremes of West Texas weather. A violent hailstorm dented helmets, broke all the army's pottery (a serious loss on the plains), and scattered frightened horses. The second great barranca encountered by Coronado's army, called the Canyon of the Plains, was assuredly Palo Duro Canyon, a tremendous gorge cut in the Llano Estacado by Prairie Dog Town Creek, a tributary of the Red River (see Figure 6).[52]

At Palo Duro Canyon, Coronado decided to send the main army back to Tiguex, while he would push on toward Quivira with some thirty mounted men and a few foot soldiers. On June 1, 1541, the smaller detachment climbed out of the canyon and headed north by northeast traversing the eastern border of the High Plains to the Arkansas River.[53] Traveling "by the needle," ten to twelve degrees east of true north, Coronado's trail probably took him near the present Texas communities of Canyon, Pullman, Amarillo, Adobe Walls, Borger, Gruver, and Hitchland. Coronado crossed the Arkansas River near present Ford, Kansas, and from there traveled northeast to the vicinity of Lindsborg, Kansas. This location brought him to the eastern edge of Quivira, but instead of golden cities he found only grass huts and cornfields of the Wichita Indians. These same Indians would later migrate to Texas and adapt to the buffalo-plains cultural pattern.[54]

The Turk had been confined in chains during the journey to Quivira, and before leaving there Coronado reluctantly ordered him garroted. The Indian had lied about the land and attempted to save his skin by urging the Quivirans to slaughter the Spaniards and their horses. On the return to Pueblo country, Coronado retraced his route along the Arkansas River to where he had forded it and then traveled southwest to the present Kansas-Oklahoma border where he began to break new trail. His march crossed the extreme northwest corner of the Texas Panhandle.[55]

Shortly after reaching Tiguex, Coronado announced his intent to return to Mexico in the spring of 1542. Three religious persons and a secular, however, refused to leave with him. Juan Padilla, the only ordained priest, chose Quivira as his mission field and returned there with two Indian lay brothers, Lucas and Sebastián, and a Portuguese companion, Andrés do Campo. Fray Padilla began his teachings among the Wichitas, who received him well. Unfortunately, his efforts to explore east of Quivira ended in martyrdom at the hands of unidentified natives. His three companions did manage to escape and crossed Texas from north to south en route to safety in Mexico. Their journey was yet another remarkable example of pedestrian travel across the Texas landscape.[56]

In retrospect the Coronado expedition was the first contact of Europeans with the Plains Indians of Texas, Oklahoma, and Kansas. It crossed the Texas Panhandle, reconnoitered the land, and assessed the resources of the region. Coronado's leadership of men in the north country was generally quite good and his losses in personnel were small, especially when compared to the record of Pánfilo de Narváez and Hernando de Soto. However, his failure to discover rich lands that could be settled from Mexico caused the viceroy and other officials in New Spain to regard him as a failure.[57]

It is perhaps unfortunate that the Coronado and de Soto expeditions did not make contact with each other, for they jointly explored the north country from Florida to Arizona in the years 1539–1543. With luck they might have returned to New Spain as a single unit. There was nevertheless an ironic link between them near the end of both ventures.

De Soto, Mendoza's chief competitor in the race to claim Cíbola, approached Texas and New Mexico from the east. He had landed in Florida with some six hundred men in May 1539. The terms of de Soto's patent were indeed generous. He could select two hundred leagues of coastline as the confines of his government, and he had four years to explore before designating the frontage. His expedition was notable for the blunt assertion that its intended goal was plunder. Valuable objects obtained from natives by war or trade would be assessed the royal *quinto*, but treasure taken from graves, sepulchers, and temples would be shared equally with the king.[58]

Shortly after the landing in the vicinity of Charlotte Harbor, de Soto's army found a survivor of the Narváez expedition who had spent eleven years among Florida Indians. Reunited with his countrymen, Juan Ortiz, until his death in the spring of 1542, would serve as de Soto's chief guide and interpreter. In their peregrinations from May 1539 to May 1542, de Soto and his army covered hundreds of miles, primarily in the present states of Florida, Georgia, Alabama, Mississippi, Arkansas, and Louisiana. In all their wanderings a small chest of inferior quality freshwater pearls was the extent of the plunder that fell into their hands, and even this booty was lost during an Indian attack in Alabama.[59] After three years in the field, de Soto was struck by a raging fever that took his life within a week. As his illness worsened, he recognized the need to appoint a successor. The choice fell on Luis de Moscoso Alvarado. At the time of de Soto's death (May 21, 1542), his army was perhaps camped at the junction of the Ouachita and Mississippi rivers near present Ferriday, Louisiana.[60]

On June 5 Moscoso and his army headed westward from the Mississippi River, seeking an overland passage to New Spain. Moscoso's journey outside and within Texas, like Cabeza de Vaca's, has sparked considerable disagreement among interpreters of his route. In charting the most probable path followed by Moscoso, one should again be sensitive to time and distance traveled, geography, biota, hydrography, and mineralogy.[61] When all data are correlated, it seems likely that Moscoso crossed the Red River near the modern boundaries of La Fayette and Miller counties in Arkansas—more precisely about four or five miles below present Garland City, Arkansas. From there, Moscoso blazed a trail southwest by south, and on the third day after leaving the Red arrived at a sandy region west of Atlanta, Texas, in late August 1542. His men then marched southward near modern Jefferson, Texas, and continued on to Harrison County. Moscoso probably passed near present San Augustine and at that juncture turned westward to the Angelina River west of Nacogdoches. Beyond that river he maintained a westerly direction, reaching the Neches River near the sites of modern Alto and Weches. The farthest extent of Moscoso's penetration into Texas was probably the Trinity River in southwestern Houston County (see Figure 6). This expedition provided the first documented contact by Europeans with Indians of the Hasinai Confederacy. Moscoso and his men also gained acquaintance with an area that was vitally important in the early history of Spanish Texas.[62]

During the Spaniards' stay in East Texas, a young Indian woman encountered Moscoso's soldiers. She had previously been a "captive Indian girl belonging to Juan de Zaldívar," one of Coronado's captains, and had escaped from him while the army was camped in Palo Duro Canyon— only to fall into the clutches of other Spaniards. With just two expeditions in the entire north country, this woman has to rank as one of the unluckiest persons on record. But perhaps she unintentionally gained a measure of revenge. Moscoso, refusing to believe her story of contact with other white men, returned to the crossing of the Red River and from there marched back to the Mississippi River, arriving in late 1542. Had he given credence to the Indian woman's account, the de Soto expedition might well have reached New Spain by way of Texas and New Mexico.[63]

Shortly after his return, Moscoso decided on a water route to New Spain and began the construction of seven small craft. While skilled craftsmen had been recruited for the de Soto expedition, the creativity of Spaniards stranded in the wilderness was again remarkable. Seams were caulked with plant fibers; slave chains were forged into spikes; and sails were fashioned from skins and scraps of woven hemp.[64]

In July 1543, 322 Spaniards began the descent of the great river. Reaching the coast, they sailed the Gulf Coast shoreline from the Mississippi Delta to Pánuco without serious mishap. While harbored in an inlet during a storm on the Texas coast, Moscoso and his men discovered surfaced crude oil. Its value, other than as caulk for their leaky barges, was of course lost on them. Their journey ended on September 10, 1543, when they arrived at Santiesteban del Puerto. Only ten men had been lost since embarking on the Mississippi River. After resting, the survivors set out for Mexico City, where they were graciously received by Antonio de Mendoza. Ironically, men who had set out as rivals of the viceroy were welcomed back into the community of Spaniards by him.[65]

The Coronado and de Soto expeditions had both set off with high hopes of finding "another Mexico" or "another Peru." Both had ended in bitter disappointment. During his second winter on the Río Grande, Coronado suffered a serious head injury when a saddle girth snapped at full gallop, spilling him under the hooves of a nearby steed. After the accident, he "was never quite himself." He was certainly blameless for not finding in Cíbola and Quivira what was never there, but his remaining years were nonetheless filled with gloominess of spirit and ill health.[66] As for the de Soto undertaking, it ended with its commander dead, a 50 percent loss in personnel, and not a single peso of spoils. At a heavy cost, some knowledge of the north country and its inhabitants had been acquired by Coronado and de Soto, but little else.

The final contemporary piece of information about the land of *más allá* also fell into place in the early 1540s. Antonio de Mendoza's partnership with Pedro de Alvarado dissolved with the death of Alvarado (July 4, 1541) in the Mixtón War. Accordingly, Mendoza found himself sole heir to Alvarado's Pacific fleet. The viceroy appointed Juan Rodríguez Cabrillo, who had been second in command under Alvarado, as captain and ordered him to reconnoiter the coast of California. At the time Cabrillo set sail in June 1542, his sponsor was fully aware of Coronado's failure to find wealth. So Cabrillo's voyage was a completely independent venture.[67] The expedition was important, for it brought back the first information about the coast of Upper California and its inhabitants. Cabrillo, however, died on the voyage (January 3, 1543) due to complications from a severely broken limb. Bartolomé Ferrelo, his second in command, completed the exploration and returned to port in April 1543. Ferrelo's report, however, was all too familiar: unpromising land, poor Indians, and another dead captain.[68]

THE FIRST STAGE OF EXPLORATION AND DISCOVERY IN THE north country came to an end in the early 1540s. Unfortunately for them, Spaniards had found no booty in Florida, no riches in Texas, no wealthy Seven Cities of Cíbola in New Mexico, no Gran Quivira in Kansas, and no gold in California. It was apparent from firsthand information that a land mass of continental proportions lay to the north of New Spain, but its size was formidable, its people often inhospitable, and its soil unpromising to treasure-seeking adventurers. Future expansion toward Texas would be more measured and less dramatic, and its agents would be more prosaic than the golden conquistadors. Nevertheless, the hope of finding rich kingdoms in the north country persisted for some time.[69]

THREE

The Northward Advance toward Texas, 1543–1680

LEGENDS DIED HARD FOR SPANIARDS. DESPITE THE UNFAVORABLE reports of Coronado and Moscoso about the north country, Tierra Nueva, as it was then called, continued to attract the attention of gold-hungry men in New Spain. Within five years after Coronado's return to Mexico, the presumed wealth of Gran Quivira was again a subject of interest for colonial officials. By then Coronado had fallen on hard times, and it was commonly held that a more resourceful captain could do better.[1] How does one explain such persistent, chimerical visions?

Spaniards who came to the New World saw it "through medieval spectacles." Many of them were influenced by St. Augustine, who had devoted an entire chapter of *The City of God* to the question of whether descendants of Adam and Noah had produced monstrous and bizarre offspring. All of them remembered the facades of medieval churches that sprouted griffins, gargoyles, and a mixture of man and beast. Accordingly, beyond every mountain and horizon, Spanish captains looked for mythical and fabulous creatures. Their expectations, which included finding giants, white-haired boys, bearded ladies, human beings with tails, headless folk with an eye in their navel, and trumpet-blowing apes, were only enhanced by the very real discoveries of enormous wealth within the Aztec and Inca empires.[2] Texas, too, had its share of the fantasies that beckoned Spaniards into unknown realms. Explorers would look for the Seven Hills of Aijados, where gold was so plentiful that natives tipped their arrows and spears with it, for the Pearls of the Jumanos, and for the Great Kingdom of the Tejas.[3]

This chapter details the slow northward advance of New Spain, an impetus supplied by adventurers, prospectors, ranchers, friars, and soldiers (see Figure 7). Over the following century and a third (1543–1680), Spaniards compiled considerable information about Texas and its potential for settlement. Cast in this light, their response in the late 1680s to

FIGURE 7

*Central and northern New Spain. This map depicts the location
of major rivers, towns, and settlements that are mentioned in the text.
(Cartography by Caroline Castillo Crimm.)*

the founding of a French colony on the Gulf Coast was not entirely reflexive.

EXPANSION OF NEW SPAIN BY WAY OF THE NORTH-CENTRAL plateau had been pioneered by Nuño de Guzmán. Once Guzmán founded San Miguel de Culiacán as the northern outpost of New Galicia, he was about halfway along the direct route to the fabled Seven Cities. But instead of following the coast, Don Nuño turned eastward toward the Sierra Madre of Durango, one of the most formidable mountain barriers on the North American continent. His initial expeditions, three in total, were ultimately frustrated by impassable ramparts. Perhaps Guzmán believed his approach was the best route to Pueblo country, but that is unlikely since Indians in the region knew the proven way. His real motive for probing the mountainous area must have been to link New Galicia with Pánuco, where he had held the governorship since 1527. If successful, Don Nuño's control of northern New Spain would stretch from ocean to ocean.[4]

Guzmán's fourth attempt to penetrate the Sierra Madre came in the first months of 1533. At the head of a small force, he left Nochistlán for the long, difficult march to Pánuco. Success was assured when he broke through the mountains in the spring and founded the *villa* of Santiago de los Valles. Guzmán incorporated the settlement under his rule as governor of New Galicia, although it was in close proximity to Pánuco. By establishing the eastern boundary of New Galicia between Pánuco and modern Valles, he laid claim to a huge expanse of northern New Spain known as Gran Chichimeca. The importance of his accomplishment is best appreciated when one remembers that little more than a decade later other Spaniards discovered the rich silver mines of Zacatecas.[5]

However, Guzmán's control of access to Tierra Nueva was a reality for only a few months. The crown removed Pánuco and Valles from his jurisdiction in 1533–1534, and Guzmán himself was relieved as governor of New Galicia with the arrival of his replacement in early 1537. Coronado's departure for Cíbola and the outbreak of the Mixtón War delayed further exploration of Gran Chichimeca for several years.[6]

At the conclusion of the Mixtón War (1542), no Spaniard had yet made a profitable entrada into the north-central plateau. The effective line of settlement ran southwestward from the Río Pánuco to Querétaro, then west along the Río Lerma to Lago de Chapala. From the lake the frontier turned sharply to the northwest and followed the inner coast to Culiacán. Expansion of the frontier between the Sierra Madre Oriental and Occidental ranges was a dangerous undertaking, for it was the domain of fierce, seminomadic tribes known collectively as the Chichimeca.

"Chichimeca," often translated as "Barbarian," was a term applied to natives who ranged across a broad expanse of territory, roughly from Saltillo in the north to the Río Lerma in the south. The term encompassed four major nations: the Pames, Guamares, Zacatecos, and Guachichiles. Collectively, these warriors were noted for their proficiency with the bow and arrow and their nudity. An awed Spanish adversary commented: "In the opinion of men experienced in foreign lands, the Zacatecos are the best archers in the world. They kill hares which, even though running, they pierce with arrows; also deer, birds, and other little animals of the land, not even overlooking rats." As for nudity, the men discarded any covering of the body as they entered battle for the startling "effect" it produced on their enemies. Fueled by alcohol and peyote, their ferocity in battle, combined with terrain unfavorable to the Spaniard, discouraged European entry into Tierra Nueva. But circumstances changed dramatically in the late summer of 1546.[8]

Operating out of Guadalajara, Captain Juan de Tolosa, a small party of soldiers, and four Franciscan padres arrived at the future site of Zacatecas in September 1546. Tolosa camped at the base of a large mountain known from that time forward as La Bufa. He convinced a few Zacatecos of his peaceful intentions and in exchange for trinkets received gifts of ore. Samples from La Bufa were also collected, strapped to mules, and sent south to Nochistlán for an assay. The ore proved to be exceptionally high in silver content and gave hope of riches long dreamed of but unrealized since the fall of the Aztec capital. Mines had been worked by Spaniards in New Galicia as early as 1543, but the magnitude of the strike at Zacatecas surpassed all earlier discoveries.[9]

Joining Tolosa at Zacatecas were three prominent veterans and prospectors: Cristóbal de Oñate, acting governor of New Galicia before Coronado's appointment and during his absence in the field; Diego de Ibarra, an experienced soldier who had fought in the Mixtón War; and Baltasar Temiño de Bañuelos, who would assume leadership in the forthcoming Chichimeca wars. By early 1548 these men constituted the "big four" of Nuestra Señora de Zacatecas.[10]

Within two years after its founding, Zacatecas had become a classic boom town with sixty-one mine owners in residence. Tolosa, the original discoverer, lagged well behind Oñate in mining entrepreneurship. He possessed only one stamp mill and smelter, while Oñate owned a total of thirteen mills and smelters, 101 households of slaves, and a residence with a private chapel. Tolosa, while financially less successful than Oñate, did marry well. His bride was Leonor Cortés Moctezuma, the product of a liaison between Fernando Cortés and a daughter of the Aztec emperor, Moctezuma II. Ibarra, another member of the big four, would expend much of his accumulated wealth to underwrite the important but costly explorations beyond Zacatecas by his nephew, Francisco de Ibarra.[11]

A prominent addition to the silver aristocracy was the Zaldívar family whose patriarchs, Don Juan and Don Vicente, had figured prominently in the conquest and settlement of New Galicia. By the second generation, the Zaldívars and Oñates had entered into complex intermarriages. Juan de Oñate, the future adelantado of New Mexico and trailblazer in the Texas Panhandle, was both uncle and second cousin to the Maestres de Campo Vicente and Juan de Zaldívar, his closest associates in those undertakings. Oñate's wife, Isabel de Tolosa Cortés Moctezuma, was also the daughter of Tolosa and Leonor Cortés Moctezuma.[12]

To supply the needs of the silver aristocracy and the rich mines of Zacatecas, an arterial road ran southeastward from there, via San Felipe and Querétaro, to the capital. Other approaches to the mining town ran almost due north from Nochistlán and Guadalajara. In late 1550 a group of Hispanicized Tarascan Indians, loaded with merchandise and bound for the mining frontier, were killed by Zacatecos. This incident was the opening salvo of conflict with the Chichimeca nations, a war that would engulf the northern frontier of Mexico for nearly half a century. The course of this conflict was crucial to expansion along the north-central plateau of New Spain toward Texas.[13]

At the same time that Indian warfare retarded overland expansion, events transpired in the Gulf of Mexico that would hasten Spaniards to the shores of Texas. Eleven years after Luis de Moscoso had sailed the Texas coast in improvised barges, a sizable number of Spaniards were shipwrecked there. They were part of a flotilla containing more than twenty vessels and one thousand passengers bound for Spain from Veracruz in April 1554. After a brief stop in Cuba, the ships were caught in a severe storm and blown westward into the Gulf. Three of the craft, *Santa María de Yciar, San Esteban,* and *Espíritu Santo,* wrecked on the Texas coast near the southern extremity of Padre Island. Of the nearly three hundred survivors, about thirty apparently managed to salvage one of the ship's boats and sail it to Pánuco or Veracruz. The remaining castaways, including women, small children, and five Dominican friars, attempted to walk the coast to Santiesteban del Puerto, with Indians killing stragglers along the way.[14]

When the survivors reached the mouth of the Río Grande, they constructed rafts from driftwood. Unfortunately, in negotiating the crossing a cumbersome bundle containing the crossbows was accidentally cast overboard. The loss of these long-range weapons left the Spaniards vulnerable to the Indians' arrows. All of the shipwrecked victims save one or two were killed between the Río Grande and the Río de las Palmas. One survivor, a Dominican lay brother named Marcos de Mena, who had been left for dead by a larger party, somehow recovered from his wounds and walked to Pánuco. His account of the disaster may have prompted salvage vessels to sail to the Texas coast in the summer of 1554. The site of the wrecked vessels was reached on July 22, Magdalene's Day, and in accord with the Spanish custom of naming geographical features for religious occasions, it was designated Médanos de Magdalena. Salvage operations at Magdalene's Dunes recovered less than half of the gold and silver registered aboard the three vessels.[15]

Concern over the safety of men and ships plying Gulf Coast waters as well as military and missionary impulses designed to punish and then Christianize the coastal tribes led directly to a planned expedition to the Texas coast. Those considerations, plus the fact that Spanish presence would serve to deter foreign adventures on the Gulf Coast, were impressed upon the crown and the second viceroy of New Spain, Luis de Velasco. As a preliminary to plans for colonization, three vessels were outfitted and placed under the command of an experienced mariner, Guido de Lavazares. Armed with orders to reconnoiter the Gulf from the Río de las Palmas to the Florida Keys, Lavazares lifted anchor at Veracruz on September 3, 1558. After a brief stop in Pánuco, the ships sailed directly to the Texas coast, striking it in the latitude of present Kingsville, Texas. From that point Lavazares followed the shoreline until he came to a large body of water, apparently Matagorda Bay, which he named San Francisco. He went ashore there and claimed the region for the king of Spain. Thus, a Spaniard discovered and named the bay 127 years before La Salle arrived there under the flag of France. Lavazares continued exploration eastward beyond Mobile Bay, where contrary headwinds forced him to turn about and sail to Veracruz. A second preliminary expedition, led by Gonzalo Gayón, sailed counterclockwise along the Florida and Texas coasts in the late 1550s, but attention soon shifted from the Texas coast.[16]

In the second half of the sixteenth century, the most important Gulf Coast area was the Florida peninsula. With its long shoreline, large Indian population, and strategic importance to Gulf waters and the Bahama Straits, Florida overshadowed all other littoral regions and became the focus of intermittent military and missionary enterprises throughout the remainder of the century. This activity, as was the case with the Nar-váez and de Soto expeditions, had important ramifications for Texas.

In the immediate aftermath of the Lavazares and Gayón reconnoiter-ing expeditions, plans were finalized for settlement of the Florida penin-sula. From New Spain, Tristán de Luna y Arellano, second in command to Coronado on the march to Cíbola, was the next to try his hand where Ponce de León, Narváez, and de Soto had suffered so much misfortune. This well-prepared expedition likewise fell on hard times due to bad weather, unfavorable terrain, and de Luna's illness. A support expedition led by Angel de Villafañe failed to sustain the Florida settlement, and the last of his troops were removed in late 1561. At that juncture, "New Spain shucked responsibility" for the settlement of Florida. The penin-sula would be the focal point of bitter international rivalry between Spain and France in the 1560s and 1570s, but Spanish approaches to it would be made from points other than New Spain. These developments por-tended significantly for the Gulf Coast, for it no longer served as a lifeline to Florida. Another century would pass before Spanish navigators would again probe the mouth of the Mississippi River, but by then it was too late to avert French designs on that vital region. Meanwhile, the northern frontier of New Spain advanced along a broad front toward Texas.[17]

In theory, expansion into Gran Chichimeca fell under a comprehensive set of regulations known as the New Laws, formally approved by the emperor Charles V at Barcelona on November 20, 1542. While the leg-islation covered a wide variety of matters, provisions regarding Indian servitude had the greatest impact on the frontier of New Spain. The laws commanded "that henceforth, for no cause of war nor any cause what-soever … can an Indian be made a slave." Indians already enslaved were to be set free if they had lost their freedom "against all reason and right." Enforcement of the edict, however, was erratic throughout the colony, and it was especially lax on the distant mining frontier.[18] The New Laws also called for phasing out encomienda, a complicated institution whereby Spanish overseers (encomenderos) received free Indian vassals with work or tribute obligations. Subsequent modification of that stipulation and dissimulation on the part of colonial officials combined to perpetuate en-comienda throughout the entire colonial era. But in 1549 labor obliga-tions on the part of encomienda Indians were terminated, bringing even greater temptations to violate the interdict on Indian bondage.[19]

During the years 1550–1585, official policy toward the Chichimeca nations evolved into a contest labeled guerra a fuego y a sangre. War by fire and blood meant that concerted military pressure would be brought to bear on the hostiles. Overall, this intense struggle failed to pacify frontier natives. The nation that had defeated with comparative ease the highest Indian civilizations in Mexico and Peru had little success with the Chichimecas. In addition to their deadly proficiency with bow and arrow, these frontier cultures were decentralized and did not depend on agriculture for sustenance. Accordingly, control of native food sources, a powerful lever that worked well on sedentary cultures, was not applicable against the Chichimecas. Other impediments to Spanish policy were the Indians' knowledge of terrain and the difficulty of their languages, a circumstance that hindered Spanish communication and thwarted the missionaries as agents of pacification. Spain's wide-ranging commitments elsewhere in the second half of the sixteenth century and the lack of an agreed-upon system for funding the war further abetted Indian resistance.[20]

An initial step toward securing roads and lines of communication in Gran Chichimeca, one which figured importantly for the entire Spanish Borderlands, led to the creation of defensive towns and presidios. The first walled and garrisoned presidios were probably built in 1570 between San Felipe and Zacatecas on the most dangerous leg of the route from the capital. Additional military outposts were soon added to the original two. Eventually, dozens of garrisons dotted the frontier—from Pánuco to Durango, from Querétaro and Guadalajara to Saltillo. Overall, however, it appears that presidial soldiers did not substantially alter the course of the Chichimeca wars. While security was undoubtedly better on the roads, the conduct of poorly paid frontier captains and soldiers often served to incite Chichimeca hostility. By the early 1580s, pacification of the northern frontier by *guerra a fuego y a sangre* had clearly failed. Chichimeca resistance, destruction of property, and loss of life had actually increased.[21]

However, a new dimension in Spanish Indian policy developed during the decisive years 1585–1600. The shift in tactics emerged from an important gathering, the Third Mexican Provincial Council of 1585. Despite recommendations by colonial officials and the council's advisers that "fire and blood" policy be continued, Mexican bishops condemned its injustice. A new approach termed "peace by purchase," instituted by the seventh viceroy of New Spain, Alvaro Manrique de Zúñiga, would henceforth attempt pacification by persuasion, rather than by the sword.[22]

Viceroy Manrique began the practice of providing food and clothing for the Chichimecas in exchange for promises of good behavior. He recognized, too, that the very soldiers charged with securing the frontier were in reality agents of Indian unrest. The men squandered their salaries, then supplemented their income by goading the Chichimecas into rebellion, whereupon under a revision of the New Laws they could sell the offending natives into slavery for thirteen years. Restraints on this underhanded practice were imposed by the viceroy. More important, he moved colonies of Hispanicized and Christianized Indians from Central Mexico to the frontier, where they served as models of desirable conduct. By the later decades of the sixteenth century, Franciscan and Jesuit padres who had learned the difficult languages of the Chichimeca nations became more effective as agents of conversion and pacification. The viceroys who followed Manrique de Zúñiga accelerated his policies, and by 1600 "it could be said that the Spanish-Chichimeca War had come to an end." In fifteen years "peace by purchase" accomplished results not achieved in four decades of bloody warfare.[23]

Near the end of the conflict, the frontier of New Spain had advanced steadily toward Texas, and its most northern outposts had served as staging areas for expeditions that again brought Spaniards upon Texas soil. Contributing significantly to the expansion of the frontier were the actions of Francisco de Ibarra and, later, of Luis de Carvajal y de la Cueva. Ibarra carried out extensive exploration in the Mexican states of Sonora, Sinaloa, Chihuahua, and Durango. His active career, which spanned the years 1554–1575, may be divided into preliminary (1554–1562) and major (1563–1575) explorations.[24]

Francisco de Ibarra was the favored nephew of Diego de Ibarra. His silver-aristocrat uncle was not only wealthy but was also the son-in-law of Viceroy Luis de Velasco. The political ties of his uncle perhaps explain approval of the younger Ibarra when he was only seventeen to lead the first authorized expedition to the north and west of Zacatecas. Ibarra's initial entrada traversed the states of Zacatecas and Durango, and after an absence of three months he returned to the town of Zacatecas in late 1554. His discoveries prompted settlement of San Martín, a mining region northwest of Zacatecas, within two or three years. By the early 1560s, Viceroy Velasco had empowered Ibarra, then armed with titles of governor and captain general of Nueva Vizcaya, to carry out extensive exploration, conquest, and settlement of unknown lands to the north of San Martín. A major motive in dispatching Ibarra was the viceroy's desire to provide a missionary padre for Indian towns beyond the settled frontier.[25]

In late 1563 Ibarra founded the city of Durango and in the following year explored the upper tributaries of the Río Conchos in southern Chihuahua. Three years later in that same region Rodrigo del Río de Losa established a mining camp at Santa Bárbara in the San Bartolomé valley.

This locale would become the primary staging area for expeditions to New Mexico and Texas. Within a decade a series of settlements, revolving around mining, wheat farms, and cattle ranches, extended from Durango in the south to the village of San Bartolomé in the north. Settlers under Ibarra's command occupied the future sites of Monterrey, Cerralvo, and Monclova, but after the premature death of Francisco de Ibarra in 1575, those regions as well as Saltillo were claimed by a rival, Luis de Carvajal, and annexed to Nuevo León.

The explorations of Carvajal in northeastern New Spain were indirectly related to events transpiring in Florida and were aided by still another example of gross misperceptions of geography. Florida in the broadest sense incorporated the Gulf Coast from the peninsula to the province of Pánuco. After the bloody triumph (1565) of the great Spanish admiral, Pedro Menéndez de Aviles, over French Huguenots on the Atlantic Coast of Florida, Menéndez petitioned the crown for permission to settle the region north of Pánuco. The admiral insisted that the Río de las Palmas, the present Soto la Marina, lay only eighty leagues via the coast from Santa Elena, Florida! The Audiencia of Mexico, when consulted on the matter, was quick to point out that the actual distance was between 450 and 600 leagues, whereas the river in question was only 60 leagues from Mexico. Geographic realities notwithstanding, a royal cedula dated February 23, 1573, authorized Menéndez to settle the Palmas from a base in Pánuco and to pacify natives not then under the jurisdiction of New Spain. He died in 1574 before acting, but his settlement rights passed to a nephew.[26] This potential challenge to the Palmas from Florida, however, bestirred efforts in Mexico to expand another area of the frontier toward Texas.

The agent of defensive expansion was Luis de Carvajal, who was Portuguese by birth and Jewish by heritage. He was the son of "new Christian" parents, meaning recent converts to Roman Catholicism. In New Spain, Carvajal won a measure of fame by capturing several dozen stranded and helpless English corsairs on the coast of Pánuco. The men had been put ashore by John Hawkins in 1568 after he had suffered a near disastrous defeat by the Spanish navy. One of the Englishmen who eluded Carvajal was David Ingram. He and two companions somehow walked from Pánuco along the Gulf and Atlantic coasts to near Cape Breton, Nova Scotia, and lived to write about the trek. In many respects Ingram's odyssey across Texas and beyond is as remarkable as that of Cabeza de Vaca.[27]

In reward for his capture of English pirates, Viceroy Martín Enríquez appointed Carvajal as alcalde of Tampico and commissioned him with the task of finding a road between Pánuco and the mines of Mazapil, located to the southwest of Saltillo. Once he accomplished his primary objective, Carvajal was to swing toward the mouth of the Río Grande and then proceed down the coast, punishing Indians who had been invariably hostile toward survivors of Spanish shipwrecks. Carvajal completed his first assignment, opening the possibility of direct contact from the Río Pánuco or Río de las Palmas with the mines of Zacatecas, San Martín, Mazapil, and Santa Bárbara. He then proceeded to the Río Grande. It appears that Carvajal was the first European to cross the lower Río Grande into Texas, where he later carried out reprisals against the coastal tribes, although the latter was of "little lasting benefit."[28]

Carvajal returned to Spain in early March 1579. There he presented a grandiose plan to the Council of the Indies and Philip II. From a base in New Spain, Carvajal proposed to tie the colony to Florida by settling all Gulf ports from Pánuco to Santa Elena. His persuasiveness combined with a poor sense of geography bore fruit. Carvajal received the titles of governor and military commander of the Nuevo Reino de León. The new kingdom was an enormous "square" of land two hundred leagues on a side. With the mouth of the Río Pánuco as its reference point, Carvajal's jurisdiction extended north to the site of San Antonio, Texas, and west to include almost all of the Mexican states of Zacatecas and Durango. It also included substantial portions of San Luis Potosí, Nayarit, Sinaloa, and Chihuahua. In its entirety, Nuevo León encompassed an estimated 702,244 square kilometers.[29]

Carvajal's grant left him hundreds of leagues short of Florida proper, but it brought him, significantly, into conflict with mining properties long established by other Spaniards. The latter factor as well as his reluctance to accept viceregal authority in New Spain and to abide by a new set of royal ordinances issued in 1573 contributed to his downfall.[30] Carvajal persisted in slaving activities that ranged along the coast from Pánuco north to the Río Grande. While in the interior, he founded the settlements of Ciudad León, Villa de la Cueva, and Villa de Almadén, the latter at the site of Monclova. His encroachment on localities established by followers of Francisco de Ibarra, his overweening ambition, and his Jewish heritage led to Carvajal's arrest on orders of the Holy Office of the Inquisition. Convicted of heresy, his sentence in early 1590 included six years of exile from New Spain, but he died in prison before the end of the year. His Almadén settlement fell under the charge of Gaspar Castaño de Sosa, a minor actor on the developing stage of New Mexico and Texas.[31]

The combined activities of Francisco de Ibarra, Luis de Carvajal, and their followers had carved out the provinces of Nueva Vizcaya and Nuevo León by the late sixteenth century. At the same time, those accomplishments had been buttressed by economic enterprises on the frontier—especially mining. The treatment of Indians and the course of the Chichimeca wars, however, had influenced issuance of new ordinances in 1573, which in turn affected entradas into Tierra Nueva.

Mining of course was the favored economic activity on the frontier, for it held the prospect of instant wealth. Far more important for Texas, however, was the rapidly developing cattle industry. Cattle had arrived in the New World on the second voyage of Columbus. From the Caribbean, Gregorio Villalobos and Fernando Cortés introduced the first breeding stock to the mainland shortly after the conquest of Mexico. The principal strains of Spanish cattle were the piebald, a half-wild range animal, and the *ganado prieto,* ancient black bovines related to Andalucian fighting bulls.[32]

Ranching as it developed in Mexico was a purely Spanish innovation. North American Indians had no large domesticated animals, and in Mexico, with few exceptions, natives did not farm beyond a line beginning slightly north of Veracruz and extending west by northwest past the Central Valley to the Pacific Ocean just south of Tepic. To the north of this line the lands of Gran Chichimeca were cut by barrancas and rugged mountains with grazing potential suited to the introduction of European livestock. To this end, cattle were driven north after the Mixtón War, and by 1550 the grasslands around Querétaro supported a promising and flourishing cattle industry. To aid the development of cattle ranches, the crown granted to individuals enormous 4,338-acre tracts known as *sitios de ganado mayor.*[33]

After the silver strikes of the 1540s, in some regions ranchers and miners lived in a symbiotic relationship. Beef, leather, and tallow were essentials to miners, who provided markets and much needed specie for ranchers. The Mexican states of Zacatecas, Durango, Chihuahua, and Coahuila constituted "the oldest and best cattle raising region of New Spain north of the Tropic of Cancer." Within Nueva Vizcaya, pasture lands were so lush that they attracted not only cattlemen but also great herds of feral animals that moved northward on their own accord. Managed herds increased at an astonishing rate with some ranches claiming more than 100,000 head of cattle. Bigness was so commonplace that a mere 20,000 head "was considered a small number." Where mines were absent or played out, cattle raising proved to be the dominant industry. Indeed, investments in land and cattle were among the few economic opportunities available to most settlers, clergy, and government officials.

As geographer Donald D. Brand demonstrated, Walter P. Webb's contention that cattle raising outside the Great Plains did not play a significantly important role is untenable, for Webb's thesis "completely ignores an older and highly important frontier that moved northward from central Mexico and left its indelible imprint on what is today the region from Texas to California."[34] Ranching was especially associated with missions on the frontier, where friars became part-time vaqueros. By the end of the sixteenth century, the northern fringe of ranching ran in a rough arc from Culiacán to the southern borders of Chihuahua and then dropped southward toward Monterrey.[35] Sizable herds of livestock in this region would provide essential components of future expeditions into Tierra Nueva.

As the mining and cattle frontier advanced and the Chichimeca wars intensified, differences over treatment of Indians also escalated. A general ordinance issued by Philip II on July 13, 1573, superseded all existing regulations regarding future conquests by land or sea. The regulations were a temporary victory for the advocates of benign policy toward Indians, and they extolled the benefits of Spanish civilization for natives who accepted the cross. Future encounters between Hispanic and Indian cultures must be strictly licensed by proper authorities, and the word "conquest" was stricken in favor of "pacification." If, however, all efforts toward peaceful persuasion failed, then hostiles were to be subdued with "as little harm as possible." In any event, the 1573 ordinances reinforced the injunction against Indian enslavement. While the laws of 1573 remained in force throughout the colonial era, they—like the earlier New Laws—were selectively enforced and vitiated by circumstance. The ordinances reflected, nevertheless, the considerable influence of religious persons on Spanish policymaking.[36]

While treatment of missions on the frontier will be reserved for later, it is important to note here that Franciscan padres were present in Nueva Vizcaya from its beginnings. But the mission field was so large and the number of friars so limited that Jesuits also entered the picture near the end of the sixteenth century. The first record of Black Robes visiting Durango came in 1589. Jesuits aided in pacifying the Chichimeca and were established in the provincial capital by the middle 1590s, the very time a contractual agreement was signed by Juan de Oñate for the permanent settlement of New Mexico.[37] By then the Franciscans had already suffered additional martyrs in Tierra Nueva.

The settlements of Santa Bárbara and San Bartolomé, situated at the headwaters of the Río Conchos in southern Chihuahua, were logical gateways to Texas and New Mexico. Despite prohibitions on Indian bondage in the New Laws, slaving expeditions in search of labor for mines in the region had already followed the Conchos toward its confluence with the Río Grande. In the late 1570s, an Indian captive with knowledge of New Mexico spoke of populous settlements to the north wherein the people had abundant food and raised cotton for clothing. This information jogged memories of the Pueblo country, not visited by Spaniards for nearly forty years. Fray Agustín Rodríguez, a Franciscan lay brother stationed at San Bartolomé, successfully petitioned the viceroy for permission to revisit the land of the Pueblo. Two fellow Franciscans selected to accompany Fray Augustín were Francisco López, as religious superior, and Juan de Santa María. The military commander of the expedition was an aged veteran, Francisco Sánchez Chamuscado, with Hernán Gallegos serving as second in command. In early June 1581, the small party of nine soldiers and three friars departed Santa Bárbara. After descending the Conchos to its junction with the Río Grande, the Spaniards contacted Indians there who were probably Jumanos. From La Junta the Spanish ascended the Río Grande toward El Paso and then continued along the streambed to the Tiguex pueblos near present Albuquerque.[38]

The Chamuscado-Rodríguez-López expedition explored New Mexico north toward Taos. Near present Santa Fe, Fray Juan de Santa María chose to leave the group and report directly to the viceroy. Unfortunately, a war party followed him for three days, overtook him, and crushed his skull with a rock. Later, Chamuscado marched eastward to the Buffalo Plains. Along the Pecos River, he came upon Querechos, the same prototypical buffalo hunters encountered by Coronado forty years earlier, but it is doubtful that Chamuscado reached the borders of Texas on this entrada. After westward explorations to Acoma and Zuñi were completed, Chamuscado announced his intent to return to Santa Bárbara and to file a report with the viceroy. Against his vigorous objections, the two remaining Franciscans insisted on staying in New Mexico. Chamuscado, who was nearly seventy years of ago, died on the final leg of the expedition before reaching his intended destination.[39]

The remaining soldiers under the command of Hernán Gallegos returned to Santa Bárbara in April 1582, after an absence of nearly eleven months. Gallegos's report lent information about the Indians at La Junta and in New Mexico as well as those encountered on the Buffalo Plains toward Texas. The alcalde of Santa Bárbara immediately claimed the newly explored lands for the governor of Nueva Vizcaya. Efforts by Gallegos to win possession in his own right ended when his petition, carried in person before the Spanish crown, was rejected in March 1583.[40]

While Gallegos unsuccessfully pleaded his case, events in Nueva Vizcaya led directly to a second expedition to New Mexico. Concern over the personal safety of the Franciscans who had remained among the Pueblos and the motives of a frontier captain coalesced into a follow-up effort. The captain was Antonio de Espejo, who had come to Mexico in 1571 as a familiar of the newly created Holy Office of the Inquisition. Later, Espejo and his brother acquired cattle ranches near Celaya, but in a heated dispute on one of their properties the brother killed a mestizo cowhand. As an accomplice to the crime, Antonio de Espejo drew a heavy fine and to avoid paying it fled from authorities to the frontier of Nueva Vizcaya. Hoping for royal clemency, Espejo lost little time in thrusting himself forward as leader of a rescue mission to New Mexico. Accompanying him were two Franciscan friars and fourteen soldiers. One of the troop, Diego Pérez de Luxán, was a meticulous observer and careful chronicler of the expedition.[41]

The party of seventeen left San Bartolomé on November 10, 1582, with Luxán logging a day-by-day account of the trek to and from New Mexico. It followed the Río Conchos downstream to its junction with the Río Grande. At La Junta de los Ríos, five Indian pueblos were encountered in the precise location described by Cabeza de Vaca in the 1530s. The expedition spent eighteen days among these Indians before following the Río Grande upstream. After forty-five days of marching, the Spaniards arrived at the southernmost Piros pueblos. From there, they continued upriver to Puaray, situated between modern Albuquerque and Bernalillo, where they learned with certainty that Friars López and Rodríguez had been martyred. Espejo punished the offending Indians, explored westward to the Hopi pueblos, and probed beyond them to the region of present Flagstaff, Arizona. He then returned to the Río Grande and from there marched eastward toward the Buffalo Plains. At the Pecos River, he decided to return to Mexico along the course of that river and followed it for some 120 leagues. At that point friendly Indians advised the Spaniards to alter their course of travel and to head directly toward the Río Grande. They struck the river a short distance above the Conchos junction and from La Junta retraced their route to San Bartolomé, arriving there on September 10, 1583, precisely ten months after their departure.[42]

The Espejo-Luxán expedition had brought the first Europeans into extreme southwest Texas. At a point near Pecos, Texas, where they left the Pecos River, the Luxán diary suggests a journey to the Río Grande near the contemporary Texas landmarks and communities of Toya Creek, Balmorhea, Toyahvale, Fort Davis, Alamito Creek near Marfa, and Ruidosa or Candelaria. The historical significance of the journey is underscored by the fact that no Europeans visited this region again for a hundred years. It is also interesting that Pérez de Luxán applied the name Jumanos only to Indians of this locale who had become adaptive to buffalo hunting.[43]

On returning to San Bartolomé, Espejo proposed that he pacify New Mexico at his own expense. His petition for a contract was denied, but he was granted a suspended sentence for his involvement in the death of the mestizo vaquero until the case could be reviewed by the Council of the Indies. En route to Spain to defend himself, Espejo died in Cuba. His highly exaggerated report of the potential riches of New Mexico and Arizona, however, stimulated interest in the regions that continued until the crown approved a formal contract in 1595.[44]

While Espejo was still in the field, the crown on April 19, 1583, authorized the pacification of the Pueblo country. The royal cedula was issued in response to viceregal reports of the Chamuscado-Rodríguez expedition. Conditions to be met by applicants were private financing, approval of contract by the Council of the Indies, and agreement to abide by the Royal Ordinances of 1573. For complex reasons, no formal agreement was reached for a dozen years. In the meantime, two unauthorized expeditions again brought Spaniards to Texas.[45]

The first "bootleg" expedition was led by Gaspar Castaño de Sosa, a close associate of Luis de Carvajal. Castaño departed from Villa Almadén in 1590, crossing northern Coahuila with a retinue of 170 persons. At the Río Grande, he followed the Pecos River upstream, the first wagon train crossing of southwest Texas. After reaching the pueblo of Pecos in New Mexico, Castaño marched westward to the Río Grande and established his headquarters at Santo Domingo, north of modern Albuquerque. His unauthorized expedition ended when Juan Morlete, a viceregal agent, pursued and arrested Castaño for violating the colonizing laws of 1573. Returned in chains to Mexico, Castaño was tried, convicted, and exiled to the Philippines. He later died at sea in a slave revolt.[46]

A second "bootleg" venture under the joint leadership of Francisco Leyva de Bonilla and Antonio Gutiérrez de Humaña left Nueva Vizcaya in 1593. Details of this expedition are sketchy, but it did probe the Buffalo Plains into the Texas Panhandle and perhaps beyond to Kansas. A dispute between the leaders led to the fatal stabbing of Leyva. Later, almost the entire party was killed by Indians on the plains.[47]

The continuing lure of New Mexico, the fact that it attracted rank adventurers, and crown insistence on formal settlement led to extended contract negotiations with several aspirants. The eventual winner was

Juan de Oñate, son of the silver aristocrat and veteran administrator, Cristóbal de Oñate. The younger Oñate triumphed in competition that can best be described as Byzantine. His successful application may be attributed in large measure to support from friends and relatives, who ranked among the foremost families of New Galicia and New Spain. Oñate's choice for second in command was his nephew, Juan de Zaldívar, as *maestre de campo;* his recruiting officer and *sargento mayor* was another nephew, Vicente de Zaldívar.[48]

Under the terms of his contract, Oñate received impressive titles and a salary to be paid by revenues in New Mexico. He was to recruit a minimum of two hundred men, including missionaries, and to provision at his expense an expedition with several thousand head of horses, cattle, sheep, and goats. Other supplies included food, sowing wheat, weaponry, medicines, tools, and gifts for Indians. A series of delays postponed Oñate's departure for nearly three years. In the end Oñate was unable to satisfy all stipulations of his contract, although final approval did come from the viceroy's agent in early 1598. On January 26, 1598, the assembled party with its supplies and livestock began leaving San Gerónimo, a small outpost near Santa Bárbara.[49]

On previous occasions explorers had descended the Conchos to its confluence with the Río Grande and then followed the latter river upstream to New Mexico. This established route assured water along the way. But Oñate, made impatient by delays, sought a shortcut. He dispatched Vicente de Zaldívar and a small party toward that end. Zaldívar was gone for nearly a month before returning with knowledge of a more direct route through formidable sand dunes with some accessible water. After a hard march, the full expedition reached *el paso,* the ford in the Río Grande, on May 4, 1598.[50]

Oñate completed the occupation of New Mexico in the late spring and early summer of 1598, but the experience proved disappointing for most of his followers. Life on the frontier obviously lacked the amenities of New Spain, and readily exploitable wealth was not evident. The Pueblo Indians were sullen and resentful toward friars, soldiers, and colonists alike. A serious revolt at the sky pueblo of Acoma on December 4, 1598, took the life of Oñate's kinsman and second in command, Juan de Zaldívar, along with twelve other Spaniards. Under Oñate's orders, Vicente de Zaldívar crushed the revolt in early 1599 and inflicted brutal punishment on the Acomas. Oñate, however, recognized the pressing need to seek augmentations in personnel and supplies from Mexico, which he deemed necessary to reconnoiter the surrounding country and perhaps even to hold the province. When the relief expedition finally arrived on

Christmas Eve of 1600, Oñate began preparations for another journey to Quivira.[51]

Even at the turn of the century, rumors of the Seven Hills of Aijados fueled interest among Oñate's disappointed followers. Jusepe, an Indian who had survived the disastrous Humaña-Bonilla entrada, served as guide on the trek to Kansas. With about seventy men, Don Juan departed from San Gabriel, the new capital, on June 23, 1601. His party passed through Galisteo en route to the Pecos River and then reached the Canadian River west of present Tucumcari, New Mexico. It would appear that Oñate followed the course of that river completely across the Texas Panhandle. East of the contemporary Texas-Oklahoma border, he turned sharply to the north and struck the Arkansas River at its great bend east of modern Dodge City, Kansas. In the early part of his explorations, Don Juan contacted friendly Apaches, the first reference by name to these natives. But like Coronado, Oñate was singularly unimpressed with Quivira. To make matters worse, he was forced to fight a pitched battle with Indians in south-central Kansas. The troubled expedition retraced its route to New Mexico, again crossing the Panhandle from east to west along the Canadian River.[52]

Oñate's fortunes did not improve on reaching San Gabriel. Despite the protests of the lieutenant governor and the Franciscan commissary, most of the colonists at the capital had abandoned the province and fled to Mexico during Oñate's absence. After the governor's return, other settlers remained in New Mexico against their will. They were further discouraged when additional explorations failed to discover enough wealth to make the province attractive. In 1607 Oñate resigned his post as governor. He and his family had spent nearly 400,000 pesos on the New Mexico venture.[53]

Shortly before Oñate's resignation, the Council of the Indies had reassessed the situation in New Mexico and reached a decision with significant implications for Texas. A new governor would replace Oñate, the appointee must emphasize the mission program, and only friars could carry out further explorations. In 1608 New Mexico was royalized with the crown made responsible for its maintenance, and in the following year Pedro de Peralta traveled north as the first royal governor of the established province. Under orders to centralize the capital, Peralta relocated it at Santa Fe. During the ensuing decades, slow and unspectacular progress characterized the province. The Spanish population increased from a few hundred to a few thousand, and by the 1630s some two dozen friars attended twenty-five missions. Sustained more from Christianizing impulses, less from the promise of profits, New Mexico continued to serve as the primary gateway to Spanish Texas.[54]

Until 1680 passage to and from New Mexico along the Río Grande between La Junta de los Ríos and El Paso brought hundreds of Spaniards in view of Texas soil, but expeditions to the interior were rare. One of those early contacts, however, resulted from the apparently miraculous bilocations of the Lady in Blue. In July 1629 a delegation of some fifty Jumanos appeared at the Franciscan convent of old Isleta, located south of present Albuquerque. The Indians had come to New Mexico to request religious teachers for themselves and their neighbors. They demonstrated rudimentary knowledge of Christianity and when asked who had instructed them replied—the "Woman in Blue." Prior to the arrival of the Jumanos, the archbishop of Mexico, Francisco Manso y Zúñiga, had written the religious superior of New Mexico requesting information about a young nun's claims of transportations to the frontier of New Spain. The woman in question was María de Jesús de Agreda.[55]

Sister María had accepted vows in 1620 and entered the Franciscan convent of Immaculate Conception in Agreda, a small village in northeastern Spain. Throughout the 1620s María de Jesús repeatedly lapsed into deep trances, and on those occasions she experienced dreams in which her spirit was transported to a distant land, where she taught the Gospel to a pagan people. Her alleged miraculous bilocations often took her to eastern New Mexico and western Texas. There she instructed several Indian groups, including the Jumanos. For many years Sister María recounted her vivid dreams to a confessor, Sebastián Marcilla of Agreda. In the late 1620s Fray Sebastián's superior informed the archbishop of Mexico of the nun's mystical experiences, which led to his queries.[56]

The timely inquiry from the archbishop and the appearance of the Jumano delegation prompted immediate explorations into Texas. In 1629 Friars Juan de Salas and Diego López marched some 112 leagues east of the Pueblo area. The two padres spent several days in southwest Texas where they were welcomed by a large band of Indians, who claimed they had been advised of approaching Christian missionaries by the Woman in Blue. Although no permanent mission was set up among the Jumanos, in 1632 Fray Ascencio de Zárate and Fray Pedro de Ortega led a follow-up expedition to the same locale.[57]

Between these early contacts with the Jumanos, Fray Alonso de Benavides, former religious superior in New Mexico, traveled to Spain. In an effort to learn more about the mysterious Lady in Blue, Fray Alonso interviewed María de Jesús at Agreda in 1631. He described the nun's habit as brown (*pardo*) sackcloth covered by a coarse blue cloak, and in their conversations Sister María affirmed her claim of some five hundred bilocations to the frontier of New Spain.[58]

Belief in miracles is an individual matter, but the sequence of events surrounding the Lady in Blue provides an acceptable and plausible explanation for missionary endeavors to the Jumanos in 1629 and 1632. After those visitations, the Jumanos remained isolated for almost twenty years. Later expeditions appear to have been to an upper branch of the eastern Colorado River. The first of them was captained by Hernando Martín and Diego del Castillo. This venture returned to New Mexico with poor quality pearls, plus knowledge of a territory peopled by Tejas Indians and ruled by a king. The second entrada, led by Diego de Guadalajara, was instructed to search for Pearls of the Jumanos and the Kingdom of the Tejas. While those attempts at finding wealth were as frustrating as earlier efforts to the environs of Cíbola and Gran Quivira, they opened the way in succeeding years for traders and soldiers to exchange products from New Mexico for buffalo hides. But barter with the Jumanos from New Mexico was severed by the Pueblo Revolt of 1680, and at the same time those Indians were pressured by Apaches who raided settlements and carried off prisoners, developments that influenced post-1680 events in Texas.[59]

FROM 1543 TO 1680, OFFICIAL POLICIES OF THE CROWN AND the independent energies of soldiers, miners, missionaries, and ranchers directed Spanish approaches to Texas. Despite the momentum of an expanding empire, stimulated in part by persistent myths and legends, the vast land of the future Lone Star State remained largely unexplored and ignored at the time of the Pueblo Revolt. Extreme southwest Texas had long bordered the path from mines, missions, and ranches of northern Mexico to the land of the Pueblos, but most of the interior of the state remained *tierra incógnita*. When one of the most successful Indian revolts in the Hispanic empire forced abandonment of New Mexico, El Paso del Norte, where some settlement had already occurred, increased significantly in importance as the focus of Spanish presence on the frontier of New Spain.

FOUR

Río Grande Settlement and the French Challenge, 1656–1689

THE 1680s WERE A TIME OF CRISIS FOR THE NORTHERN FRONTIER of New Spain. The decade began with a massive, coordinated Indian revolt in New Mexico that claimed the lives of more than four hundred Spaniards and forced the total abandonment of a province held continuously for eighty-two years. Survivors, well over two thousand of them, retreated down the Río Grande toward El Paso del Río del Norte. Those events transformed Texas, which had been secondary in importance to New Mexico, into a focus of empire and international rivalry. Refugees were placed in camps southwest of the Río Grande, while military planning for the reconquest of New Mexico proper was begun. At the same time, Spaniards accelerated Río Grande settlement with the growth of missionary enterprises along the river. Near midpoint in the decade, however, those activities also became secondary when it was learned that Frenchmen had violated Spanish sovereignty by entering the forbidden waters of the Gulf of Mexico and by planting a colony somewhere on the coast between Pánuco and Florida. To meet that challenge, officials in New Spain organized five land expeditions in a span of four years and sent three of them into Texas. In the same time frame, they sent five sea voyages to probe Gulf Coast waters in search of the elusive French colony. These interrelated developments that preceded the founding of the first missions in East Texas are the subject of this chapter.

BY 1680 SPANISH SETTLERS IN NEW MEXICO NUMBERED approximately twenty-eight hundred. The majority of them lived in the southern district, known as Río Abajo, while a smaller number resided to the north in the vicinity of the capital at Santa Fe. Scattered among the various missions of the province were some sixteen thousand partially Hispanicized Indians and thirty-two Franciscan friars. While there was no formal presidio, regular soldiers were stationed at Santa Fe. At that time Antonio de Otermín as governor and captain general of New Mexico directed the affairs of the province.[1]

In late summer of 1680, Pueblo Indians throughout most of the province rose up against the Spanish colonists. The revolt stunned the European community, but to historians advantaged by hindsight its occurrence comes as no surprise. Although the causes of the Pueblo Revolt had little direct bearing on Texas history, they merit brief consideration, for the New Mexico experience illustrated the shortcomings of Spanish frontier policies, even among sedentary people whose cultural attainments were superior to those of any Texas Indians. Second, while in office, Diego de Peñalosa, a former governor of New Mexico, not only had contributed by his actions and conduct to the disharmony of Spanish rule but also later cast an intriguing shadow over French designs in Texas.

The fundamental issue that divided Europeans and Indians in New Mexico was a determined effort by Spaniards to suppress the religious beliefs of the Pueblos and to reshape their ancient habits and customs into European modes of conduct. This proved to be not possible, either by persuasion "or by the severity of punishments inflicted." For example, the arrest in 1675 of forty-seven native medicine men as alleged practitioners of sorcery and witchcraft and the subsequent hanging of three of them served only to worsen conditions.[2]

Other matters of lesser consequence also contributed to increasing friction that reached flash point in 1680. The decade before the Pueblo Revolt had witnessed drought conditions that produced crop failures and resultant hunger. Food shortages probably meant that Indians suffered more than Spaniards. Indeed, famine coupled with the increasing menace of Apache attacks had forced abandonment of some outlying missions, and by 1680 even Santa Fe was the target of bold raids. Earlier, the unscrupulous and self-seeking actions of governors Bernardo López de Mendizábal (1659–1661) and Diego de Peñalosa (1661–1664) had left deep scars in church-state relations "that were never entirely obliterated." Worse, public quarrels between governors and religious custodians had created a spectacle that "caused the Indians to lose whatever respect they had for Spanish authority except that inspired by force." Significantly, too, the lack of rich natural resources in New Mexico meant that the stakes were small and the competition for them often fierce between clergy and colonists. Finally, the widespread belief among Pueblo leaders that the Spaniards could be driven from New Mexico with comparative ease provided the confidence needed for rebellion.[3]

Among the medicine men arrested in 1675 was an Indian leader named Popé. His quick release that same year did little to assuage his anger toward the Spaniards, and from a base of operations in Taos, Popé made preparations for a general revolt. His plans were cloaked in secrecy and coordinated throughout the far-flung pueblos by a cord tied in knots, one for each day intervening until the target date of August 11, 1680. A breach in security, however, prompted Indian leaders to initiate the uprising one day ahead of schedule.[4]

By August 15 the Pueblo Revolt was so successful that Santa Fe itself was under siege. After six days of fighting, Governor Otermín elected to abandon the capital and to withdraw toward Isleta and the larger settlement in Río Abajo. Unfortunately for the Spaniards, the lower community had also come under attack. Maestre de Campo Alonso García, believing Indian reports that all of the Spaniards at Santa Fe had perished, summoned a council to determine the proper course of action. A unanimous decision favored immediate retreat downriver toward El Paso del Norte. Unknown to Governor Otermín, on August 14, the day before the siege of Santa Fe began, Isleta was relinquished to Indian control.[5]

The Río Abajo settlers moved southward to a place called Fray Cristóbal, situated below the inhabited portion of New Mexico but still some sixty leagues north of El Paso. There word arrived of Otermín's retreat, then in progress down the Río Grande. The larger contingent waited at Fray Cristóbal until Otermín's division overtook it on September 13. After a general council, the combined refugees continued the retreat toward the Spanish settlement at El Paso.[6]

At La Salineta, located four leagues from El Paso on the Texas side of the Río Grande, Otermín ordered a general muster on September 29. Survivors totaled 1,946 when the review ended in early October, but before the count was finished, scores of refugees had slipped away without permission into Nueva Vizcaya. The muster revealed only 155 Spanish men under arms; the remainder were unarmed men, women, children, and 317 partially Christianized Piro Indians. After the assemblage, a council, composed of cabildo members of Santa Fe, military officers, and friars, considered the question of whether to attempt the immediate reconquest of New Mexico. The decision against swift action, announced on October 5 by Otermín, was influenced by the weakness of his forces, by fears that native unrest in Nueva Vizcaya might escalate into a broader rebellion on news of the Pueblo Revolt, and by the desire of Otermín to receive instructions and reinforcements from the viceroy of New Spain. Accordingly, the entire camp at La Salineta continued downriver and crossed the Río Grande at El Paso del Norte.[7]

Refugees from New Mexico were settled in three camps near the church of Nuestra Señora de Guadalupe. They were obliged to live in improvised wooden huts, but these mean conditions were viewed as temporary. Otermín was especially intent on acquiring authorization to found a presidio for the protection of the civilian communities. In January 1681 officials in New Spain empowered the governor to carry out his proposal, but unavoidable delays prevented him from doing so. A year later, during the winter months of 1681–1682, Otermín returned to El Paso after an unsuccessful effort to reconquer New Mexico. By then it was clear that extended campaigns would be needed to restore control over the former towns and missions. Settlers at El Paso were relocated into several small villages; plans were made for planting crops; and the makeshift settlements were given a degree of permanence. Events over the next few years "served to make them entirely permanent."[8]

With the loss of New Mexico proper, parts of present-day Texas would become the northern outposts of New Spain. For the refugees, it was indeed fortunate that sporadic settlement and exploration along the western fringes of Texas had been in progress for some time. Otherwise, the New Mexico outcasts would have found no haven short of the mining and ranching frontier in Nueva Vizcaya. To this juncture, the focal areas of settlement had been the El Paso and La Junta de los Ríos regions. Their importance was recognized as early as 1630 by the custodian of New Mexico, Fray Alonso de Benavides, who had noted that both were vital way stations between Nueva Vizcaya and New Mexico as well as important centers for conversion and indoctrination of Manso and Suma Indians, but Spaniards made no attempts to settle either site until the 1650s.

In 1656 Fray Juan Pérez and Fray Juan Cabal, both from New Mexico, founded a small temporary church near El Paso del Norte and began baptisms and religious instruction among the Manso Indians. A resident mission, Nuestra Señora de Guadalupe, was finally begun in 1659. Construction of a permanent church was under way by 1662, and the completed structure was dedicated on January 15, 1668. From this place of worship, missionaries carried out conversion efforts among the neighboring Sumas, but a permanent mission for them was not in operation prior to 1680.[9] Initial work among these primitive Indians may have come from friars en route to New Mexico, but sustained missionary efforts were the product of actions taken by Pérez and Cabal.

Baptismal, marriage, and burial records kept at the church of Guadalupe indicate the presence of a small Spanish population antedating 1680. Prior to the Pueblo Revolt, fourteen priests had served in the El Paso region for varying lengths of time, but their efforts, according to available statistics, "were not remarkably successful." In addition to the Mansos and Sumas, a few Jumanos, Piros, Tanos, and Apaches also fell under the tutelage of the friars.[10]

Simultaneous with early settlement in the El Paso region, Spaniards from bases in Coahuila and Nuevo León began to penetrate lands north of the lower Río Grande. By 1660 Indians in northern Mexico and from beyond the Río Grande had successfully raided frontier outposts near Saltillo, Monterrey, and Cerralvo. The desire to avenge these attacks and the need for labor in the mines prompted a punitive expedition. To this end, men recruited from Saltillo and Monterrey were placed under the command of Juan de la Garza in October 1663. With 100 men and 800 horses, de la Garza marched seventy leagues to the vicinity of present Eagle Pass, where he engaged Cacaxtle Indians. In a pitched battle his force killed nearly 100 natives and captured 125 prisoners. Whether de la Garza crossed the Río Grande on this occasion is undocumented.[11]

The first definite crossing of the river in the Eagle Pass area came in 1665. Continued Indian attacks prompted a second entrada led by the *alcalde mayor* of Saltillo, Fernando de Azcué. Again, men were recruited from the towns of Saltillo and Monterrey. Azcué's company of seventy-three men, bolstered by three hundred Indian allies, penetrated twenty-four leagues north of the Río Grande where an all-day battle was fought with the Cacaxtles. At the conclusion of hostilities, more than one hundred natives were killed and another seventy captured.[12] The de la Garza and Azcué campaigns, aimed at frontier security, were complemented by new missionary activity in northern Coahuila. For reasons that remain unclear, some of the Indian nations in Coahuila and from lands north of the Río Grande actively sought missionaries, while others remained unreceptive. Nevertheless, requests for men of the cloth first struck a responsive chord in the Franciscan padre, Juan Larios.[13]

In 1670 when Larios was returning to the province of Jalisco from a visit to his sister in Durango, two Indians confronted him and demanded his immediate presence as a missionary among their people. Responding, Fray Juan began work among hunting and gathering tribes some thirty miles to the north of Monclova. For three years Father Larios labored alone. He studied the languages of those peripatetic natives and during that time set up the first mission among them. His pioneering efforts bore dividends in 1673, for in that year conversion of tribes in Coahuila and beyond into Texas was entrusted to Larios's fellow Franciscans of the Jalisco province. Larios was named superior at his mission and was assigned two assistants, Father Francisco Peñasco de Lozano and Brother Manuel de la Cruz.[14]

On separate occasions in 1674, Father Francisco and Brother Manuel journeyed beyond the Río Grande. The latter reconnoitered the region of present Maverick, Val Verde, and Kinney counties for some three weeks. Father Francisco likewise traveled a few leagues north of the river to a campsite of the Manosprietos Indians. Both religious returned with neophytes for the Coahuila mission, among whom were a few Tejas Indians.[15]

Repeated requests for missionaries from tribes in Texas led to a major undertaking in 1675. In that year Antonio Balcárcel, the *alcalde mayor* of Coahuila, outfitted an expedition headed by Fernando del Bosque. It consisted of ten soldiers and two missionaries, Fathers Juan Larios and Dionisio de San Buenaventura. The party set out on April 30, 1675, and arrived at the Río Grande on May 11. It crossed the river at a disputed site, but a likely ford was Paso de Francia, near the future location of mission San Juan Bautista.[16]

The Bosque-Larios expedition apparently visited the same region of Texas explored earlier by Brother Manuel. It traveled forty-one leagues beyond the Río Grande and gave names to six localities. At two sites Indians were congregated and told to await the coming of missionaries. Thus a portion of extreme south central Texas came under the jurisdiction of Balcárcel in Coahuila and was staked out as an extended mission field of the Franciscans. On the return trip, Bosque probably marched down the east bank of the Pecos River to its junction with the Río Grande. He completed his trek in mid-June of 1675.[17]

After the return of the Bosque-Larios entrada, Bosque suggested to Balcárcel that three mission districts, including land and Indians north of the Río Grande, be established. Conditions in Coahuila, however, did not permit implementation of the proposal. Indian hostilities and jurisdictional disputes with Nuevo León precluded action for a decade.[18] By then the focus had shifted to East Texas to counteract the French challenge. Similar considerations would likewise short-circuit missionary efforts directed from El Paso.

During the winter months of 1681–1682, the unsuccessful campaign of Governor Antonio de Otermín had determined that the reconquest of New Mexico would be a long and difficult process. That realization further enforced a reluctant sense of permanence on the El Paso communities. Among the refugees of 1680 were a small number of Tiguex Indians from Isleta. Their ranks were swelled by additional natives from the same pueblo who returned with Otermín in 1682. The desire to congregate those Indians into a community separate from the Spanish colony led to the establishment of the first permanent European settlement within present boundaries of the Lone Star State. In 1682 Fray Francisco Ayeta founded the mission and pueblo of Corpus Christi de la Isleta. It was located a few miles east of El Paso at the site of modern Ysleta, Texas (see Figure 14).[19]

In the following year, delegations of Jumano Indians twice visited the Spanish community at El Paso. On the first occasion, they asked that traders be sent among them. Commerce had existed between these natives and settlers in New Mexico on an irregular basis since the 1650s, but no action was taken on the initial request. The second appearance of Jumanos in 1683 came shortly after the arrival of the newly appointed governor of New Mexico, Domingo Jironza Petris de Cruzate. That delegation was led by Juan Sabeata, who had been baptized at Parral but lived at La Junta de los Ríos. Sabeata shrewdly calculated that an appeal for missionaries would be more likely to bring results than would the prospect of acquiring buffalo hides. To make his request more attractive, the Jumano leader concocted a story of a cross miraculously falling from the heavens, and he spun out an enticing lure when he spoke of the Kingdom of the Tejas, a populous realm some fifteen to twenty days' travel to the east of La Junta. Only once did the Jumano leader mention that his people needed allies to counter the growing menace of Apache attacks. Of interest, the interpreter for Sabeata was Hernando Martín Serrano, a co-captain of the 1650 expedition from New Mexico.[20]

Jironza forwarded Sabeata's request to the viceroy, but a more immediate response came from Fray Nicolás López, custodian of the El Paso missions. Accompanied by Fray Juan Zavaleta and Fray Antonio Acevedo, Father López set out for La Junta. After thirteen days' travel, the three friars reached their destination and began missionary work. The results of their proselytizing is uncertain. It appears that some instruction took place in mission pueblos, but no sustained religious activities occurred until a later period. Meanwhile, Jironza, also sensing the urgency of the situation, authorized preparations for an expedition without waiting for viceregal approval. His choice for command fell on Juan Domínguez de Mendoza, one of the most experienced frontier captains and a member of the Domínguez de Mendoza clan, the wealthiest family in New Mexico.[21] His first experience in the land of the Jumanos had come in 1654, when he served as a member of the Diego de Guadalajara expedition. Later, he earned a reputation in New Mexico as an able administrator and capable leader in the local militia. On several occasions Domínguez led successful reprisals against marauding bands of Apaches. After the Pueblo Revolt, he captained the first military action north of Isleta (New Mexico), advancing as far as Cochiti, southwest of Santa Fe.

Mendoza's wide experience and proved leadership made him a logical choice of the governor. He was commissioned to look for pearls, to teach Indians respect for the friars, and to explore possibilities of trade.[22]

At the head of a troop of soldiers, Domínguez de Mendoza left El Paso in mid-December of 1683. He moved downstream along the south bank of the Río Grande until he reached its junction with the Conchos. At La Junta he added Fathers López and Zavaleta to his entourage. Leaving Acevedo in charge of mission activities, Mendoza set out for the plains. He traveled seventy leagues north to the Pecos River and then followed it downstream for nine leagues to a point near Horsehead Crossing. From the Pecos, he marched eastward across a dry plain and after forty leagues of travel arrived at a stream, perhaps the Middle Concho. The course of that river was followed eastward for more than twenty leagues until it joined the Colorado. Mendoza remained for six weeks in this locale, most likely at a site to the south of the Colorado River where his party killed over four thousand head of buffalo. He and the two padres erected a fortified structure and crude chapel where a few natives were baptized. Before leaving, Mendoza assured the Indians of continued Spanish presence within a year. Mendoza then returned to La Junta, where he proclaimed the north bank of the Río Grande part of New Mexico. Fathers Acevedo and Zavaleta remained at La Junta; Mendoza and López returned to El Paso. From there the two men traveled to Mexico City, where in 1685 they strongly urged the occupation of Jumano lands with soldiers and missionaries. Their pleadings fell on deaf ears once intelligence of French designs in the Gulf of Mexico reached the viceroy.[23]

By that time El Paso del Norte had been firmly established as a permanent outpost of New Spain. To secure the settlement, Governor Jironza established the presidio of Nuestra Señora del Pilar y el Glorioso San José and located it some seven leagues from the pueblo of El Paso. Indian revolts in the spring of 1684, however, forced him to move the garrison closer to the mission. The danger of Indian attacks, crop failures, and the dim prospects of returning to New Mexico proper had caused agitation among the settlers, many of whom sought permission to leave. It was denied. Instead, El Paso became the nerve center of missionary and pioneering enterprises extending southeastward to La Junta.[24] With settlement along this stretch of the Río Grande, with penetration north of the lower river from Coahuila and Nuevo León, it is arguable that the future Lone Star State would have been colonized without the stimulus of foreign challenge. But it is also clear that Spanish occupation of East Texas was hastened by international ambitions of France and a great French explorer, René Robert Cavelier, Sieur de la Salle.

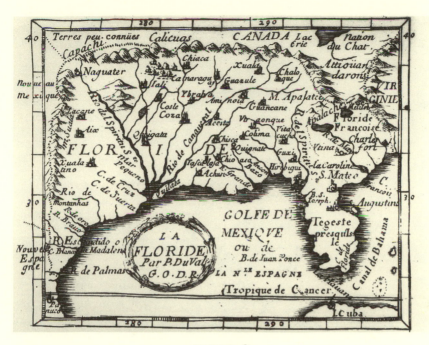

FIGURE 8
The Gulf Coast as understood in 1663. The Gulf Coast as depicted in
Pierre du Val, Le Monde ou la Géographie Universelle *(Paris, 1663).*
(Courtesy of Peter H. Wood.)

La Salle, the son of a Norman boilermaker, was born at Rouen in
1643. At an early age he studied with padres of the Jesuit order, but
monastic life was alien to his adventurous nature. He left a religious calling and journeyed to Canada, where in 1666 he acquired a land grant
and interest in the fur trade. In 1669 La Salle heard of a great waterway
flowing southward whose course was almost completely uncharted (see
Figure 8).[25]

The first descent of the Mississippi by the French, however, was effected not by La Salle but by Père Jacques Marquette and Louis Joliet in
1673. The two men canoed downstream to the junction with the Arkansas River. There they learned from Indians that the Mississippi dis-
charged its waters into the Gulf of Mexico, not into the Gulf of California
as the French had hoped, for they had been optimistic that the Mississippi would provide an avenue to the Orient. On their return to Canada,
the two explorers communicated their findings to Governor Louis de
Buade, Comte de Frontenac. But neither man was able to pursue his ex-

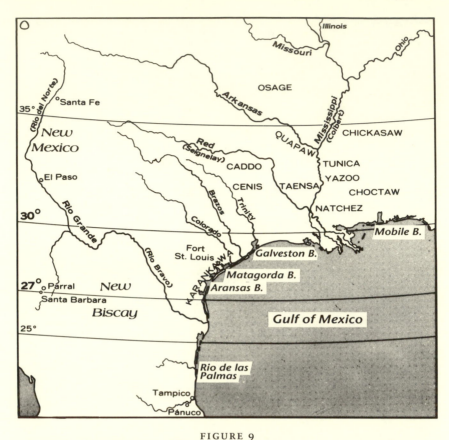

FIGURE 9
The Lower Mississippi and related regions. This map is an accurate depiction
of the Gulf Coast and adjacent areas at the time of La Salle's explorations.
Note the location of the Río de las Palmas. (Courtesy of Robert L. Williams.)

plorations. Marquette died in 1675, and Joliet was supplanted when
Frontenac backed La Salle as a rival explorer.[26]

La Salle returned to France twice in the 1670s, and on the second trip,
with Frontenac's support, he received trading concessions in the country
traversed by the Mississippi River. Back in Canada, he set out in early
1682 to follow the Mississippi to its mouth (see Figure 9). He arrived at
the Gulf in April and on the ninth of the month formally named the
region he had explored Louisiana to honor his monarch, Louis XIV. La
Salle's claims for France could hardly have been more all-encompassing,
for they included "the seas, harbors, ports, bays, adjacent straits, and all
the nations, peoples, provinces, cities, towns, villages, mines, minerals,

FIGURE 10

*The Lower Mississippi as understood by La Salle. This map depicts
the Lower Mississippi River Valley and adjacent areas, perhaps as they were
understood by René Robert Cavelier, Sieur de la Salle, in the 1680s.
(Courtesy of Robert L. Williams.)*

fisheries, streams, and rivers, within the extent of the said Louisiana." [27]
Convincing the French court to support those claims and to sustain them
against a hostile environment and determined Spanish opposition were
formidable tasks faced by La Salle. He accomplished the first but failed
the second.

From the reports of Marquette and Joliet, Frontenac had quickly perceived the importance of where the Mississippi debouched. Its mouth lay
between Spanish Florida and Pánuco. If Spain closed this gap and occupied the lower Mississippi Valley, then New France would lose its access
to the sea and be threatened from the south. But when La Salle returned
to Canada in late 1682, the political climate there had turned against him.
Frontenac had been replaced by Lefevre de la Barré, who showed little
appreciation for the explorer's ambitious scheme to control the midcon-
tinent by planting a French colony near the mouth of the Mississippi
River (see Figure 10). Frustrated, La Salle returned to France in 1683 to
lay his plan before the court of Louis XIV. At Versailles, his ideas received
a generally favorable hearing, but complications developed due to the
presence there of Diego Dioniso de Peñalosa, former governor of New
Mexico.[28]

Following his turbulent tenure as governor, Peñalosa returned to Mexico City, where he tried to interest the viceroy in a plan to conquer the provinces of Gran Quivira and Teguayo. These two regions, which he claimed to have visited during his residence in New Mexico, were situated somewhere between the northeastern borders of New Spain and the Mississippi River. The journal of Peñalosa's alleged expedition is clearly fraudulent, for he was on a visitation of the Hopi pueblos in Arizona at the very time he claimed a march to the east. While still in the capital, Peñalosa was arrested for blasphemy on orders of the Mexican Inquisition. His trial, loss of property, and banishment from New Spain in 1668 left him, in the words of historian France V. Scholes, "a ruined man."[29]

After exile Peñalosa traveled to the Canary Islands and from there booked passage to London, where he offered his services to the English. When rebuffed, he passed to Paris in 1673 where he married and lived for five years. By the early 1680s, the artful former governor had insinuated his way into the inner circles of the French court, where he gained the confidence of the influential Abbé Claude Bernou. Again Peñalosa spun out his elaborate plans for the conquest of Gran Quivira and Teguayo. From a base at the mouth of the Río Grande, he claimed, some of the world's richest gold and silver mines would easily fall into French coffers. Bernou laid the Peñalosa proposal before the Marquis de Seignelay, who was in effect minister for the colonies. Seignelay was not as enthusiastic as Bernou, but he thought the plan had some merit. At that juncture, La Salle arrived with his proposal for a French colony at the mouth of the Mississippi.[30]

For a time, much to the dismay of La Salle, Seignelay contemplated combining the two suggestions presented to him. Then international considerations worked to La Salle's advantage. Louis XIV began to weigh the advisability of ending a war then in progress with Spain. If that came to pass, the king did not wish to pursue the more provocative Peñalosa plan, which would have landed the French on territory that was clearly part of New Spain. In the final analysis, Louis XIV undoubtedly favored a Frenchman with proven credentials over a turncoat Spaniard of questionable veracity. Accepting La Salle's petition, the king provided four ships—*Le Joly, L'Aimable, La Belle,* and *St. François*—instead of the two originally requested. The royal grant for supplies and munitions was equally generous.[31]

Final preparations for La Salle's expedition to the Gulf of Mexico were made with the utmost secrecy. The Spanish knew of Peñalosa's presence at the French court and suspected his involvement in promoting an attack on their empire. They were likewise aware that French agents in America had studied Spanish defenses and that an aggressive strike would likely come. But where? When La Salle's flotilla, containing nearly three hundred soldiers and sailors, left the port of La Rochelle on July 24, 1684, even the naval commander, Sieur de Beaujeu, did not learn its destination until the ships were well under way. Beaujeu deeply resented La Salle's lack of trust, and the two-month voyage across the Atlantic increased his hostility. Beaujeu's ship, the *Joly,* could easily outsail the other vessels, all of which were heavily laden with supplies. The commander was forced to tack constantly in order for the other three vessels to keep pace, an inconvenience he peevishly blamed on La Salle.[32]

When the ships reached Santo Domingo, the two leaders again quarreled over where to anchor. Beaujeu sailed to another part of the island, and during his absence the *St. François,* loaded with irreplaceable supplies, provisions, and tools for the colony, was captured by Spanish privateers. Bad luck continued. La Salle fell victim to a near-fatal illness; several members of the expedition deserted; others contracted deadly venereal diseases. It was the deserters, however, who would eventually alert Spanish officials to La Salle's secret mission. After La Salle's recovery, the three remaining vessels resumed the voyage in late November 1684. As the ships passed into the Gulf of Mexico, they entered "a forbidden sea from which all foreigners were excluded by royal Spanish decree."[33]

LA SALLE'S UNSUCCESSFUL SEARCH FOR THE MOUTH OF THE Mississippi River has generated a host of speculative arguments that center around whether the French explorer landed on the coast of Texas by accident or by design. But in reality, "neither of these standard alternatives hits the mark."[34] In sailing Gulf waters, La Salle and Beaujeu shared a common problem with all seventeenth-century explorers. There was no way to determine longitude, "except by measuring east-west distance from a known location."[35] La Salle's voyage down the Mississippi River in 1682 had determined conclusively that the river entered the Gulf of Mexico, but he was extremely vague about where it did so. He later struggled with existing maps to reconcile the location of the river's mouth. The exact maps consulted by La Salle are not known, but those that were available to him shared several common features. All of them failed to show the enormous delta at the mouth of the river with its multiple passes projecting into the Gulf to 29° latitude. The maps did show the north coast of the Gulf running east-west at about 30°, roughly accurate; a mythical large bay, Espíritu Santo, where several streams emptied; and a series of rivers that flowed southeast and east into the western

portion of the Gulf. One of those rivers, the Escondido, with forks upstream to the north and west, had features similar to the actual Río
Grande. It entered the Gulf near 27° latitude in the region now known as
the Texas Coastal Bend. When La Salle was at the mouth of the Mississippi in 1682, his latitude sighting was calculated at 27°, off two degrees
or nearly 140 miles. Significantly, too, he concluded that in its final journey to the sea the great river approached the coast in a southeastward
direction, thus positioning it in western Gulf waters. It is also important
to remember that while at the mouth of the Mississippi, La Salle explored
only the eastern passes of the river and did not learn of the delta's true
configuration. Had he gained accurate knowledge of it, he could not have
misidentified the river two years later.[36]

La Salle's misperceptions and reliance on faulty maps obviously influenced his decisions. At French Santo Domingo, sailors more familiar with
Gulf waters than were Spanish mariners had warned La Salle of the powerful eastward flow of Gulf currents toward the Florida Straits, a tug that
unless counteracted would carry him off course. Accordingly, in sailing
toward his destination, La Salle compensated for the current, in fact,
overcompensated. When he arrived at Matagorda Bay in early 1685, La
Salle believed he was at the entrance of lagoons where the Escondido
emptied, and he concluded that the Escondido was also the Mississippi.
If that were the case, he was excitingly close to Spanish settlements in
New Spain. In the plan that La Salle had presented to his king, he envisioned a French colony within striking distance of mines in New Spain.
Matagorda Bay suited those plans quite nicely. Unfortunately for La
Salle, he had no way of knowing that he was still hundreds of miles short
of the nearest mines in Coahuila.[37]

An earlier miscalculation of latitude at the mouth of the Mississippi,
inaccurate maps of the northern Gulf Coast, his desire to establish a
colony near New Spain, and navigational errors in overcompensating for
Gulf currents—all caused La Salle, who intended to establish his colony
in the western portion of the Gulf in any event, to overshoot the actual
Mississippi River by some four hundred miles. Given those combinations
of circumstances, "he had no reason to look in the area where we now
know the base of the river to be."[38] By the time La Salle discovered that
"his river" was not where he had landed, he was stranded by circumstances on the Texas coast and was the object of a resolute Spanish
manhunt.

In large measure La Salle's precarious situation was again the product
of bad luck. During the search for the Mississippi, he and Beaujeu became separated in Gulf waters. Predictably, when the ships were reunited,

each man blamed the other. A second vessel was lost when the *Aimable* ran aground in Matagorda Bay. Its cargo for the most part was also destroyed because of a rising storm. Finally ashore, La Salle's colony was ravished by dysentery and venereal disease. Ironically, by then relations between Beaujeu and the explorer were finally amicable, perhaps because the naval commander had fulfilled his mission. Beaujeu put to sea in mid-March and sailed the *Joly* back to France. Later, La Salle's one remaining vessel, the frigate *Belle,* was caught in a sudden squall and destroyed on a sand bar. As a result, "the ill-fated French colony was left irrevocably stranded in an uncharted wilderness where it had never meant to be."[39] The hostile environment of Matagorda Bay and the sorry state of the French survivors were bad enough, but in late summer of 1685 Spanish officials learned of the French intrusion.

Disclosure came from the deserters at Santo Domingo. Many of them had joined privateers who carried out a bloody raid on the Yucatán peninsula under the French buccaneer Michel de Grammont. On the passage out of San Francisco de Campeche, Grammont lost two ships to Spanish vessels of the Armada de Barlovento. Among the 120 prisoners were several who had sailed from France with La Salle more than a year before. A young Frenchman named Denis (Dionisio) Thomas was the most knowledgeable of the captives about the French explorer's secret plans. Thomas had gleaned enough information to know that La Salle's destination was a place named "Misipipi." Spanish officials searched their maps and concluded that the river must enter the Gulf through the bay of Espíritu Santo. A hostile French colony there would pose a threat to all Spanish commerce in Gulf waters as well as to settlements in northern Mexico. If the French gained a toehold on the Gulf, they would certainly reinforce it with additional supplies and manpower as soon as possible. Urgency dictated that the viceroy of New Spain not wait for crown authorization; instead plans were immediately formulated to extirpate the foreign colony.[40]

Response by sea could be carried out most expeditiously. Two experienced pilots of the Armada de Barlovento were selected to command the first search for La Salle. On January 3, 1686, Juan Enríquez Barroto and Antonio Romero sailed from Havana on a chartered vessel. Along the Florida coast, Barroto and Romero rediscovered Pensacola Bay, then explored Mobile Bay before arriving at the North Pass of the Mississippi River. There was nothing about the mud-and-driftwood-choked river that resembled the Espíritu Santo as portrayed on existing maps. Reconnaissance ended abruptly when bad weather forced the ship toward Veracruz.[41]

To ensure a more thorough search for the French colony, officials at Veracruz were granted permission to organize a land expedition as a complement to the Barroto-Romero voyage. Unable to find a person in their midst who was familiar with the coast of northeast New Spain, the search quickly broadened to Nuevo León, where there was rumored to be a frontiersman experienced in the region of the Río de las Palmas. That person was Alonso de León, Jr.

The younger de León was born in the town of Cadereyta, Nuevo León, in 1639 or 1640. His father of the same name was a man of letters, a seasoned Indian fighter, and a friend of the provincial governor. At the age of ten, Alonso, Jr., journeyed to Spain, where he attended school and later joined the Spanish navy. His career at sea must have been brief, for he was back in Nuevo León by 1660. Over the next two decades, de León led a series for entradas that traversed the northeast coast of New Spain as well as the banks of the Río de San Juan. In 1682 he petitioned the viceroy for a franchise to work salt deposits along the San Juan, open trade with neighboring settlements, and search for mines. His efforts won a fifteen-year concession. And when the search for a captain broadened beyond Veracruz and Tampico, Alonso de León was a logical choice. Over the next four years, his career focused on "probing the wilderness in quest of the French intruders."[42]

De León's initial reconnaissance was organized from two companies of men formed at Monterrey and Cadereyta. Fifty soldiers, plus servants, an Indian guide, and a chaplain began the overland search for La Salle in the summer of 1686. De León's party followed the Río de San Juan north and east toward its confluence with the Río Grande. Striking the larger river, he marched the right bank to the coast. There he turned southward toward the Río de las Palmas. Along the shoreline, he found flotsam from a wrecked vessel and a flask that he judged to be non-Spanish, but de León found no solid evidence that Frenchmen had visited the region. He retraced his route to Cadereyta, having spent almost the entire month of July in the field.[43]

A second land expedition led by de León set out in late February 1687. De León forded the Río Grande, probably near the present town of Roma – Los Saenz. This effort crossed the southern tip of Texas and reached the coast on March 20. Ironically, the object of the search, René Robert Cavelier, Sieur de la Salle, had been murdered in East Texas on the previous day. It appears that de León advanced up the Texas coast to Baffin Bay, southeast of Kingsville, Texas. But again he found no evidence of the French and no Indians with knowledge of them. His second expedition was as fruitless as the first.[44]

The second sea expedition closely coincided with de León's march to Baffin Bay. It was organized and dispatched by Viceroy Conde de Monclova, who arrived in New Spain on September 13, 1686, with specific orders from the crown to deal swiftly with the French threat. On the recommendations of Barroto and Romero, two shallow-draft vessels equipped with sails and oars were quickly constructed and provisioned. These piraguas were captained by Martín de Rivas and Pedro de Iriarte, with Barroto and Romero serving as chief pilots. In late December 1686, the ships left Veracruz bound for the Texas coast. At the mouth of the Río Grande, unfriendly natives discouraged entry, prompting the explorers to continue along the Padre Island shoreline. An Indian canoe captured near a stream named the Río Flores contained parts of a large vessel, obviously wrecked nearby, as well as weapons of French manufacture. Those discoveries confirmed the prior presence of the French between Corpus Christi and Matagorda bays.[45]

Exploration of the latter bay, which the Spaniards named San Bernardo, brought positive results, for within its waters were found the remains of the *Belle*. Fleur de lis emblazoned on the stern were irrefutable proof of its origin. Hostile Karankawas, however, prevented a thorough exploration of Matagorda Bay's tributaries, thus the miserable survivors of La Salle's ill-fated colony, located only a few miles up Garcitas Creek, escaped any chance of detection. Further sailing along Galveston Bay and Sabine Pass failed to reveal likely sites for a French colony. Later, the voyagers did explore the huge Mississippi Delta, arriving there in mid-May. After a brief run to Florida for fresh provisions, the Rivas-Iriarte expedition completed its circumnavigation of the Gulf and returned to Veracruz on July 3, 1687. It had not lost a man.[46]

Despite the success of Rivas and Iriarte, they were out of touch with the viceroy for seven months. Their absence had caused increasing concern for the Conde de Monclova. By late spring of 1687, he ordered that two ships suited for coastal exploration be outfitted and sent over the same route followed by the second sea expedition. And on June 20, a pair of frigates (*pataches*) lifted anchor at Tampico. Several days later, the first of the overdue piraguas arrived at Veracruz. Its arrival, however, was too late to recall the third surveillance by sea in search of La Salle, and the entire voyage of Rivas and Iriarte was duplicated. This somewhat superfluous expedition was captained by Andrés de Pez and Francisco de Gámarra (June 30–September 4, 1687). Their careful log and latitude recordings confirm reconnaissance of Mustang and St. Joseph islands as well as Corpus Christi, San Antonio, Matagorda, and Galveston bays. They found no physical evidence of the French but did provide reference points for future voyages and detailed information on the Mississippi Delta.[47]

Still, in the summer and fall of 1687, optimism among the Spaniards ran high. Two searches by sea and two land expeditions to the lower Río Grande had failed to find any French. At that time, the viceroy received a report from Spain, based on pirated French documents acquired by the Spanish ambassador in London. The information was a compendium of Beaujeu's report to the French court on the status of La Salle's colony. By the naval commander's own admission, he had left the colony "in very bad condition," without potable water, racked by disease and dysentery, menaced by Indian attacks, and endangered by lost provisions.[48] The viceroy's sanguinary assessment of the situation was soon shattered, however, by reports from the frontier of New Spain. The surviving Frenchmen were among the Indian nations of Texas.

On July 13, 1687, ten days after the return of Rivas and Iriarte, the younger Alonso de León was named governor of Coahuila. He assumed his duties in October, taking up residence in the village of San Miguel de Luna near the site of Monclova. From the first days of his governorship, de León's attention was focused on Indian attacks directed at missions, towns, and haciendas in the province. The offending Toboso Indians were severely punished in a series of campaigns and executions. Then came ominous news that a white man was organizing Indian tribes north of the Río Grande. At the head of a small detachment of soldiers, de León marched northeastward toward the Río Grande to investigate. He crossed the river at Paso de Francia and after some difficulty found a large settlement of Indians presided over by an aged and tattooed Frenchman, Jean Géry. Géry was sent to Coahuila, where interrogation heightened concern that his countrymen were marshaling Indians in Texas for sinister purposes. The captive Frenchman was subsequently sent to Mexico City, where his confused and mendacious testimony undermined the viceroy's optimism and spurred further efforts by land and sea to find La Salle's colony.[49]

Simultaneous with the capture of Géry, Indians arriving at the Franciscan missions near La Junta reported "other Spaniards" living among the Tejas in East Texas. This vague report, however, failed to alert the padres. A year later (September 1688), Indians again brought stories to the missions about a lone white man, obviously Géry, who had lived among hunting and gathering tribes of the Texas Hill Country. Like de León, the governor in El Parral was sorely pressed by hostile Indians, but he elected to send a small troop of soldiers north of the Río Grande under the command of Juan de Retana. Delayed for several months, Retana had

not progressed beyond La Junta when information concerning the fate of
La Salle's colony in Texas reached him on March 3, 1689. Scouts and
Juan Sabeata, the same chieftain who in 1683 had led a Jumano delegation to El Paso, informed him that local Indians had attacked and destroyed the last remnants of the French settlement. This intelligence was
forwarded to the governor at El Parral, who recalled Retana on April 12.[50]
Meanwhile, renewed efforts to find La Salle's colony had been launched
from Coahuila and Veracruz.

The fourth effort by sea in search of La Salle (March–April 1688) was
of little importance in Gulf Coast exploration. It was prompted by fabricated testimony extracted from two English captives, John Philip Vera
and Ralph Wilkinson, and resulted in another voyage by Pez and Barroto
to Mobile Bay. That body of water was believed to be the elusive Bay of
Espíritu Santo. Wilkinson's claim that he could lead Spaniards to La
Salle's settlement was exposed as a hoax, and he paid for his deception
by drawing a life sentence in the galleys.[51]

In a similar vein, the interrogation of Jean Géry in Mexico City led
directly to the fifth and final sea expedition. The viceroy was suspicious
of Géry's veracity but determined to leave nothing to chance. The Conde
de Monclova again sought the advice of experienced seamen. Rivas and
Pez insisted that the north coast of the Gulf had no port deep enough to
accommodate large ships. They did, however, suggest thorough reconnoitering of the Río Grande. If that failed to produce results, then careful
exploration of San Bernardo Bay (Matagorda), where the wrecked *Belle*
was spotted, should be the next priority.[52]

The same piraguas used in the second voyage left Veracruz on August 8, 1688. On board the two vessels were small launches capable of
probing rivers and shallow bays. From the mouth of the Río Grande, the
first thorough exploration of the river by water advanced about one hundred miles upstream to a latitude of 26° 24′ near present Roma, Texas.
Finding no French but many uncooperative Indians, the launches returned, and coastal navigation continued. At Matagorda Bay, extensive
exploration revealed pieces of the *Aimable* and information on Tres Pa-
lacios Bay, but the searchers did not discover the entrance to Lavaca Bay.
That oversight again prevented any chance of finding La Salle's colony.
A return trip to Veracruz completed the fifty-four-day voyage. While the
search was under way, the Conde de Monclova had received orders to
leave Mexico and take up duties as viceroy of Peru.[53]

One of Monclova's final actions in New Spain was the assignment on
July 23, 1688, of Alonso de León as commander of still another land
expedition into Texas. After the appointment, Jean Géry was sent north

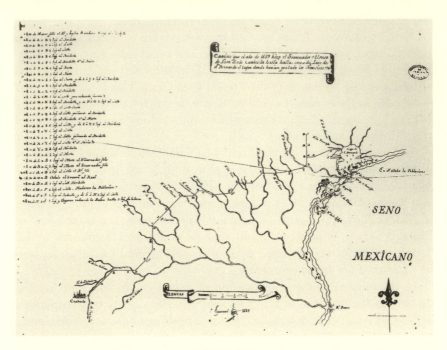

FIGURE 11

*Log of the Alonso de León expedition of 1689. This sketch map records the
daily progress of Alonso de León from Coahuila to the site of La Salle's colony
near Matagorda Bay. (With the permission of the Archivo General de Indias,
Seville, Spain; Mapas y Planos, México 86.)*

to Monterrey to serve as de León's guide. Men were drawn from presidios
in Nuevo León and Nueva Vizcaya with leadership supplied by Coahuila.
Rendezvous of the combined force was delayed, however, until late
March 1689. It totaled 114 men, including Chaplain Damián Massanet
of the mission at Caldera, soldiers, mule drivers, and servants. De León,
recently promoted to the rank of general, was well provisioned with
eighty-five loads of supplies.[54]

From the Río Sabinas, de León headed northeast and on April 2 again
forded the Río Grande at Paso de Francia. The march toward Matagorda
Bay followed the inner coastal plain, thus avoiding broad streams near
the coast. Charting de León's path across Texas, however, is at best pure
guesswork because his latitude sightings were consistently thrown off by
a damaged astrolabe (see Figure 11). Géry apparently proved worthless
as a guide, for the commander relied increasingly on the advice of local
Indians who knew the French. On April 20 de León carefully righted his

broken astrolabe and took a sun shot five miles east of the Guadalupe River. The computed latitude was 28° 41', which, if accurate, placed him about eight miles southeast of present Victoria, Texas. Two days later the expedition began a march down Garcitas Creek. Shortly before noon, it came upon the ruins of the French settlement. Four years of searching had finally borne results.[55]

De León, recognizing that he must file a detailed report with the new viceroy, recorded a scene of utter devastation. A fort near the creek and five crude houses made up the dwellings. The houses had been sacked, furniture smashed, dishes broken, books and documents torn apart and scattered. What the Indian attackers had not wanted or carried off, they had destroyed. Three corpses, one apparently a woman, lay among the ruins. After services conducted by Father Massanet, the remains of the French colonists were interred in a common grave.[56]

One day after the grim discovery, de León set out to explore the waterways south of Fort St. Louis. He discovered Lavaca Bay and pieces of the *Aimable,* the same wreck viewed by Rivas and Iriarte in 1687 and by Rivas and Pez in 1688. Returning to a camp near Garcitas Creek, de León found a reply to a letter he had dispatched to the land of the Tejas, inviting any surviving French there to surrender. Two men, Jean L'Archevêque and Jacques Grollet, accepted. On the return trip, they were contacted at the Colorado River in the Smithville–La Grange area and accompanied the expedition back to Coahuila, arriving there with the main force in May 1689. L'Archevêque and Grollet were sent to Mexico City for further questioning along with de León's report of his march to Matagorda Bay. At that juncture, only three Frenchmen had been found in Texas.[57] What had been the fate of La Salle and the others? Significantly, La Salle's initial exploration from Matagorda Bay had been toward the west, not the east, indicating a desire to reconnoiter Spanish settlements in New Spain. That decision also underscores the explorer's belief that he was situated in western Gulf waters. On reaching the Río Grande, which La Salle named La Maligne, he ascended the riverbanks for a considerable distance, perhaps as far as the site of modern Langtry, Texas, in western Val Verde County. In March 1686, La Salle and the remnants of his troop struggled back to Fort St. Louis.[58]

Shortly after La Salle returned from his trek along the Río Grande, the remaining ship, *Belle,* and most of its crew were lost. This final naval disaster canceled any plans to explore rivers by sea or send for assistance from the Caribbean islands. Limited in his options, La Salle chose another contingent of men and set off to the east on April 22, 1686. His second overland effort was a desperate attempt to locate the Mississippi

River, travel upstream by it and the Illinois River, and return to Canada. Therein lay the best hope of succoring his colony. On his initial exploration into East Texas, La Salle contacted the Tejas and Cenis Indians of the Hasinai Confederacy. He apparently reached the Trinity River before returning to Fort St. Louis in August. On the homeward journey, the dangers of the wilderness were dramatized when one of La Salle's servants, while swimming the Colorado River, was attacked and killed by an alligator.[59]

The colony at Fort St. Louis had been reduced to less than forty-five people when La Salle decided to redouble efforts to reach Canada. In early January 1687, the third expedition left Garcitas Creek on a fatal march to East Texas. Included in a group of seventeen were Henri Joutel, La Salle's brother, two nephews—one of whom was the hot-tempered Moranget—as well as Pierre Duhaut, the surgeon Liotot, a German former buccaneer named Hiems, and Jean L'Archevêque. After an arduous march to the Trinity River, frustrations and old animosities surfaced. Following a quarrel over the division of buffalo meat, Moranget, La Salle's Indian hunter, and a servant were ax-murdered in their sleep by Liotot and another conspirator. On the following day (March 19, 1687), La Salle, who was camped some distance away, investigated the disappearance of his nephew. Near the banks of the Trinity River, as he approached the scene of violence, the French explorer's "head was well-nigh blown away" by Pierre Duhaut.[60]

Ultimately, only fifteen or sixteen people survived La Salle's ill-fated colony on the Texas coast. Six of them returned to France while nine were captured by the Spaniards. Only one of the six, Father Anastasius Douay, returned to America with the Iberville expedition of 1699. Of the nine captives, the three adults became Hispanicized and settled in New Mexico after the reconquest was completed in the 1690s by Diego de Vargas. The remaining six survivors, five of whom were brothers and a sister of the Talon family, were all children spared by the Karankawas in their final assault on Fort St. Louis.[61]

How serious was the French challenge, and how appropriate was the Spanish response? La Salle's belief that "his river" was near the mines of northern Mexico made his plan potentially dangerous to the Spanish. The French explorer's greatest consistent strength was his ability to befriend and mobilize Indians. The success of the Pueblo Revolt had demonstrated the depth of anti-Spanish feeling in New Mexico. A persuasive man such as La Salle with his linguistic skills and wide experience among natives west of the Mississippi could have created havoc on the frontier. Serious Indian unrest already plagued both Coahuila and Nueva Vizcaya at the very time that the French menace materialized. Given the imperial rivalry between Spain and France in the second half of the seventeenth century, La Salle's plan of 1684 was not far-fetched.[62]

In retrospect, as Robert S. Weddle has noted, La Salle failed because of bad luck, hostile environment, disease, deadly Karankawa arrows, and the enmity of Frenchman toward Frenchman. Had he been able to find the mouth of the Mississippi, La Salle would have planted his colony there. Spaniards would have searched for the settlement until they found it and probably could have destroyed it. More important, discovery of the great river, which eluded all five sea explorations, would have impressed its strategic location on the Spanish. That this did not occur had enormous importance in shaping the course of history. Because La Salle overshot the Mississippi, Spain reacted to the accidental landing of the French "on an obscure, unnavigable bay on the Texas coast."[63]

Spain's response would center attention on the Tejas Indians in East Texas, where success was hard to come by, and the failure of the French colony in Texas diverted attention from the more serious French threat in Louisiana. Within a decade, that focus would allow the French to penetrate and settle the lower Mississippi Valley, driving a wedge between Spanish Texas and Florida. Spain's response had also served to short-circuit the missionary enterprises of Juan Larios in extreme south-central Texas, thereby delaying settlement of that region.

FIVE

International Rivalry and the East Texas Missions, 1689–1714

THE LAST THIRD OF THE SEVENTEENTH CENTURY MARKED A crisis in the effectiveness of Spanish imperial policy. Symptomatic of the problem was a malaise of government rooted in the king himself, for on September 17, 1665, a four-year-old sickly child "retarded by rickets, and mentally subnormal" ascended the Spanish throne. Charles II was the tragic product of incestuous marriages that had linked the Hapsburg families of Spain and Austria for nearly two centuries. Seven of the king's eight great-grandparents were direct lineal descendants of one woman, the psychologically unstable Spanish queen, Juana la Loca (1479–1555). Known in history as *el Hechizado* (the Bewitched), Charles was incapable of ruling and of fathering an heir. During his reign (1665–1700), Spain had been viewed as a corpse, picked at by internal parasites and foreign marauders. This conventional picture is no doubt overdrawn, for the country began a slow, painful upturn in the 1680s.[1] Recovery, however, would take decades. By 1695 the moribund Spanish government felt obliged to auction the top offices in the viceroyalties of Mexico and Peru to the highest bidder from the ranks of the wealthy nobility. To make matters worse, Spain was a pawn in the ambitions of the French king, Louis XIV. The first three wars of the Sun King made France and Spain almost constant enemies.[2] That enmity was also reflected in America. With the death of Charles II in 1700, Louis XIV maneuvered his grandson, the Duke of Anjou, to the Spanish throne as Philip V. The union of Spain and France under the same ruling family created a preponderance of Bourbon power in Europe as well as in America. The ensuing War of Spanish Succession (1702–1713) made allies of the former antagonists, but on the North American continent the two countries continued to compete for control of the lower Mississippi Valley and Texas. The establishment of the first missions in East Texas, their subsequent failure, and the stimulus to reestablish them should be viewed against this backdrop of internal conditions in Spain and shifting international alignments.

ALONSO DE LEÓN'S BRIEF ACCOUNT OF HIS SEARCH FOR AND
the fate of the French colony at Matagorda Bay and his diary of the expedition were forwarded from Coahuila to the viceroy on May 16, 1689.
Two French captives, L'Archevêque and Grollet, in the custody of Francisco Martínez, accompanied the reports to Mexico City. Martínez
arrived in the capital in late June or early July and interrogation of the
French captives began immediately. News of the complete failure of La
Salle's colony created instant optimism and quickened religious fervor,
for the Conde de Galve and his advisers viewed the disaster at Fort St.
Louis as renewed proof of God's "divine aid and favor."[3]

The viceroy was especially impressed with de León's secondhand report on the Tejas. The Indians maintained that in the past *una mujer* had
visited their ancestors, imparting religious instruction to them. In response to her teachings, the Indians had effected religious accessories
such as a chapel, with its interior illuminated by a perpetual flame fed by
deer fat, an altar, images of saints, and a cross. These appearances of
Christianity were interpreted in the capital as additional evidence of miraculous visitations by the Lady in Blue. De León's assessments of the
land and people in East Texas were perhaps overly sanguine, for he reported a level terrain with many varieties of trees, a good climate, and an
abundance of bison and other game animals. He also portrayed the Indian governor of the Tejas, whom the Spaniards would name Bernardino,
as a man of reason. Without firsthand observation, de León noted that
the Indians lived in nine settlements of wooden houses and that they had
a governmental organization comparable to culturally advanced Indians
of New Spain. He further recorded that the Tejas sowed abundant crops,
such as corn, beans, pumpkins, watermelons, and cantaloupe. Finally, de
León reported that the Indians had expressed a desire that missionaries
be sent them to impart religious instruction, and he further informed the
viceroy that his companion, Father Damián Massanet, as well as the
brethren of the Colegio de la Santa Cruz in Querétaro, would gladly
volunteer their services if missions were authorized among the Tejas.[4]

The viceroy submitted Massanet's suggestion to an advisory council.
That body likewise interpreted the entire La Salle episode as evidence of
divine prompting, which called for determined efforts to save the souls of
the pagan Tejas. It recommended that Massanet's proposal be accepted,
and it ordered Alonso de León to file a report outlining his suggestions
as to how conversion of the Tejas could best be accomplished.[5]

A series of letters sent to the Conde de Galve in August 1689 endorsed
the proposed missionary effort in East Texas. The bishop of Guadalajara
recommended that conversion of the Tejas be assigned to the Colegio de

Santa Cruz, and he stressed the advisability of taking steps to avoid another penetration of the French at Matagorda Bay. The bishop's recommendations of August 3 were followed closely by enthusiastic endorsements from Fathers Massanet and Miguel de Fontcuberta, guardian of the college of the Holy Cross.

In compliance with his orders, Governor de León filed a report (August 12) that reflected wisdom acquired from years of experience among frontier natives. Had his suggestions been accepted, the subsequent disasters in East Texas might well have been lessened, if not avoided. De León recommended that presidios be constructed to bridge the gap between the Coahuila settlements and the proposed new mission field. Military outposts should be positioned on the Río Grande, the Frio, and the Guadalupe; a fourth garrison should also be erected near the mission site itself.[6] De León's advice was largely ignored, primarily because officials in Mexico City believed that a substantial military presence would impede spreading the Gospel. That decision was also influenced by an acute shortage of funds in New Spain.[7]

Officials in the capital nevertheless regarded the French intrusion as a serious matter, especially in the light of renewed war in Europe between Spain and France. Although resisting the notion of converting the natives in an atmosphere of military might, they authorized de León to choose a sufficient number of soldiers to prevent any further French penetrations into Texas. Their objectives in the words of the *fiscal* were "to destroy and flatten all vestiges that remained of the French nation and to extend the reach and favorable influence [of Spain] over all Indians from Coahuila to Texas." The size of de León's company, however, at 110 men would become a sore point with Father Massanet, who saw the governor as arrogating personal and military ambitions over peaceful missionary goals. This issue sparked strained relations between the two men and a mutual distrust borne primarily by Massanet.[8]

Initial preparations for founding a mission among the Tejas took place in Mexico City in late 1689, and Massanet was called there to participate in the planning. Officials in the capital assigned responsibility for manning the missionary effort to the Franciscan college at Querétaro and gave Massanet control over religious aspects of it. In all, the college selected six padres for the Texas enterprise: Damián Massanet, Miguel de Fontcuberta, Francisco Casañas de Jesús María, Antonio Bordoy, Francisco Hidalgo, and Antonio Perera.[9]

In January 1690 the six friars made final preparations at Querétaro for their trip north toward Texas. Accompanying them on the journey with provisions and other necessaries was Captain Francisco Martínez. In Coahuila they experienced a short delay, for soldiers assigned to the enterprise from Nueva Vizcaya had not arrived. On March 26 the expedition departed Santiago de Monclova without waiting longer for the still absent troops. However, two of the friars, Francisco Hidalgo and Antonio Perera, remained behind at the mission of San Salvador de la Caldera.[10]

De León followed a route similar to the one he had taken in 1689. From the Guadalupe River crossing, he led a detachment of twenty men and again descended on Fort St. Louis, arriving there on April 26 (see Figure 12). The wooden fort was burned, allegedly by the hand of Massanet. On that same day, a reconnoitering of the mouth of the Lavaca River revealed two distant objects, which the governor believed to be buoys marking a ship channel. Lacking a canoe to investigate, de León could only report his suspicions to the viceroy. His failure to determine the nature of the objects and the growing criticisms of him by Massanet would later serve to discredit the veteran commander.[11]

Rejoining the main camp on the Guadalupe, de León marched the full expedition to the Neches River, where on May 22 he encountered a settlement of the Tejas. After a brief search for an ideal site, the foundations for the first mission in East Texas, San Francisco de los Tejas, were laid, and mass was celebrated in the new church on June 1.[12] Of particular interest to de León was any information the Tejas might have of Frenchmen in the area. He learned that only recently four white men had approached an Indian settlement seeking friendly contacts with it. The Tejas chieftain had refused to receive them, for he professed friendship to the Spaniards, then en route to East Texas. The Frenchmen had subsequently withdrawn eastward toward the Mississippi River. These men were undoubtedly members of Henri de Tonti's expedition. In fact, one of them was probably Tonti himself. De León made no attempt to pursue the retreating Frenchmen, believing that the mission as an intelligence-gathering outpost could monitor their activities.[13]

The viceroy had left the number of troops to be stationed in East Texas at the discretion of de León and his officers, with consultation from Massanet. The governor's initial decision to leave fifty men under the command of Nicolás Prieto was unequivocally opposed by Massanet, who insisted that only three soldiers should remain at the mission. De León did not press the matter and on June 1, after completion of the church and residence for the padres, departed for Coahuila. Massanet left on the following day, after securing a promise from the Indian governor that he

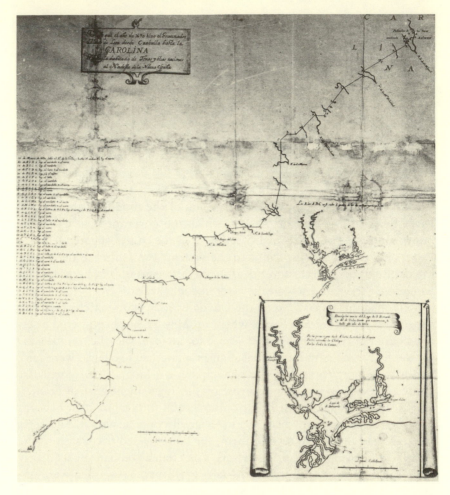

FIGURE 12

Log of the Alonso de León expedition of 1690. This sketch map records the daily progress of Alonso de León and Damián Massanet from Coahuila to the Tejas villages in East Texas. (With the permission of the Archivo General de Indias, Seville, Spain; Mapas y Planos, México 88.)

would not mistreat the three friars who would remain at the mission, but subsequent events would reveal the hollowness of that pledge. In reality, "the experienced and reasonable Alonso de León knew Indians much better than the visionary and impetuous Massanet."[14]

On the outward trip to the Neches, de León had recovered two French youths from Indians near the Colorado River crossing. Pierre Talon and Pierre Meunier had been spared from the general massacre at Fort St. Louis, and they accompanied the governor and Father Massanet on the return march to Coahuila. As the command approached the Guadalupe crossing, de León learned of additional French children living as captives among coastal Karankawas. He again detached a small force from his troops and descended toward Matagorda Bay. A dispute with the Indians over the amount of ransom to be paid for the children led to hostilities and to the death of four natives, but the rescue mission was a success. Robert, Marie Madelaine, and Lucien Talon were reunited with their older brother, Pierre. De León's actions, however, drew criticism from Massanet, who maintained that lack of discipline among the soldiers had provoked the clash.[15]

After rejoining the main body of his troops at the Guadalupe River, de León marched to the Río Grande, arriving there on July 4. He found the river swollen by floodwaters, which delayed his progress until July 12. On that date the commander drafted his account of the 1690 expedition. De León again painted a highly favorable portrait of East Texas and its Indian occupants and described the Tejas as affable folk who raised abundant quantities of food. The Indians lived in houses furnished with wooden benches and raised canopied beds, and they possessed a large quantity of pots and earthen jars for cooking *atole* and tamales as well as stones for grinding corn into meal. To the north and the northeast of the Tejas settlements were villages of the Kadohadachos, who also raised abundant crops and managed their food supply to last throughout the year. The governor's report and his *diario,* however, contained ominous news concerning the continued presence of French interlopers in Texas. In addition to learning that four Frenchmen had retreated to the east as his party approached the Neches River, he had been informed by coastal Indians that a ship had stopped to pick up firewood and fresh water. De León strongly recommended that permanent Spanish settlements be founded on the Guadalupe River and at Matagorda Bay. Failure to do so, he argued, was to risk having Frenchmen seize the coastal and interior regions of Texas. De León also requested that friars be sent to spread the faith among the infidel natives, and he recounted his recovery of the five young survivors of La Salle's colony. Captain Gregorio de Salinas Varona, accompanied by Pierre Meunier, carried the governor's reports to Mexico City; the main body of the expedition returned to Monclova.[16]

By the fall of 1690, the viceroy and his advisers in the capital had two plans recommended to them, the first by de León (July 1690) and the second by Father Massanet (September 1690). In the previous year, as Massanet had moved northward from Coahuila into Texas, he recorded various native groups encountered by the expedition and the levels of their cultures. He listed and named many Indian nations, most of which have never been identified. They ranged from natives who lived off the fruit of the land to others with cultivated fields, fixed houses, and organized government. His intent was to bring as many infidels as possible into contact with Christian teaching at minimum expense to the crown.[17]

In all, Massanet requested fourteen priests and seven lay brothers for the Texas mission field. The brothers were to be assigned to the houses of priests, thereby preventing the introduction of Indian women as household servants, and they were to assist in teaching the Indians. Father Massanet also asked the viceroy to request that the commissioner general of the order not impede volunteers for the new missions from the Franciscan provinces under jurisdiction of the Colegio de Querétaro. He supported the recommendation of de León that a Spanish settlement be established on the Guadalupe River, a strategic location situated halfway between Coahuila and the Texas missions. Military and civilian presence in Texas would guard against foreign entry at Matagorda Bay and would ensure that the French, who were skilled in Indian languages, would not cause mischief among the Texas tribes. The padre further advised that military personnel stationed in Texas be paid the usual stipend for presidio soldiers as well as supplemental wages for service on the frontier and that they be paid regularly in cash, rather than in other forms of compensation. He specifically cautioned that soldiers not be permitted to live in Indian towns, recognizing the potential for trouble if poorly paid soldiers lived in close proximity to Indian communities. As for the Tejas, Massanet requested neither soldiers nor a presidio. Instead, civilian craftsmen such as carpenters and masons were urgently needed to build living quarters and chapels. A protector of Indians should be appointed for Texas to control the civilians and soldiers and to assist the natives. This position need not add to crown expenses, for the protector at Saltillo was essentially without a job because no Indians were left there to protect. Finally, Massanet suggested that children might be sent to Texas to grow up there and mingle with the Tejas under the supervision and instruction of priests.[18]

Viceregal officials in Mexico City studied the proposals of de León and Massanet, and they elected to implement most of the latter's suggestions. The Massanet plan was considerably less expensive. The seemingly friendly attitude of the Tejas, the optimistic assessments of the padre, and the decline of de León's reputation were factors militating against the governor's recommendations. The *fiscal* endorsed Massanet's proposal on October 10, and that decision was confirmed by the Junta de Hacienda on November 16. The military settlement on the Guadalupe River, however, was deemed premature, and in any event an expenditure of that magnitude required approval of the king and the Council of the Indies. Soldiers, it was decided, would be provided for Texas only on the recommendations of the padres. In accordance with Massanet's request, eight missions were authorized for the Texas province: three among the Tejas, including San Francisco de los Tejas, four among the Kadohadachos, and one for the tribes near the Guadalupe. The fourteen priests and seven lay brothers proposed by Massanet were also approved. All supplies needed for the enterprise were to be provided by funds from the royal treasury, and instructions to implement the expanded missionary program were dispatched to the frontier.[19]

The suspected buoys sighted by de León near the mouth of the Lavaca River were of particular concern to the viceroy. He closely questioned Salinas Varona and Pierre Meunier about the suspicious objects and the possibilities of French penetration to the east of the proposed missions. Salinas Varona defended de León against charges that the governor had been remiss in not investigating the precise nature of the distant objects, for he was handicapped by not having a boat or a canoe. Nevertheless, with the concurrence of an advisory junta, the viceroy took immediate steps to outfit a sea expedition to Matagorda Bay. Selected as captain was Francisco de Llanos, an experienced officer of the West Indian fleet; the pilot was Juan de Triana, a man familiar with Gulf waters; the mapmaker was an engineer, Manuel Joseph de Cárdenas, who had recently completed work on the fortress and prison at San Juan de Ulúa in Veracruz harbor; and the commander of land operations was Salinas Varona, a man obviously experienced in the region. Salinas was to ascertain whether the site of La Salle's colony was suitable for a Spanish presidio. If so, the buried French cannon were to be left in place, and if not, they were to be dug up and sent to Veracruz.[20]

The expedition departed Veracruz on October 12, 1690, and sailed directly to Matagorda Bay. Close inspection from a launch on December 1 revealed that the troublesome "buoys" were upended logs embedded in silt. They were removed, and efforts were directed toward a careful mapping and reconnaissance of Lavaca Bay and its tributaries. No navigable river toward the interior, which would have provided an important link with the missions in East Texas, was discovered, but the resulting drawings by the careful engineer, Cárdenas, pinpointed the location of La Salle's colony on Garcitas Creek (see Figure 13).[21] After a month of exploration, the Llanos-Cárdenas expedition returned to Veracruz on December 9, 1690, where a report was filed with the viceroy.

As the expedition sailed homeward, final preparations were under way for a new entrada into Texas. The viceroy and an advisory junta diplomatically removed Alonso de León from consideration as commander. His presence in Coahuila was deemed essential to the continuing security of that province. In reality, one of the finest servants of Spain in America had fallen into disfavor. He was blamed for failing to remove all traces of French occupation at Lavaca Bay; his frank and honest nature had offended officials in the distant capital; and he was the target of Massanet's frequent complaints. Alonso de León died in March 1691, shortly after the appointment of a new governor for Texas. He remains the most able and dedicated soldier-administrator of early Spanish Texas and Coahuila.

On January 23, 1691, the Conde de Galve appointed Domingo Terán de los Ríos as the first governor of the province of Texas. Terán was a thirty-year veteran in the Spanish colonies, having served in Peru and New Spain, and during the 1680s, he had gained administrative experience as the governor of Sinaloa and Sonora. Terán was ordered to establish seven additional missions among the Tejas and neighboring tribes, to explore the province thoroughly, and to ascertain the truth of lingering rumors about French presence in the region. He was also instructed to keep a diary of his travels and experiences, and he was informed that his authority was subordinate to that of Massanet's in formulating policy. To support this new land expedition into Texas, the viceroy decided to send provisions by sea to Matagorda Bay.[22]

Terán's departure was delayed for several months by careful preparations regarded as necessary for the success of the undertaking. On May 16, 1691, his army moved out of the base camp at Monclova. However, the full complement of priests and lay brothers, as requested by Massanet, had not been recruited. Ten friars and three brothers made up the religious contingent; the soldiers numbered fifty. It is important to note that the first four land entradas of de León had been of a protective and defensive nature with no intent to accomplish political or religious settlement of Texas. The expedition of 1690, which had led to the founding of San Francisco de los Tejas, was almost exclusively missionary in intent; but, by the very nature of its size, provisions, and instructions, the

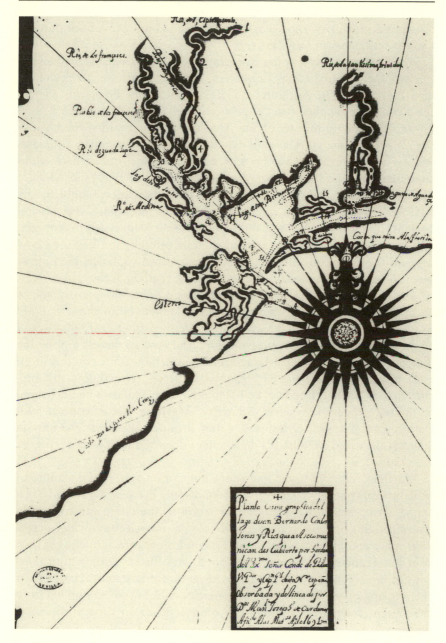

FIGURE 13

Matagorda Bay and the location of Fort St. Louis. This map, drawn in 1691 by Manuel Joseph de Cárdenas, depicts the Matagorda Bay area and establishes the location of La Salle's colony on Garcitas Creek (Río de los franceses). (With the permission of the Archivo General de Indias, Seville, Spain; Mapas y Planos, México 89.)

Terán undertaking of 1691 was clearly intended to bring about the permanent settlement of East Texas.[23]

Terán's party arrived at the Río Grande on May 28 and remained encamped there until June 3. Consistent with his penchant for renaming almost everything he encountered in Texas, including the province itself, the commander applied Río del Norte to the stream. By June 13 he had advanced to the future site of San Antonio, and he reached the Guadalupe River on June 19. There his expedition met a huge party of Jumano Indians and their allies, among whom was the much-traveled chieftain Juan Sabeata. The Indians bore two letters from the padres at Mission San Francisco, and the news within the communications could hardly have been worse. Massive sickness had broken out among the mission Indians; illness had also claimed the life of Father Miguel de Fontcuberta. The Jumanos and their allies seemed friendly enough, but they somehow aroused the suspicions of Terán. Despite increased vigilance, the natives were able to steal seventy-five horses from the remuda as they departed.[24]

The Terán expedition reached the Colorado near the present site of Austin on June 26 and camped for several days. From there Captain Francisco Martínez and a detachment of twenty soldiers were dispatched to the coast to attempt a rendezvous with the support vessels sent by the viceroy. Martínez reached Matagorda Bay on July 7 but could find no trace of any ships. He waited for five days before retreating to the interior. Before leaving the coast, he left a letter with Indians to be delivered to the sea expedition when it did arrive. Martínez missed contact with the ships by a matter of hours, for they dropped anchor at the bay on July 12, the same day that his detachment departed for the camp on the Colorado.[25]

Martínez returned to the main encampment on July 17. His failure to find the supply vessels triggered a heated dispute between Terán and Massanet. Terán wished to send another troop to the coast and to remain encamped until he was resupplied. Massanet insisted that further delays were unacceptable, given the desperate conditions known to exist at mission San Francisco. The padre prevailed, and the expedition continued toward the Neches, but at a pace so slow that it irritated Massanet. At the crossing of the Trinity, the missionaries, without informing Terán of their intent, hurried on ahead of the soldiers. Their arrival at the mission was much welcomed by the two surviving priests, Fathers Bordoy and Jesús María. Terán followed at his own pace and camped near mission San Francisco on August 4, 1691. He entered the settlement two days later and distributed gifts to the Indians and their governor. The combined soldiers and priests then heard mass in celebration of their safe arrival.[26] During their months of isolation in East Texas, the padres had founded a second mission about five miles east of San Francisco de los Tejas. Santísimo Nombre de María was specifically the inspiration of Father Jesús María. Later, the sullen and indifferent attitude of the natives had likewise caused conditions there to deteriorate badly.

Enthusiasm surrounding the arrival of Massanet and Terán quickly subsided and relations between Spaniards and Indians worsened. The Tejas committed petty thievery and stole horses and mules. The weather, so typical of Texas in August, was torrid. Terán also became increasingly apprehensive over failure to contact the supply vessels. He tolerated the situation for twenty days and then took action. On August 24, with most of his command following, Terán set out for Matagorda Bay. His intent was clear. If the ships had not arrived on the coast, he would march back to Coahuila. Perhaps to his disappointment, for Terán was clearly unhappy with conditions in East Texas, when he arrived at the site of La Salle's colony, he found Captain Salinas Varona camped there with news that the ships were anchored nearby in the bay. Worse, Salinas carried new instructions from the viceroy. It was imperative that Terán explore the province thoroughly before returning to Monclova. Terán accepted supplies, added Salinas's troops to his own, and turned "back to the country of the Tejas, which he had hoped never to see again." [27]

When Terán arrived at the mission, he found that conditions there had deteriorated alarmingly. Cattle and horses disappeared daily; the Indians were openly insolent; some of the priests had become thoroughly discouraged; and the Indian governor, Bernardino, had gone off to punish a hostile tribe, warning that when he returned the Spaniards should not be among his people. Still, Terán knew what he had to do. In compliance with the viceroy's orders, he must further explore the province.[28]

On November 6, 1691, Terán, accompanied by a few soldiers, Massanet, and two other priests, set out toward the country of the Kadohadachos. The expedition was plagued by snow and cold, slowed by sick and dying horses, and imperiled by inadequate clothing and provisions. Terán reached a Kadohadacho settlement on the Red River near the end of the month, and the bitter march was mitigated somewhat by the friendly welcome extended by the Indians. Terán explored the riverbanks, took a few soundings, and determined that the Red was navigable, but he lacked a boat or canoe to explore the waterway. Given the wretched condition of the Spaniards, even the zealous Massanet agreed that it was out of the question to establish even one mission among the Kadohadachos, much less the four specified in viceregal instructions. Most of December was spent on the painful return trip to Santísimo Nombre de María.[29]

Terán had honored only perfunctorily the viceroy's orders to explore the province, but he had become thoroughly disaffected with the region. Almost all of his horses were either dead or had been stolen by Indians. His request for animals from the mission's herd to aid his retreat toward Matagorda Bay was adamantly refused by Massanet. After a bitter quarrel with the padre, Terán ordered his soldiers to round up some of the mission's horses and cattle for the use of the army. Six of the missionaries also shared Governor Terán's discouragement and elected to leave East Texas with him. As he withdrew toward the coast, only three religious and nine soldiers remained at the struggling missions.[30]

The march from mission San Francisco to Matagorda Bay occupied Terán for nearly two months (January 9–March 5). When he arrived at the site of La Salle's old fort, fresh supplies from Mexico awaited him. Terán released his command to Captain Francisco Martínez, who bore responsibility for marching the army back to Coahuila. Terán, however, boarded the *Santa Margarita de Buena Vista* for a pleasant voyage to Veracruz. En route he marshaled defense for his actions in Texas in the form of a lengthy interrogatory with supporting testimony from sympathetic witnesses.[31]

Contrary to Terán's contention, his expedition was a near total fiasco. No new missions were founded; supplies and livestock had been decimated by theft; and with the exception of an entrada to the Red River, the enterprise added little by way of new information about the province. Both Governor Terán's diary and the report forwarded to the king by the viceroy reflected the magnitude of failure.[32]

Despite Terán's report on the dismal state of affairs in East Texas, officials in Mexico City did not rush to resupply the fledgling missions. The Conde de Galve had written to the crown in April 1691 requesting more religious to missionize the Tejas and secure the province, but he waited until the late spring of 1692 before taking positive action. At that juncture, he ordered the acting governor of Coahuila, Captain Diego Ramón, to report any news of events transpiring in Texas. Ramón responded with information gleaned from peripatetic Indians, namely, that the missionaries were healthy but that their supplies were running low. He advised that twenty men from Monclova be dispatched to reprovision the missions, a suggestion quickly endorsed by the viceroy. Actual implementation, however, would be carried out by Gregorio de Salinas Varona, the newly appointed governor of Coahuila. Substantial supplies and gifts for the Indians were sent north from Monclova in May and arrived at San Francisco de los Tejas in June. The timely arrival of Salinas Varona temporarily prevented the impending abandonment of the mission, for conditions there had become desperate. Crops had failed; food was in short supply; and pestilence had again broken out among the Indian population. Worse, from Massanet's perspective, was the obvious indifference of the Indians for the doctrine imparted to them; even his roseate view of the Tejas had been eroded by bitter experience.[33]

Massanet suggested three courses of action to secure the enterprise: first, a presidio was essential to command the Indians' respect for the padres; second, additional missions should be established at favorable sites; third, the Indians must be congregated in pueblos to facilitate religious instruction.[34] His recommendations were forwarded to the viceroy by Governor Salinas Varona on his return to Coahuila. Ultimately, the fate of the East Texas enterprise was considered by the royal *fiscal* and a general junta in Mexico City. Official policy was shaped by the belief that the use of force was contrary to sound theology, that the French threat had not materialized, that the province appeared unsuitable for permanent settlement, and that abandonment would not adversely affect strategic considerations in the Gulf and Florida. The conclusion was unequivocal. Salinas Varona must again proceed to mission San Francisco to escort home the missionaries and soldiers stationed there.

The rescue effort, however, never reached Texas. It was delayed by the onset of winter, while at the same time deteriorating conditions at the mission approached flash point. The Tejas had become openly insolent and threatened bloody rebellion under the leadership of their governor. Secretly, the missionaries began packing their sacred belongings in the fall of 1693. Large objects such as mission bells and military cannon were buried. On the night of October 25, mission San Francisco de los Tejas was set ablaze by the padres themselves as they hurriedly retreated toward the safety of Coahuila. Unfortunately, the small party was soon lost in the wilderness. After forty days of wandering, it struck the coast where someone finally reconciled its bearings. En route, four soldiers elected to desert, opting for life among the Tejas. The battered remnants of Spain's first missionary effort in Texas did not reach Monclova until February 17, 1694. Father Massanet and his fellow religious were soon reassigned to their college in Querétaro, and the East Texas mission field was abandoned for the next two decades.[35]

The difficulties of sustaining missions in East Texas had proved overwhelming. The religious outposts had been situated more than four hundred miles beyond the nearest settlement in northern Mexico. Their survival depended above all on winning the continuing friendship and cooperation of the natives, a situation that never developed. Other considerations incident to success were the patience of the missionaries, the arrival of supplies, and the size of the military guard. Since Massanet and the officials in Mexico City would never approve the stationing of a large contingent of soldiers near the mission, the latter circumstance helped doom the enterprise. This is not to suggest, however, that the first missions in East Texas had served no useful purpose. The experience had familiarized Spaniards with the terrain, rivers, and coastline of the future Lone Star State; and it served to convince officials, viceroys and bishops alike, that conversion and Hispanization of even the most tractable of Indians must be attempted by a combination of coercion and persuasion.[36]

At the very time the East Texas missionary effort was tested most severely, the defense of Pensacola Bay also served to divert attention away from the western Gulf shores. In the search by sea for La Salle's elusive colony, the Spanish had rediscovered Pensacola Bay and renewed their interest in it. Pensacola was viewed as the most favorable bay on Gulf waters, better than Mobile and far superior to Matagorda, where the French colony had experienced so much misery. Spanish officials expected the French to try in the near future to gain a new toehold on the Gulf Coast. The initial suggestion to occupy Pensacola Bay, made shortly after Alonso de León discovered the ruins of Fort St. Louis, had come from the experienced mariner, Andrés de Pez.[37]

The recommendation of Pez experienced in full measure the trials of formulating Spanish policy in the 1690s. It was debated endlessly in Spain by royal advisers, the Junta de Guerra, and the Council of the Indies; it involved suggested retrenchment at St. Augustine, Florida, with savings reallocated to Pensacola; it called for a thorough exploration of the bay, ably performed by the Mexican savant, Carlos de Sigüenza y Góngora; and it experienced inevitable procrastination and changed plans. Not until 1698 was a final order drafted, hastened then by the aggressive designs of Louis XIV following the Treaty of Ryswick (1697). The plan called for the establishment of a military garrison at Pensacola, thereby contesting French efforts to renew La Salle's old project.[38]

Construction of Presidio San Carlos de Austria began at Pensacola in late 1698. It was hampered by unusually cold weather, mutinous workers, food shortages, and damaging fires. But as events turned out, the timing was excellent. The death of La Salle and the course of King William's War, as it was known in America, had forestalled French designs to colonize the lower Mississippi River Valley. La Salle's grand enterprise, however, was kept alive by his faithful lieutenant, Henri de Tonti. Tonti had traveled to Versailles, where he pressed the French court to resurrect his friend's plan. A colony on the mainland, he argued, would discourage English designs in the region, and it could serve as a base for attacks on the rich silver mines of New Spain. His persistent entreaties and the end of war in Europe again focused attention on the Gulf Coast. While the Treaty of Ryswick stipulated status quo ante bellum regarding the territories of England, Spain, and France in America, none of the three powers was prepared to honor that agreement.[39] The French in particular concluded that they must act quickly or face foreign occupation of an area critical to the security of Canada. Louis XIV's minister of marine and colonies, Louis Phelypeau, Count of Pontchartrain, was as enthusiastic for the new venture as the Marquis de Seignelay had been in backing La Salle. His choice as leader of the French enterprise was Pierre Le Moyne d'Iberville.

Iberville was born in Canada, where he trained for a career in the French navy. By the end of the seventeenth century, he was an experienced explorer, diplomat, and combatant. He was joined in the venture by four of his brothers, the most famous of whom was Jean-Baptiste Le Moyne de Bienville, the future "father of Louisiana." Iberville's instructions granted him wide discretionary powers in deciding the route to follow in reaching the Mississippi, except for a mandated stop in Santo Domingo, where he was to receive assistance. On arrival at the great river, he was to select a site and fortify it. Iberville sailed from Brest on October 24, 1698, and arrived in Santo Domingo on December 4. Despite his best efforts, he could find no one who knew the exact location of the Mississippi Delta. Accordingly, as he entered Gulf waters, he was obliged to explore the entire coastal region carefully. When he reached Pensacola Bay on January 26, 1699, he found it already occupied by the Spanish. His request to enter the bay was denied by polite but firm posturing on the part of the presidio captain. The French commander's assurances that he posed no threat to Spanish possessions, for he was operating under limited orders from his own monarch, were to no avail. On January 30 his vessels unfurled sail and were under way. Determined to avoid La Salle's mistakes, Iberville closely examined the coast west of Pensacola Bay. He entered and made note of Mobile Bay and then from repeated anchorages carried out exploration of the coast by canoes. On March 2, 1699, the river that had eluded La Salle was found and entered, and in April a temporary fort was constructed at Biloxi. Having planted a colony near the mouth of the Mississippi, Iberville returned to France to receive additional instructions regarding the king's intent.[40]

Iberville's insistence that his squadron had come to the Gulf only to expel Canadian adventurers and pirates did not deceive the commander of San Carlos de Austria. It was clear to Andrés de Arriola that the French, finding Pensacola Bay occupied, would establish a settlement elsewhere on the Gulf Coast. Arriola sailed for Veracruz on February 2 to alert the viceroy of the impending threat, but when he arrived in Mexico he found that news of renewed French designs in the Gulf did not receive top priority. Instead, the viceroy was intent on investigating rumors that a contingent of Scots was headed for Panama to establish a colony there. Only when that threat failed to materialize did attention slowly shift to the French menace and the sorry plight of the soldiers at Pensacola. And even then the viceroy decided not to reinforce the Florida outpost or take action against the French. Reticence on the part of the Conde de Moctezuma can be explained in part by the abominable conditions of government finance incident to the last days of the reign of Charles II. The matter was referred to Madrid to await a decision by the king and his advisers.

Repeated rumors of a new threat, however, this time from English in the Gulf, finally prompted the viceroy to take action. He dispatched instructions to Arriola, who had returned to Pensacola, ordering him to organize a thorough search of Gulf waters. Embarking for Mobile Bay, Arriola indeed spotted a small boat flying the English flag, but a closer investigation revealed Frenchmen aboard the craft under the guise of the Union Jack. It quickly became apparent that a clever hoax had been perpetrated by members of Iberville's colony. From interrogation of the French, Arriola learned of the fort at Biloxi and of two other outposts upstream on the Mississippi, whereby direct communication could be established with Canada. When Arriola arrived at Biloxi, he was graciously provided with food and given assurances that the French had occupied the lower Mississippi River Valley only to prevent its falling into the hands of the English. All pretense of hostilities evaporated when both the Spaniards and the French agreed to await orders from Madrid and Versailles.[41] Spain's ineffectual response to French occupation of the lower Mississippi River Valley can also be explained by uncertainty following the Treaty of Ryswick. The imbecilic Charles II finally died in November 1700, bringing an end to the Hapsburg dynasty in Spain. The newly crowned monarch was a French Bourbon, the grandson of Louis XIV. Philip V ascended the Spanish throne with intent to resolve continuing problems between his adopted country and his native France.[42]

Diplomatic initiatives by the French stressed the strength of England's Atlantic colonies. It was argued that France and Spain should cooperate in securing the Gulf Coast lest it fall into the hands of Englishmen intent on seizing approaches to the rich mines of New Spain, at best a deceitful proposal on the part of the French. It was likewise argued that the Iberville expedition was solely intended to forestall English expansion and to provide a vital link with Canada. In diplomatic exchanges between the two countries, the Spanish insisted on maintaining Pensacola Bay, which the French had offered to control, but there was tacit agreement that French settlements in the lower Mississippi River Valley would go un-challenged as long as they were not expanded at the expense of Spanish realms.[43] International considerations as well as matters of public finance serve to explain why French occupation of Louisiana was not effectively opposed by Spain.

By early January 1700, French presence in Louisiana had been strength-ened with the arrival of fresh supplies and reinforcements at Biloxi. Ac-companying Iberville on his second voyage into the Gulf was a cousin, Louis Juchereau de St. Denis, a Canadian-born adventurer who would change the course of Texas history. St. Denis was born in or near the city of Quebec on September 17, 1676. In his early youth, he had been sent to Paris, where he obtained some formal education. Soon after his arrival in Louisiana, St. Denis carried out important upriver explorations, rang-ing into the country beyond the Red River. His experiences made him familiar with Indian languages, customs, trade, and government as well as with the geography of the region. Those early assignments combined with his extraordinary talents would make him the best-informed and most-powerful man on the eastern borders of Texas. His administrative experiences in Louisiana were command of Fort St. John, a new garrison on the Mississippi, and in the second decade of the eighteenth century, control of the fort at Biloxi.[44]

At the time of St. Denis's second appointment, the crown colony of Louisiana had suffered neglect due to resumption of the costly diplomatic and military adventures of Louis XIV, known in Europe as the War of Spanish Succession, 1702–1713. In an effort to reduce royal expenses, Louisiana was assigned as a proprietary colony for a period of fifteen years to a wealthy Frenchman, Antoine Crozat. Crozat's choice for gov-ernor of the colony fell on Antoine de la Mothe, Sieur de Cadillac, who arrived there on May 13, 1713. Cadillac's duties were obvious: he must run the colony in a businesslike manner and find a way to turn a profit. He quickly concluded that the desired avenue of riches lay in establishing trade with New Spain, a commerce he knew to be forbidden by Spanish mercantile restrictions, even though amicable relations existed between France and Spain.[45]

At first Governor Cadillac directly challenged the Spanish prohibition on international trade. He loaded a ship with goods brought from France and sent it to Veracruz, where he hoped to effect an exchange for live-stock. This approach was totally rebuffed by Spanish officials, who warned the governor to keep his merchandise out of New Spain. At that juncture, Cadillac received a letter, drafted more than two years before, from the zealous Franciscan missionary, Father Francisco Hidalgo. Hidalgo had despaired of winning support from the Spanish crown for his plans to reestablish missions in East Texas. His letter specifically asked the French governor to assist him in accomplishing that goal, a request that quickly stirred interest in the French colony.[46]

Governor Cadillac saw an opportunity to do God's work and his own. He knew of only one man in Louisiana skilled in diplomacy and Indian languages and familiar with the approaches to East Texas, and so he summoned St. Denis from Biloxi and outfitted him for a journey into the land of the Tejas. Clearly the invitation by Hidalgo would be used as a device to introduce goods on the frontier of New Spain, where mercantile restrictions might be vitiated by distance and scarcity. A passport, bearing the date September 12, 1713, was issued to St. Denis, who was dispatched to the Red River country in late September with twenty-four men and a retinue of Indian servants. St. Denis traveled up the Mississippi River to the mouth of the Red River and at the site of Natchitoches constructed two storehouses for the safekeeping of a part of his merchandise. After crossing the Sabine River, the French group traveled for twenty-two days before reaching the first Tejas villages. Trade for livestock and buffalo hides began on a modest scale, but the French adventurer had more ambitious goals. He would push on toward Spanish settlements, justifying his actions by the fact that he had not found Hidalgo living among the Indians, and he would carry word that the Tejas Indians earnestly desired the return of Spanish missionaries.[47]

As St. Denis moved southward toward contact with Spanish outposts on the Río Grande, he passed through the future site of San Antonio, and he traversed a land that had been virtually ignored by Spain for two decades. However, during that period, developments on the frontier of New Spain had not been completely static. With glacial slowness, Spain had moved to establish a presidio and mission some thirty-five miles south of present Eagle Pass, Texas. San Juan Bautista del Río Grande would become "the gateway" to Spanish Texas. Its founding and the personnel stationed there would entwine with the timely arrival of St. Denis in July 1714 to bring about the permanent occupation of Texas.

SIX

The Permanent Occupation of Texas, 1714–1722

THE APPEARANCE OF LOUIS JUCHEREAU DE ST. DENIS AND HIS forbidden merchandise at San Juan Bautista del Río Grande touched off a series of events that led to the permanent occupation of Texas. Once again Spain, as in the late 1680s and early 1690s, reacted defensively when confronted with foreign influence in the future Lone Star State. Whereas the search for La Salle had launched an almost chimerical manhunt, there was no denying the reality of the self-assured and flamboyant St. Denis. Aware of the viceroy's interdict against the entry of foreign merchandise or traders into New Spain, Commandant Diego Ramón had little choice but to arrest St. Denis and confiscate his goods. He forwarded to Mexico City St. Denis's papers and Father Francisco Hidalgo's letter to the French governor of Louisiana. While Ramón awaited instructions from the viceroy, he "incarcerated" St. Denis in his home. This pleasant arrangement accorded the Frenchman an opportunity to gain favor with Ramón's family and win a promise of marriage from the commandant's beautiful granddaughter, Manuela Sánchez.[1] St. Denis was subsequently sent under guard to the capital, where he charmed the viceroy and won his freedom. Indeed, he was appointed as commissary officer and guide for the expedition that would reestablish Spanish missions in East Texas. This chapter details the extraordinary role of St. Denis, the work of resolute friars and conscientious military captains, and the contributions of pioneer civilian settlers—all of whom helped lay the enduring foundations of Spanish Texas.

WHILE TEXAS WAS UNOCCUPIED BY SPANIARDS FOR MORE than two decades (1694–1715), it was not entirely forgotten nor unvisited. It especially remained on the mind of Father Francisco Hidalgo, who made unfinished work among the Tejas Indians a consuming passion. After his sojourn in Texas, Father Hidalgo labored in small villages near his college of Santa Cruz in Querétaro. In 1697 one of the college's founders, Father Antonio Margil de Jesús, returned there as guardian. Margil, perhaps the most renowned Franciscan missionary to enter Spanish Texas, had gained wide experience as a missionary in Central America and Yucatán. During his thirteen-year absence from the college, its field of apostolic work had broadened northward from Querétaro to include such outlying areas of New Spain as New Mexico. However, little by way of missionary activity had occurred in Coahuila. Determined to correct that omission, Margil in 1698 dispatched Fathers Francisco Hidalgo and Diego de Salazar to the region. For Hidalgo, "it was the first big step on the road back to the Tejas."[2]

With the support of the governor of Coahuila, the two padres began work on the mission of Santa María de los Dolores and from those meager beginnings founded a second mission to the north of it on the Río Sabinas. The latter was the first to be named San Juan Bautista, and it represented another milestone in Hidalgo's master plan of returning to Texas. Margil encouraged those initial efforts by assigning two more Franciscans to the area, Fathers Antonio de San Buenaventura y Olivares and Marcos de Guereña. For undocumented reasons, the first San Juan Bautista did not thrive. It was replaced by a second mission of the same name located nearer the Río Grande.[3] Aiding in the construction of this gateway mission, which was begun on January 1, 1700, was Diego Ramón, who would be associated with the mission and a soon-to-be-built presidio until his death in 1724 (see Figure 14). The positioning of mission San Juan Bautista had roots in explorations carried out along and north of the lower Río Grande in the second half of the seventeenth century and in the river crossings used by Alonso de León and Domingo Terán de los Ríos.[4]

The new mission was still another step in Father Hidalgo's goal of returning to the land of the Tejas. On March 1, 1700, a second mission, destined to loom large in the history of Texas, was founded in the same locale. San Francisco Solano was established for Coahuiltecan tribes a short distance west of the Río Grande channel. It would remain in that locale until 1718, when it was removed to San Antonio. A third mission, San Bernardo, was likewise associated with San Juan Bautista mission and presidio.[5]

Shortly after the establishment of mission San Juan Bautista, José de Urrutia, a former soldier who had opted for life among the Indians in 1693, appeared there. Urrutia's years in East Texas made him an invaluable guide and interpreter, and his talents were quickly utilized by Father

Olivares. He was persuaded to accompany Olivares and a small armed guard that advanced beyond the Río Grande to the Frio River. There the eagerness of Coahuiltecan tribes to receive religious instruction impressed Olivares. Although he returned to San Juan Bautista, where he believed his assistance was essential in securing the gateway mission, Father Olivares, along with Hidalgo, became a determined champion of missions north of the Río Grande.[6]

The mission and presidio of San Juan Bautista, both located a short distance west of the Río Grande, would serve as the final staging area for expeditions into Texas as well as a source of supplies for future settlements there. They and the two nearby missions also served the native population of the Río Grande area and ministered to roving hunting and gathering tribes to the north of it. The latter groups in particular kept the padres informed about events transpiring among the Tejas and Apaches. Unfortunately, the coming of Spaniards to the region brought with it the scourge of smallpox, which struck the native population in 1706. When the epidemic had run its course, the three gateway missions stood virtually depopulated. An expedition to recruit neophytes advanced to the environs of present Crystal City in March and April of the following year. Captained by Diego Ramón with Father Isidro Félix de Espinosa serving as chaplain to a force of thirty-one soldiers and civilians, the entrada, which was in the field for twenty-six days, resulted in a clash with natives and the capture of a few Indians who helped replenish the missions.[7]

In August 1707 Gregorio de Salinas Varona, the Spanish commander at Pensacola, informed the viceroy that the French in Louisiana were intent upon introducing merchandise and establishing trade with Spanish dominions. A council of war in Mexico City dispatched instructions to the provincial governors and presidial commanders, ordering them to prevent the entry of foreign merchandise and of foreigners themselves. The council also recommended that contacts be made with the Tejas and other Indian nations to dissuade them from accepting the goods of French interlopers.[8]

The orders and recommendations of the *junta de guerra* especially influenced the settlements at San Juan Bautista. Friars at the college of Santa Cruz discussed the possibility of using the moment to reestablish missions among the Tejas, and they asked for advice from Father Espinosa, who on December 11, 1708, gave his endorsement to an entrada north of the river. The viceroy in the meantime had approved a new entrance into Texas. He ordered Father Olivares, who had returned to the missionary college at Querétaro, to proceed to San Juan Bautista,

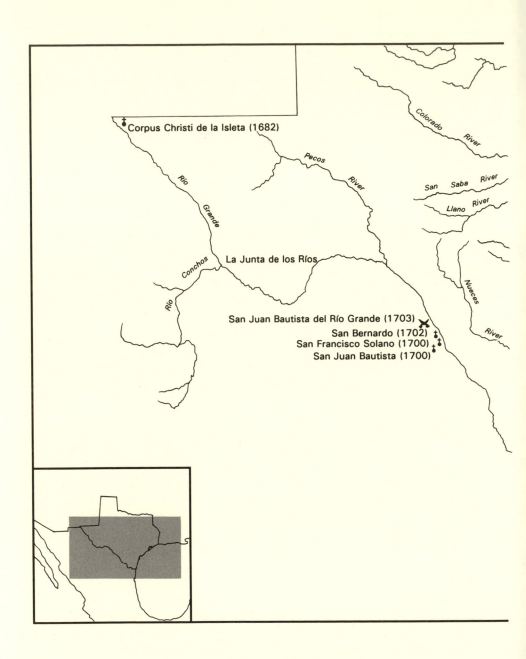

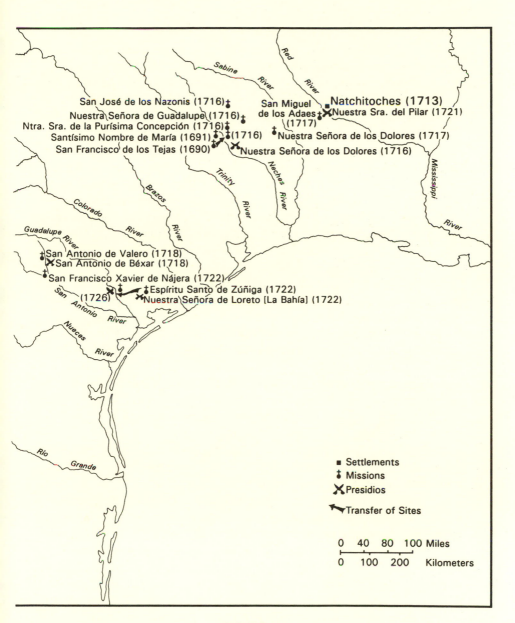

San José de los Nazonis (1716)

Nuestra Señora de Guadalupe (1716)

Ntra. Sra. de la Purísima Concepción (1716)

Santísimo Nombre de María (1691)

San Francisco de los Tejas (1690)

(1716)

San Miguel de los Adaes (1717)

Natchitoches (1713)

Nuestra Sra. del Pilar (1721)

Nuestra Señora de los Dolores (1717)

Nuestra Señora de los Dolores (1716)

San Antonio de Valero (1718)

San Antonio de Béxar (1718)

San Francisco Xavier de Nájera (1722)

(1726)

Espíritu Santo de Zúñiga (1722)

Nuestra Señora de Loreto [La Bahía] (1722)

Red River

Sabine River

Neches River

Trinity River

Brazos River

Colorado River

Guadalupe River

San Antonio River

Nueces River

Río Grande

Mississippi River

■ Settlements

† Missions

✖ Presidios

↖ Transfer of Sites

0   40   80   100 Miles

0   100   200   Kilometers

FIGURE 14
*Missions and presidios, 1682–1726. This map locates Spanish
missions and presidios from El Paso del Norte to present-day Louisiana.
(Cartography by Caroline Castillo Crimm.)*

where he would be escorted beyond the Río Grande by a company of soldiers. Command of the undertaking was assigned to Pedro de Aguirre, a temporary replacement of Diego Ramón as commandant.[9]

With Fathers Olivares and Espinosa serving, respectively, as chaplain and diarist, the Aguirre expedition left San Juan Bautista on April 5, 1709. It traveled to the future site of San Antonio, where the padres were much impressed with the land and availability of water. The river there was named San Antonio de Padua, the same as it had been designated by Terán de los Ríos in 1691. From the San Antonio River, the expedition pushed on to the Colorado, where it was rumored that Tejas Indians had moved their habitations in order to be closer to the Spaniards. The report proved unfounded, and from information supplied by a Yojaune chief, it was learned that Bernardino, the old Tejas chieftain, was still ill disposed toward the Spaniards and their faith. The expedition proceeded no further, for it had reached the extent of Aguirre's instructions, and it was clear that the Tejas would not willingly serve as buffers against the French.[10]

On April 28, 1709, the Espinosa-Olivares-Aguirre expedition returned to San Juan Bautista. It had increased familiarity with the land and lent a favorable impression of the San Antonio River as a promising site for future settlement but contributed little else. Indeed, it is likely that the immediate effect of the 1709 entrada was to delay the reestablishment of missions among the Tejas, for it effectively dispelled the notion that the Tejas were eager for renewed contact with the Spanish. Furthermore, two of the principals in the expedition, Fathers Espinosa and Olivares, soon left the gateway missions. Espinosa returned to his college where he remained for years, while Olivares journeyed to Spain to make special pleadings for the case of the Tejas missions. It remained for Father Hidalgo, still stationed at the Río Grande, to champion the cause on the immediate scene. After years of frustration, he devised a plan that bordered on treason. Why not use French presence in nearby Louisiana to stimulate the lethargic Spanish crown? Thus his letter, drafted in 1711, requested that the French governor assist in reopening Spanish missions among the Tejas. Hidalgo's single-minded determination to return to the East Texas mission field coincided nicely with Governor Cadillac's imperative need to make Louisiana a profitable proprietary colony. If the governor could not introduce French goods into New Spain proper, then he must bring Spaniards closer to Louisiana. St. Denis's appearance at San Juan Bautista in July 1714 represented a timely convergence of French mercantile interests and Spanish evangelism.[11] He also presented a vexing problem for Commandant Diego Ramón.

Ramón asked guidance from Mexico City in deciding what to do with St. Denis, thereby reflecting his doubts about enforcing royal edicts. Spain and France had been allies in the recently concluded War of Spanish Succession. Was it possible that mercantile restrictions had been eased but not yet publicized on the northern frontier? Ramón's uncertainty and the resulting delay in sending St. Denis to the capital worked to the French cavalier's advantage. He would use that opportunity to become a close friend of the extended Ramón family and the husband of the commandant's granddaughter.

After a pleasant stay at San Juan Bautista, St. Denis was ordered to Mexico City by viceregal authorities. When interrogated by them, he defended himself ably. He professed ignorance of trade barriers between French and Spanish colonies, and he steadfastly maintained that he had gone to the land of the Tejas seeking Father Hidalgo. Not finding him among the Indians and learning of their desire for his return, he had pushed on to the Río Grande settlements. His testimony buttressed the position set forth by Hidalgo and his Franciscan brethren over two decades: the missions in East Texas should be reestablished. While officials in the capital objected to Father Hidalgo's unauthorized overture to the French, they also recognized the expressed preference of the Tejas for the return of Spanish missionaries. What could not be ignored was the absolute necessity of setting up enough missions and presidios in East Texas to counter French influence.[12]

In a lengthy report, the *fiscal* reminded the viceroy that Salinas Varona, writing from Presidio Santa María de Galve in Florida, had warned of French penetration westward from Mobile. By piraguas and canoes, French traders had already entered Spanish realms and begun contacts with the Indians. The *fiscal* cautioned that such illicit commerce must be checked before it spread to Nueva Extremadura and Nueva Vizcaya, or it would place the silver mines there in "grave and notorious danger."[13]

Officials in Mexico City decided in the late summer of 1715 to initiate a substantial effort to reoccupy Texas. The experiences of the 1690s, however, were not lost on them, for they authorized four missions supported by a garrison of twenty-five soldiers. Command of the military unit was assigned to Domingo Ramón, a son of the commandant at San Juan Bautista. As mentioned earlier, St. Denis received appointment as commissary officer and guide for the expedition. He announced his intention of marrying Manuela Sánchez and of going into business on the frontier as a Spanish subject.[14]

St. Denis's motives in assisting Spain's reoccupation of Texas have been the subject of much speculation. Did he favor French or Spanish presence in East Texas? It seems clear that he was determined to bring Spanish settlement close enough to Louisiana to facilitate trade but not to promote its advancement any further. He kept his French superiors apprised of his actions, and there is no evidence that he was ever censured by them. It also seems likely that Governor Cadillac was more interested in promoting business opportunities for the proprietary colony than in advancing French claims to Texas. Indeed, the establishment of Spanish missions near Louisiana probably figured importantly in St. Denis's original goals for coming to Texas as well as in those of his sponsor. Whatever his underlying motives, St. Denis also provided a valuable service to Spain. His role in reestablishing missions in East Texas substantially influenced whether the area would be Spanish or French and whether the future boundary between the United States and Spain would be the Sabine or the Río Grande. The realization that France might occupy Texas from Louisiana brought a Spanish reaction, which is perhaps what Father Hidalgo had anticipated all along.[15]

Domingo Ramón and St. Denis received their appointments on September 30, 1715. Supplies included gifts for Indians, military equipment, hand tools, and various kinds of seeds. Unfortunately, the crown agent pared the request for gift items by 40 percent. Any Frenchman experienced in Indian affairs would have advised against this false economy. Soon after his appointment, Ramón left for Saltillo to collect livestock and recruit soldiers. St. Denis, on the other hand, returned to San Juan Bautista in the fall and married Manuela Sánchez in late 1715 or early 1716.[16]

Domingo Ramón was delayed at Saltillo until February 17, 1716, when he departed for the Río Grande. The march to the gateway presidio took just over two months. After his arrival there, he immediately began transporting equipment, supplies, and livestock across the river, and on April 27, 1716, the expedition set out for the land of the Tejas (see Figure 14). The entrada eventually included nine priests, three lay brothers, twenty-six soldiers, three Frenchmen, and several dozen civilians—in all an entourage of seventy-five persons. Interestingly, seven of the soldiers were married and brought along their families. Their wives were the first recorded female settlers in Texas. Responsibility for reestablishing missions in East Texas was divided equally between friars from the missionary colleges of Querétaro and Zacatecas.[17]

The college of Querétaro was represented in Texas by its president, Father Isidro Félix de Espinosa, along with four other padres, the most prominent of whom was Father Francisco Hidalgo; the college of Zacatecas also sent its president, Father Antonio Margil de Jesús, as well as three additional priests. Margil, however, did not accompany the Ramón expedition into East Texas. Due to illness, he remained at San Juan Bautista and did not join his companions until shortly after the founding of the first four missions.[18]

The 1716 expedition reached the land of the Tejas in late June and was greeted with much enthusiasm and celebration by the Indians. Beginning in early July, four religious outposts were founded among tribes of the Hasinai Confederacy. With the assistance of Ramón and St. Denis, mission San Francisco was reestablished on July 3 for the Neche Indians and neighboring tribes. Renamed Nuestro Padre San Francisco de los Tejas, the new mission was apparently established to the east of the original (1690) site. It was entirely appropriate that Father Hidalgo received appointment as minister at this first site.[19] A second mission was established a few days later. Nuestra Señora de la Purísima Concepción was located about fifteen miles west of present Nacogdoches on the Angelina River. This mission, which became the headquarters of the Querétaran friars, was positioned at the main village of the Hainai, the head tribe of the Hasinai Confederacy. Ramón then led the Zacatecan friars eastward to the site of modern Nacogdoches, where he founded a third mission, Nuestra Señora de Guadalupe, at the main village of the Nacogdoche tribe. A fourth mission, San José de los Nazonis, was set up among the Nazoni Indians for the Querétaran friars and completed their religious establishments in East Texas. It was probably located a short distance north of present Cushing, Texas (see Figure 14).[20]

The new missions in East Texas were set up in the very locale where two had failed in the 1690s. They were also far removed (more than four hundred miles) from San Juan Bautista, the nearest Spanish settlement. Nevertheless, this was a venture worth the risk. The Tejas were the strongest and most influential Indians between the Río Grande and the Red River. If the Spanish could gain influence over them, the activities of the French in East Texas might be checkmated. Conversion of the Tejas might also serve to influence the weaker tribes toward an acceptance of Spanish religion and dominance. And by erecting missions and later a presidio, "the Spaniards put forward an incontrovertible claim to the possession of Texas—that of occupation."[21]

St. Denis played an active part in establishing Spanish presence in East Texas, and his skill in Indian relations and willing cooperation with the padres made a favorable and lasting impression on them. In later years St. Denis would become a thorn in the Spanish crown, but his critics and detractors did not include the early mission builders. After completion of the first four missions, St. Denis and Diego Ramón II journeyed to Natchitoches and then on to Mobile, where they arrived in early September 1716. The Frenchman had much to tell: of his trip to the Río Grande and Mexico City, his marriage into an influential Spanish family, and his role in bringing potential customers closer to Louisiana. Although Governor Cadillac was much impressed, his problems remained the same: he had to find a way to make Louisiana profitable for the company. Another commercial invasion of Mexico might provoke a serious international incident and result in the loss of all the merchandise, but St. Denis's connections could perhaps ward off those possibilities. The value and quantity of goods packed on the backs of mules purchased by Diego Ramón II suggest considerable financial backing for St. Denis's second venture into Texas. He and Ramón left Mobile in October and arrived back at the East Texas missions before Christmas. The situation there, however, was hardly festive.[22]

From the beginning, the two dozen soldiers and twelve missionaries had recognized the precariousness of their situation. While the natives were friendly, their attitude could change at any time. Should they turn hostile, the nearest source of assistance was hundreds of miles away on the Río Grande. In a report written to the viceroy on July 22, 1716, Domingo Ramón and the Franciscans had outlined their requirements. If the missions were to become permanent, they needed an additional twenty-five soldiers to perform guard duty and an annual appropriation of six thousand pesos a year to buy suitable gifts for the Indians. By December, when St. Denis and Diego Ramón II returned from Louisiana, conditions at the four missions made this report to the viceroy seem prescient. While still friendly, the Indians refused to congregate or give up their idols and religious temples. To attempt forced compliance with the wishes of the padres seemed foolish, for the strength of the military escort had been reduced by death and desertions. It became increasingly evident that unless a halfway station were established between the Río Grande and the East Texas settlements, the reoccupation of Texas seemed destined to go the way it had gone in 1693.[23]

The return of St. Denis helped bolster the morale of the Spaniards. In early 1717 two additional missions were founded for the Zacatecan friars. Nuestra Señora de los Dolores was built near modern San Augustine, Texas, for the Ais Indians. It would become the headquarters for Father Margil. A sixth mission, San Miguel de los Adaes, intended for the Adais Indians, was located near the site of present Robeline, Louisiana (see Figure 14).[24] It appears that St. Denis aided in the founding of these last two missions and helped succor all Spanish settlements by providing maize from the French trading post at Natchitoches. Captain Ramón completed the East Texas establishments by founding a presidio, Nuestra Señora de los Dolores, on the Neches River. It was situated opposite San Francisco de los Tejas at the western end of the mission field.[25]

In March 1717 St. Denis left for San Juan Bautista del Río Grande. Accompanying him were Diego Ramón II and the goods acquired at Mobile. The party also carried dispatches to officials in Mexico City and to Martín de Alarcón, the newly appointed governor of Coahuila and Texas. At the gateway presidio, St. Denis's happy reunion with his wife and infant daughter was soon spoiled when Commandant Ramón confiscated all of his merchandise. Once again the governor at Pensacola had received intelligence that St. Denis was headed for Mexico with valuable, illicit cargo. That information had been forwarded to the viceroy and relayed northward to the Río Grande. Ramón no doubt felt that he must enforce the law against the entry of foreign goods and distance himself from the charge of complicity with his grandson by marriage. Even so, he did not escape a storm of controversy. St. Denis, on the other hand, reacted angrily, maintaining that he intended to become a Spanish citizen by virtue of his marriage to Manuela and that the goods were not illegal. Within a few days after his arrival at San Juan Bautista, the French cavalier, determined to carry his case in person to the viceroy, again set out on the long journey to Mexico City.[26]

It had been two years since St. Denis had charmed the Duke of Linares into releasing him and appointing him as guide and commissary officer for the reoccupation of Texas. In the interim, a new viceroy, the Marqués de Valero, had assumed power in 1716. Valero's tenure signaled a positive trend for the struggling presidio and six missions in Texas. Although he ordered the suppression of illegal trade from Louisiana, he made support for the Franciscan missions a primary objective. In implementing that policy, the viceroy was influenced by the recommendations of Father Olivares, who had returned from Spain. Olivares had written favorably of the Texas landscape and the potentially rich harvest of souls for the Roman Catholic church. The padre also set forth his plan for transferring Indians from San Francisco Solano on the Río Grande to the San Antonio River.[27] His recommendations together with the communications from Domingo Ramón and the missionaries in Texas were presented to the viceroy and his advisory council. The *fiscal de hacienda* (treasurer) strongly urged that Matagorda Bay be occupied to avert French occupation there, and the plans for a halfway mission on the San Antonio River received official support. Chosen as commander of the expedition was Martín de Alarcón, a knight of the Order of Santiago and a man of considerable experience on the northern frontier of New Spain, while Father

Olivares was charged with setting up the new mission. Olivares left for Querétaro in late 1716 to prepare for his assignment. Arriving at San Juan Bautista on May 3 of the following year, he immediately asked for a military escort. That request was denied by Commandant Ramón, who felt the need to consult with the viceroy due to the depleted condition of his garrison, thereby forcing Olivares to wait for Alarcón's arrival. The delay did little to improve the padre's rather irascible and petulant nature.[28]

Alarcón's journey to San Juan Bautista was slower than that of Olivares. He apparently left Mexico City in the spring of 1717 and arrived in Saltillo by June. He then investigated the trading activities of St. Denis and the possible complicity of the Ramón family and did not arrive at the gateway settlements until August. Final preparations on the Río Grande and the onset of winter postponed Alarcón's crossing of the river until the spring of 1718. By then relations with Olivares had deteriorated badly, and he criticized Alarcón for the poor quality of the soldiers he had recruited and the delays occasioned by his investigation.[29]

Alarcón's extended inquiry into the affairs of the Ramóns and their French in-law convinced him that a sizable contraband operation had been thwarted. He recommended that St. Denis be detained in the capital and that Diego Ramón be removed from command at Presidio San Juan Bautista, but neither of his recommendations was carried out. St. Denis's skillful defense of his actions—that his wife was Spanish and the goods were a means of supporting himself, not contraband—won his release in Mexico City and control of his merchandise. But he was forbidden to return to Texas. Later, he was forced to flee the capital to avoid arrest on unrelated charges. The Ramón family weathered the storm and remained influential in Texas for many more years.[30]

WHILE ALARCÓN AND OLIVARES WINTERED AT SAN JUAN BAUTISTA, the settlements in East Texas remained unsupplied. An attempt to provision them was initiated in December 1717, when Father Miguel Núñez de Haro and fifteen soldiers crossed the Río Grande and advanced to the Trinity River, where swollen waters halted their progress in late January of the following year. The cleric and four of the soldiers remained at the Trinity until the end of March, when they were forced to hide the supplies near a lake and return to the Río Grande. Remarkably, the cache was undisturbed by Indians and later was recovered with the items in good order. The immediate situation in the East Texas missions, however, remained desperate. By early 1718 the friars lacked food and clothing and had run out of essentials for performing their religious obligations. Those desperate straits were outlined in letters to the viceroy written by both Margil and Espinosa in February of that year. As Father Espinosa lamented, "The penury that has come to pass leaves us lacking every material necessity and vestment ... for celebrating the holy sacrifice of the mass." But relief was finally under way.[31]

After months of delay, Alarcón's entrada crossed the Río Grande on April 9, 1718. The expedition from the time of its inception was not intended as a purely military undertaking. Its charge was to found a way station between the Río Grande and the East Texas mission field, the station to include a presidio, a mission, and a civilian settlement. To populate the latter, Alarcón had recruited ten families from Coahuila and Nuevo León. In all, the entrada totaled seventy-two persons. It also included 548 horses, six droves of mules, and a variety of other livestock. Relations between Alarcón and Olivares, however, had deteriorated to the point that they refused to travel together.[32] Instead of proceeding directly to the San Antonio River, Alarcón attempted to reach the site of La Salle's former colony. His route there was so impeded by swollen streams and heavy timber that he abandoned his goal and changed course. He arrived at the San Antonio River on April 25. Olivares, with a small escort, did not leave the Río Grande until April 18. On a direct march he rendezvoused with the Alarcón party on May 1.[33]

Mission San Antonio de Valero was founded on the very day that Father Olivares reached the San Antonio River. Alarcón awarded him official possession of it on May 1, 1718. Technically, the new mission represented a transfer of Indians from the original San Francisco Solano on the Río Grande. It seems, however, that by 1718 not a single Indian was left at the original mission site. The most famous mission in Texas history (its chapel would later be known as the Alamo) began as a temporary structure of mud, brush, and straw located near the headwaters of San Pedro Creek and initially populated with three to five Indians that Olivares had raised since childhood.[34] Four days after the founding of San Antonio de Valero, Presidio San Antonio de Béxar was begun at a site about one mile to the north. The families clustered around the presidio would make up the first civilian settlement of Villa de Béxar, destined to become the most important town in Spanish Texas, leading to the first generation of native Bexareños.[35]

By the summer of 1718, Alarcón was aware that provisions cached near the Trinity River had been recovered intact and delivered to the East Texas missions. Accordingly, he proceeded beyond San Antonio at a leisurely pace. His party of twenty-nine persons set out for Matagorda Bay in early September. At the Guadalupe River, Alarcón encamped the main body of the expedition and from there led a small detachment of soldiers and three priests on to the coast. After exploring the bay, Alarcón returned to the camp on the Guadalupe and then continued the march to East Texas. He arrived at mission San Francisco in mid-October, more than six months after he had first crossed the Río Grande.[36]

Alarcón visited all of the East Texas missions, completing his assignment on November 21. While there, he confiscated goods of French origin, which included rich cloth, brocade with gold embellishments, 170 pieces of fine lace, and twenty-four pairs of blue stockings—all early evidence of forbidden trade. During his inspection, he also entertained recommendations from the friars and Captain Ramón regarding the best means by which Spain could fix a firmer hold on Texas. Overall, however, there is little doubt that the Alarcón expedition was a disappointment to the missionaries. The governor had failed to bring new families, nor had he recruited the additional soldiers that were needed to strengthen the military guard. In the words of Carlos E. Castañeda, "The missions were no better off at the close of 1718 than they had been when founded two years before."[37] The unpopularity of the governor with the missionaries and a loss of confidence in him on the part of the viceroy prompted Alarcón to offer his resignation when he returned to Mexico. Without doubt, the greatest accomplishment of his expedition had been to establish a mission, presidio, and civil settlement on the San Antonio River. The strategic importance of this way station in Spanish Texas was soon demonstrated by events that had transpired in Europe.[38]

Spain, unhappy with the settlement at the Treaty of Utrecht (1713–1714) and the loss of its Italian possessions, carried out an ill-advised invasion of Sicily in 1717 and Sardinia in 1718. An alliance of European powers, including France, subsequently declared war on Spain in defense of the treaty arrangements. Military engagements between France and Spain, which began in January 1719 and ended in February 1720, spilled over, as they frequently did, into their American possessions. During the brief war, the French seized Pensacola and launched an attack from Natchitoches on the Spanish mission at Los Adaes. Defended by only one soldier and a lay brother, Los Adaes was easy prey for Philippe Blondel and half a dozen Frenchmen. The French, however, were more concerned with raiding the mission chicken house than with guarding the lay brother, who used the diversion to make his escape.[39]

The Franciscan brother reached mission Nuestra Señora de los Dolores, the headquarters of Father Margil, on June 22. From there the news spread westward to Presidio Dolores, where Captain Domingo Ramón viewed the situation as untenable. Significantly, he and the missionaries lacked confidence in their relationship with the Indians, who were armed with French muskets and favorably disposed toward the suppliers of their weapons. As a result of the "Chicken War," the six missions and presidio were hastily abandoned, bringing an inglorious close to the second effort at establishing Spanish settlements in East Texas. While the retreat to San Antonio was precipitous, it was not continuous. Approximately three months were spent at a campsite west of the Trinity River. The main body of displaced missionaries, soldiers, and civilians did not reach San Antonio until late September or early October of 1719.[40]

Prior to these events in Texas, the Spanish government had foreseen that the war in Europe would especially threaten parts of the empire that were contested by France. A royal cedula, dated June 11, 1718, but not received in Mexico until May 29, 1719, expressed that concern. The king and Council of the Indies issued strict orders to port governors and presidial captains, prohibiting the entry of French vessels and expeditions into New Spain. Second, the missions in East Texas were to be strengthened by placement of a military guard at each of them. Third, the religious contingent at San Antonio de Valero was to be augmented by adding as many missionaries as necessary. Fourth, a fort was to be erected at Matagorda Bay on the exact site of La Salle's colony.[41]

These royal directives reinforced plans of the Marqués de Valero, who had already contemplated a new expedition into Texas. His commitment to that enterprise hardened when news of the abandonment of East Texas reached Mexico City. The viceroy's first objective was to appoint a replacement for Alarcón as governor of Coahuila and Texas, a matter he resolved in the fall of 1719. His choice could hardly have been better. It fell on a wealthy Spanish nobleman of Coahuila, the Marqués de San Miguel de Aguayo.

The Marqués de Aguayo was a descendant of an old Spanish family that boasted knights and noblemen of Aragón. His title and wealth, however, came from his wife, Ignacia Xaviera de Echeverz, who was heiress to enormous properties in Coahuila. Particularly attractive to the financially strapped viceroy was Aguayo's offer to drive the French from Texas and reestablish the abandoned missions at his own expense.[42]

This generous proposal of the Marqués de Aguayo was in fact his third attempt to become involved in Texas and lands beyond the province. In January 1715 he had requested formal authorization to lead an expedition of three or four months' duration to Gran Quivira. Then, as later, he promised that the undertaking would result in no burden to the royal treasury, but the proposal did not receive a favorable recommendation from the *fiscal,* and it was rejected by the viceroy on July 3. Not one to give up easily, Aguayo tried a new tack. In November of that same year, he reported that when José de Urrutia had lived among the Tejas, the self-imposed exile came to know an Indian who had journeyed twenty days from "a land beyond" to the north. The traveler informed Urrutia of Gran Quivira's rich lands and a large population of Indians who governed themselves within a political system. Once again Aguayo offered to underwrite all expenses for an exploratory entrada and asked only for approval in Mexico City. This proposal fared no better than the first, for the *fiscal* counseled the viceroy to reject it "with all brevity." The timing of these petitions was, of course, all wrong, since it ran counter to plans then in progress that resulted in the Domingo Ramón expedition. But Aguayo's third proposal was more propitious.[43]

In late October 1719, Aguayo formally assumed the titles of governor and captain general of Coahuila and Texas. He began immediate preparations for an entrada, but his departure for Texas was delayed more than a year by circumstances so troublesome, in his words, that "it seems that all hell" had conspired against him. He had to deal with Indian problems in Coahuila; then a severe drought killed thirty-five hundred of the four thousand horses he had purchased for the expedition. The drought was finally broken by heavy rains that slowed preparations to a standstill.[44]

By late 1720 Aguayo had assembled five hundred men, tons of supplies, and thousands of head of livestock. Final instructions from the viceroy, however, displeased the *marqués,* for he had planned an aggressive campaign into both Texas and Louisiana. He learned that France and Spain were negotiating a truce that would end the war in Europe. Accordingly, Aguayo could initiate no offensive action unless he encountered open resistance in Texas. Of interest, too, in 1719 the Council of the Indies first advanced the idea of recruiting civilian families in the Canary Islands for Texas, and it recommended the enlistment of Tlaxcalan families to serve as role models for Texas Indians.[45]

While the Marqués de Aguayo struggled with Indian insurrections and inclement weather in Coahuila, the only Spanish settlement in Texas was at San Antonio. The presidio, mission, and settlement there were strained to accommodate the East Texas exiles, among whom was Father Antonio Margil. Margil quickly saw the wisdom of founding a second mission at San Antonio and enlisted the support of the newly appointed governor. When in December 1719 he wrote to Aguayo congratulating him on his appointment, Margil also pointed out the imperative need of the Zacatecan friars for their own halfway mission between San Juan Bautista and East Texas and tactfully suggested that the religious establishment be named for the governor himself. The proposal won favor with Aguayo, despite the determined opposition of Father Olivares at mission Valero. A site with fertile lands that could be watered by building an irrigation ditch to the San Antonio River was chosen. With the aid of Juan Valdez, the military captain at San Antonio, the most successful and beautiful mission in Spanish Texas, San José y San Miguel de Aguayo, was officially established on February 23, 1720.[46]

Nine months after the founding of mission San José, Aguayo finally sent his expedition northward to the Río Grande. When the main body of his force arrived there on December 20, 1720, and found the river swollen by recent rains, he immediately began experiments to determine the best means of transporting bulky goods and animals across the current. Aguayo finally settled on a raft of ten beams, with additional buoyancy provided by empty barrels lashed between the vigas. The heavily laden raft was then pulled across the Río Grande by ropes attached to fifty Indian swimmers. Not surprisingly, this cold and arduous work took its toll on the men in the water. Despite being plied with aguardiente and extra rations of hot chocolate and food, all but four became seriously ill.[47]

Problems with the crossing delayed Aguayo until March 24, 1721. During that time, he received news from the presidial commander at Béxar that St. Denis was believed to be organizing Indians on the Brazos River for an assault on the San Antonio settlements. To forestall that possibility, Aguayo sent troops ahead to reinforce Béxar. Later, he dispatched another forty soldiers under Captain Joseph Ramón to occupy Matagorda Bay. In late March the main body of the expedition set out for the San Antonio River. The large numbers of stock made this the first big "cattle" drive in Texas history. Aguayo had acquired twenty-eight hundred horses, forty-eight hundred cattle, and sixty-four hundred sheep and goats. Although livestock had accompanied previous entradas, Spanish ranching in Texas truly began with the arrival of these huge herds in 1721.[48]

The Aguayo expedition reached San Antonio on April 4 and remained there until May 13, 1721, when it resumed its march, accompanied by the East Texas exiles. Because of swollen streams, Aguayo traveled north of the Camino Real that linked the East Texas settlements with San Antonio and the Río Grande. He did not pick up the established road until he was near present Navasota and then followed it to the former mission and presidio sites between the Trinity and Red rivers.[49] Aguayo then took steps to reestablish and secure the six East Texas missions. To that end he met with St. Denis on August 1 and agreed to accept the truce then in effect between France and Spain, provided the French commandant

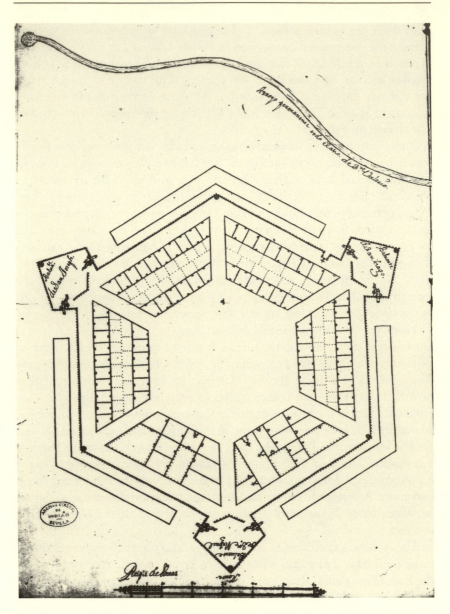

FIGURE 15.

Plan of Presidio Nuestra Señora del Pilar de los Adaes. Proposed design of the easternmost presidio founded in 1721 by the Marqués de San Miguel de Aguayo. (With the permission of the Archivo General de Indias, Seville, Spain; Mapas y Planos, México 113.)

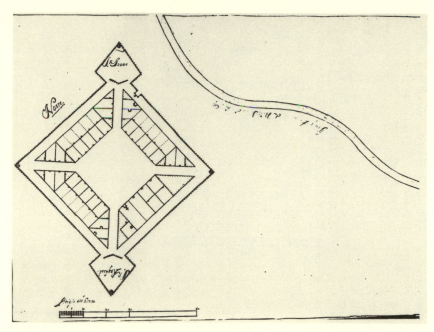

FIGURE 16

Plan of Presidio Nuestra Señora de los Dolores. Proposed design of the presidio refounded in 1721 by the Marqués de San Miguel de Aguayo. This garrison, commonly called Presidio de los Tejas, guarded the western mission field in East Texas. (With the permission of the Archivo General de Indias, Seville, Spain; Mapas y Planos, México 112.)

would evacuate Texas and retire to Natchitoches. Confronted by the size of Aguayo's army, St. Denis could do little but accede. To defend Spain's dominion, the Aguayo expedition established the presidio of Nuestra Señora del Pilar a short distance from the old mission site of San Miguel de Linares and staffed it with one hundred men (see Figure 15). In future years Los Adaes would serve as the Spanish capital of Texas, while the Río Hondo, a small stream between it and Natchitoches, would be recognized by Spain and France as the boundary between Texas and Louisiana.[50]

The six missions founded by the Domingo Ramón expedition were again placed in the hands of friars from the colleges of Querétaro and Zacatecas. As additional security and aid for the missionaries, Aguayo refounded Presidio Dolores (commonly called Presidio de los Tejas) but moved its location from the Neches River to a site near the Angelina River and mission Purísima Concepción (see Figure 16).[51]

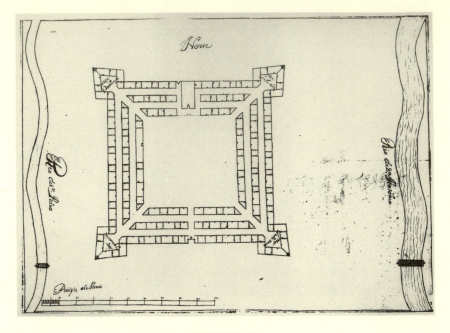

FIGURE 17

Plan of Presidio San Antonio de Béxar. Proposed design of the presidio refounded and relocated at Béxar in 1722 by the Marqués de San Miguel de Aguayo. (With the permission of the Archivo General de Indias, Seville, Spain; Mapas y Planos, México 117.)

On November 17, 1721, Aguayo began a difficult winter march back to San Antonio, arriving there on January 22, 1722. The trek was particularly hard on his horses and mules, forcing him to send agents to Coahuila for replacements. While awaiting the arrival of animals and provisions for the return trip to Coahuila, Aguayo selected a new site for the Béxar presidio and ordered its construction with adobe bricks (see Figure 17). He also directed the founding of an unsuccessful and short-lived mission, San Francisco Xavier de Nájera, to the south of mission Valero.[52]

In early March, Aguayo sent Captain Gabriel Costales to Matagorda Bay with fifty men to augment the forty previously sent there under the command of Joseph Ramón. Aguayo himself followed in mid-March with an additional forty men to ensure construction of a presidio that would guard this vital region against French incursions. The foundations of Presidio Nuestra Señora de Loreto were begun on April 6, 1722, at the precise location of La Salle's Fort St. Louis (see Figure 18). Aguayo also

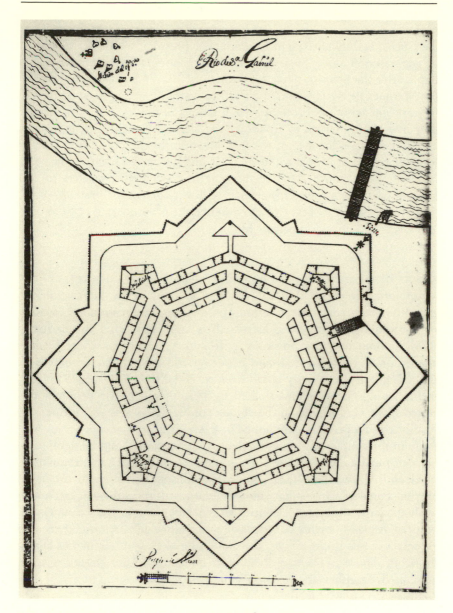

FIGURE 18

Plan of Presidio Nuestra Señora de Loreto. Proposed design of the presidio, commonly called La Bahía, founded in 1722 by the Marqués de San Miguel de Aguayo at the site of La Salle's Fort St. Louis. (With the permission of the Archivo General de Indias, Seville, Spain; Mapas y Planos, México 115.)

supervised the founding of nearby mission Espíritu Santo de Zúñiga for the Cocos, Karankawas, and Cujanes. The presidio, which was manned by a garrison of ninety men, and the mission would both be known as La Bahía after the Spanish name for Matagorda Bay.[53] By the end of April, the Marqués de Aguayo was back in San Antonio, where he was greeted by partisans who had brought a fresh supply of horses. He immediately prepared for his return to Coahuila and departed on May 5, leaving a garrison of fifty-four men at the new location for the presidio at Béxar. Aguayo arrived at Monclova on May 25 and disbanded his troops on the last day of the month. After recounting his considerable services to the king, in which he stressed his defense of Texas against the pretensions of St. Denis at Natchitoches, Aguayo resigned the governorship of Coahuila and Texas and retired to private life.[54]

AGUAYO WOULD LATER BE CRITICIZED FOR THE COST OF maintaining the presidial defenses he had set up in Texas, but overall his expedition secured, as never before, Spain's claim to the province. He had reestablished six missions, constructed two new ones, and authorized a third; he built two new presidios (both situated at points where French aggression was most feared) and relocated two others; and he increased the strength of the military guard from 60 or 70 to 268. His accomplishments would soon be undermined by peso-pinching retrenchment directed from Madrid, but in the context of his time—war in Europe, six missions and a presidio abandoned in East Texas, settlements at San Antonio in their infancy, Matagorda Bay still unoccupied and vulnerable— he performed admirably and at no small personal expense. In the words of Eleanor C. Buckley, "[The Aguayo expedition] was perhaps the most ably executed of all . . . that entered Texas, and in results it was doubtlessly the most important." Charles W. Hackett likewise praised Aguayo's work in Texas as "highly constructive and enduring." Subsequent events, especially crises in the 1730s, threatened the very continuance of Spain in Texas. Those perils may have been unavoidable but should not be attributed to either the accomplishments or recommendations of the Marqués de San Miguel de Aguayo.[55]

SEVEN

Retrenchment, Islanders, and Indians, 1722–1746

THE MARQUÉS DE SAN MIGUEL DE AGUAYO HAD ANCHORED Spanish Texas at three vital points: Los Adaes, Matagorda Bay, and San Antonio. At the first, French activities at Natchitoches were monitored and the further ambitions of Louis Juchereau de St. Denis checkmated. The second defended the coast from French incursions at the exact location of La Salle's ill-fated colony. And the third, San Antonio, secured a vital way station with the newly reconstructed presidio at Béxar. The next two decades, however, did not signal years of uninterrupted progress. Instead, they were a time of trial.

Overall, the province did not experience a "multiplication of new settlements"; death, reassignment, and retirement thinned the ranks of pioneer soldiery and clergy and led to a changing of key personnel; peace in Europe prompted retrenchment in government spending, resulting in the abandonment of Presidio de los Tejas and removal to San Antonio of the three Querétaran missions in East Texas; the presidio and mission at Matagorda Bay were scarcely four years old when they had to be moved to a more favorable location on the Guadalupe River; Indian wars began in the 1720s and greatly intensified in the 1730s; civilian settlers recruited in the Canary Islands founded the first formal municipality in San Antonio, but their coming spawned serious internal troubles at Béxar; a martinet governor and a terrible epidemic in 1739 brought near disasters to the San Antonio missions; and by the early 1740s the remaining settlements in East Texas could best be described as beggarly. This chapter chronicles Spanish Texas in those years of Job-like testing that had to be weathered before the province was stabilized and expansion could take place.[1]

AGUAYO'S RETIREMENT TO PRIVATE LIFE IN THE EARLY 1720S was symptomatic of changes already sweeping through the ranks of those who had set down the lasting foundations of Spanish Texas. Father Olivares, aged and in bad health, had retired from mission San Antonio de Valero on September 8, 1720. He was succeeded there by Father Francisco Hidalgo. In 1721 Father Espinosa had departed mission Concepción in East Texas to assume the guardianship of his college in Querétaro. Father Margil in the following year was likewise summoned from Texas to serve as president of his college at Zacatecas.[2]

At the presidio at La Bahía, Domingo Ramón died prematurely in late 1723, the victim of a stab wound inflicted by an enraged, scissors-wielding Karankawa. His father, Commandant Diego Ramón, died of natural causes at San Juan Bautista in early 1724. And in the summer of 1725, Father Francisco Hidalgo resigned his post at mission Valero in hopes of being appointed missionary to the land of the Apaches, a request that his Franciscan superiors denied. In September 1726, Hidalgo, the most resolute advocate of missions in Texas and Coahuila for more than thirty-five years, died in retirement at mission San Juan Bautista.[3] And in that same year, Father Antonio Margil de Jesús, arguably the most renowned Franciscan in Texas, also died. St. Denis, however, lived on at Natchitoches. As commandant of the French outpost, he figured tangentially in the history of Spanish Texas for nearly two more decades.

The "changing of the guard" in Texas was a forerunner of more profound adjustments already brewing in Mexico City. In October 1722 Juan de Acuña, Marqués de Casafuerte, had received appointment as viceroy of New Spain. His instructions from King Philip V included specific orders that the northern defenses of the viceroyalty be studied with a view to implementing cost-saving reforms. The maintenance of presidios on a distant frontier, where operations were suspected of being shot through with dishonesty and inefficiency, was believed to be more expensive than their usefulness justified.[4]

Twenty presidios and three mobile garrisons dotted the landscape of extreme northern New Spain. They stretched from Sinaloa and Sonora eastward to the Gulf Coast of Mexico, with four of the presidios located in the province of Texas. The suspicion of rampant corruption in many of the military outposts rested on solid ground. Presidial captains grossly overcharged their command for goods received in lieu of salary. They also assigned soldiers to duties on their private lands, thereby taking them away from their primary responsibility of service to the king. In some instances, the presidios no longer served any useful purpose, for natives in the area had been pacified by the labors of missionary friars. While these circumstances were not common in Texas, the presidios there had already cost the royal treasury 370,000 pesos.[5]

Since peace in Europe had removed the threat of French aggression from Louisiana, the presidios in Texas fell under especially close scrutiny. A former governor of Tlaxcala and temporary commander of the fortress in Veracruz harbor, Colonel Pedro de Rivera y Villalón, received military promotion and appointment as inspector general of the entire northern frontier of New Spain. His eventual recommendations for Texas would "shake the very foundations" of Spanish presence there.[6]

Brigadier General Rivera left Mexico City for his tour of inspection in November 1724. Armed with powers of inquiry that could not be ignored by presidial captains, he was ordered to file a report on each presidio, giving its exact location, the nature of the surrounding countryside, the Indian tribes in the vicinity and their general disposition, and the relationship of each outpost to adjoining presidios and missions. He began his assignment in the western regions and worked his way eastward across the vast frontier of New Spain. Rivera's commission occupied him for more than three and a half years, during which he traveled some seventy-five hundred miles on horseback. In each of the twenty-three military outposts, he compiled a three-stage report: the condition of the garrison when he arrived, its status when he left, and his recommendations for its future.[7]

The inspector general did not reach San Antonio until late winter of 1727, arriving there by way of Monclova and San Juan Bautista. On March 23 he began his inspection at Los Adaes, where he discovered no serious irregularities in the company of one hundred soldiers. At Presidio de los Tejas, however, he found quite the opposite. Discipline was lacking among the twenty-five soldiers, and the "fort" presented a dismal picture of deficient construction. As Rivera acidly commented, "a collection of huts poorly constructed of sticks and fodder did not merit the honorable name of Presidio de los Tejas." Rivera evidently made a quick judgment that the presidio was not worth preserving, especially since the nearby missions contained not a single Indian, and he did not bother to draw up a set of regulations for it. On the other hand, Presidio Nuestra Señora de Loreto, then relocated on the Guadalupe River, greatly impressed the inspector general. Discipline was excellent there, and the soldiers under the command of Joseph Ramón were well dressed and adept in the manual of arms. Except for the size of the guard (ninety men), which Rivera thought excessive, he approved of all operations at that garrison. The fourth presidio at San Antonio also impressed the brigadier general, and he commended the fifty-four soldiers for their discipline and successful resistance to Apache attacks directed against the San Antonio settlements.[8] Rivera concluded the Texas portion of his inspection on December 13, 1727. He found San Antonio, with its ample sources of water and good grazing lands that surrounded the presidio, especially to his liking. His subsequent recommendations for the entire province, however, and their implementation by the viceroy would place severe pressures on the resources of San Antonio and threaten the security of Spanish Texas.[9]

At the exact time of Rivera's inspection of the Texas presidios, another official visitor arrived on the scene. Father Miguel Sevillano de Paredes had been chosen by the commissary general of New Spain as visitor general of the Río Grande missions. Included in the survey was San Antonio de Valero, no doubt because of its origins as a Río Grande mission. Father Sevillano was an old hand in Texas, having entered the province in 1716. His most recent assignment had been at mission Valero, where he served until 1727. At the time of his commission, Sevillano was en route to Querétaro to assume the office of guardian. It is likely that both the commissary general and his appointee knew the direction of Rivera's impending recommendations. A report to the viceroy that presented a perspective different from that of a military man might be crucial to the future of the Texas missions. In October 1727 Father Sevillano returned to San Antonio to inspect the mission he knew from firsthand experience.[10]

At that time San Antonio de Valero had been situated at its third location for only three years. It served a total of 273 Indians, comprising sixty families from five tribes. The new church had been built of mud, straw, and branches, and work was under way on an aqueduct to irrigate the mission's fields. The primary concern of the missionary fathers, however, was security. Apaches had twice raided their livestock herds. Through Sevillano's report, the padres expressed the urgent need for a church of stone construction that could serve as a defensive bastion. At the same time, they acknowledged that it would be difficult to lure stone masons to a remote and dangerous frontier.[11] Father Sevillano completed his inspection at San Antonio in mid-October and then proceeded to the larger task of inspecting the Río Grande missions. In early November 1727, he concluded his visitation and filed a report with the viceroy that would counter the major recommendations of Brigadier General Rivera. But it was all to no avail. The king had ordered retrenchment, and retrenchment it would be.[12]

Rivera drafted his long report on Texas in March 1728. His recommendations included closing Presidio de los Tejas and reducing significantly the size of the guard at the other three garrisons. One year later, after consultation with his advisers, the viceroy ordered changes in Texas that were in keeping with those proposed by Rivera. The garrison at Los

Adaes was reduced from 100 to 60 men, at La Bahia from 90 to 40, and at San Antonio from 54 to 44. In accord with Rivera's recommendations that Presidio de los Tejas "ought to be extinguished," the garrison there faced closure. The overall troop strength in Texas was ordered diminished by 125. As implemented, the viceroy's mandate left only 144 soldiers in the entire province, with the presidios at La Bahía and San Antonio manned at 40 and 44 soldiers, respectively. The reorganization, however, was devastating to the padres stationed at the three Querétaran missions in East Texas.[13]

The friars at missions Concepción, San Francisco, and San José immediately protested the closing of Presidio de los Tejas, arguing that the military outpost was absolutely essential to the survival of the three missions. Without it they would be isolated some 60 leagues from Los Adaes and 150 leagues from San Antonio. Potentially dangerous Indians in the area, armed with guns and powder supplied by the French, made the situation even more precarious. Should, however, the viceroy's decision prove to be irrevocable, the padres requested permission to move their missions to a more favorable site or to return to their missionary college at Querétaro.[14]

The urgent pleadings of the East Texas missionaries did not evoke the desired response in Mexico City. After completing his massive tour of inspection, Pedro de Rivera assumed a special post as counselor to the viceroy. In that capacity he was able to deflect a flood of protests over the validity of his draconian recommendations, and he prevailed on the viceroy to order the immediate closure of Presidio de los Tejas. Rivera did agree that the three Querétaran missions could be moved westward to the Colorado River, provided that this could be accomplished without cost to the royal treasury.[15]

In July 1730 the missions were removed to the Colorado and located at present Barton Springs in Austin, where they remained for only a few months. Abandonment of religious outposts at the western edge of the mission field in East Texas brought an end to fourteen years of effort and led to the loss of influence among nearby Indians. From March to May 1731, the three missions were relocated again, this time along the San Antonio River, where they would become permanent fixtures (see Figure 19). Their transfer strengthened Spanish presence at San Antonio, but it also brought pressures on the settlements at a time when Apache raids threatened them and at the very time they were obliged to integrate civilian settlers from the Canary Islands.[16]

The presence of five missions at San Antonio meant that large numbers

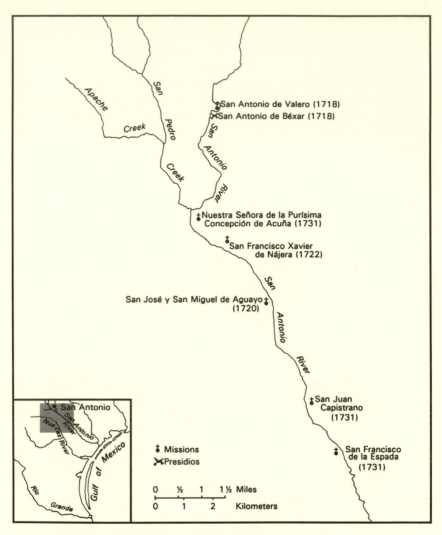

FIGURE 19

*Presidio and missions at Béxar. This map locates presidio and mission sites at
San Antonio in 1731. Mission San Francisco Xavier de Nájera, founded in 1722
by the Marqués de San Miguel de Aguayo, had ceased operations in 1726.
(Cartography by Caroline Castillo Crimm.)*

of Indians would be congregated there. Until the three new religious establishments could become self-sustaining, they were dependent on provisions, especially corn and cattle, supplied from Saltillo by way of San Juan Bautista. Because frontier travel was dangerous, a guard of twelve soldiers stationed at Saltillo had regularly provided security for the missionaries and supplies that traversed the road to Texas. In another move toward economy, the Saltillo guard was abolished and responsibility for the safety of travelers transferred to the Monclova presidio. Escort service, however, was limited to only four trips per year. The pressing need for food and supplies at San Antonio meant that the missionaries could not wait for the guarded quarterly trips.[17]

Unsecured journeys between San Juan Bautista and San Antonio invited raids by the Apaches. Attacks in the first six months of 1731 resulted in the death of a woman and two soldiers, the capture of a child, and the loss of horses and baggage. Rivera did respond to these obvious dangers. He ordered the presidios at Béxar and San Juan Bautista to provide a nine-man escort whenever it became necessary to reprovision the San Antonio missions.[18] Serious problems with the Apaches, however, were by no means solved. They had, in fact, been building for many years. Much of the difficulty stemmed from the fact that the Apaches were bitter enemies of the Tejas. Traditionally, native Texas tribes east of the middle Colorado had been allied against the Apaches. Spaniards, because of their close association with the Tejas, naturally inherited this enmity. For example, Apaches menaced San Antonio from the time of its founding in 1718. From Coahuila, the Marqués de San Miguel de Aguayo had endeavored to make peace with them in 1720, but he was unsuccessful. On his journey from Monclova to San Antonio, he had skirmished with Indians believed to be Apaches. While in Texas, Aguayo still pursued a policy of conciliation that bore no results whatsoever. After his return to Coahuila, the Apaches continued to harass San Antonio and to steal horses.[19]

In April 1722 Captain Nicolás Flores y Valdez assumed command of Presidio San Antonio de Béxar. Some sixteen months later (August 17, 1723), Apaches carried out a successful raid on the garrison and stole 80 horses. Flores pursued the offending Indians, and after traveling 130 leagues fought a six-hour battle with them, perhaps near present Brownwood, Texas. He killed thirty-four Apaches, recovered 120 horses and mules, and captured twenty Indian women and children.[20]

Relations with the Apaches by the mid-1720s were marked by attempts at peace and a dispute over policy between Flores and Father Joseph González, a missionary at San Antonio de Valero. The commander believed that the captive women and children gave him a bargaining tool with the Indians, while the missionary regarded them as impediments to peace. With some justice, González also contended that Flores wished to keep the hostages as slaves. Differences between the two men led to the temporary removal of the presidial commander.[21] Troubles with the Apaches, however, continued throughout 1724 and 1725, despite Spanish attempts at conciliation. Peaceful overtures were apparently motivated by the desire to use the Apaches as a barrier against the northern tribes and French influence along the Red River. For reasons that are still unclear, the years 1726–1730 were a time of relative quiet in Spanish-Apache relations.[22]

Near the conclusion of this peaceful interlude, Viceroy Marqués de Casafuerte, with the concurrence of Pedro de Rivera, decided to reconnoiter the Río Grande country and its inhabitants between San Juan Bautista and La Junta de los Ríos. Selected to lead this difficult undertaking was Joseph Berroterán, the commander of Presidio de Conchos, who was to travel to San Juan Bautista and then explore upriver toward his home base.

Berroterán began his assignment with seventy soldiers and six Indian auxiliaries on January 13, 1729. Rather than follow the course of the Río Grande, Berroterán felt it necessary to traverse extremely rough country to the south of the river channel, and along the march he lost horses and mules almost daily. The shortage of water for his men and a remuda of more than three hundred animals was especially critical. For example, on one stretch of thirty-two leagues without water, twelve horses and two mules died of "fatigue." Hostile natives added anxiety by their almost constant shadowing of the expedition, but in April, Berroterán encountered friendly Pacuache Indians who were on their way to kill buffalo. Finally on May 16, as he neared his destination, the commander force marched his men through the night to avoid further dehydration and expedite access to water. Nevertheless, in his words, "We abandoned twenty horses and mules, and the rest of the herd arrived overheated and worn out because of the lack of water." After resting for three days, Berroterán returned to Presidio de Conchos, where he signed his diary on May 22. His exploration had traversed some of the most difficult terrain along the confines of Texas. Nevertheless, he was severely rebuked by Pedro de Rivera for not simply following the Río Grande upstream to its junction with the Conchos. Despite testimony from witnesses who insisted that such a path was not feasible because of steep-sided canyons, Berroterán was officially denounced to the governor of Parral on June 17, 1730. Rivera was often a man difficult to please.[23]

Within a few months of Rivera's censure of Berroterán, the illusory peace with the Apaches was shattered by their raids on San Antonio. The attacks began in early January 1731 and reached their height in the spring. Enlarged settlements there, occasioned by the transfer of three East Texas missions and the arrival of Canary Islanders, undoubtedly proved tempting. But the Apaches themselves were being pressured by implacable Indian foes—the Comanches. The latter would eventually drive the Apaches from their northern hunting grounds and spread terror throughout the South Plains.[24]

The Comanches, who were of Shoshonean origin, were relative late-comers to the South Plains. According to their traditions, they originated north of the headwaters of the Arkansas River, probably in the mountainous country of contemporary Colorado and Wyoming. By 1700 the Comanches had apparently followed the Arkansas to the plains of eastern Colorado and western Kansas. They were positively identified in New Mexico in 1705, when they began devastating raids on the eastern Pueblo settlements, and by the early 1720s they had reached northwestern Texas, where they initiated a long but successful war against the Apaches. In their adaptation to the plains and a horse culture, the Comanches "were true warrior nomads" for whom sedentary life was intolerable. At best they quartered in a general area within which they moved about continuously. There is no doubt that their intrusions into Texas pushed the Apaches southward toward the Spanish settlements at San Antonio.[25] Unfortunately for the soldiers, missionaries, and expanded civilian population at Béxar, the Apaches were particularly ill suited to withstand that pressure.

The enlarged contingent at San Antonio included fifty-five Canary Islanders, who completed their long journey to Texas on March 9, 1731.[26] Their arrival was the final act in a historical process that began in 1719, when the Council of the Indies first suggested that two hundred families be recruited from the Canary Islands and the kingdom of Galicia in Spain. These families would be sent by way of Veracruz or Campeche to New Spain, where they would become the first of a series of civilian settlements, beginning at Matagorda Bay and extending down the Texas coast. The king, however, did not accept the council's recommendation, believing that families already in New Spain could be recruited at less expense and with greater ease. The idea lay stillborn for a few years but was resurrected in the early 1720s. Recruiting civilian settlers was then viewed as a way to obviate the necessity of maintaining expensive presidial guards on the frontier. Once in place, civilians would defend their lives and property out of self-interest. This consideration was at the very heart of suggestions made by the Marqués de San Miguel de Aguayo in 1722. The fact that the Canary Island settlers finally wound up at San Antonio was due more to changing circumstances than to original intent.[27]

The twelve-year delay, between the inception of the idea to recruit civilians and the arrival of the Canary Islanders at Béxar, may be explained by a clogged Spanish bureaucracy that moved with glacial slowness; by difficulties in finding ships bound for the desired ports of New Spain; by opposition from Brigadier General Pedro de Rivera, who believed that a settlement at Matagorda Bay would be too isolated and costly; and by his specific recommendation that the Canary Islanders be sent to San Antonio.[28]

Viceroy Casafuerte echoed Rivera's sentiments in a letter to the king, drafted after the Islanders were already in Béxar. He strongly advised against sending any more Isleño (Islander) families to populate Texas, even though the monarch had expressly commanded that a total of four hundred be transported across the Atlantic. The viceroy's arguments against the continuation of royal policy hinged on finances. Casafuerte portrayed the Islander men as total incompetents in handling the realities of life in New Spain, and he complained of the "absolutely useless incapacity" of the women and children. In short, the transplanted Isleños had to be supervised, fed, clothed, and cared for like infants. The viceroy calculated the expense for fifteen families at 30,082 pesos, with items listed and appraised right down to socks and handkerchiefs. Those expenses, he argued, if applied proportionately to four hundred families would cost the royal treasury 802,186 pesos. It was a telling argument to a budget-conscious crown.[29] Meantime, the immigrants were adapting to life in Texas.

Juan Antonio Pérez de Almazán, the presidial commander, welcomed the fifteen Isleño families to San Antonio. He urged the new settlers to give priority to clearing fields and planting crops, rather than to the founding of the new city government, and they agreed to do so. Their first crops consisted of corn, beans, oats, cotton, melons, chili peppers, and other vegetables. Farming without irrigation at San Antonio had proved to be risky, but conditions were favorable for that first harvest.[30]

After gathering their crops, the Islanders participated in the formal establishment of the *villa* of San Fernando de Béxar. Those formalities, begun on July 2, 1731, involved laying out the plaza, selecting sites for lots and public buildings, and designating pasture lands that adjoined the municipality. They concluded with the selection of the municipal government itself. Almazán appointed Juan Leal Goraz, the eldest of the settlers and spokesman for them, as first councilman. Other councilmen, a sheriff, a scribe, and an administrator of public lands completed the appointments. On July 19 Captain Almazán read a proclamation, issued by the viceroy in November of the previous year. In accord with the Laws of the Indies, the Isleños and their descendants, as first settlers of a new municipality, were designated as persons of noble lineage (hidalgos) in perpetuity. When the cabildo convened, it elected from within its ranks two alcaldes, with the position of first alcalde conferred on Juan Leal. On October 24, 1731, the viceroy approved the appointments and elections.[31]

What was intended as the vanguard of civilian recruitment for Texas proved, instead, to have been the final episode. The recommendations of the Marqués de Casafuerte and Pedro de Rivera against sending additional families reached the Council of the Indies in March 1732 and received official approval. As indicated, the experiment had already proved costly. Perhaps the clinching argument was assurances from the viceroy that should it become necessary to introduce more civilians on the frontier, they could easily be found in New Spain and at much less expense. Thus ended an undertaking which, if implemented, would have brought several hundred Spanish settlers to Texas. Its failure, in the words of Carlos E. Castañeda, accounted "in no small degree, for the slow development of the province in subsequent years. . . . It is to be regretted that the plan to establish civil settlements in Texas should have been abandoned just as it was being put into execution." The decision to recruit no more civilians for Texas meant that the province would have to depend in large measure on its own resources and manpower. Supplies did arrive periodically from Saltillo by way of San Juan Bautista, but Texas remained little more than a buffer outpost on the northern frontier of New Spain.[32]

The status of the struggling settlements at San Antonio during the 1730s has often been misunderstood or misrepresented. For example, T. R. Fehrenbach argued that with just a little effort San Antonio could have become "a flourishing community." Referring to the Canary Islanders, he wrote: "The settlers tended to go native. They became hunters, fishers, loafers, and in some cases, thieves. It was possible to raise a few beans without much effort, and also the ubiquitous Spanish cattle now dotted the fields around Béxar. The Spanish could eat without great difficulty, and meanwhile, enjoy what was indeed a splendid climate, amid beautiful scenery."[33] The reality of life in San Antonio was quite different.

Over the next decade, the problems at Béxar severely tested the community. Settlers there were exposed to Indian depredations, which made defense "at least a part-time occupation for the entire male population." Quarrels between the Islanders and the older settlers were a constant source of trouble. The climate at San Antonio was capable then, as now, of being torrid or cold, punctuated by periods of drought and the danger of wind storms. At times the entire population was faced with severe food shortages. Internal disputes arose over the assignment of mission guards, the ownership and use of land, the loss of mission cattle, and the labor of mission Indians. All of these problems, however, paled in comparison to continued Apache attacks.[34]

During the summer months of 1731, when the Islanders were tending and harvesting their first crops, there was a temporary lull in Apache attacks on San Antonio. This peaceful interlude was broken by a daring midday raid on September 18 that drove off sixty horses from the presidio's herd. In attempting to punish the Indians, Captain Almazán entered into a battle that nearly cost his life and the loss of most of the presidial guard. Outnumbered and completely surrounded, the troop was saved when the Indians suddenly broke off the attack and rode away. Had the soldiers perished, the entire guard at San Antonio de Béxar would have been reduced to only three or four men.[35]

Almazán reported the dangerous situation to Mexico City, and on December 29, 1731, Pedro de Rivera recommended a punitive campaign against the Apaches. Due to delays, however, the campaign was not launched until October 22, 1732. On that date the new governor, Juan Antonio Bustillo y Ceballos, left San Antonio with a command of 157 soldiers and 60 Indian allies from the missions. After weeks of marching, Bustillo's force found the Apaches and fought a battle on the San Saba River. It resulted in a temporary victory for the Spaniards and the capture of some 30 Indian women and children. The expedition, harassed by Apaches throughout the march, returned to San Antonio, arriving there on December 22. In early 1733 a truce was arranged with the Indians that permitted them to enter San Antonio freely. That arrangement ended abruptly in late March, when Apaches approaching Béxar turned on two soldiers, killing them and mutilating their bodies in full view of the presidio. The incident so shocked the community that soldiers requested the right to move their families to safety. And at the missions, the padres found it difficult to keep their neophytes from fleeing to the safety of the surrounding countryside. Governor Bustillo himself expressed the fear that the entire settlement at San Antonio was in danger.[36]

The government in Mexico City responded by taking "some feeble measures for the greater security of San Antonio." It appointed José de Urrutia as captain of the presidio, primarily because of his long experience with friendly tribes to the east of San Antonio, and it authorized detaching fifteen soldiers each from Presidios La Bahía and Los Adaes. Overall, these changes appear to have made few improvements in security. From 1734 to 1738, a succession of Apache raids on San Antonio cost additional lives and resulted in the loss of livestock. Urrutia, whose personal experience with Indians spanned half a century, reported that the inhabitants of Béxar lived in almost constant terror and that some families had moved away. The danger, he noted, had continued to worsen until some settlers refused to leave the confines of the municipality to tend their livestock. Urrutia expressed considerable empathy for the fears of the Béxar residents: "Their timidity does not surprise me (although I do not let them know it), for he who is not warned by the ill-fortune of others must be considered rather foolish. . . . Those who can enter a presidio at night as far as the center of the plaza and who without being heard can safely remove the horses from the corral in which they are tied to the doors of the houses are to be feared." [37]

Urrutia, perhaps to alleviate the situation at San Antonio, carried out a sizable campaign against the Apaches in the winter of 1739. It resulted in the capture of many Indians who faced the prospect of being sold into slavery. The expedition was opposed by Father Benito Fernández de Santa Ana, president of the Querétaran missions. Santa Ana insisted that the purpose of the campaign was solely for material gain under the guise of serving the crown. His criticism of the presidial commander was only a small indicator of the serious disharmony that characterized relationships within the Béxar community during the 1730s. [38]

Integrating the Canary Islanders into the older civilian-military-religious population lay at the core of those problems. Between 1720 and 1731, forty-seven couples had married, and 107 children had been baptized at mission Valero alone. While some of the nuptials undoubtedly united people from other settlements, it is clear that a viable civilian population existed at Béxar by 1731. [39] The older Bexareños quickly came to resent the new settlers with their titles of nobility and their exclusive privileges within the city government of Villa San Fernando.

The Canary Islanders, on the other hand, did little to ingratiate themselves with the older residents at San Antonio. Despite their small numbers and generally similar background, the Isleños proved to be both internally and externally fractious. For example, they jealously sought to exclude other civilians from residency in their new town, although the motivation here may well have been their belief that additional Islanders would be forthcoming to San Antonio and that space must be reserved for them. But their record of civil and criminal suits against each other, as well as against the missions, presidial commanders, and governors, clearly reveals their contentious nature. [40]

There is also no doubt that the older settlers at San Antonio viewed the Islanders as raw, inexperienced novices who did not belong on the frontier. The newcomers were mostly peasants who were unaccustomed to stock raising and unskilled in the handling of horses. On the trek to San Antonio, they had proved particularly insensitive to the condition of their mounts, losing 125 horses to "fatigue." The Islanders' lack of equestrian skills and their total ignorance of horse gear made them utterly useless in mounted warfare against the Apaches. It also determined that the Isleños would become farmers not ranchers. That, too, would be the source of much disruption in the Béxar community.[41]

 Ranching at San Antonio had been initially developed by the missionaries. After the dangers from French incursions had subsided in the 1720s, the padres gathered up the surviving stock that had accompanied every expedition into Texas since the 1680s. The missionaries took care of the animals and saw that they multiplied. They also had the wherewithal to conduct large-scale ranching, possessing as they did "extensive grants of land, visionary leadership, and cheap labor."[42] As implied, the coming of the Islanders certainly did not challenge the early dominance of stock raising by the missionaries in San Antonio.

As former laborers, farmers, and fishermen, the Canary Islanders felt more comfortable, at least initially, tilling the soil. They cleared fields near the San Antonio River and San Pedro Creek and enjoyed a bountiful first harvest in the summer of 1731. Their fields, however, soon proved tempting to grazing livestock that belonged to the older military and civilian families. The predictable consequences of unherded livestock and unfenced fields led to almost constant bickering. In defending their crops, the Islanders killed and maimed the offending animals, while the older settlers fumed over their losses. Both sides complained bitterly to the governor.[43]

A reasonable solution, of course, was for the Islanders to build fences around their fields or for the stock owners to employ herders. Neither would cooperate. The Islanders insisted that building fences would be unnecessary if the animals were under control, while the stock owners refused the expense of hiring herders. Complicating the problem was the constant menace of Apache raids, which made it dangerous for the stock raisers to seek more distant grazing lands. By the mid-1730s the Islanders had been forced by necessity to build fences to protect their crops, but they were not well constructed or maintained. Although lessened, incidents of crop damage and maimed livestock continued to occupy the attention of the governor and to divide the community. For the Canary Islanders, however, farming without irrigation while defending their crops from hungry livestock was a chancy undertaking. At mid-decade they were reported as starving in the midst of a land of potential abundance—hardly the idyllic circumstances described by Fehrenbach.[44] Those desperate circumstances also brought trouble between the Isleños and the missionaries.

As the foremost ranchers, the missionaries faced the problem of what to do with excess cattle. With no available market, the animals multiplied and left the confines of the mission pastures to become semiwild. At first this did not present a problem. When the missions held joint roundups, these cattle were divided in an equitable manner and brands applied. But Apache raids in the 1730s made systematic ranching precarious. It was dangerous to pursue half-wild cattle much beyond the confines of San Antonio. Furthermore, these feral animals were wantonly slaughtered by the Apaches and by *carneadores,* professional meat hunters who saved only the choicest parts of a carcass for drying and sale at San Juan Bautista. All of this placed a premium on tame cattle, with prices soaring "to an unheard-of 25 pesos a head in the villa."[45]

To cope with food shortages, the inexperienced Islanders joined the ranks of mounted *carneadores,* but they soon discovered that it was much safer to prey on the herds of tame mission cattle rather than to risk death at the hands of Apaches. Recognizing the Islanders' plight, the missionaries did not at first protest nighttime raids on their herds. But when the Islanders became so brazen that they carried out daytime raids on mission stock, the padres understandably protested.[46] Problems with the Isleños would continue, but they were merely part of a series of crises that faced the San Antonio missionaries during the late 1730s and early 1740s.

During the formative years of Villa San Fernando (1731–1745), more than twenty priests and an undetermined number of lay brothers labored at the five missions. In the ranks of religious leadership, the most prominent name was the aforementioned Benito Fernández de Santa Ana. Father Santa Ana arrived in 1731 and for the majority of the time until 1750 served as president of the four Querétaran missions. Of near equal importance was Francisco Mariano de los Dolores y Viana, who entered San Antonio in 1733 and remained on the scene until 1763. In the later years of his tenure, Father Dolores succeeded Benito de Santa Ana as president. Two other religious from the period, Fathers José Ganzábal and Alonso Giraldo de Terreros, figured importantly and tragically in future efforts to expand missionary enterprises beyond San Antonio.[47] Under the leadership of the padres, the mission Indians not only cared for livestock but also farmed productive lands along the San Antonio River. Their skills in the latter area also created problems with the Canary Islanders.

The Isleños, no doubt impressed with their titles of nobility, came to resent the hard work involved in tilling the land. They sought, unsuccessfully at first, to force the padres into releasing neophytes for work in their fields. Their prospects of acquiring agricultural laborers improved with the arrival of a new governor, Carlos Benites Franquis de Lugo, in 1736. That Franquis de Lugo was ill disposed toward the missionaries is indisputable; that his policies toward the missions, as Carlos E. Castañeda charged, "were not half as detrimental" to their progress as continued Apache depredations is questionable.[48]

Franquis de Lugo himself was a Canary Islander, a native of Tenerife. He had been sent to Mexico as the royal appointee for the governorship of Tlaxcala, but since the term of the actual governor had not expired, the viceroy made him ad interim executive of Texas. It was an unfortunate choice for the province. The new governor was short-tempered, petulant, and impetuous. He arrived at Béxar on September 16, 1736, and quickly proceeded to alienate the clergy. In a complaint brought against Franquis after he left office, the religious charged that he had used "indecorous words" in referring to them. If only a portion of the allegations were true, this was a classic case of understatement. In remarks to soldiers of the presidio, the governor allegedly called the missionaries "usurpers of the royal treasury" and "sons of satan." Worse, the padres contended that the governor had defamed them with three nouns strung together—any one of which was horrifying blasphemy.[49]

Franquis de Lugo also informed the missions that the three guards stationed at each of them would be reduced to one. This was a serious blow to the well-being of the religious establishments, for the guards helped maintain discipline, assisted in carrying out daily tasks, and aided in the return of runaways. Franquis further irritated the padres by intercepting their outgoing letters and engaging in petty quarrels over areas of civil and religious jurisdiction.[50]

Despite the governor's efforts at censorship, the Querétaran friars were able to inform the guardian of their college, Father Pedro Muñoz, of the deteriorating situation at the San Antonio missions. Muñoz registered a formal complaint with the viceroy in early January 1737. On January 11 the viceroy commanded the governor to restore the mission guards, but when the order arrived in San Antonio, Franquis refused either to acknowledge or to implement it. A subsequent warning by the viceroy in May to the effect that Franquis de Lugo's continued excesses in office would result in suspension, and a strict order to restore the mission guards brought no more results than did the first directive. Franquis stuck to his policies until he was removed from office in September 1737.[51] By then the San Antonio missions had been largely depopulated.

The exodus had begun in April 1737, and the padres were powerless to stop it. At that time Governor Franquis de Lugo had removed all guards from the missions. Spring was a time when the neophytes became most eager to resume "their roaming ways." They were probably enticed by the passing of cold weather and were anxious to avoid the rigors of spring planting. By June 8, 1737, mission San Francisco was completely abandoned. A total of 230 Indians had "returned to their former barbarous freedom." Mission San Juan Capistrano also lost most of its neophytes, while the other religious establishments experienced serious losses. There is little doubt that widespread desertions in the spring and summer of 1737 threatened the continued success of the San Antonio missions.[52]

Persistence and hard work on the part of the padres as well as the arrival of a more sympathetic governor contributed to the recruitment of replacement neophytes, but in 1739 smallpox and measles epidemics swept through the Indian population. The five missions were once more decimated by death and desertion, with three of them suffering more than 50 percent losses. After the epidemics had run their course, the friars again sought replacements from the surrounding countryside, and by 1740 the missions had recouped a sizable number of neophytes.[53]

The losses suffered by the missions in no manner discouraged the Islanders' determined efforts to force the friars into providing agricultural workers for their farms. In 1739 two members of the cabildo, Vicente Alvarez Travieso and Juan Leal Alvarez, were sent to Mexico City to argue the issue before the viceroy-archbishop. The Isleño delegates misrepresented the situation in San Antonio and won favor with the chief executive, Juan Antonio Vizarrón y Eguiarreta. They scored an important, temporary victory for the Islanders when the viceroy issued an order permitting the hiring of mission Indians for work on Isleño farms.[54]

The chief executive also forbade presidial captains from buying grain at the missions—thereby providing, simultaneously, a guaranteed market for the civilian farmers, while depriving the missions of needed income. This decree was not rescinded until January 4, 1745, when Viceroy Pedro Cebrián y Agustín's order gave presidial commanders the option of buying corn from either the missionaries or civilian farmers and prohibited the hiring of mission Indians as farm workers. The viceroy likewise commanded the Islanders to fence their fields and to cease the slaughter of mission cattle. At this time, however, defeat for the Islanders caused less bitterness than before, thanks primarily to progress made toward a sense of community at San Antonio and to improved conditions in the province as a whole.[55]

The arrival of Governor Tomás Winthuysen at San Antonio on June 2, 1741, had signaled a positive trend for Spanish Texas over the two and a half years of his tenure. His appointment was especially important for the beleaguered outposts in East Texas. The new governor "proved to be a dynamic and energetic leader." He first gave attention to continued Apache depredations, which frightened the mission Indians and contributed to their flight. In the company of Father Mariano Francisco de los Dolores y Viana from mission Valero, Winthuysen journeyed to the Trinity River, where he helped induce Atakapa and Tonkawa Indians to take up mission life. His most important contribution, however, came at the Los Adaes settlement.[56]

Winthuysen found incredibly bleak conditions in East Texas. The military and civilian dwellings were in disrepair, and the population did not even carry on subsistence farming, forcing its dependence on basic foodstuffs purchased at Natchitoches from St. Denis on his terms. Settlers at Los Adaes were so impoverished that they could process "neither wills nor the estates of people who died intestate." Winthuysen took immediate action. He ordered the construction of new palisades for the presidio and five new barracks for most of the military personnel. He also provided proper uniforms, equipment, horses, arms, and ammunition. Winthuysen, like many of his predecessors, recognized the cost and inconvenience of importing food from Saltillo and ignored the viceroy's injunction against trade with the French. Accordingly, the new governor authorized the importation of beans, corn, and other staples from Natchitoches. At the same time, he urged Spaniards to redouble their efforts toward farming.[57]

Overall, Winthuysen encouraged close cooperation between the military and civilian segments of the population, thereby ensuring in the long run less dependence on the French. His report on the missions of East Texas, however, reflected the pitiful state of those nearly forgotten outposts. Nuestra Señora de Guadalupe de los Nacogdoches, Nuestra Señora de los Dolores de los Aix, and San Miguel de los Adaes did not have among them a single resident Indian. Worse, in Winthuysen's view, the Tejas, despite being the most industrious of the East Texas Indians, were a completely hopeless cause for the missionaries. In his words, "They are all irreducible to political life and to submitting themselves to the missions. Since every effort that has been made to this end has failed, it is now considered an impossible undertaking."[58] Winthuysen's judgment of the Tejas may be questioned by some critics, for he was an inexperienced observer on the frontier, but his administration won high praise from his successor and from many elements of the Spanish population. Approval from the Canary Islanders, however, was probably not forthcoming. He was highly uncomplimentary of Villa San Fernando, regarding it as "not at all progressive, since its settlers are more given to prejudice than to progress."[59] Still, when Winthuysen left office in late 1743, San Antonio had demonstrated progress toward becoming a viable community.

Despite problems that characterized the 1730s, the passage of time produced a melding of older Bexareños and Canary Islanders. Intermarriage, the common need for economic ties and military protection, and the shared dangers of life on a remote and dangerous frontier had served to erode the Islanders' exclusiveness. By the early 1740s, the older settlers were accepted as magistrates in the *villa* and eventually as councilmembers. Differences between the missionaries and the Isleños were also ironed out. On August 14, 1745, a historic meeting between Father Santa Ana and the cabildo brought sensible compromises and concessions on issues that had split the community. The Islanders agreed that civilians could buy grain from the missions and that they would desist from their efforts to hire mission Indians as laborers. For their part, the missionaries agreed to a division of disputed lands that favored the Isleños. Both sides acknowledged the wisdom of avoiding "the delays and inexcusable expenses of lawsuits."[60]

Problems with the Apaches, however, continued. A massive nighttime attack on San Antonio, carried out on June 30, 1745, by about 350 men, women, and children, was repelled with the aid of 100 Indians from mission Valero. The assault on Béxar was apparently in retaliation for a military campaign conducted against the Apaches to the north of San Antonio in the previous April.[61] It gave impetus to a growing desire on the part of Franciscan padres to attack the problem at its source—missionary efforts must be extended beyond San Antonio. The attack also signaled progress at mission Valero, where its neophytes had been willing to stand and fight rather than flee to the surrounding countryside.

San Antonio had clearly survived its years of trial and divisiveness and emerged stronger for it. A growing sense of community meant that its population could finally look beyond its internal problems to foster new missionary enterprises, activities that had remained dormant for over two decades. But even these accomplishments at Béxar, important as they were, would not ensure success. The Franciscan friars were about to launch a series of disastrous undertakings: the founding of missions on the San Gabriel River, on the lower Trinity River, and at the San Saba River in Apachería. Their misfortunes, however, were at least partially offset by the extraordinary accomplishments of José de Escandón in carving out the province of Nuevo Santander.

EIGHT

Mission, Presidio, and Settlement Expansion, 1746–1762

EXPANSION BEYOND SAN ANTONIO AND THE STRUGGLING settlements in East Texas characterized the nearly two decades that preceded the Peace of Paris (1763). Plans to spread the Gospel and secure the broader foundations of Spanish presence in Texas were presented to viceregal authorities in Mexico City between 1746 and 1749. Targeted areas included the San Gabriel River to the northeast of San Antonio, the San Saba River in central Texas, the coastal area between the second site of La Bahía and the lower Trinity River, and the lower Río Grande and coastal region of extreme south Texas. The majority of those undertakings resulted in failures. This chapter examines the circumstances that surrounded three unsuccessful enterprises and a single successful one (see Figure 20). The chronology spans only a brief period, with the events and participants often related.

MARIANO FRANCISCO DE LOS DOLORES Y VIANA WAS PRIMARILY responsible for selecting the site for missions established on the San Gabriel River, near present-day Rockdale, Texas. The river itself was reasonably well known to Spaniards in Texas. In 1716 the Domingo Ramón expedition had discovered the stream and named it San Xavier. The San Gabriel valley was traversed by the Aguayo expedition in 1721, and in the early 1730s it was penetrated by Governor Bustillo in a campaign against the Apaches.[1]

Father Dolores had arrived in Texas in 1733, and in the following year, while pursuing deserters from mission San Antonio de Valero, he first came into contact with future tribes of the San Gabriel missions. In 1741 he had also accompanied Governor Tomás Winthuysen on an expedition to the Trinity River, where the friar unsuccessfully implored the Deadose and Mayeye Indians to take up mission life. His efforts finally paid dividends in 1745.[2]

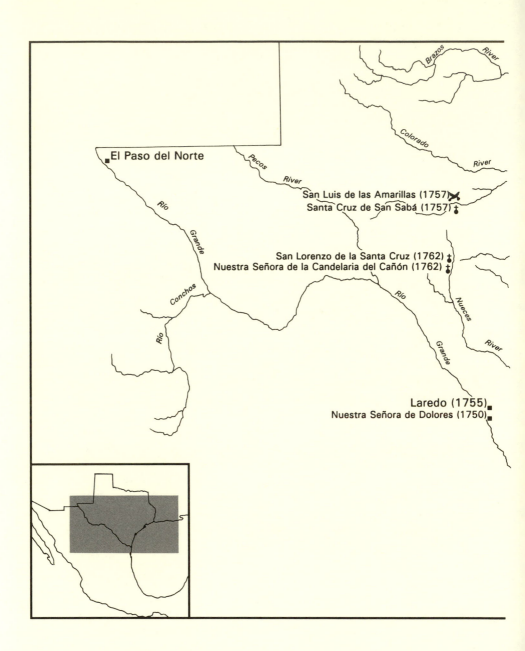

El Paso del Norte

San Luis de las Amarillas (1757)
Santa Cruz de San Sabá (1757)

San Lorenzo de la Santa Cruz (1762)
Nuestra Señora de la Candelaria del Cañón (1762)

Laredo (1755)
Nuestra Señora de Dolores (1750)

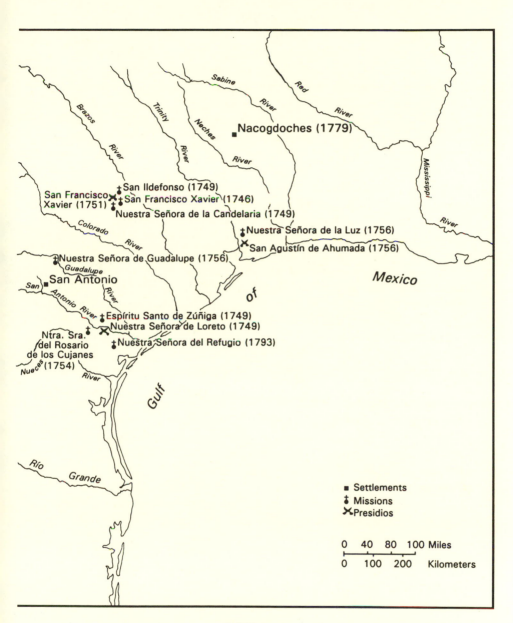

FIGURE 20

*Expansion of Spanish missions, settlements, and presidios. This map
depicts the founding of missions, civil settlements, and military garrisons from
1746 to 1793. (Cartography by Caroline Castillo Crimm.)*

In June a delegation of Indians, including the Deadose and Mayeye, traveled to San Antonio to request a mission for tribes within a hundred-mile radius of the San Gabriel River. This opportunity so impressed Father Dolores that he wrote enthusiastically about it to Father Alonso Giraldo de Terreros, guardian of the college of Querétaro. From the inception of the idea, Father Dolores intended to establish more than a single mission. The large number of potential converts and the diversity of tribes in the region influenced that decision.[3]

On November 22, 1745, Father Dolores set out to meet a group of prospective neophytes, promising to remain with them until a mission was established. However, the proposed rendezvous, east of the Brazos River, could not be reached because of rain-swollen streams. The cleric turned back, but a delegation of soldiers and mission Indians pushed on to a second location recommended by local natives. This alternate site on the San Gabriel River impressed the Spanish party, and its members reported favorably on it in San Antonio.[4]

Encouraged by the soldiers' report, in January 1746 Father Dolores scheduled another rendezvous, this time with natives on the banks of the San Gabriel. The padre came prepared to establish a mission. He brought along several presidial soldiers, mission Indians from San Antonio, agricultural tools, and presents for the neophytes. On arrival at the river, he must have been pleased to find present not only the original petitioning tribes but also members of the Coco, a Karankawan tribe of the lower Colorado River.[5]

Father Dolores set to work. He chose a site for mission San Francisco Xavier near the confluence of the San Gabriel River with Brushy Creek, supervised the tilling and planting of fields, selected locations for the buildings, and began the construction of a church. His enthusiasm for the enterprise was evident in a letter sent to Father Santa Ana in San Antonio. The San Gabriel missionary spoke of terrain that was ideal for irrigation, of ample water in the river, of abundant game and wild berries, and of plentiful timber and stone for construction materials. A sobering part of this otherwise glowing account, however, contained reference to hostile Apaches in the area as well as mention of French and English influence among the local tribes. To counter those threats, a presidio would be needed to provide security for the mission's neophytes.[6]

The Franciscan college at Querétaro quickly endorsed the San Gabriel project and dispatched a favorable recommendation to the viceroy, but winning official approval and necessary financial support involved lengthy and complex negotiations. At the core of the problem were conflicting recommendations from two former governors. Juan Antonio Bustillo, with firsthand knowledge of the region, took exception to the Franciscan's sanguine view of the locale and its native inhabitants. On the other hand, Bustillo's predecessor, Melchor de Mediavilla y Azcona, came to the friars' defense and supported "the San Gabriel proposal as passionately as Bustillo had challenged it."[7]

The viceroy delayed a definitive decision on the undertaking for several months. He sought the advice of others experienced in Texas and again received mixed recommendations. But in February 1747, the chief executive of New Spain gave formal approval for the establishment of three missions and a presidio on the San Gabriel River. Compliance with the viceregal order, however, was not immediately forthcoming. Delays were caused in large part by the acute shortage of soldiers in Texas.[8]

In December 1747 the viceroy reissued his order, commanding that three missions be founded at government expense on the San Gabriel within six months. That decision was soon reinforced in January 1748 by a royal decree from Ferdinand VI (1746–1759). The king had been petitioned directly by Father Francisco Xavier Ortiz, official inspector of missions at San Antonio during the early months of 1747. Father Ortiz shrewdly played upon political considerations, while not ignoring the obligation to extend the faith. In particular, he pointed out that fertile and bounteous lands to the north of San Antonio were coveted by foreign nations. Should Spain not respond quickly, the natives of the area would likely fall under the influence of French colonists who would ply them with guns, ammunition, and other goods. It was a tried and proved argument, used repeatedly on the crown since the 1680s. A corollary proposition was the also familiar "domino theory." If the northern frontier were not secured, then Texas itself as well as New Mexico would be threatened.[9]

As the wheels of bureaucracy inched forward in Madrid and Mexico City, Father Dolores faced a deteriorating situation on the San Gabriel that blunted his initial optimism, and in April 1748 he suffered an injury that forced him to return to San Antonio. Before he withdrew, Father Dolores placed a confrere, Francisco Cayetano Aponte, in charge. Father Cayetano appears to have been rather inept, but he can scarcely be blamed for Apache attacks already directed against a poorly equipped and defended mission. In all, the Apaches raided the mission four times in 1748, killing three soldiers and four resident Indians. While those losses were not insupportable, the frightened neophytes began to consider fleeing to the safety of surrounding woods.[10]

When reports of worsening conditions reached San Antonio, Father Dolores implored Captain Toribio de Urrutia, the son of the deceased

José de Urrutia, to assist the beleaguered mission by assigning additional soldiers to its defense. Urrutia was sympathetic, but his troop strength had been significantly reduced by the assignment of sixteen soldiers to La Bahía, where they were to join the escort of the newly arrived governor, Pedro del Barrio y Espriella, then en route to Los Adaes. Urrutia nevertheless endorsed the petition of Father Dolores in a letter dispatched to the governor. For his efforts, Urrutia was upbraided with the caustic reminder that the king needed his sword more than his pen. The governor's rebuff of Captain Urrutia presaged his subsequent dealings with Father Dolores, and it was a harbinger of serious state-church difficulties that would plague the San Gabriel enterprise.[11]

Given the shortage of troops in San Antonio and the sharp rebuke of Toribio de Urrutia, Father Dolores had little choice but to return to the San Gabriel River as soon as his health permitted. He brought with him only one additional soldier and a few mission Indians from San Antonio. During his absence, the situation at San Gabriel had deteriorated badly. Most of the Indians had fled, vowing not to return until they were guaranteed adequate protection. Within a few days, however, Father Dolores's persuasiveness lured many of the frightened natives back to the mission.[12]

In spite of his reproof of Captain Urrutia, Governor Barrio nevertheless informed Father Dolores that he would hasten to San Gabriel, and he was true to his word. Barrio arrived at the mission on May 20, 1748, to conduct a two-day investigation. At the end of his inspection, the governor filed a report with the viceroy that was highly critical of the entire San Gabriel venture. Barrio condemned the Indians for their unwillingness to work or tend crops, and he later ordered the soldiers stationed at the mission to send their wives and children to safety, a prudent recognition of the Apache menace. Barrio was especially critical of the San Gabriel site, pointing out that the river was subject to flooding during the rainy season, only to subside into stagnant pools during the summer.[13] The governor's unfavorable assessment in no way discouraged the Franciscans. In March 1748 their college at Querétaro had assigned six new missionaries to Texas, the most famous of whom were Alonso Giraldo de Terreros and Domingo de Arricivita. The viceroy himself had prompted those appointments with his decree of December 1747, but the six-month timetable could not be honored. Delays occasioned by lack of supplies, forays by Apaches, and opposition from Governor Barrio postponed increased missionary activities for almost a year.[14]

The new missionaries did not arrive in San Antonio until June 1748. In accordance with the plans of their college, three of the six later traveled on to the San Gabriel River, where they added strength to the initial mission, San Francisco Xavier. A second mission, San Ildefonso, was completed in February 1749; a third, Nuestra Señora de la Candelaria, in July of the same year (see Figure 20). The three missions sensibly grouped Indians on the basis of tribal and linguistic similarities. San Xavier contained Tonkawas; San Ildefonso congregated Orcoquizas, Bidais, and Deadoses; while Candelaria sheltered the coastal Cocos and their allies. By the summer of 1749, the number of Indians congregated at the first two missions stood, respectively, at 209 and 238.[15]

The padres who administered the three missions were initially optimistic. They reported favorably on the fertility of the soil and the availability of potable water. Problems, however, were not long in coming. Separated from their families, the soldiers began the unsettling practice of fraternizing with Indian women. The men were especially unhappy with their assignment, for they were "poorly fed, miserably housed, [and] far distant from their paymasters." Until the autumn of 1749, their commanding "officer" was only a corporal. The soldiery, as charged by the clerics, were so unhappy with their duty that they likely contributed to the collapse of the missions as their best means of escaping a bad assignment.[16]

Still lacking at San Gabriel was a presidio. The padres had consistently maintained that a formal military garrison housing men with their families was essential to the success of the religious establishments, but the governor had opposed the idea. When Barrio was unable to find substantial support in San Antonio for his objections to the missions, he carried out a second inspection in July 1749, and in his formal report to the viceroy he once again counseled against the establishment of a presidio. His continued opposition to the San Gabriel enterprise no doubt fueled the unhappiness of soldiers stationed there.[17]

In the fall of the same year, Governor Barrio reluctantly appointed the first commissioned officer, Lieutenant Juan Galván, to command at San Gabriel. The governor remained convinced that the missions should be abandoned, and he recommended their transfer to the San Marcos River. His negative attitude, according to the religious, was pervasive. It contributed to the disgruntled soldiers' lack of respect for the friars and the military's refusal to enforce discipline on the mission Indians. In October the entire assemblage of potential converts deserted San Ildefonso, the largest of the San Gabriel missions. When petitions for aid went unanswered by the governor in San Antonio, the Franciscans elected to take their case in person to the viceroy.[18] To air the order's grievances, Father Benito Fernández de Santa Ana made the long trek to Mexico City. There he raised doubts about the fairness and impartiality of Governor Barrio in the minds of the viceroy and his advisers, but to Santa Anna's dismay the viceroy ordered still another inspection before he would grant authorization for a presidio.[19]

Lieutenant José Joaquín de Ecay Múzquiz of Presidio del Sacramento arrived at San Gabriel in late June and began his inspection on July 12, 1750. His visitation was thorough: he recorded the exact depths of Brushy Creek and the San Gabriel River and noted the precise location of the missions relative to each other and the streams. Ecay Múzquiz also recorded the number of catechumens and baptized persons at each mission; he reported favorably on crops of corn, beans, and chili peppers; and he commented on the abundance of buffalo, fish, and wild fruits.[20]

Ecay Múzquiz's favorable impressions did not entirely capture the situation at the struggling missions. In the previous spring, a terrible smallpox epidemic had broken out among an encampment of San Ildefonso converts as they foraged for food. Father José Ganzábal, the first regular missionary at San Ildefonso, witnessed the contagion and ministered to the afflicted Indians. By his account the disease was so virulent that within a few days it simultaneously killed and putrefied the bodies of forty victims.[21] Those who survived, undoubtedly disfigured with pockmarks, were part of the number listed by the inspector. Despite this tragedy, the favorable report of Ecay Múzquiz and the replacement of Governor Barrio with Jacinto de Barrios y Jáuregui in late 1750 seemed to portend well for the San Gabriel complex, but that would not be the case. The new governor, like his predecessor, quarreled with the missionaries and threatened to remove soldiers from guard duty. His intransigence, however, did not prevent the founding of the long-awaited presidio.

On March 30, 1751, after consultation with his advisers, Viceroy Conde de Revilla Gigedo approved the establishment of Presidio San Francisco Xavier de Gigedo (see Figure 20). The garrison commander, Captain Felipe de Rábago y Terán, had already been selected by the king. Rábago was a weak and vain man, and his assumption of the post would mean that the hard-won victory of the padres was illusory. In the words of Father Juan Agustín Morfi, "They were yet to see the work of several years destroyed in four days, their beloved Indians scattered, the missions ruined, their honor stained, and their blood shed by the very person to whom the king had entrusted their safety."[22]

En route to San Gabriel, Rábago stopped at Querétaro and struck an agreement with the college officials. If a dispute arose between himself and the missionaries at San Gabriel, it would be settled locally without appeal to the viceroy. It was an unfortunate arrangement for the Franciscans, for the commander was an irresponsible rake. As he passed through villages on his way to San Antonio, Rábago scandalized the religious by his promiscuous conduct with women, and at San Antonio he seduced the wife of Juan José Ceballos, a member of his command. As Rábago continued onward to San Gabriel, the cuckolded husband threatened him and wound up in chains for his efforts. On reaching the missions, Rábago placed Ceballos in stocks and later confined him to a cell.[23]

In fairness to Rábago, he inherited appalling conditions at San Gabriel. Only eighteen soldiers were present, for most of the garrison had either deserted or been reassigned to Los Adaes. The missions were in equally bad shape, with only 109 neophytes at San Xavier, 25 at Candelaria, and none at San Ildefonso.[24] The new commander ordered a survey of the area and selected a site for the proposed presidio, but matters between him and the friars quickly worsened. Much of the fault was Rábago's. He continued relations with Ceballos's wife, and when the padres intervened by ordering the woman back to San Antonio, Rábago's conduct became outrageous. He ordered Ceballos tightly bound, placed a cot in the cell, and then ravished the wife in full view of her husband. The humiliated soldier later escaped from his cell and sought sanctuary in the chapel of mission Candelaria. When Rábago learned of the incident, he violated ecclesiastical sanctuary by riding his horse into the church. Therein he apprehended Ceballos and later tortured him for good measure.[25]

In his official reports sent to the viceroy, Rábago condemned the entire San Gabriel enterprise and urged its relocation to a more favorable site on the San Marcos River. The missionaries—ignoring the prior agreement—responded by venting outrage to their college and by direct appeals to the viceroy. To ease the situation, the college appointed Alonso Giraldo de Terreros as president of both the San Antonio and San Gabriel missions and enjoined its missionaries on the San Gabriel River to stay strictly out of military affairs. But it was all to no avail.[26]

The San Gabriel missions, which seemed doomed from their inception, were already in death's throes. With example set by their commander, the immorality of the soldiers with Indian women, single or married, knew no bounds. In February 1752 the outraged priests excommunicated the entire military complement. But there was still worse to come.[27]

In May 1752 Ceballos, then living at Candelaria, and Father José Ganzábal were both shot to death inside the mission. Rábago placed the blame on Coco Indians, but the perpetrators were almost certainly soldiers of the presidio. Following the murders, priests and Indians alike fled. For all practical purposes, the San Gabriel undertaking had ended, although some contact with Indians in the area continued for another three years. As if to signal nature's concurrence with the demise of the missions, in the summer of 1753 the San Gabriel River ceased to flow, depriving the area of potable water and irrigation. In 1755 missionary functions and the presidio were transferred to the San Marcos River, and in the following year all assets of the San Gabriel project were earmarked for a new mission among the eastern Apaches in central Texas.[28] As for Rábago, he was relieved of command, incarcerated, and subjected to eight years of investigation before finally being cleared of charges arising from the murders of Ceballos and González.

THE HOPE OF FOUNDING MISSIONS FOR THE APACHES WAS A late-life passion of Father Francisco Hidalgo, but his superiors had denied him that opportunity. However, subsequent raids on San Antonio by Apaches in the 1730s again raised the issue of pacifying these mounted plains people. The military cadre at San Antonio offered their solution to the problem, but punitive expeditions carried out in 1732 and 1739 had accomplished little other than to familiarize Spaniards with the country along the San Saba River and sow discord among civil and religious personnel. For their part, the padres could never accept killing or enslavement as deterrents to Apache attacks, while the governors and military commanders insisted on a forceful solution.[29]

In 1745 Toribio de Urrutia led another thrust against the Apaches that may also have penetrated to the San Saba River. This third expedition, accompanied by Father Santa Ana, stirred up extreme bitterness in the padre, for it was allegedly "little more than a slave-hunting expedition."[30] As a result of the campaign, Santa Ana and his religious brethren became even more convinced that the Apaches could be reached only with patience and understanding, brought to them by the spiritual sons of St. Francis. These same humanitarian impulses that had spawned the troubled San Gabriel missions would soon give rise to even more tragic consequences at San Sabá.

Near the end of the San Gabriel enterprise, Father Alonso Giraldo de Terreros experimented with the first mission for the troublesome Apaches. In late 1754 at a site located west of San Juan Bautista, he began an ill-fated venture that lasted less than a year. It ended when the neophytes revolted, burned the buildings, and fled the mission. Undeterred, the Franciscans petitioned for the establishment of a new mission in the heart of Apachería.[31] The proposal of the padres came at a time when the

Apaches themselves had begun to reassess their independent status. That they possessed no affection for the Spaniards is well documented by their raids on San Antonio in the 1730s. However, by the late 1740s it was clear to the Apaches that they must try to befriend the Spaniards, a decision forced on them because of relentless pressure from Comanches and their allies. In 1749 the Apaches negotiated a peace treaty at San Antonio, and their conduct toward the Béxar community improved accordingly. By Captain Toribio de Urrutia's own admission, the Apaches "had maintained peace in this province from March to today [November 25, 1749]." Three years later, and after considerable debate, the authorities in Mexico City ordered the exploration of Apache country with a view to selecting an ideal mission site, but the ongoing crises at San Gabriel delayed implementation of the order for approximately a year.[32]

In 1753 Juan Galván and a few soldiers, accompanied by Father Miguel de Aranda of mission Concepción, explored the country along the Pedernales, Llano, and San Saba rivers to the northwest of San Antonio. Both Galván and the priest were favorably impressed with the availability of water and fertile soil at the San Saba. While there, they also contacted friendly Apaches who promised to reside at a mission if one were founded for them.[33]

Galván's report, possibly written by Father Aranda, referred to the richness of mineral deposits in the area, to the bright prospects of gaining Apache neophytes, and to the advisability of setting up a garrison to protect against the Comanches. When this favorable assessment of the San Sabá region reached Mexico City, the viceregal staff sought the advice of Father Santa Ana.[34]

Long an advocate of missionizing the Apaches, Santa Ana's enthusiastic endorsement of a San Sabá enterprise comes as no surprise. Still, the viceroy was not satisfied. He ordered Pedro de Rábago y Terán, a former governor of Coahuila and relative of the infamous military commander at San Gabriel, to conduct a follow-up exploration. In late 1754 Rábago, who had succeeded his nephew as commander at Presidio San Xavier, explored the same general area covered by Galván and confirmed the accuracy of Don Juan's report. By then the settlers at San Antonio likewise endorsed the San Sabá enterprise. The Apaches had kept the peace for five years, and many Bexareños no doubt saw the advantages of a buffer settlement within Apachería. Governor Barrios, however, was not so enthusiastic. He ordered his lieutenant governor, Bernardo de Miranda, to conduct yet another reconnaissance of the region.[35]

In early 1756 Miranda began his assignment with a thorough exploration of the Llano River country in present Llano County. There on

February 27, he discovered a huge mound of red hematite that would excite prospectors for some time. Miranda also contacted Apaches who assured him that a mountain of pure silver lay at the end of six days' journey to the north, and once again Spaniards found their attention directed to the waters of the San Saba River near present Menard, Texas.[36] The improvement of defensive posture, the lure of wealth, and the potential harvest of souls had long served as inducements for the northward expansion of New Spain. In similar fashion, San Sabá focused those same motives.

The proposed settlement of the San Sabá region quickly won the support of the new viceroy, the Marqués de las Amarillas, after whom the garrison to be constructed there would be named. In late 1755 Amarillas had assumed the reins of government, and in the following May he appointed Colonel Diego Ortiz Parrilla to succeed Pedro de Rábago y Terán, who had died in an epidemic at San Gabriel. The viceroy also ordered that all properties of the San Gabriel missions be transferred to the new site.[37]

Parrilla was an experienced soldier who had entered the king's service in 1734 and a former interim governor of Sinaloa and Sonora. He was arrogant, incapable of admitting mistakes, and probably anxious to carve his name in the history of the frontier province. Parrilla succeeded in the latter but hardly in the manner envisioned by him. It was his extreme misfortune to have "come at the wrong time to the wrong place." The disasters that would strike the San Sabá mission can hardly be attributed to his personality or lack of leadership.[38]

A second forceful person associated with the San Sabá enterprise was Father Alonso Giraldo de Terreros. Like Parrilla, Terreros was a man of wide experience. He had served as guardian of the college at Querétaro and later as president of the Río Grande missions, and he had also founded the short-lived mission for the Apaches in Coahuila.[39]

Terreros traveled to Mexico City in the spring of 1756 for an audience with the viceroy, and while in the city he learned that a wealthy cousin was considering the sponsorship of missionary efforts among the Apaches. The cousin, Pedro Romero de Terreros, had proposed that if he financed the venture, Father Alonso must be placed in charge of the neophytes. By July the details appear to have been ironed out. Pedro Romero would bear all mission expenses for three years, after which responsibility would pass to the civil government. Military expenditures, on the other hand, would be borne from the beginning by the royal treasury. From its inception, the San Sabá enterprise was to be directly responsible to the viceroy, not the governor of Texas.[40]

The missionaries to be sent among the Apaches would be recruited from the college of Querétaro and the newly founded college of San Fernando, and they would be placed under the jurisdiction of Father Alonso. It was further agreed that the assets of the then suppressed San Gabriel missions would be purchased at a fair price by Romero de Terreros and handed over to his cousin.[41] With these essential details out of the way, in September 1756 Colonel Parrilla received instructions for transferring the San Xavier presidio, still located on the San Marcos River, to the banks of the San Saba. He was urged to treat the missionaries at the new site with respect, a reminder no doubt prompted by the disastrous events associated with the San Gabriel enterprise.[42]

Parrilla and Terreros proceeded separately to San Antonio. Accompanying Father Alonso were four priests, two each from the colleges of Querétaro and San Fernando. On arrival at San Antonio, the padres found Parrilla already there, with plans under way for continuing on to the San Marcos. At the river Parrilla inspected the miserable, ragtag remnants of Presidio San Xavier, which he moved to San Antonio in late December 1756.[43]

Mission San Xavier had been temporarily relocated on the Guadalupe River. Its stubborn advocate was still Father Mariano de los Dolores, but he could not convince Father Terreros to bring the beleaguered mission under the umbrella of his cousin's generous financing. Unfortunately, this circumstance led to bitter feelings that divided the Franciscans on the eve of the San Sabá undertaking. Father Dolores also resented the authority of Terreros in that venture, for he had sought approval to set up missions among the Apaches for fifteen years—only to lose out, as he saw it, to a man advantaged by a wealthy cousin. As the feud worsened at San Antonio, those who gathered around Father Dolores included Colonel Parrilla.[44]

Matters worsened in the months ahead. In early 1757 at the invitation of Spaniards in San Antonio, a delegation of Lipan Apaches visited that settlement. For Parrilla it must have been an unsettling experience. The Apaches seemed interested only in the gifts presented to them and the prospects of gaining an ally against the Comanches. The commander voiced his concerns in a letter dispatched to Pedro Romero de Terreros: "The state in which we have found the Apaches is so different from what I expected that I assure you the method of their pacification is a major concern to me." From the statement, it seems probable that Parrilla's apprehension extended beyond the attitude of the Apaches and their disinterest in being missionized, for he objected to the coequal authority of the military and religious in the San Sabá enterprise.[45]

In any event, time and again Parrilla found reasons to delay the departure for central Texas: the livestock needed fattening, the supplies were inadequate, the plans were incomplete. To Father Terreros, Parrilla's dalliance was inexcusable, and this served to worsen an already serious schism. Finally, in early April 1757, the expedition set out for the San Saba River. It included soldiers, their families, missionaries, Indian allies, food, supplies, fourteen hundred head of cattle, and seven hundred sheep.[46]

As Robert S. Weddle has noted, "The story of the Mission Santa Cruz de San Sabá is one of Apache perfidy, Spanish gullibility, and the disastrous consequences of both." Despite repeated assurances from the Apaches that they would welcome a mission among them, not one Indian was present when the entourage arrived at the San Saba River on April 17. After five days of exploration by Parrilla, he still had not seen a single Apache, and at that point the commander was ready to pull stakes and return to San Antonio. The six Franciscans, however, would not hear of it. At their insistence, mission Santa Cruz de San Sabá and Presidio San Luis de las Amarillas soon took shape near present Menard, Texas (see Figure 20). Mindful of the unsettling influence of soldiers on mission Indians, the padres deliberately positioned the mission three miles downstream from the presidio. Its location reduced the possibility of meddling by troops of the garrison, but it also made defense of the mission a serious problem.[47]

During its brief existence of less than a year, mission Santa Cruz de San Sabá failed to attract a single resident Apache neophyte. At one time some three thousand Apaches appeared on their way north to hunt buffalo, but none would enter the mission on that occasion. Had the Indians consistently shown no inclination whatsoever of submitting to mission life, the Spaniards would no doubt have given up hope and returned to San Antonio, thereby avoiding the impending disaster. However, such was not the case. The Apaches by their demeanor and occasional appearances offered tantalizing hope for the padres. Even so, three of the religious became so despondent over the lack of potential converts that they returned to San Antonio, and the original plans to build a second and third mission were scrapped.[48]

The personnel of the newly constructed presidio and mission suffered through a cold winter of 1757–1758. The soldiers and their families represented no small commitment, for three hundred to four hundred people lived at the presidio, including more than two hundred women and children. But in the late winter of 1758, events moved toward a tragic climax. It is clear in retrospect that the Apaches had enticed the Spanish to the San Saba River and influenced their staying there as a convenient bulwark against the northern tribes. The Apaches in carrying out raids on their bitter enemies also seem to have deliberately left behind items of Spanish clothing, such as shoes, as clear evidence of their ties to the San Sabá mission; furthermore, spies for the northern tribes may have reported that the Apaches were in close league with the Europeans. All of this served to infuriate the Comanches and their Indian associates.[49]

By early March 1758, there was unmistakable evidence that hundreds of hostile Comanches, Bidais, Tejas, and Tonkawas were converging on San Sabá. Colonel Parrilla, concerned for the safety of 237 women and children at the presidio, could spare only a few soldiers to guard the mission, and he requested that the three priests there move to the garrison—all to no avail. Fathers Terreros, Miguel de Molina, and José de Santiesteban insisted on remaining at the mission.[50]

In the early morning of March 16, the padres found themselves completely surrounded by Indians armed with muskets, swords, and lances. In the words of Father Molina, "I saw nothing but Indians on every hand . . . arrayed in the most horrible attire. Besides the paint on their faces, red and black, they were adorned with the pelts and tails of wild beasts, wrapped around them or hanging down from their heads, as well as deer horns." Once admitted inside the mission gate, the Indians began stealing horses and all manner of goods. They shot Father Terreros and perhaps decapitated Father Santiesteban while he was still at the altar. After killing a total of eight, the Indians set fire to the buildings and continued their looting. Miraculously, Father Molina and perhaps two dozen others escaped one by one from the inferno and eventually made their way to the presidio.[51]

Colonel Parrilla braced for an attack on the presidio itself, but it never came. The Indians tried repeatedly to lure the soldiers outside the fort, but when their ruses failed they withdrew to the north on March 18. On that same day, Colonel Parrilla inspected the awful carnage at the mission. In their fury the Indians had scalped some of the victims, decapitated others, or gouged out eyes; they had even killed the cats and oxen, sparing only a few sheep. Santa Cruz de San Sabá, the only Texas mission destroyed by outright Indian attack, was never rebuilt.[52] In the immediate aftermath of the attack on San Sabá, Colonel Parrilla asked for aid from the other presidios, but none was forthcoming. Those garrisons, fearing for their own safety, refused to release any men. In official reports to the viceroy, both Parrilla and Father Molina favored moving the presidio and mission to more favorable locations. Parrilla further recommended that thorough preparations be made if a punitive expedition were contemplated.[53]

The matter was studied at length in Mexico City. Officials there ruled out abandoning the San Sabá site, since to do so would give the appearance of retreat, inspire contempt for Spanish authority, and lead to future attacks. Plans, however, for an expedition to punish the offending Indians were left to a junta that would convene in San Antonio.[54] Parrilla departed San Sabá and participated in the junta, which met in January 1759. This special committee recognized that manpower would be a critical concern and asked for support from the governor of Nuevo León. Citizens there and elsewhere, however, refused to volunteer. Projecting the need for a total force of five hundred men, the junta then decided to recruit sizable numbers of militia and mission Indians as well as presidial soldiers.[55]

The committee forwarded its recommendations to Mexico City. There opinion divided over the merits and expense of the expedition, estimated to cost more than fifty-two thousand pesos. But in the final analysis, it was decided that the Indians must be taught the lesson that "even in their most remote haunts they would not be secure from the long arm of Spanish vengeance." Still, recruiting hundreds of men, many of whom came from the Costa del Seno Mexicano and Nuevo León, proved lengthy and troublesome.[56]

While arrangements for a punitive expedition were in progress, Indians "all armed with guns" raided the San Sabá horse herd on March 30, 1759, killing twenty soldiers and stealing the entire assembly of mounts and pack mules. All of the victims died of bullet wounds, almost certainly fired from muskets supplied by the French, since the Spanish could not legally sell firearms to Indians. As Colonel Parrilla bitterly reported, "Not one arrow was seen among the Indians," and the presidio was left with only twenty horses. This costly raid lent additional support to the arguments for punishing the offending natives.[57] Parrilla was to have launched the retaliatory undertaking from San Sabá in June, but he was still in San Antonio in August. He had waited there hoping to recruit more soldiers, but he finally accepted a motley collection of presidial soldiers, militiamen, Tlaxcalan auxiliaries from central Mexico, mission Indians, and Apaches. His total force numbered in excess of five hundred men, supported by sixteen hundred horses, mules, and cattle.[58]

From San Sabá, Colonel Parrilla reached the north bank of the Brazos River on October 2 and encountered the first hostilities. His force killed several Indians and took 149 captives, some of whom agreed to serve as guides. On October 7 the Spanish commander came under attack by a band of 60 or 70 Indians. He repulsed the onslaught and pursued the Indians through a wooded area. As he cleared the edge of the woods, Parrilla was astonished to see a fortification on the south bank of the Red River. Associated with the fort were cultivated fields and a palisaded village, and from within the walls flew the flag of France![59]

In a clash that lasted for hours, Parrilla was unable to subdue the enemy. His attacks were met with concentrated fire, and the day ended in stalemate. On the following day, Parrilla considered renewing the battle, but the condition of his troops dictated otherwise. He had suffered losses, including dead, wounded, and missing, totaling fifty-two, and had also lost cannon, muskets, saddles, and other equipment. He ordered an immediate retreat and reached San Sabá on October 25, 1759. The expedition had convinced him of the dangers of French influence on the Red River. He had seen the flag of France and heard the sound of fife and drums. As was his custom, Parrilla expressed bitter disappointment over the sorry quality of his troops, blaming them for his disastrous defeat. He, however, as he later reported to the king, had served with "zeal, valor, and exemplary conduct . . . in inflicting punishment on the enemy."[60]

Although the presidio remained in existence for another ten years, missionary enterprises at the San Sabá site had ended. In the words of Henry E. Allen, "Not only did the mission fail to attract those for whom it was intended, but the project aroused the hostility of the numerous northern tribes, all of whom were mortal enemies of the Apaches." When the mission was razed and two of its priests martyred, the Spanish chose to punish the offenders. That, too, ended in failure. Again to quote Allen, "Even with all its troubles the campaign . . . should have been successful, but the Spaniards ran into a different kind of Indian, in spirit and arms, than they had previously encountered on the northern frontier. Consequently they met defeat."[61]

THE LITANY OF FAILED ATTEMPTS TO EXPAND BEYOND SAN Antonio and the East Texas settlements saw little abatement in efforts to occupy permanently the lower Trinity River basin. Despite Spanish presence in East Texas, the geography and topography of the lower basin were virtually unknown until 1746. That ignorance almost certainly would have continued for some time except for rumors of French incursions reported to the viceroy in 1745 by the presidial captain at La Bahía. Joaquín Orobio Basterra's letter served to alert officials in the capital who ordered a reconnaissance.[62]

Orobio first attempted to descend the Guadalupe River to the coast, but rough country and high water discouraged him. In late 1746 he used a different tack. He took the road to Los Adaes as far as the Trinity River crossing, and from there intended to follow the river to the coast. At the crossing, Orobio changed his plans. Indians in the region could tell him nothing about the country toward the coast, so he continued on to Los Adaes. En route he observed unmistakable evidence of French influence among the natives. They possessed firearms, clothing, and trinkets—all of French origin. The Indians, however, insisted that these foreign items had come from the French outpost at Natchitoches, not from the coast. Still, the natives admitted hearing of French traders settled near the mouth of the Trinity River.[63]

After consultation with the governor at Los Adaes, Orobio headed southward along a trail used by the Bidai Indians. His encounters with Bidais and Orcoquizas supplied details and confirmation of French activities along the lower Neches, Trinity, and Brazos rivers. While the French visiting the area had promised to settle at a site on the San Jacinto River, as of 1746 their presence had been limited to periodic traders who arrived by sea. Armed with this information, Orobio returned to La Bahía and filed a report with Governor Francisco García Larios.[64]

No further attempts to counter French influence in the lower Trinity region came until the administration of Governor Jacinto de Barrios y Jáuregui. Personal agents of the governor regularly visited the Bidais after 1751, carrying such items as tobacco, knives, and firearms—all obtained illegally from the French at Natchitoches. They returned to Los Adaes loaded with corn, hides, and horses, the latter almost certainly stolen by Indians from other Spanish settlements. Spanish laws were broken twofold by supplying weapons to the natives and disposing of the hides at Natchitoches, but smuggling and illegal trade had long been a way of life in East Texas.[65]

Spanish settlement of the lower Trinity River, however, did not come until the mid-1750s. In September 1754 Governor Barrios sent Lieutenant Marcos Ruiz and twenty-five soldiers to investigate a report that the French had opened trade with the Orcoquizas from a post near the mouth of the Trinity. Ruiz marched to the coast and in October captured Joseph Blancpain, two other Frenchmen, and two black slaves at the village of a local chieftain. Ruiz also confiscated contraband goods, including clothing and munitions. The governor ordered the five captives sent to Mexico City for interrogation and moved to shore up defenses by stationing perhaps twenty soldiers at El Orcoquisac. Posting these men during the summer months of 1755 initiated Spanish settlement at this site.[66]

Meanwhile, interrogation of the three Frenchmen and two young blacks in Mexico City failed to spur action from the central government, despite the fact that their depositions revealed the existence of substantial trading operations among the Bidais and Orcoquizas. Even more alarming, Blancpain carried a patent and passport signed by the governor of New Orleans, which specifically authorized him and his associates to bring cattle to the city. Beef, of course, had to come from Texas.[67] Nevertheless, matters remained at an impasse until the arrival of the Marqués de las Amarillas in late 1755. The new viceroy brought matters concerning the settlement of the lower Trinity to a head. He issued a decree ordering the establishment of a garrison of thirty soldiers and a supporting mission manned by two friars from the Franciscan college at Zacatecas.[68] The viceroy also called for the creation of a *villa* populated by fifty families, but that proviso was never realized.

Governor Barrios tried to comply with the viceroy's decree. On two occasions in early 1756, he dispatched Lieutenant Domingo del Río among the Orcoquiza and Bidai Indians to learn their reaction to the arrest of Blancpain. While del Río found no French settlements, the Indians assured him that Frenchmen had been among them and intended to return. Before the lieutenant returned from his second exploration in June, Barrios had sent another troop under the command of Marcos Ruiz to begin the construction of Presidio San Agustín de Ahumada. Later in that same summer, Domingo del Río and Bernardo de Miranda made independent surveys to determine the site for the proposed *villa*. By the end of the year, mission Nuestra Señora de la Luz was built at a site near the presidio (see Figure 20).[69] Both structures, often called El Orcoquisac, were located near the present town of Anahuac in Chambers County, but they were destined to be short-lived.

Conditions at the mission must have been among the worst in Texas. The usually stoic padres complained of flies, mosquitoes, and undrinkable water, circumstances that inevitably led to suffering from dysentery. In addition, the mission and presidio were chronically short of food, clothing, and supplies; and the Indians were intractable. A description of local conditions at La Luz in 1760, given by Father Anastacio de Romero during an inspection ordered by the governor, perhaps says it all: "The Río Trinidad is very quick to overflow its banks and flood the fields. . . . the tide of the river is so that, I have heard said it is possible to go fishing inside the houses. . . . Flies . . . torment the inhabitants as in Egypt of old."[70]

This situation did not improve over the next two years. In 1762, when Louisiana passed to Spain near the end of the French and Indian War, the presidio was no longer needed for reasons of defense, but it remained viable for some years. The continued settlement of the lower Trinity River region, however, was threatened by Gulf storms, weakened by the dwindling numbers of catechumens at the mission, and undermined by strong suspicions in Mexico City that the soldiers of the presidio were engaged in widespread contraband trade, a mistrustfulness resting on solid ground. Permanent occupation of El Orcoquisac by Spaniards came to an end in 1770 when the presidio and mission were both removed.[71]

UNLIKE THE MISSIONS ON THE SAN GABRIEL AND THE SAN SABA rivers, one major enterprise in the 1740s and 1750s enjoyed success. Significantly, that undertaking was not centered in Texas with its sparse population, although the province profited from it, and it was not solely tied to the founding of missions among recalcitrant natives. However, the project did originate, at least in part, from the need to pacify coastal Indians who were raiding settlements in Nuevo León.[72]

The targeted region, known as Nuevo Santander of the Costa del Seno Mexicano, stretched from Matagorda Bay in the north to Tampico in the south, and it focused the extraordinary talents of José de Escandón y Elguera. However, Escandón was not the first to propose settlement of the northern portion of the Costa. In 1738 and 1739 three petitioners had come before the officials of New Spain and the Council of the Indies. Responsibility for selecting one of the aspirants bounded back and forth between Spanish officials on both sides of the Atlantic. In 1739 the crown remanded the matter to Mexico and called for the creation of a special junta, composed principally of the viceroy and members of the audiencia. The committee was specifically charged with choosing one of the petitioners and providing assistance as needed.[73]

Nevertheless, no action was forthcoming. The matter was studied for four years, during which two of the applicants understandably dropped out of competition. At that point the decision should have been easy, but such was not the case. Even a royal cedula in 1743, urging the junta to select a candidate, did not expedite matters or improve the case of the last petitioner, Antonio Ladrón de Guevara of Nuevo León. The junta stubbornly sought a better choice. One appeared seven years after the committee had received its initial charge.[74] On September 3, 1746, Viceroy Revilla Gigedo, newly arrived from Spain, approved an accord with José de Escandón, making him the colonizer and governor of the proposed new province. The decision came at the very time that Father Dolores sought official support for the San Gabriel missions, and there is no doubt that the Escandón enterprise received priority consideration over other plans for expansion.[75]

Escandón was a man who brought first-class credentials to the task at hand. As Weddle has written, he possessed qualities that set him "apart from a host of other explorers and colonizers who operated on New Spain's frontiers with less impressive results." In the mid-1730s Escandón had been a sergeant major stationed at Querétaro. There he established a reputation for fairness and firmness in dealing with both Indians and Spaniards, especially in a series of campaigns designed to pacify natives in the nearby Sierra Gorda. Most of his accomplishments, except for the salaries of soldiers, were financed at his personal expense, and for his services he later received the title Count of Sierra Gorda. Thus, Escandón's credentials and the esteem with which he was held by Spaniards and natives alike made his selection for the larger task of settling Nuevo Santander a logical one.[76] Initially, Escandón eschewed the offer of immediate assistance from the public treasury, preferring to make a preliminary inspection at his own cost. He did accept a viceregal proposal that would direct cooperation from officials in the surrounding provinces and in 1747 readied himself for a tour of inspection.[77]

Escandón originally intended to found a total of fourteen new settlements and an appropriate number of missions. His approach to colonization had been shaped by his prior experience in the Sierra Gorda. Emphasis would be placed on civil rather than military establishments, and he intended to transfer families from older settlements to form the nuclei of new ones. Inducements for the settlers would include farm and pasture lands and a one-time cash bonus for the purchase of supplies and implements. For reasons of security, soldiers would be assigned to the new towns but for only two or three years. Each town would be independent of existing frontier political units and their officials, and each would contain a mission to serve the needs of the Indians and settlers.[78]

The location of the new towns and missions would be determined by the need to secure the coast against foreign intruders and to pacify the Indians, especially the coastal Karankawas in Texas and shoreline groups extending into Mexico. Escandón intended to divide religious responsibility between the colleges of San Fernando and Zacatecas, while civil authority would rest with the viceroy and the audiencia in Mexico City. To plan and coordinate an undertaking of this magnitude required a masterful organizer.[79] Escandón conceived of a series of expeditions that would simultaneously explore the new province from various points along an arc running from Tampico to La Bahía in Texas. The place of rendezvous for several entradas would be near the mouth of the Río Grande. All plans were in place by January 1747. Escandón, himself, left Querétaro on January 7, while the supporting expeditions departed from various locations in the same month.[80]

Tampico and Valles were points of departure for three southern expeditions. In the north, one troop from Coahuila, led by Miguel de la Garza Falcón, marched along the north bank of the Río Grande; another column, which drew troops from La Bahía and Los Adaes, moved down the coast to the mouth of the Río Grande. The Texas contingent included fifty soldiers led by Captain Joaquín Orobio of La Bahía presidio. It was accompanied by Father Juan González, who directed mission La Bahía.[81]

Escandón's reconnoitering of Nuevo Santander from diverse starting points was a brilliant success. In the words of Lawrence Hill, "With few exceptions each unit had only a short distance to travel to accomplish its task. . . . The mountains, valleys, streams, salines, bays, and natives were noted with great care and . . . included in a detailed report to the viceroy." These undertakings become more remarkable when it is noted that they involved 765 soldiers, yet there was no loss of life during the entire period of three months.[82]

Of the twenty-four villages and fifteen missions established in the Costa del Seno Mexicano by 1755, only two of the former were within the borders of present Texas. In August 1750 José Vázquez Borrego, a rancher from Coahuila, founded Nuestra Señora de los Dolores, situated some ten leagues downstream from present Laredo; and in May 1755 Tomás Sánchez, a lieutenant of Escandón, established the town of Laredo. Earlier, Escandón had been personally responsible for moving mission and presidio La Bahía (1749) from the Guadalupe River to the present-day site at Goliad on the San Antonio River.[83]

La Bahía benefited from its better location and the new pueblo established at the site. Within five years a new mission for the Karankawas, Nuestra Señora del Rosario de los Cujanes, was founded upstream from the presidio (see Figure 20). After a shaky start, mission Rosario, unlike those at San Gabriel and San Sabá, survived for many years. While not founded by Escandón, it was nevertheless a direct outgrowth of his policies to reorganize the lower Gulf Coast and subdue the Karankawas.[84]

By the time Escandón retired in 1755, he had helped relocate more than six thousand Spaniards and congregate nearly three thousand Indians, and he helped lay the foundations of the cattle industry in the lower Río Grande Valley. In the same year of his retirement, the Marqués de las Amarillas assumed office as viceroy. This energetic executive, after whom the presidios at San Sabá and El Orcoquisac were named, ordered a comprehensive investigation of Nuevo Santander to determine the nature of its needs. To carry out this assignment, the viceroy commissioned José Tienda de Cuervo.[85]

Cuervo's inspection of Camargo and Dolores are of particular interest. At the former site, he found seventeen ranches within a radius of five leagues. The ranches contained an estimated sixty-five hundred horses, twenty-six hundred cattle, and seventy-two thousand sheep. One of the ranches, owned by Captain Blas María de la Garza Falcón and his father-in-law, extended north of the Río Grande with stock counted in the thousands. At Dolores, Cuervo found nothing but a single ranch owned by Vásquez Borrego. It was the residence for twenty-three families of laborers and contained eight thousand head of horses, mules, and cattle. Borrego's ranch even provided its own security, performed by eleven uniformed and armed vaqueros mounted on red ponies.[86]

WHY DID THE ESCANDÓN COLONIZING VENTURE ENJOY LONG-range success when the three mission outposts ultimately failed? Escandón was a thorough, well-organized, and skillful planner. He was advantaged by the proximity of Nuevo Santander to the heartland of New Spain, and his undertaking was not as dependent on the cooperation of recalcitrant natives. On the other hand, the purely missionary undertakings, especially at San Gabriel and San Sabá, were handicapped by disputes between religious and military officials, long distances from other Spanish settlements, the extremes of climate, and the mutual antipathy of the Apaches and the northern Indian nations. During the years 1745–1762, Escandón's accomplishments were a refreshing departure from the disastrous events associated with the San Gabriel and San Sabá endeavors, but it would be misleading to conclude that the older missions in Texas had also suffered serious setbacks. These same years witnessed significant progress at San Antonio.[87]

In March 1762, near the end of the French and Indian War, the commissary general of the Franciscans called for a comprehensive report on all of the order's missions in New Spain. That document reflected steady growth for five of them located at San Antonio. By 1762 more than forty-four hundred Indians had been baptized at the Querétaran missions, with half that number baptized within the last seventeen years. The physical structures of the missions and associated buildings, although they had not reached their pinnacle in architectural elegance, were then being built of more permanent materials, including quarried stone. Furthermore, the town of San Antonio itself was well on its way toward becoming a more viable community.[88]

By contrast, the missions in East Texas "continued to lead the same helpless existence which they had experienced since the outset." The near resignation of friars there was echoed in the report of Father Simón Hierro, guardian of the college of Guadalupe of Zacatecas: "If we had not taken note of the fact that the Son of God in his gospel does not command us to convert, but only to preach, and that according to the Apostle the work of conversion is not that of the one who plants nor of the one who waters, but only of God, who gives the increase, it would have been an intolerable toil of forty years . . . for, in all those years, if the time has not been altogether lost; it is because in the fulfillment of the divine decrees they have sent many infants to glory by means of baptism."[89]

The next twenty-one years (1762–1783) would bring about profound changes in Texas. Reorganization of the northern frontier of New Spain would, in fact, eliminate the deplorable conditions in the East Texas missions and presidio but hardly in the manner envisioned by those who lived there. Change is often unsettling and unpopular, and it loomed on the horizon of Spanish Texas.

NINE

Texas and the Changing International Scene, 1762–1783

NEAR THE END OF THE FRENCH AND INDIAN WAR (1754 – 1763), France by diplomatic agreement transferred the Louisiana Territory to Spain, its Bourbon ally since early 1762. The cession encompassed a vast expanse of rich lands that lay west of the Mississippi River, but it was an acquisition viewed with mixed emotions by Spanish officials. On the one hand, they recognized that Texas had been transformed from a buffer province against French expansion to an interior one; on the other, they knew that Louisiana had been a drain on the French treasury and that it would be no less burdensome for them. In reality, the Spanish had little choice but to accept the French offer. Rejecting Louisiana would soon bring aggressive Englishmen to the borders of Texas and New Mexico. Spaniards saw the threat of Anglo influence and control over the northern Indian nations as unacceptably dangerous, and they worried about the security of silver mines on the frontier of New Spain. In response to the radically changed international scene, brought about by the Treaty of Paris (1763) and the removal of French possessions on the North American continent, Spain felt obliged to institute wide-sweeping reforms and energetic measures to protect its American empire, then challenged only by the English. Spain was fortunate to have Charles III (1759–1788), arguably the best monarch in the long history of that nation, holding the reins of power. The new dictates of foreign policy mandated by Charles would have a profound political and religious impact on northern Mexico and the Spanish Southwest. This chapter discusses the implementation of those changes, especially as they affected the lives of Spaniards and Indians in Texas.

IN THE EARLY YEARS OF HIS REIGN, CHARLES III, WORRIED BY the faltering position of France in the French and Indian War, abandoned the policy of peace that had been followed by his half-brother, Ferdinand VI. He renewed (1761) the Bourbon Family Compact, an offensive and defensive alliance between France and Spain. This agreement signaled a reversal of the strained relations that had persisted between the two powers since the days of La Salle.

In the following year on January 11, 1762, Spain declared war on England, but the Bourbon alliance did little to stem the tide of English successes. As an active combatant, Spain suffered the loss of both Havana and Manila. Near the conclusion of a war that was essentially lost by the Bourbon allies, diplomats from England, France, and Spain approved the preliminaries of a peace treaty on November 3. On the same day, Louis XV of France signed papers ceding Louisiana to Spain. By then Spain, on condition that it regain Cuba, was willing to transfer Florida to the English rather than to see them acquire Louisiana, even though the latter had never yielded a sou of income to France. As for the French, they wanted out of the war and needed Spanish support to end the fighting; the French also hoped that a quick truce would permit them to retain important sugar islands in the Caribbean and to continue the alliance of the Bourbon courts.[1]

At the conclusion of the French and Indian War, France urged Spain to take immediate control of Louisiana, but that would not be forthcoming. Citizens and militia units in New Orleans opposed the transfer, resisted the first Spanish governor, and delayed effective control of Louisiana by Spain until 1769. By then significant plans were under way for reorganizing the northern frontier of New Spain.

The removal of France from the North American continent had altered the balance of power there, for it meant that Spain alone faced England. To meet this challenge, Charles III was not long in directing his attention to the northern limits of New Spain and to the defense of New Spain proper. He dispatched Juan de Villalba to Mexico with orders to organize a regular army and colonial militia structured along the lines of European military units, and by 1765 Villalba commanded troops stationed in Mexico. In that same year the king commissioned José de Gálvez and the Marqués de Rubí to carry out tours of inspection in New Spain.[2]

Gálvez as visitor general for public finance spent six years in New Spain. His overarching powers even exceeded those of the viceroy, and when the Marqués de Cruillas objected, he was replaced with the more compliant Marqués de Croix. The inspector was particularly concerned about the immense distances between Mexico City and the northern provinces and the threat to those realms posed by English and Russian ambitions. In 1771 Gálvez returned to Spain, where he later assumed the important post of minister of the Indies, from which he would institute sweeping administrative changes for the Spanish empire in America.[3]

Appointed separately from Gálvez on August 7, 1765, was the Marqués de Rubí, who was specifically commissioned to inspect the presidios on the northern frontier of New Spain. He was to examine the status of the garrisons, inspect the guard, determine whether fair prices existed on goods sold in each presidio, and judge whether the military outposts served the best interests of government and defended the realm against hostile Indians and foreign encroachments.[4] A field marshal in the Spanish army, Rubí arrived in Mexico in early 1766. He hastened to the frontier to carry out an inspection of presidios from California to East Texas. His thorough investigation lasted for three years, during which he traveled seven thousand miles in the company of Nicolás de Lafora, a sharp-eyed engineer who logged firsthand observations in his diary.[5]

There had been no comprehensive visitation of the frontier since the Pedro de Rivera inspection of the late 1720s, and the belief in Spain that some of the presidios and accompanying missions had outlived their usefulness was well grounded. Just as the Rivera inspection had reported more than thirty-five years earlier, widespread abuses and corruption still existed in most of the military outposts. As Rubí would discover, by the 1760s those malpractices had become as commonplace in Texas as they were elsewhere on the frontier. Abuses included payment to soldiers only in goods, for which they were grossly overcharged, and enlistment practices whereby a soldier entering duty at a presidio was relieved of service obligations only by death, desertion, or his commander's permission. For the most part, a soldier's tour of duty at a frontier garrison meant unrelenting poverty, poor nutrition, and labor obligations on the private lands of the presidial commander.[6]

Rubí began his inspection tour in New Mexico, moved to California, and then returned to Coahuila. He arrived in Texas in July 1767, and in general he did not like what he saw there. He was particularly appalled by conditions at San Sabá. In his official report, Rubí declared San Luis de las Amarillas to be the worst presidio in the entire kingdom of New Spain.[7] Accepting for the moment the inspector's harsh assessment, how had the largest military garrison in Texas fallen on such hard times?

After his defeat in the Red River campaign of 1759, Diego Ortiz Parrilla had demonstrated a firm grasp of the overall situation in Texas. He saw serious problems that contained three components: the poor quality of presidial soldiers and militia forces; the danger of foreign influence on the northern tribes; and the increasing threat posed by Indians who possessed firearms and munitions and the skills to use them. Parrilla had witnessed firsthand the inadequacies of men under his command, and he feared that a general alliance of the French with the Norteños would mean the destruction of Spanish settlements in Texas. In a report filed in San Antonio, Parrilla especially emphasized the importance of maintaining the military garrison at San Sabá.[8]

Parrilla also recognized that the successful attack on the San Sabá mission in 1758 had been a sobering experience for the Lipan Apaches. Their northern enemies had destroyed the mission, demonstrating that the Spanish were not as powerful allies as the Lipans had hoped. From their perspective, Spain's insistence that her real enemy was France, not the northern nations, meant that the Apaches must consider other ways to use the Spanish to their advantage. The Lipans were under pressure from many intruders on the land, including the Spanish; and since their alliance with the Spaniards was less than satisfactory, the Indians had to reassess the situation and react accordingly.[9] Ultimately, their strategy would be to request new missions on the upper Nueces River and to use the Spanish as pawns in a desperate game of survival.

Parrilla forwarded his assessment of the situation in Texas to the viceroy in late 1759 and asked permission to come to Mexico City to lend further weight to his report. Ordered to the capital, he learned upon his arrival in the summer of 1760 that Viceroy Marqués de Cruillas had removed him as commander at San Sabá and appointed him to the governorship of Coahuila. A conscientious, competent captain would be replaced at San Sabá by a scoundrel, Felipe de Rábago y Terán, the former infamous commander at Presidio San Xavier![10] After Parrilla learned of his reassignment, the viceroy asked him for a detailed assessment of the situation on the northern frontier. In particular, Cruillas sought information on three points: to what extent were the northern tribes being influenced by the French; were those same tribes also being aided by the English; and what was the status of Spanish outposts on the San Saba and San Antonio rivers?[11]

Parrilla's reply to these queries was an honest appraisal of the situation as he saw it. He believed he had seen considerable evidence of French influence among the Wichitas. Not only were those Indians armed with muskets and lances of French origin but also their employment of stockades, moats, and defensive strategies certainly indicated European contacts. On the second point, Parrilla could only repeat rumors of English successes in the French and Indian War. He had also heard that the English were distributing firearms among the Wichitas. On the final point, Parrilla could again call on personal experience. He knew that peace overtures from some of the northern tribes had been communicated through Father José de Calahorra at Nacogdoches. Those Norteños had promised to be friendly if missions were founded among them and to respect all Apaches who were congregated in other missions, but Parrilla doubted the sincerity of the offers. He counseled that it was in the best interests of the Spaniards to maintain peaceful relations with the Lipans and to missionize them. Thus, Parrilla advocated a continuation of Indian policy that had been in place since the late 1750s. He was particularly insistent that troop strength at San Sabá be augmented by stationing forty men near the Los Almagres mine on the Llano River. The increased presence of Spanish military forces would offer the Apaches greater protection and encourage them to accept mission life. San Sabá, like La Bahía, would serve to secure Texas against foreign penetrations, spread the faith, and protect Spanish lives.[12]

To have enacted Parrilla's suggestions would have required a considerable increase in royal expenditures, which the viceroy was not prepared to authorize. The overall situation in Texas would remain much the same until the implementation of the radical proposals of the Marqués de Rubí in the mid-1770s. Meanwhile, the new commander at San Sabá would be far less capable than Parrilla, and he would make many mistakes.

The appointment of Felipe de Rábago y Terán understandably touched off a storm of protest among the Franciscan clergy. When Francisco Xavier Ortiz, guardian of the college of Querétaro, learned of Rábago's exoneration in the deaths of Father José Ganzábal and Juan José Ceballos and his impending command at San Sabá, he could scarcely contain his outrage. There was, of course, no hope of reversing Rábago's acquittal, but Father Ortiz in a letter penned to the viceroy pleaded that Rábago not again be sent to Texas because of his "bad conduct in the time he served as commandant of San Xavier." And the guardian implored the viceroy to select another leader "known to have zeal in the salvation of souls" among the Apache nations. Added to the chorus of complaints were those of Father Mariano Dolores, who traveled to Mexico City to oppose the appointment, and Colonel Parrilla, who believed Rábago to be unworthy of command. It was all to no avail, for the Marqués de Cruillas remained unswayed and ordered Rábago to the San Saba River.[13]

For those who believe that leopards don't change their spots, Rábago's conduct over the next decade is only partially reassuring. He at least gave the appearance of trying to conduct himself more responsibly. En route to Presidio San Luis de las Amarillas, Rábago blazed a new trail from the Río Grande to the San Saba, thereby avoiding contact with his detractors at San Antonio, and on October 31, 1760, he assumed com-

mand of his new post. The new commander's report of conditions at
the presidio, where the soldiers lacked food, clothing, munitions, and
supplies, was uncharacteristically generous. Rábago placed none of the
blame for those circumstances on the man he had replaced. Instead, he
attributed the sorry state of affairs to the quality of soldiers who served
in frontier posts and to the constant vigil demanded by the threat of
Comanche attacks, for the latter had regularly impeded the acquisition
of supplies.[14]

Over the next several months, Rábago was a whirlwind of activity,
although some of his policies violated specific instructions from the viceroy. The new commander sent expeditions to the west of present Menard
as far as the Pecos River, and he collected information on the various
Apache nations. Like Parrilla, Rábago recognized the importance of his
post and that it must be maintained at all cost. To do otherwise, he insisted, would imperil Spanish settlements in New Mexico, Nueva Vizcaya, Coahuila, and Texas.[15]

Rábago dispatched expeditions, which traversed portions of Texas not
visited by Spaniards since the expedition of Juan Domínguez de Mendoza
in the 1680s, that were intended to explore the plains region between
Texas and New Mexico. Those efforts proved conclusively that the distance between the two provinces was much greater than was generally
believed and that the area was filled with hostile Indians. Cruillas had
charged Rábago with finding a trail to New Mexico, but he did not pursue that goal further because of discouraging information gleaned from
the reconnoitering expeditions.[16]

While exploration of the plains was in progress, Rábago began the
physical improvement of Presidio San Luis. The wooden walls of the
stockade were replaced with quarried stone; a moat was dug; and log
cabins for the soldiers were supplanted with rooms incorporated into the
stone walls. He thought the completed structure resembled a castle, and
he gave it a new name—Real Presidio de San Sabá. Without doubt, it
was the most impressive military garrison in Texas, and thanks to Rábago's efforts it soon contained a full complement of well-armed and well-
mounted men.[17]

Remarkably, given his conduct at San Gabriel, Rábago was enthusiastic about missionizing the Lipans. Even his critics were puzzled by his
religious fervor. Being charitable, Father Agustín Morfi speculated that
Rábago's motives were perhaps an attempt "to eradicate the perverse
memory of his conduct, or . . . because he wished to make amends to
religion for the damages he had occasioned as a result of his previous

scandals."[18] Whatever his intent, Rábago's plan to spread the faith among the Apaches was ultimately his undoing.

The viceroy had charged Rábago with missionizing the Lipans at or near San Sabá. In accord with his instructions, Don Felipe inspected the charred ruins of the former mission but ruled out the possibility of re-building at that site. At the same time, important Apache chiefs were regular visitors to the presidio. They convinced Rábago, who was apparently skilled in his relationships with the Lipans, of their willingness to congregate if a suitable mission were founded for them, but they also insisted that San Sabá was not an acceptable location. Rábago, taking liberty with his instructions, permitted the chiefs to choose their preferred location, which was along the upper Nueces River. The site, about half way between San Sabá and San Juan Bautista, was located at the northern edge of present Camp Wood in Real County.[19]

Recognizing the ill will of the padres at San Antonio, Rábago appealed directly to Father Diego Jiménez at San Juan Bautista, asking him to supervise the new mission that was founded for the Lipan Apaches in January 1762. The padre accepted. Rábago assigned a guard of twenty men to protect the religious outpost, named San Lorenzo de la Santa Cruz. Later, at the request of another chief, a second mission, Nuestra Señora de la Candelaria del Cañón, was set up ten miles below San Lorenzo, and the presidial commander assigned an additional ten men to it (see Figure 20). Both missions were established without the approval of the viceroy.[20]

The Marqués de Cruillas had been especially interested in securing the frontier to the northwest of San Sabá, thereby protecting both Texas and New Mexico from French incursions. In violating his specific instructions, Rábago had virtually ensured that both Presidio San Luis and the new missions at El Cañón were doomed. The presidio was weakened by the permanent detachment of thirty men to the upper Nueces, and it was further sapped by having to share its provisions with the new missions. Worse, just as they had done at San Sabá, the Apaches directed the wrath of the northern tribes toward Spaniards at Real Presidio de San Sabá and the El Cañón missions.[21]

In association with their buffalo hunts, the Apaches would raid Comanche villages and intentionally leave behind articles of European clothing and other evidence of their contact with the Spaniards. Conversely, the Lipans would acquire the physical accoutrements of their enemies in these same raids and leave them during forays perpetrated against Spanish settlements. These actions caused the Comanches and their allies to blame the Spanish for being in league with the Apaches, while the Spanish, at least initially, implicated the Comanches for depredations that were in fact carried out by the Apaches. But such perfidy was soon detected, and it does much to explain the evolution of Spanish Indian policy that was later aimed at exterminating the Lipans.[22]

For the moment, however, Rábago struggled to befriend the Lipans and ward off the Norteños. In five years he spent more than twelve thousand pesos on provisions, clothing, and livestock for the presidio and the two missions. Because of Indian attacks and intercepted supply trains, many of these items did not reach their destinations. Even the stone walls of the presidio came under siege for periods as long as two months, and the "continuous state of warfare went on for years."[23] Rábago's pleas for assistance from Mexico City fell on deaf ears, especially after the Peace of Paris when he could no longer play on fears of the French. Without official support, the missions struggled on, but they and the presidio were doomed. When Rubí arrived for his tour of inspection in August 1767, these outposts had been reduced to a beggarly existence.

Rubí was particularly critical of the presidio at San Sabá. Its commander, although still a young man at forty-five, was broken in health, his body covered with sores. The location of the garrison, in Rubí's opinion, had been poorly chosen to defend against Indian attacks, and the moat was worthless. He likened the effectiveness of the presidio to that of a ship "anchored in mid-Atlantic . . . [to prevent] foreign trade with America."[24]

Paradoxically, after pointing out that the presidio at San Sabá served no useful purpose whatsoever, Rubí forecast the dire consequences of its closure on San Antonio. He predicted that the northern nations would sweep unimpeded on the missions, presidio, and *villa* there. Since the presidio at Béxar had only twenty-nine men, with fifteen of those assigned to the missions, the settlement would be unable to withstand attacks by large numbers of Norteños. At the same time, Rubí warned that the Lipans, displeased by their tenuous situation, would likewise direct assaults on the San Antonio settlements and endanger their continuation. To avoid this potential catastrophe, Rubí recommended that troop strength at Béxar be increased to fifty-one.[25]

Following the Rubí visitation, Indian attacks on San Sabá began anew. While the Indians were never able to force entry into the presidio, they intercepted supplies and destroyed spring crops in 1768. The resulting deficiency in the diet of the soldiers and their families probably contributed to an outbreak of scurvy and a growing mutinous attitude toward Rábago. In June of the same year, Rábago relocated the garrison to the site of mission San Lorenzo. When the viceroy learned of the unauthorized move, he ordered Rábago back to San Sabá, but the commander refused to comply and resigned his post. Rábago was replaced by Lieutenant Manuel Antonio de Oca y Alemán. Although ordered to reoccupy San Sabá, Oca remained there only briefly and then moved the presidio a second time to the upper Nueces. The site near Menard was abandoned in 1770 and never again occupied by the Spanish. In 1771 the military and mission outposts at El Cañón were also withdrawn. The remaining troops on the upper Nueces were assigned to San Antonio and a new presidio, San Fernando de Austria, south of the Río Grande.[26]

Rubí, after providing his damning assessment of the missions at El Cañón and the presidio at San Sabá, had meanwhile in the late summer of 1767 continued his inspection tour of other military garrisons in Texas. The diary kept by Nicolás de Lafora does much to illuminate the status of those military establishments. The inspector found San Antonio to be in pleasant contrast to the sorry conditions he had just observed. Indeed, San Antonio with its presidio, *villa,* and five "rich" missions flourished beyond anything he would see elsewhere in Texas. Rubí found the presidio at Béxar to be well maintained, although undermanned at twenty-two men, since the garrison regularly stationed three guards at each of the five Franciscan missions.[27]

From San Antonio, Rubí traveled to Los Adaes, the capital of Texas, and began his inspection on September 14. At Presidio Nuestra Señora del Pilar, he found abominable conditions. The garrison contained sixty-one men, but there were only twenty-five horses fit for service and two functional muskets. None of the soldiers possessed uniforms: all were dressed in rags, many without hats, shirts, or shoes. In the words of Alférez Pedro de Sierra, a witness testifying before Rubí, "This company lacks arms, horses, coats, and in a word everything necessary to carry out its obligations." The wretched circumstances of the troop was in large measure the fault of former governor Angel de Martos, who was "absolutely arbitrary" in fixing the price of goods supplied to his command, often demanding a 1,000 percent profit. Martos also had kept a detachment of soldiers at his ranch, where he worked them as cowhands. When Rubí arrived in East Texas, Hugo O'Conor as ad interim governor had already dispatched Martos to Mexico City to face charges of contraband trade and fiscal mismanagement. Despite the improvement in governors, Rubí saw no reason to maintain the capital and presidio at Los Adaes or the moribund East Texas missions.[28]

Two more presidios, El Orcoquisac and La Bahía, awaited the critical eye of the inspector. The former and its accompanying mission, Nuestra

Señora de la Luz, had been founded in the late 1750s to thwart the activities of French traders among the local Indians, but neither was viable. In 1764, three years before the arrival of Rubí, the presidio had been the scene of a sordid incident involving its commander, Captain Rafael Martínez Pacheco, and Governor Angel de Martos. Martos, angered that Martínez Pacheco was a direct appointee of the viceroy, accused the commander of so badly abusing personnel under his authority that nearly all of them felt compelled to desert. Forcing the issue, the governor decided to replace Martínez Pacheco. He sent Lieutenant Marcos Ruiz to occupy the garrison, but the commander and two of his servants barricaded themselves within and refused to surrender. In defiance of Ruiz and his command, the presidial captain fired a cannon, killing a corporal, and in the ensuing firefight wounded two of Ruiz's soldiers. Ruiz finally drove Martínez Pacheco from the garrison by burning it to the ground! Needless to say, Rubí was not impressed with the charred ruins of the presidio or with the neighboring mission that contained not a single Indian.[29]

By contrast with El Orcoquisac, Rubí found more encouraging conditions at the presidio at La Bahía, even though the soldiers and civilian settlers there suffered from malaria, and the two nearby missions were hardly flourishing. But 93 Indians lived at mission Espíritu Santo, and another 101 resided at Nuestra Señora del Rosario. Favorably impressed, the inspector decided to make La Bahía the eastern terminus in a proposed line of presidios that would extend from Sonora to the Gulf of Mexico.[30]

Rubí completed his responsibilities in Texas in November 1767 and crossed the Río Grande at Laredo. The town, founded in 1755 by a lieutenant of José de Escandón, contained some sixty huts on both banks of the river. From Laredo, Rubí proceeded to San Juan Bautista, the last presidio on his tour of inspection. The original gateway to Texas had passed its heyday, but its garrison of thirty-three men was still active in pursuing and punishing marauding bands of Lipan and Mescalero Apaches. Far from recommending the closure of the presidio, Rubí envisioned an increased role for it in frontier defense.[31]

Upon the completion of his inspection, Rubí's report to the crown was devastatingly blunt. He saw that portion of the Spanish empire stretching from the Gulf of California to the Gulf of Mexico as mostly a fraudulent operation. In the words of Elizabeth A. H. John, Rubí had found that "with rare exceptions, the northern frontier presidios were military mockeries: crumbling structures, incompetently and corruptly managed; garrisons of untrained soldiers short of basic equipment, skills, and morale; each outpost so entangled in the mechanics of its own survival as to be nearly useless against the swift-moving *indios bárbaros*." Similarly, many of the frontier missions were also not viable. Why, Rubí asked, should they continue to exist at crown expense when after years of operation they contained not a single Indian convert? Furthermore, because the military garrisons were so poorly managed and the commanders so abusive in their practices, these outposts did not serve their intended purpose. As a case in point, the destruction of mission San Sabá within three miles of a fully armed and manned garrison had demonstrated the ineffectiveness of the presidial system as it was then structured.[32]

The deplorable conditions observed firsthand by Rubí and the changed international scene occasioned by the cession of Louisiana prompted him to recommend the reorganization of presidial defenses below a "real" rather than "imaginary" frontier. Stationed along the new defensive cordon, which would stretch from the Gulf of California to the mouth of the Guadalupe River in Texas, would be fifteen presidios, each spaced approximately one hundred miles apart. Although Santa Fe and San Antonio lay to the north of this line, Rubí recognized that it would be impossible to abandon them. Both entailed too many responsibilities to people, their property, and converted Indians.[33]

Rubí also recommended that only two presidios, those at San Antonio and La Bahía, be maintained in Texas and that East Texas be totally abandoned. The latter's population and settlements should be moved to San Antonio, with Béxar designated as the new capital. Finally, he concluded that the Apaches had long been guilty of perfidy and duplicity. As allies of the Spaniards, they had requested the founding of missions in their lands but refused to enter them once they were established. In Rubí's view the trouble with the northern Indian nations stemmed from Spanish efforts to befriend and missionize their mortal enemies, the Apaches. Accordingly, Rubí recommended a war of extermination against the latter. Such a conflict would break the power of the Apaches, while earning the friendship of the Norteños. However, as events would demonstrate, Rubí's recommendations were overly simplistic.[34]

Rubí's unvarnished report on frontier conditions did not prompt quick results, for the Spanish bureaucracy continued to move with glacial slowness. Hesitancy on the part of Charles III to assume immediate control of Louisiana is perhaps a case in point, although the situation there did dictate caution. With customary lack of dispatch, Spain sent Antonio de Ulloa, the first Spanish governor of Louisiana, to take formal possession of the new colony in January 1767. However, with only 90 soldiers under his command, Ulloa could not establish control over the rebellious French citizenry, who in October 1768 forced him to withdraw. Not until the summer of 1769 with the arrival of Alejandro O'Reilly and 2,056 Spanish soldiers was Spain able to seize effective control of Louisiana.[35]

The new province with its French population and French traditions presented problems unlike those of the older Spanish realms. To further complicate matters, the king decided not to incorporate the administration of this vast territory into the already overburdened government of New Spain. Instead, Louisiana was assigned to the captaincy general of Cuba. While this political arrangement made sense, it would nevertheless create serious problems in matters such as trade and Indian policy that impinged on both Texas and Louisiana.[36]

Even though Ulloa had experienced failure in Spain's initial efforts to govern Louisiana, he did lay the foundations for a dramatic change in his country's Indian policy. He quickly observed the close bonds of French and Indians in those areas traditionally contested by France and Spain, and he wisely chose French agents to continue those ties for Spain. For example, in the Natchitoches trade center he employed the talents of Louis Juchereau, son of the late St. Denis. More important, Ulloa believed that the mission-presidio approach to controlling and converting frontier Indians, which Spain had employed since the Chichimeca wars of the sixteenth century, would have to be scrapped, and he ignored long-established but seldom-enforced legal strictures on trade between Louisiana and the East Texas settlements.[37]

Ulloa's sensible policies on trade had been opposed by Hugo O'Conor when he served at Los Adaes in 1767 as ad interim governor. O'Conor was a stickler for obedience to the law, as reflected by his actions in dispatching Angel de Martos to Mexico City to face charges of contraband trade. Worse, O'Conor banned all French traders from the East Texas settlements and Indian villages. The Indians were especially outraged, but peace was maintained largely through the conciliatory efforts of the younger St. Denis. This tense situation in East Texas eased somewhat when the inflexible O'Conor left to take up residence in San Antonio, for his leadership was needed there to help defend the town against increased Indian attacks in the summer of 1768. With O'Conor's departure for Béxar and Spain's effective control of Louisiana coming in the following year, Spanish Indian policy as it evolved in East Texas became a mirror image of earlier French practices in Louisiana.[38]

French policy had depended on the employment of traders and annual gifts in the name of the king. Once Louisiana became a Spanish possession, a large number of French skilled in Indian relations automatically became de facto Spanish subjects. As Herbert E. Bolton remarked, "To continue the French system was, therefore, but to follow the line of least resistance." That Spain was willing to alter the mission-presidio approach also reflects the willingness of Charles III to experiment with "any kind of reform which promised success, no matter how radical and regardless of tradition."[39]

On the borders of Texas and Louisiana and along the Red River, Spain began the employment of licensed traders who had consistently been on good terms with the Indians. Many of these were private businessmen who also served as government agents. They were instructed to inform the natives that Spaniards and Frenchmen were now brothers who honored the same king, and they were enjoined to expel all unlicensed traders and vagabonds. The agents were likewise commanded to sell goods, excluding alcohol, at fixed and reasonable prices and to try to influence the natives toward the acceptance of a settled, Christian life. Although not always enforced, a significant departure from French policy specified that no individual could monopolize trade with any Indian tribe.[40]

In reality the new thrust in Indian policy was a part of Spain's overall approach to the Louisiana territory. After 1763 the Mississippi River became the main line of defense, with Indian tribes to the west of the river becoming the sole responsibility of the Spanish monarch. In particular, Spain sought to make sure that those Indians did not become allies of the English. Spain also tried to avoid the enmity that certain tribes, such as the Osages, had traditionally felt for the French while simultaneously working to maintain good relations with those nations that had been amicable to the French, such as the Comanches, Tonkawas, and Wichitas. Since the latter groups were entering Texas in increasing numbers, they "like the Apache, must be expelled, exterminated, or brought to Spanish allegiance."[41] Winning the adherence of the Norteños was especially desirable, since they were the mortal enemies of the Lipans.

To serve as diplomat to the northern tribes, Spain employed the talents of Athanase de Mézières, one of the most able men to serve the Spanish empire. De Mézières was a former son-in-law of the elder St. Denis, and his role in the second half of the eighteenth century was comparable to that of St. Denis's in the first half. In late 1769 De Mézières became lieutenant governor of Natchitoches. Fluent in perhaps half a dozen Indian languages, this Paris-born gentleman began his services for Spain with an expedition to the Red River in the fall of 1770. In the following year, he successfully negotiated treaties with the Kichais, Tawakonis, and Taovayas, and by their proxy, with the Tonkawas.[42]

While De Mézières worked at gaining the allegiance of the northern tribes, a new governor had assumed office in Texas. Appointed in Spain by the king, Juan María, Barón de Ripperdá reached Mexico in 1769 and from there proceeded to San Antonio, where he arrived on February 4, 1770. Ripperdá was the first governor to establish his headquarters at Béxar, and he was exceptionally loyal to his monarch. Throughout his long tenure in office (1770–1778), he was especially committed to the welfare of the province.[43]

Like O'Conor before him, the new governor's primary concern was to defend San Antonio against the increased incidence of Indian attacks. Even at this late date—more than fifty years after the permanent settlement of San Antonio—Ripperdá feared that Villa San Fernando would soon be abandoned. In a letter to the viceroy, he expressed those concerns: "I wish to make manifest to your excellency the sad state in which this province, that exists only in name, presents itself." He further reported that the citizenry near Béxar had lost so many cattle, horses, and mules to Indians that they had abandoned their haciendas and cattle ranches. Circumstances were so bad that residents could not travel beyond the confines of San Antonio without risk to their lives. Fortunately, Ripperdá was able to bolster the military guard with the arrival of twenty-two soldiers from the defunct presidio at El Cañón. The original plan had been to reassign an equal number of men from Presidio Béxar to Coahuila, but on appeal of the citizenry, Ripperdá agreed to keep the extra troops at San Antonio.[44] The presidial guard was further augmented with the arrival in February 1771 of a few soldiers from the burned and deserted presidio at El Orcoquisac.

In April of the same year, Barón de Ripperdá opened a new military outpost known as Arroyo or Fuerte de Santa Cruz de Cíbolo. This station, located some forty miles southeast of San Antonio on the road to La Bahía, was staffed with as many as twenty men to protect farmers and ranchers in the area from Indian depredations.[45] However, the various energetic measures adopted by Ripperdá in the first months of his governorship paled in significance to impending changes mandated in Spain by Charles III.

On September 10, 1772, a royal order commonly known as the "New Regulations for Presidios" (see Figure 21) called for the abandonment of all missions and presidios in Texas except those at San Antonio and La Bahía; the strengthening of San Antonio by designating it the capital of the province and by moving to it the soldiers and settlers in East Texas; and the inauguration of a new Indian policy aimed at establishing good relations with the northern nations at the expense of the unfortunate Apaches, who were to be exterminated. In short, nearly all of the recommendations of the Marqués de Rubí, made some five years earlier, now carried the weight of royal edict. To ensure strict compliance with

FIGURE 21

Title page of New Regulations of 1771–1772. First printed in Mexico, the New Regulations, which largely implemented recommendations of the Marqués de Rubí, called for the reorganization of frontier defenses from the Gulf of California to Texas. (With the permission of the Archivo General de Indias, Seville, Spain; Guadalajara 274.)

the king's orders, on January 20, 1773, Hugh O'Conor, former governor ad interim of Texas, received promotion to the rank of lieutenant colonel and became commandant inspector of presidios on the entire northern frontier.[46]

Governor Ripperdá received the "New Regulations" at San Antonio on May 18, 1773. On orders of Commandant O'Conor, he set out for East Texas to implement the removal of its entire population and to effect the transfer of the capital from Los Adaes to San Antonio. The forced evacuation was distasteful to Ripperdá and painful to the settlers. In the six years that had passed since the Rubí inspection, the population had actually increased from perhaps two hundred to five hundred. The new residents were a mixture of Spanish, French, Indians, and perhaps a few blacks who had migrated to Texas from Natchitoches. An edict from a distant king in a distant land required all of them to forsake homes, ranches, and tilled fields.[47]

The most prominent citizen in the East Texas settlements was Gil Antonio Ybarbo. Ybarbo, a trader and rancher who lived near the Ais mission, would soon become the chief spokesman for the repatriated Texans. For the moment, however, Ripperdá ordered all settlers to be prepared for the march to San Antonio within five days. Actual responsibility for the evacuation was placed in the hands of Lieutenant José González, whereupon the governor returned to Béxar to lay plans for the arrival of the East Texas contingent. González granted the settlers a few days' extension to collect their movable assets, after which they began the three-month march to the new capital. It appears that a few dozen settlers avoided the forced abandonment of their homes by fleeing to the woods, but most East Texans accepted the king's mandate.

As the González party left the region, the presidio and mission at Los Adaes, as well as the missions at Los Ais and Nacogdoches, ceased to exist. Since 1689 Spain had followed an on-again, off-again commitment to East Texas. Spanish actions had been largely reflexive, dictated by changing perceptions of French designs on the region. The elimination of French control in Louisiana in combination with the then urgent need to strengthen San Antonio once again brought matters full circle.

Imperial policy, formulated with little regard for the lives of those it affected, had dictated the abandonment of East Texas. The former settlers turned refugees suffered horribly on the march to San Antonio. It was an ordeal that claimed many lives, including that of Lieutenant González. Those who survived the trek were so footsore and broken in health that thirty of them died in San Antonio within ninety days.[48] Unfortunately, almost all of the displaced East Texans found San Antonio not to their liking. They complained about the unavailability of suitable lands, formally voicing their unhappiness to the governor in a petition signed by seventy-five men. The petitioners wanted nothing less than permission to return to their homes. Ripperdá was again sympathetic, but his hands were tied by a royal decree. He did agree to support an appeal to the viceroy, asking for a reversal of crown policy. Two spokesmen, Ybarbo and Gil Flores, another prominent East Texan, carried the request to Mexico City. There Viceroy Bucareli, over the objections of O'Conor, reacted favorably to the petition. The viceroy was apparently swayed by the belief that the reoccupation of East Texas would have a favorable influence on the Indians of the region. He nevertheless awarded the two petitioners less than they had asked for. Ybarbo, Flores, and the other expatriates could return to East Texas and settle "in a suitable place," but the site could not be located closer than one hundred leagues to Natchitoches.[49]

Those who returned to their homeland were mostly former residents from the Adaes region. In 1774 under the leadership of Ybarbo, the Adaesaños began construction of a town on the right bank of the Trinity River at a crossing called Paso Tomás. The new settlement bore a hybrid name, Nuestra Señora del Pilar de Bucareli, evoking memories of Los Adaes while honoring the viceroy. However, as the settlement grew, it became such a center of contraband trade with Indians and forbidden commerce with Louisiana that it likely would have been suppressed by Bucareli or O'Conor, but in early 1777 Texas passed under the control of a new administrative unit known as the Interior Provinces. That political reorganization apparently gave the town of Bucareli an extended period of grace.[50]

As it turned out, the fate of the town was not determined by Bucareli or O'Conor but by a series of Comanche raids in 1778 and by rising floodwaters in early 1779. Without authorization the settlers pulled stakes and moved to the site of the former mission at Nacogdoches. From 1779 onward the town of Nacogdoches was permanently settled. This growing and viable community immediately supplanted the historic role of Los Adaes, even though the townspeople were forced to defend themselves until the arrival of Spanish troops in 1795. In future years when Nacogdoches would serve as a counterweight against Anglo-Americans, its influence would rival even the importance of Béxar.[51]

San Antonio, even before its designation as the capital of Texas, had experienced remarkable growth and had been the scene of important social changes. At the end of the 1740s, the estimated total population for Béxar was between 437 and 560 persons. However, expansion in the late

1740s and the decade of the 1750s had siphoned off soldiers as well as their families to man the mission and military outposts at San Gabriel, San Sabá, and El Orcoquisac. Concern for the security of San Antonio and economic losses occasioned by the diminished market for local produce had nonetheless caused the civilian and military leaders of Béxar to exaggerate their losses. In 1762 the governor's count revealed that despite a few setbacks the total population of Béxar had actually increased to between 514 and 661 individuals.[52]

It may be assumed that San Antonio continued to grow slowly throughout the 1760s, but by the late years of that decade and the early 1770s, crown policies contributed to a virtual population boom. For example, the town council in 1770 estimated the total population at 860 men, women, and children. The increase from 1762 may be explained in part by the failure of the missions for the Apaches at El Cañón, the closure of the presidio there, and the evacuation of El Orcoquisac. After 1770 the transfer of the civilian population from East Texas to San Antonio assuredly produced a surge in Béxar's growth. True, the majority of the Adaesaños returned to East Texas in 1774, but sixty-three of them remained behind and became permanent residents of Béxar, and the complement of men at the presidio remained at eighty. More important, the designation of San Antonio as the new capital in 1773 meant that the Spanish government would henceforth concentrate its resources on Béxar.[53]

The first formalized census report of Texas, made in 1777 in response to a royal order of the previous year, reflected the continued expansion of San Antonio's population. It recorded a total of 1,351 individuals, and in 1780 the figure had increased to 1,463. Assuming the figure of 860 for 1770 is correct, the population of Béxar had increased 70 percent over the decade.[54] By 1782 the racial composition of San Antonio reflected substantial changes brought about over some three generations. In general the early population of Béxar had consisted of settlers from other frontier regions of New Spain, a changing number of mission Indians, and a small group of Canary Islanders. The social tensions of the 1730s and 1740s, caused primarily by the Isleños, had eased considerably over the decades. Ethnic categorization was particularly in flux in Texas, although the situation there differed only in degree from societal changes transpiring in the heartland of New Spain.

Initially, race had been the sole criterion for social categories in colonial Mexico. The elite were the European-born Spaniards, the slaves were blacks, and the peasants were Indians. For the most part, these three groups lived apart. However, by the middle of the eighteenth century, when racial mixture and residential mingling had been in progress for more than two hundred years, the socioeconomic dimension of race "was no longer as straightforward as it had been before." At that juncture, five basic terms were used to designate race: Spanish, black, Indian, mestizo, and mulatto. And race categorization was increasingly determined by social perceptions as well as biological origins. As Patricia Seed has noted, an individual's social race "was related to the combination of physical appearance, economic status, occupation, and family connections, in other words, to his overall socioeconomic positions as well as to physical features."[55]

Throughout New Spain, and especially on the frontier that included Texas, more and more people regularly "passed" from darker- to lighter-skinned categories, and "toward the middle of the colonial period, it became increasingly difficult to determine racial mixture on the northern frontier simply because it had become a matter of status that could be altered."[56] Nevertheless, it should not be assumed that there was total racial harmony in Béxar. Certain racial designations such as "mulatto" were used pejoratively, and as Jesús F. de la Teja has noted, evidence suggests that punishments handed down to lawbreakers were more severe for mixed-race persons.

Restructuring of the presidial system, which had brought large numbers of soldiers and civilians to swell the population of San Antonio, was only a part of the consequences of wide-sweeping administrative changes ordered by Charles III. As mentioned earlier, José de Gálvez, appointed in the same year as Rubí (1765), remained in New Spain for six years. Part of his charge was to formulate an overall plan for reorganizing the defenses of New Spain's northern provinces. In particular, Gálvez was concerned about the immense distances between Mexico City and the northern provinces and the threat to those realms posed by Russian and English ambitions.[57]

After his return to Spain, Gálvez assumed the influential post of minister of the Indies. In that capacity he was able to persuade the Council of the Indies to enact a major reorganization of the northern frontier provinces. On May 16, 1776, the council created the Provincias Internas, a huge new administrative unit that included Texas, Coahuila, Nueva Vizcaya, New Mexico, Sinaloa, Sonora, and the two Californias. The Interior Provinces, so named because one had to go inland from New Spain to reach them, were initially detached from the jurisdiction of the viceroy of New Spain and brought under the control of a commandant general. In later years the Provincias Internas would undergo substantial political reorganization, but for the moment its creation spelled important changes for Texas.[58]

On August 22, 1776, Charles III appointed Teodoro de Croix, a man already experienced in New Spain, as commandant general of the Provincias Internas. Croix had accompanied his uncle, Viceroy Marqués de Croix, to Mexico in 1766 and had served as governor of Acapulco and inspector of troops. In 1771–1772 the younger Croix returned to Spain with his uncle and remained there until his selection to head the Interior Provinces.[59]

Authorized to report directly to José de Gálvez or the king, Croix's powers made him virtually independent of Viceroy Bucareli. Croix arrived at Veracruz in early December 1776 and spent the next eight months studying documents and reports relating to the northern frontier. By then O'Conor had already relocated well over a dozen presidios in line with the recommendations of the Marqués de Rubí, and Viceroy Bucareli expressed the view that the inspector general's reorganization had greatly improved security on the frontier. Croix disagreed. The lack of accord between the two men was the beginning of consistently strained relations. Reports from the frontier clearly indicated to Croix that Indian attacks had actually increased after the realignment of the presidios. The commandant general believed the military outposts to have been situated too far apart, and he criticized the troops stationed in the garrisons for their lack of discipline and military skills. Recognizing that it was probably not possible to relocate the presidios again, Croix asked for an additional two thousand men from the viceroy and recommended the creation of a second line of defense formed by a string of fortified towns. This request was denied by Bucareli, who undoubtedly harbored ill feelings over the loss of half the territory under his jurisdiction and resented the suggestion that O'Conor, his principal adviser on Indian and military affairs in the north, was an incompetent.[60]

Croix, believing it impossible to work further with Bucareli, left Mexico City in late 1777 for a personal inspection of the northern frontier. Accompanying him as his personal chaplain was Father Juan Agustín Morfi, already an accomplished man of letters and a future historian of Texas. At Monclova and again at San Antonio in January 1778, Croix held councils of war. Persons appearing before the assemblies were unvarying in their recommendations: the Apaches were the scourge of the frontier, and they must be exterminated.[61]

Those testifying before Croix characterized the Apaches as having waged war on Spanish settlements in northern Mexico for more than forty years. These accusations were undoubtedly true, for the Apaches had been forced southward by their Indian enemies in Texas and by Spaniards as well. The councils heard bitter complaints that the fertile provinces of New Spain were being turned into "the most horrible deserts," and if unchecked, the Apaches would soon drive as far as the vicinity of Mexico City. Additional testimony before the councils condemned the various bands of Apaches, especially the Lipans. In summation the final verdict of the councils read: "The perfidy of the Lipanes is exposed, and the necessity to divide and confound that nation, whose wisdom, rapacity and industry are always dismal and indecorous to the progress of the arms of the king and the tranquility of these possessions." [62]

To support these assertions, Croix asked the local justices of Nueva Vizcaya to assess the damages and loss of life from Indian attacks between 1771 and 1776, roughly the period of O'Conor's administration. In the words of Alfred B. Thomas, "The totals were staggering: persons murdered, 1,674; persons captured, 154; haciendas and ranches abandoned, 116; livestock stolen, 68,256." [63] It is little wonder that persons speaking before the assemblies were determined to break the back of the Apache nations. That objective could best be realized by Spaniards forming an alliance with the Comanches and the northern tribes, and the key to such diplomacy lay in the hands of Athanase de Mézières, already familiar with the Norteños. De Mézières was under the command of Bernardo de Gálvez, the governor of Louisiana, but Gálvez agreed to release him and to assist his commission in Texas. [64]

De Mézières reached San Antonio in February 1778. In a letter to Croix, he expressed optimism that an alliance could be forged with the Norteños because of their hatred for the Apaches, and he proposed the use of Taovaya villages as rallying points for over one thousand Indian allies. Once the native forces were assembled, the Frenchman intended to lead them to the Colorado River, where they would be joined by three hundred Spanish troops drawn from Louisiana and the Interior Provinces. [65]

To effect the agreed-upon arrangements, De Mézières traveled extensively over the next year: to the town of Bucareli, to the vicinity of Waco to contact Tawakoni Indians, to the Red River villages of the Taovayas, and even to New Orleans. During his stay in New Orleans, the East Texans without authorization moved their town from the Trinity to the site of Nacogdoches. On his return trip to Texas, between the abandoned post of Los Adaes and Nacogdoches, De Mézières suffered a severe injury when thrown from his horse. After recovering his strength but not his health, he continued on to San Antonio, arriving there in September 1779.[66]

When he reached the capital, he learned of impending changes that would elevate him to the governorship of Texas. In May of the previous year, José Rubio, an assistant to Croix and commandant inspector of presidios for the Interior Provinces, had died suddenly. The commandant general intended to replace Rubio with Domingo Cabello, then governor of Texas, and to appoint De Mézières to that position. Croix praised De Mézières as a man who "has learned to win over the Nations of the North" and ironically commented that he was "very robust" for a man of nearly sixty years.[67] However, the proposed changes in administration did not come about. De Mézières remained gravely ill and asked to be spared the responsibilities of office. He died on November 2, 1779, having never recovered from his injuries, and the proposed general alliance with the Comanches and Norteños was never realized.[68]

Shortly before the death of De Mézières, Teodoro de Croix learned that Spain on June 21, 1779, had entered the war for American independence as an ally of France. The news meant that Spanish resources would henceforth be funneled into the defense of Florida and the Gulf Coast, not into the protection of the Interior Provinces. In any event, Croix's plans for a general offensive against the Apaches had by his own admission been seriously handicapped by the untimely death of De Mézières. Furthermore, other news from Texas was generally not good. Croix received intelligence that the Norteños were becoming increasingly unhappy over strictures on trade with Louisiana, that authorities in Texas were worried about a possible alliance between the northern tribes and coastal Karankawas, and that the Comanches had launched a series of devastating raids on Texas cattle ranches and farms. The latter Indians had even breached the corral at Presidio La Bahía and stolen 246 animals on the night of May 10, 1781. In the following month, a force of three hundred Comanches returned and attacked the presidio itself but were repulsed.[69]

The "good tidings" from Texas brought word that the Comanches had scored significant victories over the Lipans. That circumstance, coupled with the successful campaigns waged in Coahuila by Governor Juan de Ugalde, who had forged an alliance with the Mescaleros against their Apache brethren, had brought the Lipans to their knees. In 1780 a peace treaty formalized the temporary defeat of the very Indians who had been the object of Spanish mission programs since the days of Father Hidalgo.[70] But singular attention directed to the resolution of Indian affairs had undoubtedly retarded the development of the province.

Teodoro de Croix visited San Antonio in 1781, and his cryptic comments about Texas reflected his extreme displeasure with circumstances there: "A villa without order, two presidios, seven missions, and an errant population of scarcely 4,000 persons of both sexes and all ages that occupies an immense desert country, stretching from the abandoned presidio of Los Adaes to San Antonio, . . . does not deserve the name of the Province of Texas . . . nor the concern entailed in its preservation." Fortunately, Texas was not representative of the Interior Provinces as a whole.[71]

Hampered by the realities of Spain's international commitments, Croix was nonetheless able to accomplish a great deal. With limited resources, he developed mobile patrols, or "flying companies," which, along with local militia units, increased frontier security. In a line of seventeen presidios stretching from La Bahía and San Antonio to the Gulf of California, the two Texas garrisons, each with 96 men, formed the eastern anchor. By 1783 Croix had established presidial and militia units totaling 4,686 men.[72]

Throughout his tenure in office, which coincided exactly with the war for American independence, Croix recognized that the Spanish crown worried far more about Russians in California and the English east of the Mississippi River than it did about marauding Indians in the Interior Provinces. But the commander general knew the real enemy that endangered the lives of farmers, ranchers, and town dwellers from Texas to Sonora. In the final analysis, when faced "with a choice between imaginary foreigners and real, live Apaches, the practical-minded Croix naturally devoted his energies to the problems that stared him in the face." In his own words, he had sought "to open the door to a general peace, the preservation of which is the primary objective of my concerns, or a decisive war [against the Apaches] that would bring about the desired results."[73]

Thanks to international developments, the creation of the Provincias Internas, the wise and energetic policies of men such as Barón de Ripperdá and Teodoro de Croix, the development of a vigorous and integrated community in San Antonio, and the formation of a viable town at Nacogdoches, Texas had made considerable progress over the two decades that preceded the second Peace of Paris. However, that same span of years had essentially spelled the end of the mission system in Texas, a fact perhaps recognized early on by at least some of the Roman Catholic clergy.

The dramatically changed relationship of state and church in Texas prompted Carlos E. Castañeda to choose "The Passing of the Missions" as the subtitle for the fourth volume of *Our Catholic Heritage in Texas*. For the implementation of Rubí's drastic recommendations by the "New Regulations" of 1772 and the adoption of the French approach to Indian relations generally signaled the end of the Texas missions. The college of Querétaro, which administered four of the five missions in San Antonio and the two at San Juan Bautista, asked to be relieved of those responsibilities. This request by the Querétarans was justified on grounds that the college was short of qualified friars and overcommitted in its missionary enterprises. Because the neophytes at the six missions in Texas and Coahuila were not yet prepared for secularization, the Querétarans proposed that their Indian charges be assigned to the college of Zacatecas and the Franciscan Province of Guadalajara. The viceroy reacted favorably to the petition, and in early 1773 missions San Antonio de Valero, San Juan Capistrano, San Francisco de la Espada, and La Purísima Concepción de Acuña became the responsibility of the Zacatecan padres.[74]

Since the first days of Spain in America, state and church, sword and cross, had labored together, at least in theory. That cooperation had essentially ended by 1782. The future security of Spanish Texas would depend almost entirely on the sword, and the sword would prove inadequate.

Ironically, by entering the war of the American Revolution, Spain contributed to the destruction of British possessions south of Canada and east of the Mississippi River. In doing so, it helped bring aggressive citizens of the United States to the borders of Louisiana and Texas and consequently faced its greatest challenge on that frontier.

TEN

Anglo-American Concerns and the Decline of Missions, 1783–1803

THE SECOND TREATY OF PARIS (1783) FINALIZED THE BIRTH of a new American nation, a nation of expansion-minded citizens who would soon exert increasing pressures on Spain's North American holdings. Over the next two decades, which ended with the Louisiana Purchase, Spain faced an impending crisis of empire. Its expanded responsibilities included the defense of Florida, obtained from Great Britain at the conclusion of the war for American independence, and Louisiana, where it had exercised effective control for only fourteen years. Protecting the latter against Anglo-Americans would require significant reorganization and new policies. Unfortunately for Spain, Charles III died in 1788, and the dictum that great monarchs are seldom succeeded by equally great sons held true. One of Spain's best monarchs was followed by one of her worst: Charles IV (1788–1808). The immigration policies formulated by the new king and his chief minister, Manuel Godoy, for the defense of Louisiana proved ineffective, but they would nonetheless be repeated in Spanish and Mexican Texas.

As Anglo-Americans of questionable loyalty entered Louisiana, conservative officials in New Spain regarded Texas and New Mexico as critical areas of defense. To this end Spanish officials thought it important to address the Indian situation in those provinces and to secure the loyalties of the more powerful tribes, lest they fall under foreign influence. In its dealings with the Norteños and the Comanches, Spain continued to employ the recently adopted French approach. At the same time, the general absence of Indians in South and East Texas who were willing to accept life on Spanish terms essentially doomed missionary enterprises. Mounting secular influences in the late 1700s, which ended the missions at San Antonio, are also evidenced by the emergence of viable communities at Nacogdoches, La Bahía, and San Antonio and an economy dominated by ranching and farming. Finally, continuing concerns over Anglo-American activities convinced Spanish officials of the importance of establishing direct lines of communication between San Antonio and Santa Fe. These foreign and domestic developments that significantly shaped events in Texas on the eve of Mexico's struggle for independence are the subject of the following chapter.

IN LATE 1783 A FRENCH INDIAN AGENT, JUAN GASIOT, SENT A remarkably prescient warning to Felipe de Neve, the new commander general who had replaced Teodoro de Croix. Gasiot warned that the attainment of independence by Britain's North American colonies spelled grave new dangers for Spanish interests. He characterized citizens of the American Confederation as "active, industrious, and aggressive people" who had been freed from the burden of war against the founding country. Those same Anglo-Americans, Gasiot continued, "will constantly menace the dominion of Spain in America and it would be an unpardonable error not to take all necessary steps to check their territorial advance by strengthening the outposts of Spain, particularly in Texas, Coahuila, and New Mexico." Gasiot also predicted that Anglo-Americans would be tempted by trade with unsettled Indian tribes and that they would eventually establish forts among them.[1]

The French agent further cautioned that Anglo-Americans with their newly established freedom represented a grave new dimension in international relations. "Their republican government," he wrote, "has great influence over the individual. The voice of public interest binds them and moves them as one, and in this union of action their strength is found. Such a people may be exposed to suffer more internal disturbances than any other, but they are likewise capable of undertaking and accomplishing greater things than any other."[2]

Similar concerns had been voiced earlier by the Count of Aranda, Spanish ambassador to France during the American Revolution. Aranda, speaking of the new American nation, had written: "This federal republic is born a pigmy. [But] a day will come when it will be a giant, even a colossus. . . . Liberty of conscience, the facility for establishing a new population on immense land . . . will draw thither farmers and artisans from all the nations. In a few years we shall watch with grief the tyrannical existence of this same colossus."[3] Again, a Spanish official had demonstrated remarkable insight.

In the first year after the Treaty of Paris, an estimated fifty thousand American settlers crossed the Appalachian mountains, and by the fall of 1785 they needed an outlet for their crops of wheat and tobacco. Transporting bulky goods eastward across the mountains was impractical, if not impossible. Accordingly, the right to navigate the Mississippi River and to deposit goods at New Orleans, preparatory to their shipment by sea to the Atlantic Coast, became the foremost need of trans-Appalachian farmers.[4]

Extended negotiations between John Jay, secretary of foreign affairs for the Confederation, and Diego de Gardoqui, Spanish minister to the American states, produced nothing of lasting consequence. In 1785–1786 the two diplomats reached a preliminary agreement whereby Spain would practice "forbearance" regarding use of the Mississippi in exchange for a commercial treaty, but the proposed accord failed to win the necessary approval of nine states in the Confederation Congress.[5] Jay then stalled for time, hoping that a new American government in the making at Philadelphia in 1787 would create a stronger union and lead to more successful negotiations with Spain. As for Spain, continued control over navigation on the Great River and the right to deposit goods at New Orleans gave it a powerful bargaining chip in dealing with Anglo-American settlers of the trans-Appalachian region. To ensure that it maintained the upper hand, Spain also worked at establishing good relations with Indian nations to the east and west of the Mississippi.

Spain's first objective was to win the confidence and allegiance of the trans-Appalachian tribes. From Natchez and New Orleans, its agents enjoyed the rare advantage of speaking the truth. Spain did not covet the lands of the Indians; the Anglo-Americans did. Further, Spain openly urged the tribes to maintain themselves as independent buffers against the tide of American western expansion, and at the same time it accelerated efforts to ensure the loyalties of the most powerful Indian nations of Texas and New Mexico.

For the most part, those efforts represented a continuation of official policy, begun a few years earlier, aimed at exterminating the Apaches while winning the friendship and support of the Norteños and Comanches. In the last years of Teodoro de Croix's administration, the Lipans had been pressured into temporary submission by a combined force of Spaniards and Comanches, but they did not remain peaceful for long. Croix, faced with limited resources because of Spain's entry into the war for American independence, ordered that some six hundred Lipans be granted amnesty at San Antonio. The commandant general hoped to use improved relations with the Lipans as a barrier against increased Comanche attacks on Spanish settlements in Coahuila and Nuevo Santander. Thus, the policy of extermination was momentarily halted, and erstwhile Apache enemies would be used to the advantage of the Spaniards. However, the plan did not work as intended.[6]

By the late 1770s, relations with the Comanches in Texas had reached a low point. It was Comanches who attacked the new town of Bucareli and contributed to its demise in early 1779. But in late summer of that same year, Governor Juan Bautista de Anza of New Mexico in alliance with Ute Indians delivered a crushing blow to the western Comanches. Ironically, Anza's victory, while important to the security of New Mexico, forced the Comanches to redirect their activities toward the weaker province of Texas, and by late 1780 Governor Domingo Cabello reported that his jurisdiction was beset by their attacks.[7]

At the same time, the Lipans broke the peace. Through trade with coastal Karankawas, the Apaches began to arm themselves with weapons and ammunition by way of Louisiana. Cabello felt powerless to deal with either the perfidy of the Apaches or the boldness of the Comanches. As he reported to Croix, Comanches raiders had stolen so many horses and mules from the military garrison that he could not mount retaliatory campaigns. Croix could offer nothing but sympathy and advice. He recommended that both Indian groups be shown the benefits of peace by bestowing presents on them and by overlooking their depredations. This approach galled Cabello, who was especially unhappy with the Lipans. When they were not threatened by the Comanches, the Lipans raided Spanish settlements. Conversely, when imperiled by their mortal enemies, they rushed to the protection of the Spaniards.[8]

Peace by persuasion, while less than satisfactory to Cabello and the settlers in Texas, eventually worked, but it was initially a failure. In 1783 Comanche attacks increased with awful intensity, and they continued until 1785. As an example of the Indians' contempt for Spanish defenses, in December 1784 Comanches stole horses at San Antonio, not only from the corrals of civilians but also from the presidial compound. Cabello could do little, for Commandant Felipe de Neve again reminded him of the king's intent to treat the natives with clemency and to overlook their transgressions.[9]

Given the strictures under which he had to operate, Cabello's approach was entirely appropriate. In the summer of 1785, he sent emissaries among the Comanches, inviting them to a conference at Béxar. Three chieftains accepted, and a treaty was signed in October. Its salient provisions called upon Spaniards and Comanches to cease hostilities; the Comanches were to understand that the proviso for peace extended beyond Texas to all subjects of the crown; Spanish captives among the Indians were to be ransomed exclusively to Spaniards; foreigners would not be welcomed into Comanche villages; friends and enemies of both parties would remain friends and enemies; the Comanches could continue to make war on the Apaches and carry the conflict as far as Coahuila with permission from the governor of Texas; and annual presents would be distributed to the chiefs and principal tribe members.[10]

Despite the prospect of peaceful relations with the Comanches, Spanish officials believed a constant vigil was necessary. They must continue to operate trading posts among the natives, which would monitor Indian activities and serve as intelligence-gathering centers. Experience had demonstrated the untrustworthiness of the Indians, and crown agents feared that the treaty might be broken at any time. Those fears, however, proved unfounded. With few exceptions, the remarkable accord of 1785 lasted over the next thirty years and essentially marked the end of warfare with the Comanches for the remainder of Spanish rule in Texas. Like most enduring treaties, this one lasted because it worked to the mutual benefit of both parties. The Indians were particularly interested in receiving annual gifts that came to include knives, razors, glass beads, mirrors, tobacco, shoes, and articles of clothing. Gifts of apparel would become especially popular with the Comanche chiefs, who would soon be decked in brightly colored stockings, shifts, and frock coats. The chieftains were especially honored with gifts, such as medals, flags, and staffs of command, that reflected their positions. After a time, the confidence of the Spaniards was such that they even supplied the Indians with muskets, powder, and shot. For the Spanish, good relations with the Comanches meant increased security for Texas farmers, ranchers, and townspeople.[11]

The generally peaceful relations that prevailed with the Comanches, however, did not extend to the Apaches. After their defeat in Coahuila in 1780, the Lipans had been forced to move northward into the region bounded by Laredo, San Antonio, and Goliad. There, under the guise of friendship and amnesty granted by Croix, they continued their marauding activities. Near the end of 1781, the Mescaleros and Apaches proper reconciled their differences with the Lipans. This general accord posed serious problems for Texas and northern Mexico. In 1781 and 1782 Governor Juan de Ugalde of Coahuila carried out vigorous campaigns against the Apaches in the northwestern Coahuila and the lower Pecos region, but he was unable to stop their depredations. For example, in a single month (June 1784), the Apaches killed forty-six people and stole six hundred horses and mules.[12]

In 1785 Bernardo de Gálvez, who had distinguished himself as governor of Louisiana and captain general of Cuba, succeeded his father as viceroy of New Spain. While his tenure was brief (he died in 1786), Gálvez outlined a forceful policy against the Apache nations. The new viceroy viewed the Apaches as the worst menace in the entire Interior

Provinces, calling them "the enemies most to be feared because of their treachery, their warlike customs, their habit of stealing for a livelihood, and their knowledge of our strength."[13] Gálvez ordered increased vigilance and immediate reprisals on offending bands, rather than a formal war against all Apache nations. He also made it incumbent on settlers, when necessary, to assist soldiers in mounting punitive campaigns. If civilians did not offer their services voluntarily, they were to be conscripted by the governors of Texas and Coahuila. However, Gálvez stopped short of ordering the total extermination of the Apache nations. After they had been thoroughly chastised and forced to petition for peace, the Spanish were to grant them reasonable terms that, they hoped, would ensure the Apaches' good conduct.[14]

Although Gálvez did not live to see his policy implemented, it nonetheless brought important results. In pursuit of Mescalero and Lipan Apaches, Ugalde marched an expedition from Monclova to the site of the former San Sabá presidio, arriving there in late 1789. The governor's forces were soon joined by fifty-two civilian volunteers and eleven soldiers from San Antonio, all of whom were well armed and mounted. With these reinforcements and a sizable number of Comanche, Tawakoni, and Wichita allies, Ugalde in early January 1790 inflicted a stunning defeat on a huge band of Mescaleros and Lipans. The battle, fought at Soledad Creek to the west of San Antonio, effectively broke the back of Apache resistance in Texas. By 1790 relations between Spaniards and Lipans were generally stabilized, although the latter would occasionally revert to their marauding ways.[15]

Overall, the Spanish enjoyed considerable success in their policies toward the Comanches and Apaches, but that would not be the case in their efforts to pacify the Karankawas and other coastal tribes. By the late 1780s, mission La Bahía sheltered only a few neophytes, and the nearby mission at Rosario had been closed in 1781 as a result of Indians fleeing the site. But in 1789 Franciscans of the college of Zacatecas were given new hope. Former residents of Rosario appeared at La Bahía and asked that the mission be reopened. Their request was endorsed by the padres and forwarded to officials in Mexico City, but without waiting for formal authorization Father José Mariano Reyes of La Bahía reestablished mission Rosario and gathered there almost one hundred Indians.[16]

Unfortunately, Reyes was not well thought of by the president of the Zacatecan missions. His religious superior charged him with mismanagement as well as insubordination and asked the viceroy to remove him from Rosario. The viceroy complied. Reyes was sent southward to Zacatecas to answer charges and was replaced at the mission in 1791 by

Father José Francisco Jáudenes. Jáudenes was a capable padre, and the Indians accepted the change. But he was never able to satisfy the demands of the natives for material things, and they absolutely refused to work.[17]

In the same year that Jáudenes took charge at Rosario, the Franciscans made one last attempt to breathe life into the faltering missions of Texas. The college of Zacatecas chose Fathers Manuel Julio de Silva and José Mariano de la Garza, both proved workers in the field, to carry the cross among the Comanches and Norteños. The plan miscarried because the padres could not move without military escort through lands occupied by unreduced Apaches.[18]

Disappointed, Silva and Garza then turned their attention to the Texas coast and proposed a plan to convert the Karankawas. To support their religious undertaking, the padres sought the necessary approval of both the commissary of their college and the viceroy. While awaiting an answer, they visited several proposed sites for a mission. Formal approval came in January 1792, and on February 8 of the following year, Garza with the support of Governor Manuel Muñoz gathered 138 Indians at the junction of the San Antonio and Guadalupe rivers.[19]

The opening of Nuestra Señora del Refugio (see Figure 20) marked final efforts to revitalize missionary activities in Texas, but the results were again disappointing. The Karankawas' newfound enthusiasm for mission life at Rosario and Refugio was in no small measure influenced by their desire for protection from Lipan Apaches, and mission Refugio had been founded at an unhealthy location. In 1794 Father Silva moved it to a second site on Mosquito Creek near the mouth of the Guadalupe, but this placement also proved unacceptable. A third site chosen in 1795 at Rancho de Santa Gertrudis (present Refugio) was a marked improvement over the earlier ones, but the mission still did not prosper. Karankawas would remain there only when it suited them. Frequent desertions disheartened the padres, and the religious were unable to change significantly the life-style of those primitive Indians.[20] Nevertheless, mission Refugio did serve the useful purpose of keeping a watchful eye on the Karankawas, and it probably influenced them toward more peaceful behavior.

In marked contrast to increased missionary activity along the Texas coast, the oldest religious establishments in Texas were in their final throes. In 1772–1773 missionaries of the college of Querétaro had surrendered control of their four missions at San Antonio to friars of the college of Zacatecas, who had been at San José from the beginning. Shortly thereafter, all five missions experienced a decline that continued unabated for two decades. By the late 1700s, all of the missions at Béxar operated within buildings of permanent construction, but those structures contained diminishing numbers of neophytes. Traditionally, the missions had been peopled with hunting and gathering tribes, but by the last quarter of the 1700s only a small number of these natives had not been Christianized. At the same time, the conversion process within the missions was essentially completed. For example, Indians in residence at San Antonio Valero "were neither neophytes nor Indians but well-instructed Christians [of mixed parentage] . . . and there were practically no more pagan . . . Indians within a radius of 150 miles."[21]

This circumstance was reported in September 1792 by Father José Francisco López, president of the Texas missions, to his superiors of the college of Zacatecas. López recommended that mission Valero be secularized completely and that the administration of secular affairs for the other four missions be assigned to officials appointed by the government.[22] The proposal proved attractive to Viceroy Revilla Gigedo II, for if implemented it meant that the government would be relieved of all financial responsibility for the religious establishments at La Bahía and San Antonio. Mission Indians at those locations would henceforth become Spanish citizens with tax-paying obligations rather than remain as wards of the state.

In 1793 Revilla Gigedo ordered the complete secularization of San Antonio de Valero and in the following year commanded that all other Texas missions in existence for more than ten years be likewise turned over to the state. However, Governor Muñoz protested implementation of the decree at La Bahía and Rosario, arguing that those neophytes were not prepared for the full obligations of citizenship. On reflection, the viceroy concurred with Muñoz and exempted those two missions from the decree. The four remaining missions at San Antonio were "partially secularized." San Juan Capistrano and San Francisco de la Espada were permanently closed, and the few Indians then in residence at those sites were transferred to Purísima Concepción and San José.[23]

In advocating secularization in Texas, the Franciscans had by no means given up their goal of spreading the faith among unconverted Indians. Rather, it was a matter of releasing the order's missionaries for more productive endeavors elsewhere in New Spain. With ever-decreasing numbers of neophytes, the remaining missions in Texas struggled on for some years. Their eventual demise was the result of official policy that eschewed congregating Indians and the diminished numbers of Texas Indians willing to accept mission residence.

Other signs of strong secular influences were increased attention given to ranching and farming and the growth of urban communities. These developments also had roots that antedate 1783. Early in his tenure as commandant general, Teodoro de Croix had noted the large number of unbranded livestock in Texas. In those animals he astutely saw a source of revenue for the financially strapped royal treasury. While in San Antonio, Croix posted a decree, dated January 11, 1778, which gave the owners of stock four months to corral and brand their animals. After May 12 all unmarked livestock would automatically become the property of the king. Croix's decree also mandated that all brands be of different design and that they be registered with the governor. He further specified fines and punishments for rustlers and established fees for capturing feral or half-wild cattle and mustangs. As an additional source of revenue, the commandant general established an export fee of two pesos for each head of cattle or horses driven from the province.[24]

In May, Croix's unpopular decree went into effect, although it required the approval of the king before it could become permanently operative. That realization raised a storm of protest among settlers and missionaries in Texas. Ranchers and clergy objected through petitions and letters directed to the monarch and, after years of complaint, eventually won his ear. The royal revocation of Croix's initial order and all subsequent modifications of it finally reached Texas in early 1786. But ownership of the thousands of unbranded animals there was not resolved until 1795, when the matter received the attention of a council meeting in Mexico City. Albeit belatedly, the council exonerated anyone from debts to the crown for animals acquired during the period in which Croix's decree was in force. However, the council again assessed small fees for the capture of wild cattle and horses.[25]

Implementation of Croix's orders had coincided exactly with the eight-year governorship of Domingo Cabello (1778–1786). During his tenure, Cabello drew the wrath of ranchers and missionaries alike for his rigorous enforcement of the cattle laws and his alleged profiteering. Cabello's critics maintained that the governor seized thousands of head of livestock under the pretext of defending the king's property and then defrauded his monarch by selling the animals into Louisiana and pocketing the money. While those charges were never proved, ranchers in Texas were especially pleased to see Cabello replaced by Rafael Martínez Pacheco, the former commander at El Orcoquisac.[26]

Martínez Pacheco's governorship began soon after news reached Texas that the king had repealed Croix's decree. In January 1787 the new governor orchestrated the first big roundup in Texas. Initial planning for the rodeo involved some of the most prominent names in early Texas ranching as well as padres representing La Bahía and four of the missions at

San Antonio. The goal was to mark unbranded cattle located in a huge triangular area that lay between Béxar and the west bank of the Guadalupe River. The roundup was also intended to achieve the "best union and peace" between private ranchers and missionaries, for it would establish boundaries between disputed land claims. Signers of the resultant agreement protested Croix's earlier judgment that unbranded strays belonged to the king. They argued that systematic control of herds had been impeded by the threat of Indian attacks and continuing disputes over mission and private lands.[27]

The first rodeo was followed closely by a second in either 1777 or 1778, but neither involved active participation by any of the missionaries at Béxar. Their inability to field men or horses reflected the deplorable conditions that beset the five San Antonio missions as they approached secularization. While La Bahía was actively involved, the roundups nonetheless indicate the predominance of privately owned ranches over the missions. The latter had pioneered ranching in Texas, but by the last quarter of the eighteenth century the absence of neophytes had rendered the Béxar missions incapable of rounding up a single stray or mustang.[28] Once range cattle were branded and brought under more effective control, as was the case by the 1780s, it was much easier to prevent rustling. By law, punishment for stealing livestock carried the death penalty, but as Jack Jackson has noted, "Such extreme reprisals were rarely if ever taken. . . . New Spain needed men on her exposed northern frontier too desperately to subject them to capital punishment, certainly not for cattle theft." More common punishment, especially if the offender were an Indian or a mestizo, was a severe public whipping. Similar offenses by Spaniards usually resulted in nothing more serious than a requirement to perform public or military service.[29]

Despite government restrictions and taxation, if not outright control, cattle ranches in South Texas flourished in the last quarter of the eighteenth century, but surplus cattle and horses had little or no cash value within the province. While cattle drives northward from Texas in the post–Civil War era have long captured the attention of historians and novelists, the first organized drives were to Coahuila and Louisiana and occurred a century earlier.

During Teodoro de Croix's administration, Governor Bernardo de Gálvez of Louisiana had dispatched Francisco García to Texas and commissioned him to buy fifteen hundred to two thousand head of cattle. Trade between Louisiana and the Commandancy General was forbidden by royal decree, but Croix deliberately bent the law. He justified illegal commerce on the grounds that the Gulf of Mexico was likely to become

a war theater with the British and that Gálvez would need adequate supplies of beef. Accordingly, Croix ordered Governor Cabello not only to
supply the cattle requested by Gálvez but also to provide an escort of
soldiers for the livestock as it was driven eastward. Because cattle were
scarce in Louisiana and Coahuila, it became profitable for vaqueros in
Texas to round up unbranded animals, pay the export fee if they were
scrupulous, and drive them to market through the pine forests of East
Texas or southward across the Río Grande. It was this same abundance
of livestock, especially horses, that would later direct the attention of
Philip Nolan and other Anglo filibusters to Texas. And the proliferation
of cattle there during the last decades of the eighteenth century meant
that beef was the most common item in the daily diet of soldiers, civilians, and Indian raiders.[30]

Far less glamorous than ranching, farming has not generally attracted
the attention of historians or novelists. In the early history of Spanish
Texas, missionaries scratched out fields and constructed irrigation ditches
at locales such as San Antonio and San Gabriel, where surface water was
available but rainfall inadequate. Corn, as elsewhere in New Spain, was
the staple cereal, and it was regulated by price controls enforced throughout the Spanish American empire. For example, in 1789 Governor Martínez Pacheco set the price of corn at no more than two and one-half
pesos per *fanega* (1.6 bushels). Other crops included beans, garden vegetables, and chili peppers. Despite the abundance of land and some irrigation, farmers in Texas seem to have practiced agriculture on a less than
satisfactory basis. In years of plenty—largely because there were no markets for agricultural produce—they left surplus crops unharvested; in
lean times they begged for government assistance. Census data for San
Antonio in 1795 indicate only a slight preference for ranching over farming. Occupations included sixty-nine ranchers, sixty farmers, thirty servants, ten merchants, nine tailors, six shoemakers, six cart drivers, four
fishermen, four carpenters, two blacksmiths, and so forth. Also present
were government officials such as tax collectors and notaries.[31]

Despite the prevalence of ranching and farming in South and East
Texas, the province was still sparsely settled. Between 1777 and 1793,
twelve general and local censuses reflected the dearth of residents. By the
late eighteenth century, Texas remained one of the least populated regions
of New Spain. Overall, the Interior Provinces averaged six inhabitants
per square league (approximately six square miles), but both Texas and
Coahuila had slightly less than two. Only the desert region of Baja California, at one person per square league, had less. Including the residents
of missions, the total population for settled regions of Texas in 1777 was

3,103. It had risen only to 3,169 in 1790. While the census for 1804 recorded a total of 3,605 persons, that figure was probably inflated by recent immigrants from Louisiana who entered Texas at least temporarily to remain under the flag of Spain. In any event, a population figure of 3,122, given by Governor Manuel de Salcedo for 1809, indicates that the province had not experienced significant growth in the number of permanent residents since the first census of 1777.[32]

The relatively small number of settlers in Texas can perhaps be explained by the rigors of frontier life with its hostile Indians, limited diet, and virulent epidemics. San Antonio, of course, contained the largest concentration of population in the province. Interestingly, La Bahía reached its peak in numbers with 1,138 persons in residence there by 1796. From that year onward, it lost population steadily, probably caused by the lack of irrigation and dangers posed by Gulf Coast Indians. Contrariwise, Nacogdoches doubled in growth between 1779 and 1810, reaching a total of 655 inhabitants in the latter year. This growth is readily explained by the influx of Spaniards from Louisiana after 1803 as well as by the presence of foreigners such as Americans, British, and French.[33]

By the 1790s roughly two-thirds of the adult population in Texas was married. Single men outnumbered single women, with disparity most noticeable in towns containing military garrisons. Most immigrants and soldiers married women from the local community, thereby providing continuity and stability for frontier societies. As elsewhere in the Spanish Borderlands, the practice of men and women living together out of wedlock was fairly common in Texas. Illegitimate births increased steadily in the late 1700s and reached 20 percent of all births by 1799. Baptismal records indicate an abundance of foundlings, "children of the church," and bastards. There was also a high percentage of widows, to be expected given the premature death of soldiers and other males in Indian campaigns.[34]

The ethnic structure of Texas during 1777−1793 reflected that the largest percentage of the population, approximately 50 percent, was classified as "Spaniards," followed by settled Indians. The latter category, however, decreased in percentage from 29.5 in 1777 to 8.6 in 1793, the year in which secularization began at San Antonio. Additional ethnic groups included mestizos, other mixed colors, and blacks. Blacks, most of them probably slaves, made up less than 1 percent (twenty persons) of the total population in 1777, and the percentage rose only to 2.2 by 1793. Furthermore, there is no reason to believe that the slave population increased during the last thirty years of Spanish Texas. In fact, in 1819

San Antonio and La Bahía together reported only nine persons of "African origin." As Randolph B. Campbell has observed, "The number of bondsmen in Spanish Texas was always far too small to give the institution a significant hold on the province."[35]

In general, the population of Texas at the close of the eighteenth century reflected ethnic mobility. The marriage of white men with women of mixed origin started the process of racial amalgamation, and children of those unions often "passed" as whites. In the words of Alicia Tjarks, "The most positive deduction arising from all these trends . . . [was] a marked racial diversification, combined with and induced by an active biological and cultural miscegenation. As an immediate consequence, these factors encouraged a strong social and ethnic mobility, tending toward a free and heterogeneous society, which a few decades later was ready to break away from the old order."[36]

Spain itself by the late eighteenth century had begun to recognize the problems of maintaining the loyalties of citizens who lived far from crown and court and of defending sparsely settled provinces on the frontier of its North American empire. To this end, it sought to tie the provinces of Texas and New Mexico closer together with better transportation routes and began to experiment with an immigration policy in Louisiana that allowed the entry of large numbers of foreigners: English, Irish, French, and even Americans after 1783.

Travel between Santa Fe and San Antonio had traditionally been a long, dangerous, and circuitous undertaking. For example, from Santa Fe one had to detour southward by way of El Paso to Nueva Vizcaya and from there go eastward to Monclova or San Juan Bautista, before turning northward to San Antonio. Spanish officials had long recognized the importance of direct communication between the provincial capitals, but all attempts to link them, including those of Felipe Rábago from San Sabá, had failed.[37]

For reasons of commerce, a direct passage between Santa Fe and San Antonio was important, but it was also imperative that Spain establish contact with Indians living in the intervening region. Failure to do so would risk the influence of foreigners, especially Americans, over those tribes. The French agent, Juan Gasiot, had again articulated growing concern on this matter: "We will see citizens of the United States of America, lured by the advantages offered by the uncontrolled Indians in the territories lying between their frontiers and our provinces of New Mexico and Texas, make frequent incursions in order to establish trade with the natives. Thus the natives will become attached to them by bonds of interest. The trail blazers will next establish forts among them and continue to advance in this manner until they reach the limits of our borders, where they will have to be stopped. But by that time they will have become irresistible, drawing great strength from their new acquisitions and the establishment of alliances with numerous Indian nations."[38]

Pedro (Pierre) Vial, a Frenchman who had traded with Indians along the Red River from Natchitoches to the Wichita villages, first accepted the task of finding a direct route between San Antonio and Santa Fe, and in 1786 he was commissioned to this effect by Governor Cabello. In the company of Cristóbal de los Santos, a native of San Antonio, Vial left on October 4. He was to keep a diary of his travels—recording distance covered, Indians encountered, and the size of their encampments. Soon after his departure, Vial became ill and perhaps disoriented. In any event, his path was hardly on a direct line to Santa Fe. He traveled northward by way of Tawakoni villages near present Waco and then continued on to the Red River. From there, Vial turned westward and eventually reached Santa Fe on May 26, 1787. En route he had established important contacts with Indians over the course of his more than one-thousand-mile journey.[39]

The governor of New Mexico was equally eager to establish a direct route with Texas, and to this purpose he quickly commissioned José Mares of Santa Fe and dispatched him on July 31, 1787. Accompanying Mares were Cristóbal de los Santos and Alejandro Martín, a Comanche interpreter. The three men traveled eastward through the region near contemporary Tucumcari and entered the West Texas plains, perhaps in the vicinity of present Dimmitt and Tulia. Mares continued on to the Red River, where he and his companions camped among the Taovaya Indians and from there marched southward to San Antonio, reaching the capital on October 8, 1787. But again the most direct route had not been found.[40]

Mares expressed his immediate intent to return to Santa Fe and in January 1788 left Béxar in the middle of winter. On this occasion he traveled toward Santa Fe on a generally northwestward march. His path took him by way of the San Saba and upper Colorado rivers, and he probably passed through the locale of modern Amarillo. From there Mares crossed the high plains of Texas and New Mexico. He then crossed the Pecos River to the east of Santa Fe, arriving at the capital on April 27, 1788. In all, he had traveled some 325 leagues, or roughly 810 miles. This newly established route was by far the shortest link between the two capitals.[41]

Less than two months after his arrival at Santa Fe, Mares was again in transit to Texas, this time with a commission to establish a direct route to Natchitoches, with a return course by way of San Antonio. He departed Santa Fe on June 24 with a party of soldiers and a diarist. From the Taovaya villages, he traveled to Natchitoches, arriving there on August 20, 1788. From Louisiana by way of Béxar, he returned to Santa Fe in August 1789. Mares's extraordinary trek had covered a total of 914 leagues, or about 2,300 miles.[42]

The travels of Vial and Mares had shed light on the geography and ethnology of the vast reaches between Texas and New Mexico. They revealed the distribution of Indian tribes, their languages and customs, and their general relations with each other; they also paved the way for future contacts between the two provinces.

In 1792–1793 Vial traveled over what would become the Santa Fe Trail, blazed more than half a century earlier by Canadian traders, Pierre and Paul Mallet. Vial journeyed to St. Louis and back to Santa Fe in successive summers, a round trip distance of approximately twenty-three hundred miles. His travels brought home to Spanish officials the realization that Spain's dominions were not as far from Anglo-American settlements as they might have wished and emphasized that the continued security of those lands would depend on bold new approaches, including an immigration policy that they hoped would attract loyal citizenry to Louisiana.[43]

All immigrants who entered that realm would be required to forsake their original citizenship and become Spanish vassals, which carried the obligation of honoring the king, obeying Spanish laws, and accepting instruction in the Roman Catholic faith.[44] For the most part, foreigners publicly took the necessary oaths but privately clung to their old allegiances. Spanish officials accepted such duplicity, for they were faced with a Hobsonian choice. To leave the frontier virtually unoccupied except by Indians would almost certainly ensure its eventual loss to other European nations or the United States. Accordingly, peopling Louisiana with vassals of questionable loyalty was preferable to the alternative.

Beyond the Sabine River, Texas with its sparse population represented a similar problem, but the Spanish view of foreigners there was radically different. Unlike Louisiana, with its French background, bustling port of New Orleans, and administrative ties to Cuba, officials in New Spain and the Commandancy General looked with disfavor on the entry of outsiders. To prevent the unwelcome influx of foreigners, Spanish authorities in the mid-1790s placed a permanent detachment of troops at Nacogdoches. Defending Texas was the primary responsibility of the commandant general, with his headquarters in distant Chihuahua. From that city the commandant could also look after the defenses of New Mexico, Sonora, and California, but distance and poor lines of communication often meant a considerable time lag in correspondence between the governors of Texas and their superior in northern Mexico. Nevertheless, the commandant general did dictate official policy. For example, on August 27, 1796, Pedro de Nava issued an order forbidding the entry of any foreigner into Texas, even citizens of Louisiana, unless they carried satisfactory passports. In this directive, he singled out Anglo-Americans as suspicious aliens and was especially apprehensive that foreign immigrants could upset the delicate relationship between Spanish settlers in Texas and the Indian nations.[45]

The Spanish policy of distributing gifts and dispatching emissaries among Texas Indians had not ensured the universal goodwill of all natives. Near the turn of the century, the Indian problem was still a matter of concern. Very few Indians remained within the missions, and even those neophytes were prone to desertion, often on the pretext that they needed to supplement their food by hunting and fishing. Indians outside the missions were, of course, even more difficult to control. When tribes occasionally waged wars against each other, both sides would demand assistance from their white "friends," thereby placing the Spaniards in an insupportable position. Even Indians who attacked soldiers and civilians or natives who cooperated and traded with foreign intruders went unpunished, for official policy would brook no reprisals.[46]

Complicating the situation were the repeated requests of Louisiana officials to resettle Indians, such as the Choctaws, who were already under the influence of whites. Despite serious reservations on the part of Nava and Governor Juan Bautista de Elguezábal, those Indians received official permission to enter Texas in the early 1800s. At approximately the same time, the Alabama-Coushatta Indians also resettled in the province.[47]

Increasingly, as Mattie Austin Hatcher has observed, Spanish officials in Texas at the turn of the century faced problems of incredible complexity. "[They] felt compelled to be on their guard against the Indians, whom they tried to conciliate; against Spanish vassals of Louisiana, whom they really distrusted but feared to antagonize; against the French, whom they did not feel justified in definitely classing as either friends or foes; against the English, whom they kept under constant surveillance; and against Americans, whom they feared most of all."[48] The latter concern, which had been building since the 1780s, would prove deadly for Philip Nolan.

Spain had hoped that control of the Mississippi River and the port of

New Orleans would provide an invaluable lever in its relations with American citizens who crossed the Appalachian Mountains. In particular, Spain tried to persuade Anglo-Americans in Kentucky and other western districts to disassociate themselves from the fledgling Confederation and become independent states or—better yet—part of the Spanish empire. Apparently, no small number of those settlers entertained similar sentiments. In fact, as Samuel Flagg Bemis noted, it was the Americans who first broached the idea. Spokesman for the settlers was the gifted intriguer James Wilkinson. Based on documents in Spanish archives, Bemis maintained that there is not the slightest doubt that Wilkinson was willing to detach Kentucky and as much other territory as possible from the American Confederation of States in order to deliver those lands to Spanish sovereignty. Even after the formation of the United States, Wilkinson continued to receive pensions as a Spanish informant in Louisiana.[49]

Spanish goals in America were complicated by international events that changed with bewildering rapidity between 1789 and 1793. In the second year of his reign, Charles IV witnessed the adoption of a new constitution by the United States, which gave that nation the potential to address foreign and domestic problems more effectively. Also in 1789, the French Estates General convened for the first time in 175 years, launching that nation down the road to revolution. By 1793 the French had founded a republic, executed their king, and plunged most of Western Europe into war. To prevent the spread of revolutionary precepts beyond France and to excise the curse of republicanism, a coalition of European monarchical powers arrayed itself against France. Spain, although a Bourbon ally of France since 1762, joined that political front.

The repercussions of war in Europe were soon felt in New Spain and the Interior Provinces. In late 1793 Nava ordered Governor Muñoz to dispatch an expedition to the Gulf Coast. Coastal Indians must be urged to avoid relations with French traders and to report any French activities to Spanish authorities. Shortly thereafter, it became apparent in Texas that French agents were at work among the Norteños in an attempt to subvert their loyalties to Spain. The viceroy, responsible for the overall defense of New Spain, ordered the arrest of all French nationals living on Spanish soil, but those instructions were modified in Texas because of the large number of Louisiana-born French residing in the province. They and Frenchmen married to Spaniards were exempted from the order. But other French nationals were not so lucky. Those unfortunates were subject to arrest and loss of their possessions.[50] Circumstances, however, changed again in the mid-1790s. In 1795 Spain and France by the Treaty of Basle reestablished peaceful relations. That accord did much to ease concern over the French in Spanish realms.

At the same time, however, reports of Anglo-Americans working among the northern Indian nations filtered into Texas, and Nava again ordered all-out efforts to arrest and interrogate unwelcome intruders. In July 1795 the commandant general wrote Muñoz informing him that "a royal order, sent through secret channels, has arrived ordering the utmost care to prevent the passage to this kingdom of persons from the United States of America. The king has been informed on good authority that the United States has ordered emissaries to move here and work to subvert the population. . . . For this reason you are to exercise the utmost diligence and care to avoid the entry of any foreigner or any suspected person."[51] But the international scene continued to shift.

Jay's Treaty, negotiated in late 1794 between the United States and Great Britain, had been misinterpreted by the Spanish, who concluded that the two nations had settled most of their differences and therefore posed a combined threat to Louisiana and the Interior Provinces. Those concerns influenced Spain to sign the Treaty of San Lorenzo (Pinckney's Treaty) with the United States in October 1795, which resolved several longstanding issues: principally, unequivocal rights to navigate the Mississippi River and for three years to deposit goods at New Orleans. However, that agreement scarcely lessened suspicion of American adventurers on Spanish soil, whether agents of the United States government or freelance operators. In the following year, largely because it had unilaterally withdrawn from the European coalition, Spain found itself at war with Great Britain. Strained relations between the two powers would persist until 1808, when they ended their differences and joined forces against Napoleon Bonaparte in the Peninsular War. The almost constant changes occurring in the European theater, combined with Spain's traditional xenophobia, made it particularly dangerous for Anglo-Americans entering Texas, and Philip Nolan would become a victim of that fear.

The real Philip Nolan, as Jack Jackson has noted, remains difficult to separate from the fictitious character of the same name, created by Edward Everett Hale. When he wrote *The Man without a Country,* Hale mistakenly believed Nolan's given name to have been Stephen, and only after the book was published did he learn his intentionally fabricated name, Philip, was in fact Nolan's real name.[52] The 1794 census of Nacogdoches listed Philip Nolan as born in Belfast, Ireland, in 1771, but his early life has remained a mystery. By 1789 he resided in Kentucky, where he worked as bookkeeper and clerk for James Wilkinson. It seems likely that Nolan had been associated with Wilkinson for some years, for he once referred to the general as "the friend and protector of my youth."[53]

While living in Kentucky, Nolan definitely came under Wilkinson's influence. His mentor, according to James R. Jacobs, was a consummate "political chameleon" whose "loyalty to his friends and his government endured only so long as his personal interests were served."[54] Perhaps because of Wilkinson's intercession or his own winning personality, Nolan soon moved among influential people in lands between the western United States and New Orleans. Like Wilkinson, Nolan became interested in trade with Spanish possessions. He served as the general's agent in New Orleans, where he gained experience and some skill in using the Spanish language. Nolan saw opportunities for wealth as a horse trader between Texas and Louisiana. The latter, thanks to Texas cattle drives, had a thriving beef industry but lacked horses. While commerce between the two provinces was technically prohibited, it was nonetheless commonplace. And on occasion, such as the exigencies of war, it was even sanctioned by royal decree.[55]

Nolan appears to have entered Texas for the first time in 1791, and he is the first Anglo-American known to pursue horse trading there on a systematic basis. In all, he carried out four expeditions into Texas over a period of ten years, although information on his activities between 1791 and 1796 is sketchy. Most of his ventures were supported by legal trappings, such as his first when he bore a passport and letter of recommendation from Governor Estevan Miró of Louisiana. However, those documents afforded him little protection. For example, in 1791 authorities in Texas seized him as a spy and stripped him of all personal property. Discouraged, Nolan spent approximately two years living among Indians, including the Comanches. At the end of that time, he tired of life in the wilderness, which he judged as "less pleasing in practice than in speculation."[56]

By mid-1794 Nolan was back in Nacogdoches preparing for his second trip into Texas, and he again bore a passport, obtained from Governor Barón de Carondelet of Louisiana. At that juncture, Muñoz almost certainly knew of Nolan's activities as a horse trader and gave at least tacit approval to them. When Nolan returned from this expedition, he had collected 250 mustangs, which he sold at Natchez and Frankfort, Kentucky. Significantly, Nolan kept Wilkinson apprised of conditions in Texas, information useful to a man who was both a ranking officer in the United States army and a paid informant of Spanish officials in Louisiana.[57]

Nolan's third trip into Texas in 1797 came in the midst of deteriorating relations between the United States and Spain, occasioned by problems surrounding the establishment of a western boundary line as specified by the Treaty of San Lorenzo and by Spanish suspicions of U.S. designs on East and West Florida. Nevertheless, Nolan entered San Antonio in October 1797 with a letter and passport from Carondelet. His presence in Texas was also made known to Nava by letters from Muñoz.[58]

Nolan remained in Texas for about two years, before returning to the United States in 1799 with more than twelve hundred horses. But his activities and close ties to Wilkinson had begun to alarm the commandant general. In 1800 Nava sent instructions to Governor Juan Bautista de Elguezábal, ordering the arrest and interrogation of Nolan if he should return to Texas. Nolan had also drawn the suspicion of the governor of Natchez, Manuel Gayoso de Lemos, who knew firsthand of his ties to Wilkinson. In a letter to Nava dated June 1, 1799, Gayoso recommended that Anglo-Americans not be permitted to reconnoiter Spanish territory, particularly Texas, and specifically named Nolan as the most dangerous of those nationals. Finally, Gayoso expressed his belief that Nolan had been commissioned by Wilkinson to gather intelligence on Texas. Nava did not receive the Gayoso letter until after Nolan had departed for Texas on his fourth expedition.[59]

Nolan, himself, was well aware of the distrust he had aroused in Spanish officials and the dangers of reentering Texas. José Vidal, the Spanish consul and commandant at Concordia Post, had tried to prevent Nolan's departure by carrying complaints to the supreme court of the Territory of Mississippi, but American authorities refused to act on the petition. Rebuffed, Vidal then learned almost all of the details of Nolan's intended venture into Texas, and he, too, alerted Elguezábal. Particularly concerned about Nolan's skills in Indian relations, Vidal expressed fears that the American might influence the Norteños or Comanches to break the tenuous peace.[60]

Despite the dangers inherent in such an undertaking and his recent marriage to Frances Lintot, the daughter of a prominent citizen of Natchez, Nolan embarked on still another expedition. With a band of twenty-five followers, he entered Texas in late 1800 to the north of Nacogdoches and from there proceeded to a crossing of the Trinity River. He then continued to the Brazos, where his men constructed a corral to pen mustangs and a crude "fort" for shelter. The interlopers remained in the area to the north of present Waco for several weeks.[61]

In the meantime, the military commander at Nacogdoches, acting under orders from Governor Elguezábal, had organized a small army and set out to capture Nolan and his followers. The resultant clash occurred on March 21, 1801, in the northern Hill Country, possibly near the present town of Blum. Outnumbered six to one by Spanish forces under Manuel Múzquiz, Nolan and his party stood little chance of escape. Early in the battle, Nolan was killed by a cannon ball. Dispirited by their leader's death, his men soon surrendered. For most of the survivors, one of whom was Ellis P. Bean, it would mean years of incarceration in the prisons of New Spain. For Ephraim Blackburn, his life ended by hanging at the town of Chihuahua on November 11, 1807. He along with eight others cast dice to determine who among them must die for having fired on the king's soldiers. Blackburn's "four," the lowest number of nine rolls, sealed his fate.[62]

WITH NOLAN DEAD AND HIS FOLLOWERS IN CUSTODY, TEXAS remained securely within the Spanish fold as it entered the new century, but concern over Anglo-American penetration would increase steadily over the next two decades. In 1800 Louisiana again passed under French control. However, that province with its polyglot citizenry and cosmopolitan attitudes would remain under the tricolored flag for only three years. Its purchase in 1803 by the United States again transformed Texas into a frontier region. Significantly, the eastern and northern borders of the province now adjoined a nation that had doubled in size in just fourteen years. But it was not U.S. subversion that would end three hundred years of Spanish claims to Texas. The real problem, although few could discern it in 1803, lay in the heartland of New Spain and in Spain itself.

ELEVEN

The Twilight of Spanish Texas, 1803–1821

FROM THE LOUISIANA PURCHASE IN 1803 TO JULY 21, 1821, when the flag of Castile and León was lowered for the last time at San Antonio, Texas experienced its most turbulent and bloody years as a Spanish province. Along the Sabine River, a shared but undefined border with the United States highlighted continuing problems over the extent of and rights to Spanish and American possessions on the North American continent. Throughout much of the eighteenth century, Texas had been the outer bulwark for New Spain, but in 1803 the province faced a new circumstance. For the first time its Spanish subjects stood face to face with Anglo-Americans who embodied what Julia K. Garrett called "the greatest evil to monarchy, the rising plague of the nineteenth century—ideas of liberty—theories of popular sovereignty—and revolution." A non-Indian population in Texas of less than four thousand, largely vacant and dilapidated missions, two fixed presidios, three settlements, and two roads were the only "memorials of Spain's imperial enterprises in this primeval kingdom." To Spain's credit, it gave increased attention to Texas over the better part of two decades. The indefinite boundary that separated Texas from land-hungry Anglo-Americans moved Spain to adopt a threefold approach: "First, to hold the territory with its ancient boundaries unimpaired; second, to increase its garrisons and colonize the territory with loyal Spanish subjects; and third, to keep out Anglo-American intruders." To a remarkable degree, Spain accomplished those goals, but the real danger to continuing control of Texas lay festering within Spain and its American empire.[1] The ambitions of Napoleon Bonaparte, revolution in the heartland of New Spain, and the reactionary policies of King Ferdinand VII in Spain itself spelled the loss of an entire viceroyalty. This chapter first examines critically important events transpiring beyond the confines of Texas. Then against the backdrop of revolutionary developments in Europe and New Spain, it explains the forces that weakened Texas's ties with Spain and led to its incorporation into the new Mexican nation.

IN 1808, NINE YEARS AFTER BECOMING FIRST CONSUL OF France, Napoleon forced renunciation of the Spanish throne from Charles IV while at the same time capturing his son and heir, Ferdinand VII. Charles retired to Italy; Ferdinand spent the next six years under house arrest at Valençay, the country estate of Charles Maurice de Talleyrand. By imperial decree, Napoleon's brother, Joseph Bonaparte, became monarch of Spain. On March 2, 1808, Spanish patriots, angered at the French and the loss of the genuinely popular Ferdinand, launched the first stage of the Peninsular War. Opposition to Napoleon's pretensions in Spain came from local guerrilla units, who were soon joined by British forces under the command of the Duke of Wellington.[2]

Spanish resistance to Napoleon's armies was coordinated by the Central Junta of Seville, organized in the name of Ferdinand, "*El Deseado.*" In the Americas, actions taken in behalf of "The Desired One" would complicate political events from 1808 to 1814, and they often masked the real motives of revolutionaries from Texas to Argentina and Chile.

News of Charles IV's retirement, the capture and imprisonment of Ferdinand VII, and the outbreak of war on the Iberian Peninsula reached New Spain in the summer of 1808 and produced a flurry of activity. The *peninsulares,* Spaniards born in Spain, with few exceptions had traditionally monopolized the most important positions in colonial government. Predictably, they insisted that control of the government of New Spain should remain in their hands—in the name of Ferdinand VII. On the other hand, creoles countered with the contention that the viceroyalty should be ruled by juntas—again, in the name of Ferdinand—that they clearly intended to dominate.

Viceroy José de Iturrigaray, himself a *peninsular* and a corrupt and scheming appointee of Charles IV's chief minister, Manuel Godoy, shrewdly assessed the situation and concluded that "if he played his cards right he might see a Mexican crown on his head." With that in mind, the viceroy shifted his support to the Mexican-born creoles, who outnumbered the *peninsulares* by a ratio of roughly ten to one.[3]

Unfortunately for Iturrigaray, a small group of *peninsulares* apprehended his plot. They attacked the viceregal palace on the evening of September 15, arrested the turncoat viceroy, and dispatched him to Veracruz to await passage to Spain. The *peninsulares* then elevated Pedro Garibay to the viceregency. Their chosen leader was a senile octogenarian whose chief qualifications for office appear to have been mental confusion and a willingness to take orders. With a puppet in place, the *peninsulares* then began a witchhunt, arresting creoles and handing out drumhead justice.[4]

However, the preemptive strike of September 1808 had set a dangerous precedent with implications that extended as far as Texas. A royal appointee, never mind that Iturrigaray was probably guilty of treasonous plotting, had been removed from office by force of arms. The actions of the *peninsulares* in the fall of 1808 also drove many creole activities underground and led to the formation of secret organizations such as the "literary club" of Querétaro. A key member of this group was Father Miguel Hidalgo y Costilla, destined to become known as the Father of Mexican Independence.

Hidalgo was born in 1753 to moderately wealthy parents who could afford to educate their sons. In the mid-1760s Miguel and an older brother matriculated at a Jesuit school in Valladolid (today Morelia), but the institution soon closed as a result of the order's banishment from the New World. Hidalgo then transferred to the college of San Nicolás Obispo, also in Valladolid. As a student, young Miguel excelled in theology and languages and upon graduation in 1774 began immediate preparation for the priesthood. Four years later, he received the sacrament of ordination. Like thousands of Mexican priests before him, Hidalgo broadened his education to include learning Indian languages. He also began work toward a doctorate in theology at Mexico City, while maintaining ties with his alma mater as a teacher and later as an administrator.[5]

In the eyes of his church, Hidalgo was hardly an exemplary priest. He questioned clerical celibacy, read books on the Index of Forbidden Literature, kept a mistress, fathered three daughters, and challenged the infallibility of the pope. Although it is unclear whether these nonconformities were responsible, in 1792 Hidalgo severed all ties with the college of San Nicolás. Over the next eighteen years, he labored as a parish priest but continued his irregular ways. He fathered two more daughters, referred to the king of Spain as a tyrant, and even questioned the virgin birth of Christ! It is therefore not surprising that Hidalgo would attract the attention of the Holy Office of the Inquisition. In 1800 he was summoned before the tribunal and questioned closely about his beliefs and conduct. However, no formal action was taken against him.[6]

Three years after appearing before the Holy Office, Hidalgo accepted the curacy of Dolores, where he worked hard for seven years—teaching

Indian parishioners such practical skills as carpentry, wool weaving, silk raising, and wine making. But he never lost a sense of his own importance, and he longed for intellectual discourse. To that end, Hidalgo frequently traveled to Querétaro and there joined its "literary club." As it turned out, the organization's leaders displayed little interest in discussing the finer points of Goethe, Wordsworth, or Chateaubriand. Instead, with the eventual cooperation of Hidalgo, they began to lay plans that would lead to "the separation of New Spain from the old." [7]

In Querétaro, Hidalgo's path crossed that of firebrands led by Ignacio Allende, a captain in the Queen's Cavalry Regiment. Nonetheless, except for the far-off actions of Napoleon Bonaparte and the irresolute leadership of Charles IV, it is unlikely that treasonous activities would have been contemplated, much less planned. While it is true that social and economic tensions had been rising, particularly among the creoles and lower classes, New Spain was assuredly not filled with revolutionaries eager to cut their ties with the founding country. But external events in Europe played on internal tensions in Mexico, and as sometimes happens in history, cause and effect became intertwined.

By the spring of 1810, Allende and his creole associates had formulated a plan to drive the *peninsulares* from power. It called for an uprising to begin in early December of that same year, the occasion of an annual trade fair held at San Juan de los Lagos. Details of the Querétaro Conspiracy, as it came to be known, were privy to too many people, and secrets were betrayed. By August, Spanish authorities in Mexico City knew of a revolt that was planned for the following December. In that same month, a new and capable viceroy arrived on the scene. [8]

Francisco Javier de Venegas, appointed by the Central Junta of Seville, was kept apprised of the conspiracy as he made the slow, ceremonial journey from Veracruz to the capital. On September 13 Venegas sent secret orders northward from Mexico City, calling for the arrest of the conspirators. But again there was a breach in security. Juan de Aldama, the "Paul Revere" of Mexican independence, galloped by night with news of the impending arrest and arrived at Dolores in the wee hours of September 16, 1810. The plotters had little choice but to start their revolt prematurely, for royal authorities knew their identities. In the early morning hours of September 16, 1810, Father Hidalgo delivered his Grito de Dolores to a few Indians and mestizos of his parish, situated some sixty miles to the northwest of Querétaro. Hidalgo's *grito* was a cry for social and economic justice and for good government, not an outright proclamation of independence.

With timing gone awry, the conspirators hastily recruited thousands of untrained Indians and mestizos to their cause. Their desperate situation cast Hidalgo, because of his linguistic skills and popularity with the lower classes, into a larger role than was originally intended. Unforeseen circumstances and Hidalgo's leadership would severely damage the insurgents' chances for long-term success. Despite his intellectual abilities, in every endeavor save theology Hidalgo was a dilettante. As his biographer, Hugh Hamill, Jr., has observed, throughout his life Hidalgo "became enthusiastic about one project after another. He devoted all his energies to the promotion of idea after idea, but the responsibilities of following yesterday's inspiration were frequently neglected in the exhilaration of today's pursuit. What he lacked was a sense of sober organization, long-range planning, and deep submersion into the intricacies and contradictions of any one field."[9]

The insurgents, with a neophyte general directing what was more a mob than an army, overwhelmed royalist forces by sheer numbers and captured the important town of Guanajuato in late September. For the downtrodden Indians and mestizos, victory represented a unique opportunity to unleash their deep-seated hatred of the ruling classes, and they demonstrated that fury in an orgy of murder, pillage, and plunder. Significantly, Hidalgo made no attempt to curb those base passions. Worse, in exacting vengeance on the lives and property of the whites in Guanajuato, the lower classes made little distinction between creoles and *peninsulares*. The horrifying specter of social revolution sent a wave of fear through the upper classes and quickly undermined creole support for the revolutionaries.[10]

From Guanajuato the insurgents descended on Mexico City. After a bloody battle, they defeated royalist forces outside the capital. But Hidalgo, for reasons that remain unclear, chose not to occupy the city. His failure to do so has led critics to charge that he snatched defeat from the jaws of victory. Perhaps Hidalgo was unwilling to loose an uncontrollable mob on Mexico City. Whatever his reasoning, the decision was a major turning point in the revolution, for it produced a falling out with his creole officers. It certainly alienated Indians and mestizos in the ranks. Denied the opportunity to sack the capital, many of them disappeared into the countryside and returned to their homes.[11]

Pressed by royalist forces, in late 1810 Hidalgo and his creole officers set aside their differences. In Guadalajara they rebuilt a makeshift army of about eighty thousand men. The last major battle of the Hidalgo revolt was fought on January 17, 1811, at Calderón Bridge, some thirty miles east of Guadalajara. An apparent victory for the insurgents turned into a disastrous defeat when a huge grass fire, accidently ignited by an exploding ammunition wagon, swept flames into their ranks and panicked the soldiers. Unable to rally their forces, Hidalgo and a few followers retreated northward. Subsequently in the summer of 1811, the insurgent leaders were captured and executed.[12]

After the death of Hidalgo, another parish priest seized the banner of revolution in New Spain. José María Morelos y Pavón, a mestizo, organized a small military force that effectively employed guerrilla tactics. After isolating Mexico City from both coasts, in 1813 Morelos called into session a congress at Chilpancingo. The delegates issued a definitive declaration of independence from Spain and formulated principles of social justice, such as the elimination of slavery and distinctions among classes, to be set forth in a new constitution.[13] Promises contained in this document, which was promulgated from Apatzingán in 1814, were never realized because of the impending defeat of the insurgent army and the capture and execution of Morelos by royalists in 1815.

The failure of the Morelos movement was caused at least in part by the changing political scene in Spain and the course of the Peninsular War. During his years of forced confinement in France (1808–1814), Ferdinand VII had remained genuinely popular in Spain. Because he had ruled such a short time in 1808, his true qualities were not known, but his subjects believed him to be far superior to his lackluster father. Juntas formed in Spain and New Spain during Ferdinand's absence often claimed temporary authority in the name of "*El Deseado.*"

In late January 1810, the Central Junta of Seville gave way to a Regency Council but simultaneously called for the selection of representatives to a new Cortes, or parliament. Significantly, major administrative agencies in Spanish America and the Philippines could select delegates to serve in the Cortes on an equal basis with those chosen from Spain itself. Moreover, reformist elements on the Iberian Peninsula, fueled by the political ideas of John Locke and other theorists, did not intend for Ferdinand to reclaim an absolutist throne.[14]

The resulting parliament convened in Cádiz, "the most liberal city in the peninsula at that time." In that environment the Spanish Cortes in 1812 produced a remarkably progressive constitution, "based on principles of national sovereignty rather than royal authority." While not eliminating monarchy, the constitution provided universal suffrage to householders of a specified age, ended the right of entailment, and abolished the inquisition. Significantly, freedom of press was ensured except in matters pertaining to religion, for Catholicism remained the official faith of the state and the people. In short, only those articles that pertained to entailment and the inquisition could be regarded as threatening to the

Roman Catholic church. However, the immediate future of the political process would depend on the willingness of Ferdinand to accept restrictions on his powers.[15]

Following the defeat of Napoleon in early 1814 and the end of the Peninsular War, Ferdinand returned to Spain in April to resume his reign. In the words of Stanley G. Payne, "He proved in many ways the basest king in Spanish history. Cowardly, selfish, grasping, suspicious, and vengeful, D. Fernando seemed almost incapable of any perception of the commonweal." The king immediately prorogued the Cortes, threw out the constitution of 1812, and declared absolute monarchy restored on the terms of 1808.[16] From 1814 to 1820, Ferdinand committed himself to a threefold program: extirpate liberalism in Spain, crush the wars for independence in America, and share power with no one else on earth. He ultimately failed in all three endeavors.

Over the first half dozen years of his reign, Ferdinand survived a series of plots and pronunciamentos staged by disgruntled generals and liberal sympathizers in the officer corps of the Spanish army. Finally, in 1820 a successful military uprising led by Major Rafael del Riego forced him to make concessions. The reluctant king reinstated the constitution of 1812 and reconvened the Cortes. By then Mexico was on the brink of independence.[17]

Father Morelos, like Hidalgo, had been defrocked and shot as a traitor in December 1815. Over the next five years, the course of Mexican independence lay essentially stillborn. Events in Spain, however, breathed new life into the movement. In late 1820 Agustín Iturbide, a former officer in the Spanish army and opponent of insurgency, joined with Vicente Guerrero, a dedicated revolutionary, to become the final architects of independence. With the support of conservative elements in Mexico, who wished to separate themselves from the temporarily liberal Spain, the two men were able to detach New Spain from the old by the Plan of Iguala, drafted in February 1821 and fulfilled by the Treaty of Córdoba on August 24. The Plan of Iguala contained three salient features in its twenty-three articles: independence for the Mexican nation, full protection for the Roman Catholic faith, and equal treatment for creoles and *peninsulares* in the new state. This successful formula, also known as the Plan of the Three Guarantees, brought about an independent Mexico, which by extension meant that Texas was no longer Spanish.[18]

TEXAS'S LAST TWO DECADES AS A SPANISH PROVINCE WERE profoundly affected by the aforementioned events in New Spain and

Spain itself. Imperial concerns over the expansion of the United States and the activities of American adventurers had not ended with the death of Philip Nolan and the capture of more than a dozen of his ragged followers in 1801. Two years later, Napoleon broke his pledge not to alienate Louisiana, and for the sum of approximately fifteen million dollars disposed of it to the United States. Left unsettled was the western boundary of Louisiana, a matter that would complicate diplomatic relations between Spain and the United States until 1819.

When Spain retroceded Louisiana to France by the Second Treaty of San Ildefonso (1800), language pertinent to the western boundary of the territory read: "with the same extent that it now has in the hands of Spain, and had while in the possession of France."[19] Three years later, upon the sale of Louisiana to the United States, Napoleon may well have retained vagueness in the matter of a western boundary in order to use that issue to full advantage in future dealings with Spain. Thus, his often-quoted instruction to François Barbé-Marbois—"that if an obscurity did not already exist, it would be good policy to put one there"—may in part be interpreted as Napoleon's intent to wring considerations from Spain in return for his support of its claims, whatever they might be. In this context, the equally famous comment of Talleyrand to the U.S. negotiators of 1803, "You have made a noble bargain for yourselves and I suppose you will make the most of it," may also be read as France's unwillingness to define Louisiana to the detriment of Spain and to the benefit of the United States.[20]

Among Americans who sought maximum advantages for the United States in establishing the western boundary of Louisiana, none was more aggressive than President Thomas Jefferson. In 1803 Jefferson wrote a treatise, based solely on French documents, in which he concluded that the Río Grande was the proper southern limit of Louisiana. U.S. claims to that effect soon prompted a royal directive from Charles IV, dated May 20, 1805, which called for the compilation of data and maps pertinent to determining the true boundary between Louisiana and Texas. That commission was finalized in 1808 with the appointment of José Antonio Pichardo, who undertook the completion of a massive project that occupied him day and night until his death in 1812.[21]

Without waiting for the results of scholarly disputation, Jefferson actively pursued U.S. claims to western lands. As a scientist, he was interested in plants and animals within unexplored regions, and he hoped to lay claims to untapped riches in the west before they fell into the hands of a European power. In addition to sponsoring the Lewis and Clark expedition (1804–1806), Jefferson planned other explorations. From

Natchez in 1804, William Dunbar and John Hunter set out with a seventeen-man force to follow the Red River to its origins and to explore the headwaters of the Arkansas. That expedition was barely under way when its leaders learned that Spain would resist such an undertaking, for in the Spanish view it would constitute a threat to Texas. Unwilling to risk trouble with Spanish officials, Dunbar and Hunter limited their explorations to lands along the Ouachita River and did not leave the confines of the present state of Louisiana.[22]

In 1806 a second expedition led by Thomas Freeman and Peter Custis again headed up the Red River in two flat-bottomed boats. After traveling some six hundred miles, the thirty-seven-man party was forced to turn back when confronted by several hundred Spanish soldiers from Texas and New Mexico.[23]

Americans to the east of the Sabine were particularly incensed by this display of Spanish high-handedness, since a determination of the western boundary of Louisiana had not been reached. Both sides prepared for what seemed an inevitable clash of arms. To make matters worse, Commandant General Nemesio de Salcedo had already ordered Spanish troops to take up a position east of the Sabine near the abandoned site of the presidio at Los Adaes, and he had begun to shift troops in the Interior Provinces with the intent of strengthening defenses along the Texas-Louisiana border. Spanish troops in Texas at the end of 1805 numbered 700, with 141 men stationed at Nacogdoches. However, by June 1806, shortly before the confrontation on the Red River, additional militia units from Nuevo Santander and Nuevo León brought the total troop strength in Texas to an unprecedented 1,368 men, with nearly two-thirds of that number (883) posted at Nacogdoches and its vicinity. War seemed imminent.[24]

However, by the fall of 1806, caution began to replace saber rattling. Salcedo ordered governors Antonio Cordero y Bustamante of Texas and Simón de Herrera of Nuevo León, who had been transferred to Texas, "not [to] begin the action or attack the Americans without an entire and absolute certainty of evicting them from the disputed territory." From Spain, Charles IV also commanded that every effort be made to end differences with the Americans peaceably, but the king authorized no concession on the contested territory.[25]

U.S. citizens also began to soften their stance. General James Wilkinson, commander of United States forces in Louisiana, offered a compromise on October 29. He would withdraw U.S. troops to the east of the Arroyo Hondo if Spanish forces would pull back to the west of the Sabine. Herrera agreed to Wilkinson's proposal on November 4. The re-

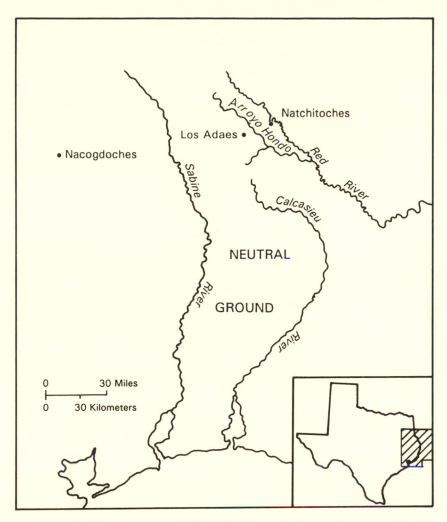

FIGURE 22
Neutral Ground Agreement. This map depicts the diplomatic agreement of 1806 between Spain and the United States whereby neither power would have jurisdiction over a strip of land lying between the Sabine River and two streams to the west of the Red River. (Cartography by William M. Holmes.)

sulting Neutral Ground Agreement preserved peace (see Figure 22). Nevertheless, it created a corridor that soon filled with an incredible assortment of thieves, criminals, fugitive slaves, and smugglers—"the refuse of both Texas and Louisiana," as Odie Faulk called them—who preyed on both provinces. At times, U.S. and Spanish authorities would occasionally find it expedient to cooperate in flushing out this human driftwood.[26] During and after the Neutral Ground controversy, Spain attempted to increase its presence in Texas by founding the small settlements of Trinidad de Salcedo and San Marcos de Neve, but neither was destined for permanency. Both had ceased to exist by 1812–1813.

In accepting a compromise, both Wilkinson and Herrera acted without the approval of their superiors. Herrera, in fact, had been guilty of disobeying orders. Nevertheless, he received praise for his good judgment from both Salcedo and the viceroy of New Spain. Wilkinson, ever the main-chance operator, quickly dispatched an aide to Mexico City who presented the viceroy with a bill in the amount of $120,000 for services rendered to His Catholic Majesty of Spain![27] Soon after negotiating the Neutral Ground Agreement, Wilkinson made haste to New Orleans, where he denounced his shadowy associate, Aaron Burr. Whatever the implications of the Burr Conspiracy to western lands of the United States and Spanish holdings in New Spain, they had no impact on Texas.[28]

Having experienced two failures in the south, the second of which had nearly brought war with Spain, Jefferson tried a different tack. In July 1806 Lieutenant Zebulon Montgomery Pike left St. Louis to probe lands upstream between the Arkansas and Red rivers. Pike was to seek friendship with Indians along the way and drive out unlicensed traders. On the Republican River in present-day Nebraska, he encountered Pawnee Indians who were disposed to cause trouble, having been visited recently by a Spanish army searching for U.S. citizens. Pike squashed such intentions by informing the Indians that "warriors of his Great American Father were not women to be turned back by words."[29]

From the Republican, Pike marched southward to the Arkansas, striking it at its Great Bend in present Kansas. He then followed the river toward its source into the Colorado country, where he searched in vain for the headwaters of the Red. In the spring of 1807, Pike crossed the Sangre de Cristo Mountains and camped on the upper Río Grande. He was arrested there by a Spanish force of one hundred men, interrogated in Santa Fe, and sent eastward to Texas by way of El Paso, Chihuahua, and Monclova. Arriving in San Antonio, Pike and his followers received cordial treatment as guests of Governor Cordero. The province drew his praise for possessing "one of the most delightful temperatures in the world." His comments on Bexareños, however, were not so favorable. In his words: "Their general subjects of conversation are women, money, and horses, which appear to be the only objects, in their estimate, worthy of consideration. . . . Their games are cards, billiards, horse-racing, and cock fighting." From Béxar, Spanish soldiers escorted Pike over the Camino Real to Natchitoches, where on July 1, 1807, he was unceremoniously deposited on U.S. soil.[30]

While Pike was under detainment, Spanish authorities had confiscated his notes and maps, but he was able to reconstruct from memory much of his extraordinary journey. His favorable impressions of Texas, with its fertile soil and grasslands teeming with game and herds of wild horses, would serve to whet even further the appetite of land-hungry Americans.[31]

The expulsion of Pike from Spanish realms did not allay the concerns of Commandant Salcedo. He believed that the real intent of Pike's intrusion had been to subvert the loyalty of Indians between Texas and New Mexico. To counter Pike's influence, Salcedo ordered Captain Francisco Amangual and two hundred soldiers to march from San Antonio to Santa Fe, reassuring Indians along the way of Spanish might and good intentions toward them. Amangual completed his assignment between March 30 and June 19, 1808, and returned to Béxar before the end of that year. In fulfilling his commission, he had contacted many bands of Comanches, but as Odie Faulk has observed, "The value of the expedition is debatable."[32]

Salcedo's concerns over the long-range implications of the Pike expedition were further reinforced by the activities of "unofficial" representatives of the United States among Indians of the South Plains and by problems flowing from the Neutral Ground Agreement of 1806. In the first instance, the appointment in 1804 of Dr. John Sibley as occasional Indian agent for the United States looms large. As Dan L. Flores has written, Commandant Salcedo's fears that Sibley was "a revolutionist, the friend of change" were well founded. From his base in Natchitoches, Sibley missed no opportunity to dispose Indians favorably toward the United States. Through John House, who had escaped capture as a member of Nolan's fourth expedition, Sibley dispatched presents to the Comanches and Norteños in the spring of 1805 and urged them to send representatives to Natchitoches. Other U.S. traders moved among the Red River tribes in the autumn of 1806 and early summer of 1807. The success of those endeavors in befriending the Comanches and their allies was soon evident. From mid-August into the fall, "one band after another . . . began arriving in the American city of Natchitoches" to attend a Grand Council.[33]

Sibley was apparently a skilled propagandist. In addressing the council, he impressed upon the Indians that U.S. citizens were "Natives of the

Same [*sic*] land that you are, in other words, white Indians." He also assailed Spanish traders at Nacogdoches, pointing out that their high prices were not the fault of the United States. Ironically, where government-sponsored expeditions had failed, Sibley and his agents, much to the consternation of Salcedo, had succeeded.[34] And the stage was set at Natchitoches for the boldest venture yet—the expedition of Anthony Glass.

From July 1808 to May 1809, Glass and several companion traders traveled from Natchitoches to the Taovaya villages on the Red River. From there they penetrated Texas as far as the Edwards Plateau to the west of present Waco, making friendly contacts with natives along the way. The return trip to Natchitoches, again by way of the Taovaya villages, completed a remarkable trek.[35] The successful overtures of Glass and others among Texas Indians from the Red River to the Colorado River made it doubly important that Spain improve its relations with the tribes to the west of the Neutral Ground.

Spanish trade in East Texas and across the neutral area that lay between the Sabine and Arroyo Hondo was carried out primarily by the commercial House of Davenport and Barr, the very traders alluded to in Sibley's harangue. Founded in 1798 and headquartered in Nacogdoches, the firm conveyed merchandise from Louisiana to Texas and transported goods such as pelts and livestock back to Louisiana. The company's principal owners, William Barr and Samuel Davenport, were both naturalized Spanish citizens who were licensed to engage in commerce.[36] An early function of the traders was to supply Indians of the region with a wide variety of gifts, thereby influencing them toward friendly relations with the Spanish. Beginning in 1800, Davenport and Barr transported horses obtained from East Texas Indians to Louisiana. The former, who was an enemy and competitor of Philip Nolan, also volunteered to serve with the Spanish forces that attacked and killed the Irish adventurer. After Nolan's death, it was again Davenport who agreed to deliver Múzquiz's report and the mustanger's severed ears to the governor in San Antonio, as he was "moved by his well known love for the king."[37]

Allowing trade with the French during the period of retrocession was one thing; permitting it with U.S. citizens once they took possession of Louisiana was another. In 1803 Commandant General Salcedo had proscribed the exportation of livestock, an endeavor that had greatly profited the House of Davenport and Barr. When Barr complained that his firm could not continue in business if forced to depend only on pelts and furs supplied by the Indians, it was exempted from the order. Encouraged,

Barr then bargained for a monopoly that would exclude all other traders in East Texas, and Salcedo again agreed to grant the company a favored position. This extraordinary concession to the House of Davenport and Barr can be explained by the company's critical role in supplying gifts to friendly Indians.[38]

In addition to providing presents for the Indians of East Texas, the House of Davenport and Barr also supplied Spanish troops at Nacogdoches with supplementary items such as flour, beef, salt, chili, and soap. Not surprisingly, the firm generally prospered in the first decade of the 1800s, but not all was as the proprietors would have wished. They had difficulty collecting trading debts from the Indians; the Embargo Act, passed in 1807 during Jefferson's second administration with the primary intent of preventing export of goods on the high seas, was enforced—spitefully in the view of Davenport and Barr—on the Texas-Louisiana frontier; and the dangers posed by bandits who infested the Neutral Ground proved especially troublesome and costly. With the repeal of the Embargo Act in 1809, the company again recouped its fortunes, and on occasion Spanish and U.S. forces cooperated in combing out the bandits. Nevertheless, the continuing problem with lawless elements would move Davenport in 1812 to complain: "The Neutral Ground is still infested by gangs of bandits, and it is impossible to carry on business. I dare not risk my interests to capture by the outlaws."[39]

Shortly after his protest to Commandant General Salcedo, Davenport would forsake his adopted citizenship and join forces designed to end Spanish rule in Texas. The genesis of that independence movement had erupted a few years earlier with the Grito de Dolores. Like a mushrooming cloud, the insurrection grew in size until it enveloped Texas and parts of the Interior Provinces.

Following the Neutral Ground crisis and the extraordinary boldness of the Glass expedition, Texas had been fortunate to receive an intelligent and vigorous governor. Appointed in 1807 by the Council of the Indies, Manuel María de Salcedo was the nephew of Commandant General Nemesio de Salcedo.[40]

Manuel de Salcedo was the product of military academy schooling in Spain. In the early 1800s he had accompanied his father to Louisiana, where the elder Salcedo served as political and military governor. Following the transfer of Louisiana to the United States, Manuel de Salcedo returned to Spain with his father in 1804. As appointed governor of Texas, Salcedo proceeded to his assignment by way of the United States, passing through Philadelphia, Natchez, and Natchitoches. His leisurely journey afforded him an opportunity to form impressions of the character and inclination of U.S. citizens. Among those whom he personally contacted were former associates of Aaron Burr and members of the Pike expedition.[41]

Assuming office at Béxar on November 7, 1808, Manuel de Salcedo quickly assessed the province and formulated a program for its development, which he submitted to his uncle in Chihuahua. Nemesio de Salcedo was not impressed. Perhaps because of his nephew's youth and inexperience, possibly because the commandant general wished to avoid any possible charge of familial favoritism, General Salcedo remained a harsh critic throughout his nephew's tenure as governor.[42]

An often-disapproving uncle as commandant general was only part of a difficult situation that faced the young executive, who, when he arrived in Texas, was obliged to share power with Antonio Cordero, the governor of Coahuila, who was still in the province on special assignment. Because of the illness and incapacity of Juan Elguezábal, Cordero had served as interim governor of Texas and remained there after the Neutral Ground crisis had passed. He also held the post of deputy commandant general. Like Cordero, Simón de Herrera, the governor of Nuevo León, was also on special assignment in Texas.[43]

One of Salcedo's first responsibilities as governor was to answer a charge of the Central Junta of Seville. On January 22, 1809, in the name of Ferdinand VII, that body "recognized the Spanish dominions in America as integral parts of the nation and declared that they should have representation in the governing junta of the kingdom." However, through no fault of the Spanish government, Texas did not choose a delegate.[44] Pedro Garibay, acting viceroy of New Spain, decided that only Durango, as the capital of Nueva Vizcaya, should send a delegate from the Interior Provinces. While that decision was challenged by an attorney for Commandant General Salcedo, it remained in effect. San Antonio de Béxar would not be represented at the Central Junta or at subsequent meetings of the Spanish Cortes between 1811 and 1814.

Governor Salcedo nevertheless prepared a report for the deputy who would be chosen to represent the Interior Provinces. While it is uncertain that his assessment of Texas in 1809 was carried to Spain, it is still a revealing document that provided a remarkable firsthand glimpse into the affairs of Texas, and it came on the eve of violent upheavals that would rack the province over the next few years. Salcedo observed that in a province noted for "its prodigious space and beautiful lands" there were only three presidial companies—actually, as he admitted, just two with fixed bases. He singled out the absence of aides to the governor, such as legal adviser, secretary, or scribe, as particularly injurious to the interests of good government. He also deplored the lack of adequate funds to administer the province. In a governmental unit the size of Texas, Salcedo seemed amazed that there were only 352 veteran soldiers and a civilian population of just 3,122 persons. The poverty of the inhabitants also drew the young governor's attention. Their mean condition meant farming without necessary tools, suffering from heat and cold, and living in houses made of sticks and straw. Worse, the populace of Texas was so poor that they could not even dress themselves decently.[45]

In a different vein, Salcedo waxed eloquently about the land, describing it as blessed with immensely rich soil that was "capable of producing anything that is planted, particularly cotton, indigo, tobacco, wheat, corn, etc." He also named the major rivers of the province and alluded to lesser streams that provided potential waters for irrigation.[46]

Governor Manuel de Salcedo next turned to the United States and its citizens, some of whom he had met en route to Texas. He assessed U.S. citizens as greatly advantaged by being "owners of the Nile of North America (thus they call the Mississippi)." Salcedo also branded as falacious "the idea that some have that we ought to hold the Americans in contempt," and he warned that "they are not to be underestimated as enemies." He continued, "The Anglo-Americans are naturally industrious. If this were not true, they would not love to live in deserts, where their sustenance depends on their industry. This very kind of life hardens them; that is to have the traits of robustness, agility, sobriety, and valor."[47]

Salcedo's recommendations for the security of Texas called for continued efforts to keep the peace with the Indian nations by supplying them with goods and trading items "better or at least equally in kind and more abundantly than the Anglo-Americans do." Additionally, he requested new regiments of heavy and light infantry, cavalry, and mounted artillery, totaling four thousand men.[48] With Texas's civilian population barely in excess of three thousand, his proposals, if implemented, would have turned the province into an armed camp. Nonetheless, the young governor sized up rather well the precariousness of Spain's presence in this frontier province, but even he could not foresee problems arising within New Spain itself. Salcedo's report, dated August 8, 1809, was drafted just thirteen months before Father Hidalgo proclaimed his revolutionary *grito*. Tragically for Manuel de Salcedo, from 1810 onward his tenure as governor would be consumed with defending his monarch from enemies outside and within Texas, and in the end devotion to duty would cost his life.

Before revolution from the south broke over Béxar, Governor Salcedo turned his attention to East Texas. In March 1810 he began an inspection of the region. The situation there was extremely complex. Unsavory characters of every description had filtered into the Neutral Ground. Other transients of questionable loyalty claimed lands in Texas without possessing any legal authority to them. Traditionally, Commandant General Nemesio de Salcedo had been adamantly opposed to all alien encroachments beyond the Sabine. However, at the very time of Don Manuel's inspection, Don Nemesio had begun to alter his stance. Perhaps, as Félix D. Almaráz, Jr., has suggested, "The last thing the commandant general needed was the precipitation of a border incident."[49]

In effect, Nemesio de Salcedo gave greater discretionary powers to the governor and deputy commandant general in Texas. Those officials, in the words of Almaráz, would be permitted to make "a sharp distinction between alien settlers who engaged in peaceful pursuits of the soil and chronic trespassers who entered for illicit purposes." At Nacogdoches, Manuel de Salcedo found that many settlers lacked documents and deeds to their lands, and to the best of his ability, he determined the intention of the squatters, granting some of them titles to lands, farms, and ranches.[50]

Upon his return to San Antonio, Governor Salcedo soon found himself confronted with the extended impact of the Hidalgo revolt. Early in the insurrection, Hidalgo and his creole officers recognized the importance of obtaining foreign assistance. To that purpose, they assigned Mariano Jiménez the responsibility of overturning Hispanic control of Coahuila and Texas. Of the two provinces, Texas was most important because of its proximity to the United States, where the rebels hoped to enlist aid.[51]

In early 1811 rebel forces south of the Río Grande captured Antonio Cordero, who had left Texas to defend his governorship of Coahuila. The capture of Cordero spread rumors and fears throughout Texas, and on the night of January 21, 1811, Juan Bautista de las Casas, a retired militia captain from Nuevo Santander, orchestrated a strike against the royalists in San Antonio. On the following morning, Las Casas and a few coconspirators seized the governor and his military staff. Elsewhere, adherents of Las Casas also enjoyed instant success in gaining control of Nacogdoches and the other settlements. In February, after confiscating the property of ardent supporters of Ferdinand VII, Las Casas sent Manuel de Salcedo, Simón de Herrera, and twelve officers under heavy guard to Monclova, where they were confined in the nearby hacienda of Lieutenant Colonel Ignacio Elizondo. Later in that same month, Las Casas received two agents of Hidalgo, Field Marshal Ignacio Aldama and Father

Juan Salazar, both of whom had stopped in Texas on their way to the United States.[52]

Unfortunately for Las Casas, he had imprudently failed to build a base of support in Texas, and he especially erred by ignoring old-line officers and descendants of Isleño families. Clandestine opposition to the Las Casas regime centered around Juan Manuel Zambrano, a subdeacon of Villa San Fernando. From his ranch well outside San Antonio, Zambrano with the aid of other counterinsurgents, including José Erasmo Seguín, formed a junta and pledged support to the king. On March 2, 1811, the royalist sympathizers surprised Las Casas and removed him from power.[53]

The counterrevolutionists quickly sent word of their success to Commandant General Salcedo, and they dispatched two dependable royalists to the hacienda of Ignacio Elizondo. A former defender of the king, Elizondo, who had joined Hidalgo, again switched allegiance. He released Governor Salcedo and the other captives and joined them in laying an ambush for Hidalgo that was aimed at intercepting the rebel priest and his straggling partisans as they approached Monclova from the south. At the oasis of Baján on March 21, 1811, royalist forces captured Hidalgo and his dispirited followers with only a few shots fired in anger.[54]

Salcedo transported Hidalgo and other important leaders of his revolt to the town of Chihuahua, where they stood trial for treason in the summer of 1811. For creole officers Ignacio Allende, Juan de Aldama, and Mariano Jiménez, death came in June with their backs exposed to a firing squad, but it took longer to dispose of Hidalgo. Under the scrutiny of his church since the inquisition case of 1800, Hidalgo was defrocked and turned over to the state for trial and punishment on charges of treason. As a priest, he was entitled to a private execution and the subtle privilege of being shot in the chest. On July 30, the "ex-priest, ex-revolutionary . . . made his peace with his Church and his country."[55]

As an indelible lesson to would-be revolutionaries, the heads of Aldama, Allende, Hidalgo, and Jiménez were severed from their cadavers and sent to Guanajuato. There the grisly relics were placed in iron cages and hung from the corners of a granary where they remained for ten years.[56] The fate of Las Casas was remarkably similar. He was tried in Monclova by a court-martial and found guilty of high treason. The verdict came on July 29, one day before the death of Hidalgo. After execution by shots in the back, Las Casas's severed head was salted and shipped in a box to Béxar for display in the military plaza.[57]

By the fall of 1811, royalists had regained effective control of Texas, although in Mexico the struggle for independence continued under the leadership of Father Morelos. Rebel sympathizers, however, had not been quashed throughout the northern provinces. One such person was José Bernardo Gutiérrez de Lara, a blacksmith and merchant from Revilla.[58] In the company of José Menchaca, another rebel partisan, Gutiérrez crossed into Texas and arrived safely in Natchitoches. From there he traveled to Washington, where in early December 1811 he was received favorably by U.S. officials in the Departments of War and State. However, Gutiérrez received little more than unofficial blessings from Secretary of State James Monroe. United States officials did provide him with a letter of introduction to William C. C. Claiborne, the U.S. military commander in New Orleans, and he was urged to "return home with all possible diligence."[59]

Gutiérrez proceeded to Natchitoches by way of New Orleans. There General Claiborne introduced the former blacksmith to William Shaler, who was to monitor his activities and accompany him to Natchitoches. In late April 1812, the two men arrived at their destination, where Gutiérrez began immediate preparations for an invasion of Texas. In the vicinity of Natchitoches, he found no shortage of volunteers willing to join the venture.[60] The province had just emerged from a series of administrative changes. A counterrevolutionary junta, headed by Zambrano, was the effective government at Béxar from March 2, 1811, to July 22, 1811. This ad hoc committee restored the confiscated property of royalists and established communication with Félix María Calleja, the royalist general who had defeated the forces of Hidalgo. In July, Simón de Herrera assumed interim control at Béxar because Manuel de Salcedo was still in Chihuahua for the trials and executions of Hidalgo and his close associates. With his return to San Antonio on September 11, 1811, Salcedo resumed the office of governor but felt his prestige had been damaged by the ease with which he had been removed from authority during the Las Casas revolt. Unfortunately for Salcedo, worse was yet to come, for the impending invasion east of the Sabine would again sweep him from office.[61]

In Natchitoches, Bernardo Gutiérrez acquired the military assistance of Augustus William Magee, a graduate of West Point and former lieutenant in the United States army. The continued support of William Shaler, in his capacity as special agent for the United States, almost certainly influenced other Americans to join the banner of the Mexican revolutionary. Gutiérrez also enlisted the services of Samuel Davenport, to whom he assigned the responsibility of obtaining support from East Texas Indians.[62] The U.S. military contingent, as Richard Gronet has argued, was not simply a filibustering expedition, rather it represented efforts by the

United States government to formulate foreign policy initiatives toward Mexico. According to Gronet, correspondence between Shaler and James Monroe makes clear that the former in influencing U.S. citizens to join Gutiérrez was following "a broadly based series of instructions from his superiors in Washington."[63]

When the self-styled Republican Army of the North crossed the Sabine on August 8, 1812, its purpose was far more important than a temporary incursion into New Spain. Although Anglo-Americans had joined Gutiérrez and Magee for reasons of "land, loot, and adventure," the goal of the army was to bring Texas into the fold of Mexican revolutionaries. Publicly, the United States expressed official protests over the invasion, a move necessitated by peaceful relations with Spain, and Monroe sent Dr. John Robinson to Chihuahua to communicate Washington's disapproval of border violations.[64]

Privately, however, Shaler would soon exult in a letter to Monroe, dated October 5, 1812: "The volunteer expedition from the most insignificant beginning is growing into an irresistible torrent, that will Sweep the crazy remains of Spanish Government from the Internal Provinces, and open Mexico to the political influence of the U.S. and to the talents and enterprize of our citizens."[65] Shaler's optimism was initially well founded, since the Republican Army quickly captured Nacogdoches, where not a single civilian answered Spanish Commander Bernardino Montero's appeal for volunteers to help defend the town. Worse, all but ten of Montero's soldiers deserted, forcing the officer and those few stalwarts to retire to Béxar.[66]

The invading army of perhaps 130 men grew to about 300 after the fall of Nacogdoches, whereupon Gutiérrez and Magee headed inland in mid-September 1812. Learning that La Bahía was poorly defended, the commanders changed course and marched directly there, whereupon its few defenders also fled. The Republican Army occupied a huge stone fort and captured two or three cannons. Three days later, a royalist army under Manuel de Salcedo and Simón de Herrera arrived at La Bahía and began a four-month siege. However, in all clashes the republicans were victorious.[67]

In early February 1813, Augustus Magee died under circumstances that remain uncertain, with explanations ranging from death by consumption to murder or suicide. However, throughout the siege the republican forces grew steadily. Volunteers filtered in from Nacogdoches and deserters from the Spanish army joined the ranks. Agents among Texas Indians were also successful in recruiting the assistance of Lipans and Tonkawas.

On February 19, 1813, Salcedo and Herrera lifted the fruitless siege and retreated toward Béxar. Two days later the republicans marched on the capital. Following the death of Magee, military command was placed in the hands of Samuel Kemper of Virginia, with Reuben Ross serving as major. To defend San Antonio, Herrera made a stand at Salado Creek, about eight miles southeast of the city.[68] The Battle of Salado, also known as the Battle of Rosillo, was a devastating rout of Herrera's forces. Anglo-Americans, Mexicans, and Indian auxiliaries defeated the royalists in an engagement that lasted no more than twenty minutes. Herrera suffered 330 killed and 60 captured, while the republicans had only 6 killed and 26 wounded.[69]

Shortly after the Battle of Salado, Salcedo and Herrera surrendered in San Antonio. A junta appointed by Gutiérrez found the two men and a dozen officers guilty of treasonous actions against the Hidalgo movement and ordered their execution, but the Anglo-American officers objected to the harsh sentences. Gutiérrez appeared to acquiesce and agreed to incarcerate the prisoners away from Béxar. On April 3 Antonio Delgado, a rebel captain, and sixty Mexican soldiers marched the bound men out of San Antonio. At the Salado battle site, the helpless captives were unhorsed, humiliated, and set upon with knives. Governor Salcedo, Colonel Herrera, and their aides died of stab wounds and slit throats! The mutilated bodies were left where they fell.[70]

When Delgado returned to Béxar, his boastful, joking remarks about the assassinations sickened many volunteers in the Republican Army. Anglo-Americans, in particular, began to desert the cause, and the terrible incident served to worsen already deteriorating relations between the Anglo-American and Mexican contingents. The murder of Governor Salcedo and his staff also moved the bureaucracy of New Spain to undertake a vengeful reconquest of Texas. In 1813 Viceroy Félix María Calleja created the Commandancy General of the Eastern Interior Provinces and filled the office of commandant with Joaquín de Arredondo, a former governor of Nuevo Santander.[71]

Meanwhile, Texas remained under the nominal control of Gutiérrez. On April 6 he declared the province independent of Spain and on April 17, 1813, proclaimed Texas's first constitution, which provided for a centralized rather than republican form of government. With the assistance of a junta, Gutiérrez governed briefly with the lofty title of "President Protector of the State of Texas."[72] Elements within the Republican Army, however, soon removed Gutiérrez from power and sent him into exile. The conspirators then installed José Alvarez de Toledo as the new com-

mander. Toledo had compiled a checkered career as a Spanish naval officer and delegate from Santo Domingo to the Spanish Cortes, but he was
a man of considerable talent and energy. His immediate responsibility
was to organize and lead a Texas army against the forces of Arredondo
and Ignacio Elizondo, who were marching from Laredo to crush the insurrection and return Texas to the Spanish fold.[73]

The two opposing armies met at the Medina River on August 18,
1813. Although they numbered perhaps fourteen hundred, the insurgent
forces were little more than a mob without discipline or organization.
The combined troops of Arredondo and Elizondo probably contained
more than two thousand men, although the commandant general placed
the number at only sixteen hundred. After four hours of battle, royalist
forces "were masters of the enemy's ground." Arredondo and Elizondo
had scored a total triumph, and their officers reported approximately one
thousand bodies of the enemy on the field of battle. Among the dead was
the son of General James Wilkinson.[74]

On September 13, 1813, Arredondo drafted his official report of the
battle to Viceroy Calleja. In his words: "The ever victorious and invin-
cible arms of our Sovereign, aided by the powerful hand of the god of
war, have gained the most complete and decisive victory over the base
and perfidious rabble commanded by certain vile assassins ridiculously
styled a general and commanders." However, near the end of his report,
Arredondo contradicted his earlier assessment of the opposition, calling
its troops "well-armed throughout, full of pride . . . and versed in military
tactics." Perhaps the commandant general did not wish to lessen the lus-
ter of a remarkable victory by contending that the enemy was totally
without military skills. He singled out the Anglo-Americans as adept
in battle but attributed their fighting qualities to lessons learned from
"traitorous Spanish soldiers," who had the benefits of training in the
king's army.[75]

Following Arredondo's victory, "the commandant general's vengeance
on Spanish Texas was swift and hard. Confiscation, detention, and execution were the methods he used to restore royalist authority." That assessment of Arredondo's policies by Félix D. Almaráz, Jr., is reinforced
by other respected historians of Texas who have charged Arredondo with
doing his work so thoroughly "that the province was virtually depopulated save for the settlement at Béxar."[76] Those appraisals of the commandant general's actions seem beyond reasonable dispute. His Draconian policies also served to erode the allegiance of the king's civilian
defenders in Texas.

After the restoration of Ferdinand VII to the Spanish throne in 1814, increasing disaffection with him and his reactionary policies spread throughout Spain as well as New Spain. It was that phenomenon, rather than the threat posed by expansion-minded U.S. citizens or the harsh retributions of Commandant General Arredondo, that ended three centuries of Spanish claims to Mexico and Texas.

Over the next six years, conditions in Spanish Texas remained peaceful but not prosperous. From 1813 to 1817, a succession of five interim executives followed the unfortunate Manuel de Salcedo. Finally in 1817 Antonio Martínez began a term that proved to be the last for Spanish governors. Throughout those dismal years, officials were far less concerned with the internal affairs of Texas than with the events transpiring beyond the borders of the province—on Galveston Island, in Arkansas territory, in Washington, and in Mexico.[77]

In September 1816 José Manuel Herrera, a would-be Mexican envoy to the United States, created a government on Galveston Island and proclaimed it part of the Mexican republic. Herrera then selected Louis Michel Aury, a former associate of South American Liberator Simón Bolívar, as his governor and naval commander. Also present on Galveston was Henry Perry, who had previously served as an officer in the Gutiérrez-Magee invasion of Texas. And in late November, those men were joined by Francisco Xavier Mina.[78]

Mina, a Spanish patriot, had fought the French in the Peninsular War until he was captured in 1810. Released in early 1814 at the time of Ferdinand's restoration, Mina soon turned against the king and his reactionary policies. Determined to become a revolutionary in Spanish America, Mina then made his way to the United States by way of London and Liverpool. In Baltimore he met José Alvarez de Toledo, the vanquished commander of the Battle of the Medina. Upon learning of Mina's plans to invade Mexico, Toledo offered to disrupt or abort them in hopes of a reconciliation with Ferdinand VII. He achieved the latter but could not prevent Mina's departure for Galveston.[79]

With a naval escort under the guidance of Aury, Mina's filibustering expedition left Galveston on April 7, 1817, and sailed to the coast of Nuevo Santander. From there Mina marched inland with a force of about 250 men to the village of Soto la Marina. Shortly thereafter, Henry Perry, who had joined Mina's ranks, detached 50 men and marched along the coast toward La Bahía. Arriving at present Goliad, Perry demanded its surrender, but the Spanish garrison was saved by the prompt actions of Governor Martínez, who virtually annihilated the fleeing remnants of

Perry's command. To avoid capture and execution, Perry took his own life.[80] Ten days before Perry's death, the formidable Joaquín de Arredondo overran Mina's defenses at Soto la Marina. Mina himself fled southward where he merged with Mexican rebels. He was captured on October 27, 1817, and executed by a firing squad on the eleventh of the following month.[81]

Almost simultaneously with Mina's filibustering expedition, Anglo-Americans approached Texas from Miller County, Arkansas territory, a vaguely defined area that claimed boundaries extending south of the Red River. This infiltration portended serious problems for Spanish Texas, as many of the nesters were land-hungry slaveholders. As early as 1816, Anglo-Americans with their slaves had located at Pecan Point to the south of the Red River. As Randolph B. Campbell has observed, "These early settlers had no legal right to be in Texas and certainly no assurances that they could hold slaves there. But they represented the first trickle of a flood that Spanish and Mexican authorities would be unable to stem."[82]

As Anglo-Americans began to penetrate south of the Red River, French exiles in the United States attempted colonization on the Trinity River at Le Champ d'Asile. Accommodation with them, however, was not negotiable. Organized in Philadelphia under the leadership of General Charles Lallemand and with the encouragement of Joseph Bonaparte— himself an exile in the United States—the expatriates planned to set up a colony on the Texas coast. From that base they hoped to liberate New Spain, secure the assistance of the new government, and free Napoleon from his island prison at St. Helena. In early 1818 the colonists led by General Antoine Rigaud arrived on Galveston Island, where they obtained vessels from Jean Laffite to transport them to the Trinity River. The French exiles propagandized the colony as an idyllic place to cultivate the olive and the vine, but it was short-lived. A combination of food shortages and news that Spanish soldiers were marching to the Trinity forced the Champ d'Asile colonists to return to Galveston, where their venture fell apart.[83]

In 1819 the Transcontinental Treaty between Spain and the United States finally resolved the ownership of Texas, a matter that had occupied officials and diplomats of the two countries since 1803. The treaty— negotiated by Luis de Onís, long-time Spanish minister to the United States, and the U.S. secretary of state, John Quincy Adams—defined the western boundary of the Louisiana Purchase, in part along the Sabine and Red rivers, and it brought Spanish Florida under the U.S. flag.[84]

The signing of a treaty whereby the United States acknowledged Spain's claim to Texas angered many Anglo-Americans, who saw the accord as an unacceptable "surrender of Texas." One such person was James Long, a merchant of Natchez who took matters into his own hands. Long organized a filibustering expedition intended to drive the few remaining royalists from Texas. If successful, he planned to form a new republican government and attract immigrants with generous land grants. With about three hundred followers, including John Sibley, Samuel Davenport, and Bernardo Gutiérrez, Long occupied Nacogdoches and set up a civil government on June 23, 1819. To strengthen his position, Long traveled to Galveston to seek the assistance of Jean Laffite. He was unsuccessful, and during his absence Spanish troops under Colonel Ignacio Pérez captured some of Long's men and drove the remainder of them across the Sabine.[85]

Undeterred by the failure of his first expedition, Long established new headquarters at Bolivar Point on Galveston Bay, where he was joined by his wife, Jane, a niece of General James Wilkinson. From Bolivar Point, Long led an expedition to La Bahía in the fall of 1821. By then Mexico had won its independence, and Agustín Iturbide controlled the capital. Forced to surrender to Ignacio Pérez, Long was sent to Mexico City, where about six months later a Mexican soldier on patrol shot and killed him, presumably an accident. Long's death marked the end of the early filibustering era in Texas and Mexico. His widow, because she bore a daughter at Bolivar Point on December 21, 1821, is often called the "the mother of Texas"—a preposterous notion that reveals ignorance of the events that have been the subject of this book.[86]

IN THE SUMMER OF 1821, AS A RESULT OF THE INDEPENDENCE of New Spain, Texas passed from Spanish to Mexican control with scarcely a protest by its inhabitants. The preceding seven years had been frightfully destructive to the province. Royalists had successfully repelled all military invasions, but Texas's defenders had also become her predators. In the words of David J. Weber, "By 1821 it must have been difficult to tell whether royalists or rebels had done the most harm." In the words of Antonio Martínez, the last governor of Spanish Texas, the king's soldiers had "drained the resources of the country, and laid their hands on everything that could sustain human life." The province, which Martínez governed for four years, had by his own admission "advanced at an amazing rate toward ruin and destruction." With Nacogdoches "nearly expired," it is arguable that Texas had less population in 1821 than reported (3,103) in the first census of 1777.[87] But one must look beyond sheer numbers, beyond a degraded and demoralized population that had suffered both foreign invasions and terrible reprisals by 1821, to appreciate the enduring legacies of Spanish Texas.

TWELVE

The Legacies of Spanish Texas

THE INDEPENDENCE OF MEXICO IN 1821 AND THE INCLUSION of Texas in that new nation did not spell the end of more than three centuries of Hispanic influence. Before joining the United States in 1846 as its twenty-eighth state, Texas experienced fifteen years under Mexican governance and another ten as an independent republic.[1] Given the state's past and its long, common border with Mexico, it is often difficult to separate Spanish and Mexican legacies, such as persistence of the Spanish language and Roman Catholicism. In those instances, it seems appropriate to blur distinctions. This final chapter assesses the lasting and important aspects of a Hispanic past, as well as the blending of Spaniards with indigenous peoples to produce the roots of Tejanos.

OVERALL, SPANISH INFLUENCES IN TEXAS APPEAR TO BE WELL out of proportion to the small number of Hispanics and Hispanicized settlers who were present in 1821. The most obvious, albeit superficial, legacy from the colonial period is Spanish names for counties, places, rivers, creeks, towns, and cities. Approximately one-sixth (42) of the 254 Texas counties have Hispanic names or Anglicized derivations such as Galveston and Uvalde. Hundreds of physiographic features like Llano Estacado, Guadalupe Mountains, or Padre Island perhaps serve as reminders of Spanish explorers and conquistadors who crossed parts of Texas well before the English settled the Atlantic Coast of North America. Every major river in Texas, with the exception of the Red, bears a Spanish name or an Anglicized derivation.[2] And there is the name of the state itself. Thanks to Indians in East Texas and the influence of a few Spanish officials who, for a change, insisted on a simple rather than complex name for the province, Tejas became Texas, not the New Kingdom of the Philippines. Surely most Texans are grateful for not being known as New Filipinos!

On a more serious note, two of the most important Spanish contributions to Texas are the legacy of literature and an astonishing bureaucratic penchant for preserving historical records. The early modern history of Texas depends almost entirely on maps, diaries, itineraries, accounts, records, and letters set down by Hispanic explorers and pioneers. A sketch map of the Gulf Coast, drawn during the voyage of Alonso Alvarez de Pineda in 1519, is the oldest known document of Texas history.

The first descriptive accounts of Texas date from the late 1530s. Shortly after the Four Ragged Castaways reached Mexico City in the summer of 1536, Cabeza de Vaca, Andrés Dorantes, and Alonso Castillo drew up a memorial of their experiences in the north country, including Texas. Their account, known as the Joint Report, contains the collective remembrances of the three European survivors of the Pánfilo de Narváez expedition. Probably within two or three years after the trek ended, Cabeza de Vaca set down his own recollections. That work, often referred to as *Los Naufragios (Shipwrecks)*, was first published in 1542.[3]

The two narratives, both of which were written from memory rather than field notes, constitute the first literature about Texas. The Cabeza de Vaca account in particular is a primary document on the Karankawas as well as inland hunting and gathering cultures, for Cabeza de Vaca lived among those groups and survived to write about the experience. No other Spaniard was able to do that. Providing insight into the Karankawas' daily lives, Cabeza de Vaca credited them with loving their children more than any other people in the world and noted that mourning the death of a child went on day after day for an entire year.[4]

His portrayals of the Mariames and Avavares, with whom he lived for about eighteen months and eight months, respectively, make them the best described Indians of southern Texas; his account is especially revealing of their cultural traditions. For example, both groups placed enormous portent on the subject matter of dreams, even to the point of destroying cherished male children. The roles of males and females in those societies and the degraded state of the elderly are clearly delineated. From experiences among the Avavares, Cabeza de Vaca remembered their fear of demons, especially an evil little man called "Bad Thing," who had terrorized these Indians in the past by tearing off arms and cutting out portions of their entrails. And Cabeza de Vaca documented male homosexuality among South Texas Indians, a repulsive practice in his view whereby a "man is married to another." He and other Spaniards labeled Indians of this sexual orientation *berdaches*.[5] Thanks to firsthand observations recorded in *Los Naufragios*, unique ethnographic information is preserved. In Cabeza de Vaca's narrative and the Joint Report, the observations of three Europeans and an African on early Texas landforms, flora, and fauna are also recorded. A careful reading and interpretation of both sources does much to illuminate the probable course of the Castaways across the Texas landscape. No other Spanish province within the present United States was described so early or with such detail.

The carefully planned expeditions of Francisco Vázquez de Coronado and Hernando de Soto contained chroniclers and diarists who provided early geographic and ethnographic information about the Panhandle and East Texas. Both regions were penetrated by Europeans for the first time in the early 1540s.

Pedro de Castañeda accompanied Coronado on his trek to the north country, and approximately ten years after their return to Mexico, Castañeda wrote a classic account of the expedition. The narrative provides core information on the first European contacts with Apaches and experiences on the High Plains. It was the landscape, however, that awed Castañeda. In his words, one could travel for sixty miles and see "nothing but cows and sky." Even the tracks of horses failed to serve as reference points "because the grass straightened up again as soon as it was trodden down." The sky was especially disturbing to Castañeda, for it appeared as a small dome clamped over the land with the horizon just a short distance away. If one became lost at midday in pursuit of game, which happened at times to Coronado's men, it was advisable to stay quietly in one place. Only at dusk did the sun provide directional orientation. Remaining stationary required great discipline, which not everyone was capable of, for "they have to be men who are practiced to do it. Those who are not, had to trust themselves to others."[6] Again, a firsthand account by a participant lends vividness to early Texas history.

Rodrigo Ranjel and a soldier known as the Gentleman of Elvas served as chroniclers of the de Soto expedition. Their narratives contain the first information on the Caddoes. In October 1541, while de Soto's army was in present southern Arkansas, a clash occurred with natives of a province known as Tula. Ranjel described these Indians as armed with "large, long poles, like lances, the ends hardened by fire, and they were the best fighting people that the Christians met with." The relationship of these natives to Caddoes was confirmed in the following summer by Luis de Moscoso's men. In East Texas they noted the similarity of Indians known to be Caddoes to the people of Tula.[7] Following these encounters, Spaniards had no further contacts with Caddoes for approximately 150 years.

In the late 1680s, Spaniards again entered East Texas in search of La Salle's colony. Alonso de León logged the progress of this journey in 1689 and again in 1690. Following the establishment of San Francisco de los Tejas in 1690 to its abandonment in 1693, and again after the reoccupation of Texas in 1716, reports from missionaries flowed southward to Mexico City. Firsthand descriptions of the Tejas came from the pens of Fathers Francisco Casañas de Jesús María, Isidro Félix de Espinosa, Francisco Hidalgo, Antonio Margil de Jesús, and Damián Massanet.[8]

Franciscan padres who labored in the missions of Texas, like those stationed elsewhere in New Spain, left behind a body of information that is truly remarkable. The best of them believed that it was necessary to learn as much as possible about their Indian charges in order to facilitate the natives' conversion to Christianity, just as a physician must first diagnose a patient's condition before administering treatment. With that in mind, friars in Texas found time to be good geographers, ethnologists, botanists, and historians, as well as servants of their faith.

Perhaps the example of Father Espinosa best illustrates the literary contributions of nonsecular clergy who served in Texas. Espinosa was a man of wide experience, having accompanied the expeditions of Domingo Ramón in 1716, Martín de Alarcón in 1718, and the Marqués de Aguayo in 1721. With his own hands, he helped build structures for churches and dwellings, and he assisted in the founding of several missions. This talented Franciscan has been called "the Julius Caesar of the Faith, for he worked all day and wrote all night."[9]

The writings of Espinosa are especially impressive. They include the biography of his friend and fellow priest, Antonio Margil de Jesús, the venerable Franciscan known as "the Apostle of Texas," who remains under consideration for sainthood by the Vatican. A second major work, Crónica Apostólica, is "the standard history of the colleges of Propaganda Fide of the Franciscans of New Spain." It is widely regarded as the best treatment of missionary work in the northern provinces of New Spain and is invaluable for the history of early missions in Texas.[10]

Apart from Espinosa, the best contemporary history of Texas in the colonial era came from the pen of another Franciscan, Juan Agustín Morfi. Father Morfi entered the Interior Provinces as a chaplain in the service of Teodoro de Croix. His work, composed in Mexico after he returned there in 1778, was intended "to prove, by presenting the facts, the unselfish character of the missionaries." The Franciscan historian, however, was far less charitable to the civil officials and soldiers in Texas, charging them with gross incompetence and moral degeneracy. Beyond obvious bias, Morfi's History of Texas, 1673–1779 provided "invaluable insights into the life in the missions, villages, and presidios, as well as the Indian tribes." Thanks to Carlos E. Castañeda's translation of Morfi's history of Texas, which contains excellent information on the eighteenth century, this work is available in English.[11]

For those who read Spanish and are skilled in paleography, the volume of original manuscript materials on colonial Texas is often overwhelming. It would be naive to suggest that Spaniards had such an appreciation of history that virtually everything that transpired from king and Council of the Indies to the lowest governmental or ecclesiastical unit was recorded and preserved. Instead, Spanish officials were thoroughly cautious bureaucrats who protected themselves by "papering over" their most minute and seemingly insignificant decisions and actions. Regardless of intent, the results were the same. For the researcher on Spanish Texas, the Archivo General de Indias in Seville, the Archivo General de la Nación in Mexico City, and the Béxar Archives in Austin, to name only the richest depositories, groan with the weight of old paper. Therein are thousands of letters, reports, lawsuits, inventories, and memorials. Few other than scholars are aware of the extent to which these holdings provide bedrock information on Spanish Texas.

By mining documentation, scholars have explored many persistent Hispanic elements in Texas. One of the earliest of these was the introduction of European livestock. Spanish expeditions dating from the 1680s brought along cattle for food on the hoof, as well as horses and mules for transportation. Some of this stock strayed or was left behind when the Spanish abandoned Texas in 1693. More than twenty years later when St. Denis passed through East Texas, he observed that the Tejas loosely managed ample numbers of half-wild horses and cattle.[12]

Systematic ranching in Texas, however, began at San Antonio in the 1720s. The Marqués de San Miguel de Aguayo first introduced large numbers of horses, mules, cattle, and sheep into the province. After his successful efforts in reclaiming East Texas from the French in 1721–1722, the two missions at San Antonio were supported by a strengthened presidio and growing civilian population. Residents at Béxar depended on beef, and the missionaries at Valero and San José, who possessed land and exercised control over Indian labor, began the care and management of open-range livestock.[13]

By the 1730s five missions at San Antonio engaged in ranching on large, vaguely defined land grants. Soldiers of the presidio, local cowhands, and Canary Islanders likewise shared in livestock management. Private ranches followed in the wake of husbandry practiced by the missions, but the earliest date of their existence is uncertain.[14] While ranching, both corporate and private, later developed around the missions and settlements of East Texas, its nucleus lay in a broad area between San Antonio and present Goliad.

Until the coming of Anglo-Americans in the 1800s, ranching was the exclusive domain of Spaniards. Much of the terminology presently used in stock raising, such as "cinch," "rodeo," "remuda," "chaps," "lasso," and "corral," is either Spanish or of Spanish derivation. Whether ranching in Texas as it developed in the nineteenth century was affected more by Anglo or Hispanic traditions is a subject of recent historiographical controversy. Terry G. Jordan credited Anglos with introducing three new concepts: the use of whips and dogs, salt for livestock, and burning the range. Jordan also maintained that Anglo practices were not significantly influenced by Hispano-Mexican traditions. Jack Jackson, on the other hand, argued that the Hispanic approach prevailed because it was already adapted to the land and climatic conditions.[15] What seems certain is that ranching in varying degrees became a composite of the two traditions. It is equally certain that the introduction of Spanish livestock and agriculture had a lasting impact on the land.

Horses, mules, cattle, and sheep subjected native grasses to concentrated grazing. As a consequence, mesquite, which was native to the lower Texas coast, began to spread inland. Thick, tall grass had historically prevented the germination of mesquite beans on the interior prairies. Pre-Spanish Indians had occasionally burned small portions of the range as a means of entrapping game, but domesticated livestock had a more pervasive effect. Original vegetation gave way to shorter standing growth. Once pastures were fenced, wooden posts made the Anglo practice of burning the range unfeasible, but enclosed, heavily grazed grasslands furthered the inland advance of mesquite.[16]

The growth of farming in Spanish Texas also permanently altered the landscape. Other than among the Caddoes, who were accomplished agriculturalists, tilling the land was a rare phenomenon among pre-Spanish Texas Indians. Like ranching, systematic farming began in the San Antonio region. From 1718 to 1731, the original civilian settlers at Béxar had engaged in some farming, but it was the Canary Islanders who made cropping their primary source of livelihood. As former peasants and fishermen, the original Isleños felt most at home tilling the land. Their efforts were soon furthered by the construction of an irrigation ditch to water their fields of corn, beans, oats, melons, cotton, chili peppers, and vegetables. While successful as farmers, the Canary Islanders were often at odds with the older Bexareños. These conflicts, however, paled in comparison to their struggles with the missionaries in the 1730s.

At that time the Franciscan missions had not yet achieved their heyday, but they, operating ideally in tandem with presidios (although this was seldom true in practice), represented one of the most important components of Spanish presence in Texas. From the founding of the first mission in 1682 to the last in 1793, there were close to forty different sites in Texas. Individual religious outposts lasted from less than a year to more than a hundred, but rarely were even a dozen in operation at any one time. They stretched from El Paso to Robeline, Louisiana, from Menard to Goliad. In colonial times outlying missions at El Paso and La Junta de los Ríos were administered, respectively, by the provinces of New Mexico and Nueva Vizcaya. Only by virtue of a flood in 1829 that changed the course of the Río Grande were the four missions at El Paso placed within the confines of modern Texas.[17]

Collectively, the missions of Spanish Texas are monuments to both idealistic and practical endeavors. As frontier institutions, they were intended to serve the dual aims of church and state. Their most obvious function was to save the souls of Indians, but they also assisted civilian settlements and presidios in extending and holding the frontier.

Civilians helped settle San Antonio as early as 1718, well before Villa San Fernando de Béxar came into existence in 1731. Chartered town settlements along with missions and presidios shared importantly in "the common goal of securing the land" against internal disturbances and foreign encroachment. Using a broad definition of civilian settlements, there may have been as many as nine or ten of them within the borders of the present state, with four still viable today. San Antonio, the oldest municipality in Texas, has expanded in size and population to become one of the ten largest cities in the United States. Simultaneous with its founding, presidio San Antonio de Béxar provided vital security to this frontier community.[18]

Antedating San Antonio de Béxar by two years, Nuestra Señora de los Dolores, the first Texas presidio, was set up in 1716 among the East Texas missions. Overall, Texas had only eight of these forts, with no more than five in operation at any one time. The restored presidio at Goliad serves to commemorate Spain's military outposts in Texas.

Historically, the presidio and the role of garrison soldiers in the hinterlands of New Spain were slighted by Herbert E. Bolton and his academic progeny, who placed great emphasis on the missionary clergy and their noble goal of winning native converts to the faith. In recent decades, however, scholars have made significant contributions to the field of military history. The works of Sidney B. Brinckerhoff, Odie B. Faulk, and Max Moorhead, supplemented in the 1980s by the publications of Thomas H. Naylor and Charles W. Polzer, provide essential balance to the wealth of publications on missions and the missionary clergy. Furthermore, over the last thirty years of the province as a Spanish possession, a predominantly military solution to existing problems was sought.[19]

The Franciscan missions as well as the friars who labored in them have earned a mixture of criticism and praise for the treatment of Indians during the mission era. It is sometimes contended that the padres did not adequately prepare their neophytes to function in the "real world." In short, when secularization began in the 1790s, mission Indians were ill suited to take their place as independent, taxpaying citizens. There may be a measure of validity in that contention. Realistically, however, Indians, except for those who intermarried or mingled with Hispanicized persons, were almost universally doomed. If one accepts the inevitability of Europeans dominating Texas, and who can argue otherwise given their superior organization and technology, then a necessary corollary is that Indians—no matter how noble or praiseworthy—would not be allowed to continue in their old ways. To argue otherwise is to deny "the inexorability of change."[20] In the long run, the choices for the indigenous people were only two: accommodation or elimination.

To be sure, Texas missions were less than perfect. Because of the incidence of infectious diseases, life within them was often perilous, but they nonetheless provided an atmosphere that was relatively more humane than any other Spanish institution. When compared to encomienda, which took a horrible death toll in the Caribbean and Central Mexico, Franciscan missions of the frontier offered surroundings that were generally benign. The friars imparted the rudiments of Christianity and European values in an atmosphere of forced confinement, discipline, and hard work. This process, which at times employed corporal punishment, made neophytes more acceptable in the eyes of Spaniards as well as those of mixed ethnicity. Therein lay the safest path to survival and assimilation. As Mardith K. Schuetz has observed, the goals of the missions were to convert "a rustic, pagan people to Christianized citizens of the Spanish crown with the same rights and privileges as other Spanish subjects." If the natives were eventually absorbed by the dominant culture, as indeed they were, the missions should hardly be "condemned for having done their job so thoroughly."[21] Schuetz's arguments provide a solid counterpoint to those who decry the failure of missions in Spanish Texas.

Fortunately, too, societal and race relations in the frontier provinces were less rigid than in the heartland of New Spain. By the 1760s intermarriage between the Canary Islanders and persons of mixed origins occurred with considerable frequency, although racial considerations were not entirely absent. Marriage and land records often made reference to an individual's ties with the original Isleño families. Those who claimed to be *españoles* (Spaniards) in the censuses of the 1780s were usually not of pure racial identification; rather, the term "served as an all-embracing label which described relative wealth, social and occupational standing, degrees of assimilation, and even the attitudes of the census takers." At the bottom of the social ladder, except for a few black slaves, were un-assimilated Indians. Many of them, however, no longer resisted contacts with Hispanics.[22]

At San Antonio, as Elizabeth A. H. John has demonstrated, "by pain-ful trial and error, Indian and Spanish communities evolved toward peaceful coexistence." John portrayed Béxar in the 1780s and 1790s as a place of interaction between Spaniards and Indian allies who came "to trade and talk, to nourish the bonds of brotherhood." But she also noted that most of these "hard-won accommodations lapsed at the turn of the century when a decaying Spain could no longer sustain its commitments on that remote northern frontier."[23] By 1821 the greater part of some three thousand nonindigenous settlers in Spanish Texas were mestizo, of mixed ethnicity. Jack Jackson has shown that caste distinctions continued in the Mexican population with the use of terms such as *español,* indio, negro, mestizo, *mulato, coyote, lobo,* and *zambo.* He also noted that many Anglo-Americans were apt to ignore these finer distinctions and lump all Spanish speakers into one "despicable" race.[24]

Social considerations aside, to what extent did Hispanic jurisprudence carry over into post-1821 Texas, and what was the legal status of men and women living in the province? Given the rather disdainful view of Hispanics and Mexicans held by many Anglo-Texans in the nineteenth century, it is perhaps surprising that so many Spanish legal practices sur-vived to become a permanent part of the state's body of law. Those influ-ences, as Joseph W. McKnight has observed, fall into three broad cate-gories: rules of judicial procedure, land and water law, and family law.

Anglo-Texas lawyers in the nineteenth century were clearly aware of the differences between Hispano-Mexican law and Anglo-American law. The latter system, which was more familiar to those lawyers, commonly involved two sets of courts: one referred to as courts of law; and the other, courts of equity. Certain remedies such as specific performance and injunction were available in the latter but not in the former. The Castilian system of civil courts, which was unitary, was in effect in Texas. There-fore Anglo-Texans favored a single "court in which all issues were con-sidered simultaneously" and perpetuated it in 1840. Accordingly, the Republic of Texas was the first English-speaking country "to adopt a permanent and full unitary system of judicial administration."[25]

Also in the area of judicial procedure, Spanish law provided that trials take place in the locale that was most convenient for the defendant. This differed from English law, which stipulated that cases be heard where the circumstance producing the dispute arose. The rationale for Anglo-American procedure was keyed to trial by jury, based on the assumption that local jurors would more likely know the facts of the case as well as the reputation of the litigants. But Castilian courts operated without juries, and therefore the place of trial was determined by the convenience of the defendant. Here again, following Hispanic precedent, the basic rule of Texas law is "that a person must be sued where he lives for *his* convenience." If the plantiff prevails, his or her convenience is also served because the defendant's property for satisfaction of the judgment will likely be located at the defendant's place of residence.[26]

Spanish law also prevailed in judicial procedures related to probate matters. Under Anglo-American law the executor of a will must obtain a court order to perform any act not specifically authorized in the testament. In Texas one can use the simple expedient of appointing an "independent executor." By the use of these words, "a testator gives his post-mortem representative the right to do without a court order what an ordinary executor could do with one." Placing trust in one's executor provides great flexibility in the administration of estates and saves time and court expenses. Years ago this Spanish judicial procedure was borrowed from Texas by Arizona and Washington, and Idaho has since copied it from Washington. Influenced by this experience, the similar provisions of the Uniform Probate Code adopted in approximately ten other states stand "as a significant Texas transmission of her Spanish heritage to other American states."[27]

In matters relating to land and water, Hispanic land titles with a substantial boost from international law persisted in Texas. A basic tenet of international law holds that when sovereignty changes, private ownership is not affected unless it is specifically altered by the new government. In short, without contravening action those who own private lands are entitled to keep them, and lands belonging to the former sovereign pass to the new one. When Texas achieved its independence, vast lands held by Mexico passed to the republic. Grants made under Spanish and Mexican rule were validated, and as a consequence approximately one-seventh of all private lands in Texas have titles emanating from Spanish sovereigns or Mexican officials.[28]

Legal guidelines regarding water are somewhat more complex in that they are a mixture of post-1840 laws adopted by the republic and those dating from the Hispano-Mexican periods. Essentially, varying laws apply to lands that adjoin seashores and banks of rivers. Both Spanish and English systems reserve seashores over which the tide ebbs and flows to the sovereign. Under Spanish practice, however, the line is drawn farther up on the shore. Where the grade is very flat, as it is along much of the Gulf Coast, pre-1840 laws reserve for the dryland owner "proportionately less of the seashore . . . than his neighbor whose grant dates from after 1840."[29]

Similar disparities apply to grants made along the courses of navigable rivers and perennial streams. Spanish law specified that the sovereign owned the beds of such waterways. Individual land grants in the Hispano-Mexican periods extended only to the edge of the streams. Post-1840 grants, however, permitted ownership of lands adjoining navigable rivers to a line drawn down the middle of the channel. In a similar vein, Spanish land grants along rivers and streams ordinarily placed more restrictions on the use of riparian waters than did post-1840 titles. Under the former they could be employed only for domestic consumption and the watering of livestock. Irrigation was not permitted unless it was specifically included in the grant.[30]

As an example of the continuing application of Spanish law in contemporary Texas, the building of Falcon Reservoir on the Río Grande in the late 1950s raised the legal issue of compensation for downstream landowners. Impounded water meant a lessened volume flowing by riverine properties. It was concluded that "since the Spanish sovereign had not disposed of these rights, the state of Texas as successor to the rights of Spain had taken nothing away for which it had to pay as a result of constructing the dam and impounding the water."[31]

Family law in Texas is especially steeped in Spanish elements. It governs the property rights of partners in marriage as well as the adoption of children, and it affects at one time or another virtually every resident of the state. The basic principle under Spanish law is that when couples enter into marriage in good faith, many of the legal consequences are the same as in a valid marriage, even if it later transpires that the union is invalid. In brief, children of marriages later deemed invalid are considered legitimate, and a fair division of the profits of marriage results as though such unions had always been valid. Legitimation of children in such instances was codified in 1841 and has been operative from that date to the present.[32]

Under English law the concept of adoption was unknown. It was not only alien as a general principle but was not even attempted in individual instances by legislation. With the advent of Anglo-American law in Texas, adoption as a legal procedure ended in 1840. However, ten years

later, after the legislatures of the republic and the state had been repeatedly petitioned to approve adoption in specific instances, the Spanish
principle was reinstated. Apart from Mississippi, "Texas was the first
Anglo-American state to institute adoption generally and permanently.[33]

The adoption statute in Texas, as McKnight has observed, had a "particularly Spanish ring" to it. It meant that an adopted child also became
an heir of the adoptive parent. Following the Spanish example, a child
acquired by adoption had the same rights as a biological offspring. As
under Spanish law, however, adopted children can still claim inheritance
from their bloodline parents unless an adoption court specifically termi-
nates that right.[34]

In the field of family law, the principle of community property is highly
significant in Texas. This familial concept, which sprang from Hispanic
precedent and frontier experience, applies to the state of matrimony,
wherein husband and wife share equally the gains of that union. Spanish
law was especially responsive to the dangers and realities of the hinter-
land. Both spouses shared harsh circumstances in remote provinces as
well as the almost constant threat of Indian attacks. In fairness, Hispanic
law held that husband and wife should reap the benefits of matrimony
equally.[35] Spanish views of the property rights of women in marriage
stood in contradistinction to the Anglo-American law that was generally
observed in English-speaking portions of the United States. "The prevailing American rule was that borrowed from the English: that during marriage the husband and wife were one, and, to use Blackstone's pithy
phrase, 'the husband was the one.'" For example, in Anglo-America the
postnuptial earnings of the wife, even from land she held title to, belonged to her spouse. On the death of the husband, the wife was protected only by a life interest in one-third of the lands of her deceased
spouse.[36]

The patent inequities of Anglo-American law as applied to married
women have been recognized and amended in many American States, but
Texas after Louisiana was the first to do so. When Anglo-American law
was generally adopted in 1840, colonists saw the wisdom and fairness of
certain aspects of the Spanish system over what they had experienced in
the United States. Accordingly, they specifically excluded the Anglo-
American law of matrimonial property.[37] While not found exclusively in
states that were former Hispanic provinces, community property law is
largely confined to those that have a Spanish heritage, such as Texas,
Louisiana, New Mexico, Arizona, Nevada, and California. As McKnight
has pointed out, even the right to file a joint federal income tax return
flows from this Hispanic principle.[38]

Finally, in the area of family law, the protection from creditors of certain essential pieces of personal property has roots in Castilian practices that date from the thirteenth century. Relying on the Spanish model, Texas adopted the first U.S. homestead law on January 26, 1839. This legislation made it possible for a debtor to protect the principal residence of the family from seizure by creditors; the law also protected such items as basic clothing, farming implements, tools of trade, beasts of burden, and ordinary household furnishings. Subsequent legislative actions, state constitutions, and judicial interpretations have strengthened these debtor exemption provisions so that Texas surpasses most other states in the United States in the liberality of its property exemption law.[39]

Again, as McKnight has observed, "The legacy of Hispanic law to the law of Texas is a considerable one. It is a striking sociological phenomenon when a people of their own free will abandon the institutions on which they have been reared in favor of foreign rules generally available only in a foreign tongue." The influences of Hispanic legal traditions and precedents probably have the greatest impact on the everyday lives of Texans, and they serve as landmarks of a significant colonial past.[40]

Also forming part of that Hispanic mosaic are notable examples of legacies in art, architecture, education, music, theater, medicine, and religion. Each deserves recognition in its own right and makes up a part of Texas's past. The "earliest extant easel painting by a professional artist depicting an event in Texas history" dates from the second half of the eighteenth century (see Figure 23). Painted in Mexico by an unknown artist, *The Destruction of Mission San Sabá,* depicting events in 1758, was commissioned by Pedro Romero de Terreros, the wealthy patron of the short-lived religious outpost near present Menard and uncle of martyred priest Alonso Giraldo de Terreros. While not accurate in all details, it nevertheless served as "a historically evocative visual document." The painting is especially significant in its attempt to convey in a single scene a sequence of events occurring over several hours.[41] Antedating the studio work commissioned by Romero de Terreros is a cartouche included in the margin of a French map published in 1705 by Nicolas de Fer (see Figure 24). This small colored drawing is probably the oldest depiction of a historical event in Texas. Its theme is the assassination of La Salle (1687) in East Texas.[42]

Hispanic contributions to architecture are still in evidence. Spaniards transferred the art of building from the mother country to the New World, where it "was adapted to new and strange conditions as it spread throughout colonial dominions. But it remained Spanish." Apart from California, perhaps the best examples of Spanish missions in the South-

FIGURE 23

Destruction of Mission Santa Cruz de San Sabá. This photograph depicts a studio painting done by an unknown Mexican artist in the second half of the eighteenth century. It is the most significant artistic representation of an event in Spanish Texas. The status of the painting is currently being disputed by the United States Customs Service. (Courtesy of Dorothy Sloan.)

west are found in Texas. The restored missions at San Antonio, all of which are much older than their California counterparts, are graceful reminders of "Spain's lasting contributions to the cultural life of the Borderlands." San José, founded in 1720 by Father Margil, should appropriately be called "the Queen of Texas Missions." Its single tower, in the words of Robert M. Quinn, "exemplifies the maturest Baroque [style of architecture] of any American mission." The historic importance of this mission and three others in San Antonio is evidenced by their designation in 1978 as a National Historical Park under the protection of the National Park Service. As Park Historian Gilbert R. Cruz remarked in 1986, "These magnificent missions are historically the first institutions to introduce Western Civilization, European values and the Christian tradition on Texas soil. They have generated an immeasurable spiritual, historical and cultural influence on the early development of the South-

FIGURE 24

The assassination of La Salle. This enlarged cartouche depicting the assassination of La Salle is a detail from a map, Les Costes aux Environs de la Rivière Misisipi, *published in 1701 by Nicolas de Fer. (Courtesy of the Special Collections Division, The University of Texas at Arlington Libraries, Arlington, Texas.)*

west." The same religious establishments are more than historic monuments, for they also serve as viable parishes in San Antonio.[43] In the heart of that city may also be found the Spanish Governor's Palace and the historic Alamo. The restored presidio and replica of the mission at Goliad along with the restructured Old Stone Fort at Nacogdoches are other notable buildings that serve as reminders of a Hispanic past.

The colonial era also witnessed efforts to provide a public school for children at San Antonio. Education outside the missions began in Béxar as early as 1746. Although it was apparently short-lived, this first school was intended to impart religious doctrines to the youth of Villa San Fernando. Near the end of the eighteenth century, as the missions declined and secularization loomed on the horizon, another school opened. This experiment in secular education, begun in 1789, likewise failed to enjoy long-range success. The teacher fled San Antonio in 1792 after becoming involved in a heated dispute with the parents of his pupils, and the school closed in the same year.[44]

The first efforts to enforce compulsory school attendance for children came in 1802, when Governor Elguezábal stipulated the assessment of heavy fines on parents guilty of noncompliance. In the following year, the commandant general ordered the founding of schools at presidial posts that were large enough to afford modest compensation for a teacher. Shortly after this decree, a tuition-free school supported by public funds opened for a few children in Béxar. However, it like all other schools in Spanish Texas led a "fitful existence." The situation became especially bleak near the end of the colonial era. As Max Berger noted, "The disorders accompanying the revolutionary period (1819–1821) eradicated all signs of formal education. Not a school in all Texas survived."[45] Frontier conditions, the scarcity of population, and the poverty of the people provide sufficient explanation for the absence of an educational system. However, the circumstances in Texas were only slightly worse than those prevailing in contemporary frontier communities of the United States. At best, Spaniards deserve "credit for their efforts to clear the ground for the later educational structure of Texas."[46]

The Spanish legacy in secular music was much more enduring than that of public education. Hispanic settlers in Texas brought musical influences from Europe. Especially notable were *romances,* or narrative ballads, which constituted the oldest type of folk songs known in the Southwest. According to Arthur L. Campa, an impressive number of these original songs with local variants are still known today. Because borderlands inhabitants "inherited the art of the troubadour along with a peninsular repertoire," they not only retained the traditional ballads of Spain but also with the passage of time composed new ones. For example, narrative ballads known as *romances corridos* were often based on life in America and told tales of love, tragedy, heroic deeds, and castastrophe. Again in the words of Campa, "No other cultural group in the United States has had as long and varied a folk-singing tradition as the Hispanic folk of the Southwest."[47]

Hispanic heritage in the realms of religious theater and music also merits consideration. Dating to the medieval period in the peninsula, *autos sacramentales,* or religious dramas, were performed both within and outside churches. In America missionaries drew upon liturgical drama, and religious plays were brought into the Southwest to transmit church doctrine to the Indians. Furthermore, folk drama, as adapted to the borderlands, allowed settlers to participate in religious activities and provided entertainment as well. An example of these persistent Spanish influences may be found in folk presentations and musical productions, especially the plays *Las Posadas (The Inns)* and *Los Pastores (The Shepherds),* still popular during the Christmas season.[48]

FIGURE 25
*Insignia of the Texas Surgical Society. This is a photograph of
an original drawing by Tom Lea. (Courtesy of the Texas Surgical Society,
John W. Roberts, M.D., Secretary.)*

Although music and drama represent a continuum from the colonial period, medicine and its practice in that era are less persistent. Apart from Cabeza de Vaca's adoption as the patron saint of the Texas Surgical Society, little else merits detailed attention (see Figure 25). The first serious attempt to establish a hospital began at San Antonio in 1805. Located in the Alamo, this infirmary "functioned with some degree of ease and efficiency at first, although difficulty was encountered in finding employees at the trivial salary named." By 1806 the Alamo hospital contained a total of eighteen patients from Béxar and other military outposts, with a waiting list of twenty others. Its personnel, including managers and physicians, remained in flux, and by 1814, near the end of turbulence associated with revolutions in Mexico and Texas, it had apparently ceased to exist. In 1819 Governor Antonio Martínez remarked that there was no hospital in the province and lamented the absence of any facility to treat the sick, whether soldier or settler. As Pat I. Nixon observed, "The end of the Spanish regime was near at hand. Political survival took precedence over all other considerations."[49]

While Spanish Texas did not survive politically, the religious underpinnings of the province remained firm as it joined the new Mexican nation. After slightly more than a century of continuous occupation by Spaniards, Texas in 1821 was thoroughly Roman Catholic in faith. That religious heritage stemmed from the efforts of dozens of resolute friars, and it was perpetuated by the Plan of Iguala, the formula by which Mexico achieved her independence. Restrictive immigration policies, initiated first by Spain and continued by Mexico in the 1820s and 1830s, stipulated Roman Catholicism as the state religion. The shortage of priests and their inability to minister to incoming Anglo-Americans, however, resulted not in persecution but widespread apathy toward religion.

Despite a nominal oath to observe Roman Catholicism, Anglo-Americans entering Texas maintained their Protestant roots. With the coming of independence, their churches gained dominance. Nevertheless, Catholicism, introduced by Spain and reinforced by Mexican influence, remains strong in the state. In 1980 that faith claimed an estimated 2,340,162 adherents, second in number only to the Southern Baptists.[50]

IT SEEMS MANIFEST THAT HISPANIC LEGACIES IN THE LONE Star State vary in importance and persistence. The range includes law, which affects the lives of virtually every Texan, and Roman Catholicism, which in the 1990s may well become the faith claiming the largest number of adherents. Of lesser importance is vernacular Spanish. Words, such as patio, plaza, and rodeo, and place names, like San Antonio, El Paso, and Padre Island, often pass one's lips with scarcely a conscious reminder of their origins. As illustrated elsewhere in the world, most recently in Canada, Yugoslavia, and the Soviet Union, bilingualism and extreme ethnicity carry a high price tag. Both are potentially destructive to national unity and identity. On the other hand, Hispanic Texans and their descendants have played and will continue to play a major role in Texas history. Understanding their past is a vital component of the state's collective experience. Even though not all Spanish influences affect the day-to-day lives of Texans, they are important enough to deserve more recognition than that traditionally given to them. As Gerald E. Poyo and Gilberto M.

Hinojosa have remarked, histories of the state "usually treat colonial Texas as a colorful, but for the most part irrelevant, prelude to the rest of the state's history." In light of the Columbian Quincentenary, it is appropriate to accord significantly more recognition to a colonial past that lasted slightly more than three hundred years, about twice the life of Texas since the birth of the republic.[51]

Governors of Spanish Texas, 1691–1821

1691–1692	Domingo Terán de los Ríos
1694–1715	Texas unoccupied but included in Coahuila
1716–1719	Martín de Alarcón
1719–1722	Marqués de San Miguel de Aguayo, Texas and Coahuila
1722–1726	Fernando Pérez de Almazán
1727–1730	Melchor de Mediavilla y Azcona
1730–1734	Juan Antonio Bustillo y Ceballos
1734–1736	Manuel de Sandoval
1736–1737	Carlos Benites Franquis de Lugo
1737	Joseph Fernández de Jáuregui y Urrutia, Texas and Nuevo León
1737–1740	Prudencio de Orobio y Basterra
1741–1743	Tomás Felipe Winthuysen
1743–1744	Justo Boneo y Morales
1744–1748	Francisco García Larios, ad interim
1748–1750	Pedro del Barrio y Espriella
1751–1759	Jacinto de Barrios y Jáuregui
1759–1767	Angel de Martos y Navarrete
1767–1770	Hugo O'Conor, ad interim
1770–1778	Juan María, Barón de Ripperdá
1778–1786	Domingo Cabello y Robles
1787–1790	Rafael Martínez Pacheco
1790–1799	Manuel Muñoz
1799–1805	Juan Bautista de Elguezábal
1805–1808	Antonio Cordero y Bustamante
1808–1813	Manuel María de Salcedo
1811	Juan Bautista de las Casas, revolutionary governor
1813–1817	Cristóbal Domínguez, Benito de Armiñan, Mariano Varela, Ignacio Pérez, and Manuel Pardo, ad interim
1817–1821	Antonio María Martínez

Commandants General of the Provincias Internas, 1776–1821

Single Administrative Unit, 1776–1786

1776–1783   Teodoro de Croix
1783–1784   Felipe de Neve
1784–1786   José Antonio Renjel

Division into Three Regions, 1786–1787

(Eastern Provinces, including Texas)
1786–1787   Juan de Ugalde

Division into Eastern and Western Regions, 1787–1790

(Eastern Provinces, including Texas)
1787–1790   Juan de Ugalde

Single Administrative Unit, 1790–1810

1790–1802   Pedro de Nava
1791–1793   Ramón de Castro served as second commandant of the Eastern Provinces, including Texas.
1802–1810   Nemesio de Salcedo y Salcedo

Division into Eastern and Western Regions, 1810–1821

(Eastern Provinces, including Texas)
1810–1813   Nemesio de Salcedo y Salcedo
1813   Bernardo Bonavía y Zapata, ad interim
1813–1821   Joaquín de Arredondo

Viceroys of New Spain, 1535–1821

1535–1550	Antonio de Mendoza
1550–1564	Luis de Velasco (the elder)
1564–1566	Mexico governed by the Audiencia of New Spain
1566–1567	Gastón de Peralta, Marqués de Falces
1568–1580	Martín Enríquez de Almanza
1580–1583	Lorenzo Suárez de Mendoza, Conde de Coruña
1584–1585	Pedro Moya y de Contreras, Arzobispo de México
1585–1590	Alvaro Manrique de Zúñiga, Marqués de Villamanrique
1590–1595	Luis de Velasco (the younger)
1595–1603	Gaspar de Zúñiga y Acevedo, Conde de Monterrey
1603–1607	Juan de Mendoza y Luna, Marqués de Montesclaros
1607–1611	Luis de Velasco (the younger), Marqués de Salinas
1611–1612	García Guerra, Arzobispo de México
1612–1621	Diego Fernández de Córdoba, Marqués de Guadalcázar
1621–1624	Diego Carrillo de Mendoza y Pimentel, Marqués de Gelves y Conde de Priego
1624–1635	Rodrigo Pacheco y Osorio, Marqués de Cerralvo
1635–1640	Lope Díaz de Armendáriz, Marqués de Cadereyta
1640–1642	Diego López Pacheco Cabrera y Bobadilla, Marqués de Villena y Duque de Escalona, Grande de España
1642	Juan de Palafox y Mendoza, Obispo de Puebla
1642–1648	García Sarmiento de Sotomayor, Conde de Salvatierra y Marqués de Sobroso
1648–1649	Marcos de Torres y Rueda, Obispo de Yucatán
1650–1653	Luis Enríquez y Guzmán, Conde de Alba de Liste y Marqués de Villaflor
1653–1660	Francisco Fernández de la Cueva, Duque de Alburquerque, Grande de España
1660–1664	Juan de Leyva y de la Cerda, Marqués de Leyva y de Ladrada, Conde de Baños
1664	Diego Osorio de Escobar, Obispo de Puebla
1664–1673	Antonio Sebastián de Toledo, Marqués de Mancera

1673	Pedro Nuño Colón de Portugal, Duque de Veragua y Marqués de Jamaica
1673–1680	Payo Enríquez de Rivera, Arzobispo de México
1680–1686	Tomás Antonio de la Cerda y Aragón, Conde de Paredes y Marqués de la Laguna
1686–1688	Melchor Portocarrero Lasso de la Vega, Conde de Monclova
1688–1696	Gaspar de Sandoval Silva y Mendoza, Conde de Galve
1696	Juan de Ortega y Montañez, Obispo de Michoacán
1696–1701	José Sarmiento Valladares, Conde de Moctezuma y de Tula, Grande de España
1701	Juan de Ortega y Montañez, Arzobispo de México
1701–1711	Francisco Fernández de la Cueva Enríquez, Duque de Alburquerque y Marqués de Cuellar
1711–1716	Fernando de Alencastre Noroña y Silva, Duque de Linares
1716–1722	Baltasar de Zúñiga y Guzmán, Marqués de Valero y Duque de Arión
1722–1734	Juan de Acuña, Marqués de Casafuerte
1734–1740	Juan Antonio Vizarrón y Eguiarreta, Arzobispo de México
1740–1741	Pedro de Castro y Figueroa, Duque de la Conquista y Marqués de Gracia Real
1742–1746	Pedro Cebrián y Agustín, Conde de Fuenclara
1746–1755	Francisco de Güemes y Horcasitas, Conde de Revilla Gigedo I
1755–1760	Agustín Ahumada y Villalón, Marqués de las Amarillas
1760	Francisco Cagigal de la Vega
1760–1766	Joaquín de Montserrat, Marqués de Cruillas
1766–1771	Carlos Francisco de Croix, Marqués de Croix
1771–1779	Antonio María de Bucareli y Ursúa
1779–1783	Martín de Mayorga
1783–1784	Matías de Gálvez
1785–1786	Bernardo de Gálvez, Conde de Gálvez
1787	Alonso Núñez de Haro y Peralta, Arzobispo de México
1787–1789	Manuel Antonio Flores
1789–1794	Juan Vicente de Güemes Pacheco y Padilla, Conde de Revilla Gigedo II
1794–1798	Miguel de la Grúa Talamanca y Branciforte, Marqués de Branciforte
1798–1800	Miguel José de Azanza
1800–1803	Félix Berenguer de Marquina
1803–1808	José de Iturrigaray
1808–1809	Pedro Garibay
1809–1810	Francisco Javier de Lizana y Beaumont, Arzobispo de México
1810–1813	Francisco Javier de Venegas
1813–1816	Félix María Calleja del Rey
1816–1821	Juan Ruiz de Apodaca, Conde del Venadito
1821	Francisco Novella
1821	Juan de O'Donojú (appointed but did not assume office)

Notes

1. Texas: The Land and the People

1. D. W. Meinig, *Imperial Texas: An Interpretive Essay in Cultural Geography*, 7; Randolph B. Campbell, *An Empire for Slavery: The Peculiar Institution in Texas, 1821–1865*, 2.

2. Terry G. Jordan, John L. Bean, Jr., and William M. Holmes, *Texas: A Geography*, 1–5. For a discussion of Texas as a southern or western state, see Campbell, *Empire for Slavery*, 1.

3. Jordan, Bean, and Holmes, *Texas*, 7.

4. Herbert E. Bolton, *Coronado: Knight of Pueblos and Plains*, 243.

5. Ibid., 284–287.

6. A. Ray Stephens and William M. Holmes, *Historical Atlas of Texas*, 4.

7. Jordan, Bean, and Holmes, *Texas*, 12.

8. Ibid., 12–14.

9. *Texas Almanac and State Industrial Guide, 1988–1989*, 143. Brewster County (6,169 square miles), the largest county in Texas, is more than three times the size of Delaware and slightly larger than the combined states of Rhode Island and Connecticut.

10. Pertinent Information on Presidios of the Interior Provinces (December 11, 1728), AGI, Guadalajara 114; Jordan, Bean, and Holmes, *Texas*, 37. By Spanish calculation, Los Adaes near present Robeline, Louisiana, was situated 230 leagues (598 miles) from San Antonio and 600 leagues (1,560 miles) from Mexico City.

11. Jordan, Bean, and Holmes, *Texas*, 28.

12. For remarks about vegetation and animals in the diaries of early travelers throughout South Texas, see Jack M. Inglis, *A History of Vegetation on the Río Grande Plain*, 16–91 passim.

13. Meinig, *Imperial Texas*, 24–26.

14. Diary of the Alonso de León Expedition (1690), AGI, México 617.

15. Anonymous Diary [1727–1728], AGI, Indiferente General 108, Tomo 3. Indians called the nocturnal birds *texolotes*.

16. Letter from Teodoro de Croix to the Viceroy (February 15, 1778), AGI, Guadalajara 267; Letter from Teodoro de Croix to José de Gálvez (January 23,

1779), AGI, Guadalajara 267; Letter from Domingo Cabello to Teodoro de Croix (June 18, 1779), BAM, Roll 13. Unfortunately, I found no evidence that any of the animals reached Spain.

17. Fanny Bandelier, trans., *The Journey of Alvar Núñez Cabeza de Vaca and His Companions from Florida to the Pacific, 1528–1536*, 102–103; Bolton, *Coronado*, 263, as quoted. For a discussion of climate in North America during the "Little Ice Age," see Hubert H. Lamb, *Weather, Climate, and Human Affairs: A Book of Essays and Other Papers*, 42–43.

18. Descriptions of the Interior Provinces by Juan Alvarez Barreiro (February 10, 1730), AGI, Guadalajara 144.

19. W. W. Newcomb, Jr., "Foreword," in T. N. Campbell, *The Indians of Southern Texas and Northeastern Mexico: Selected Writings of Thomas Nolan Campbell*, ix.

20. W. W. Newcomb, Jr., "Karankawa," in *New Handbook of North American Indians*, ed. William C. Sturtevant, vol. 10, *Southwest*, ed. Alfonso Ortiz, 359, quotation; Cyclone Covey, trans., *Cabeza de Vaca's Adventures in the Unknown Interior of America*, 61–63.

21. Covey, *Adventures*, 60.

22. Newcomb, "Karankawa," 366, quotation. Important ethnographic information on the Karankawas in the last quarter of the seventeenth century may be gleaned from the interrogations of Pierre and Jean-Baptiste Talon, survivors of La Salle's colony at Fort St. Louis. The Talon brothers lived for a time as Indians. See Robert S. Weddle, ed., Mary C. Morkovsky, and Patricia Galloway, assoc. eds., *Three Primary Documents: La Salle, the Mississippi, and the Gulf*, 2, 209–224, 259–274.

23. By the mid-1840s, remnants of the Karankawas had fled to Mexico.

24. John R. Swanton, *The Indian Tribes of North America*, 309–311.

25. Martín Salinas, *Indians of the Rio Grande Delta: Their Role in the History of Southern Texas and Northeastern Mexico*, 142, quotations.

26. W. W. Newcomb, Jr., *The Indians of Texas: From Prehistoric to Modern Times*, 33, quotation; T. N. Campbell and T. J. Campbell, *Historic Indian Groups of the Choke Canyon Reservoir and Surrounding Area, Southern Texas*, 64–65, quotation.

27. Donald E. Chipman, "In Search of Cabeza de Vaca's Route across Texas: An Historiographical Survey," *Southwestern Historical Quarterly* 91 (October 1987): 135; Campbell and Campbell, *Historic Indians*, 10. The most detailed study of Indians of the Río Grande delta is by Martín Salinas. This otherwise excellent work is marred by acceptance of the Río de las Palmas of colonial times (the Soto la Marina) as the Río Grande. Lack of agreement on fundamental points of geography has led to the placement of Spanish colonists in Texas, such as those sponsored by Francisco de Garay, when they were demonstrably not there. See Salinas, *Indians*, 22–24.

28. Campbell and Campbell, *Historic Indians*, 10–32; Chipman, "Cabeza de Vaca's Route," 147.

29. Bandelier, *Journey of Cabeza de Vaca*, 89–90.

30. Campbell and Campbell, *Historic Indians*, 5; Covey, *Adventures*, 80.

31. Covey, *Adventures*, 115–116.

32. Newcomb, *Indians of Texas*, 225–226.

33. Herbert E. Bolton, "The Jumano Indians in Texas, 1650–1771," *Quarterly of the Texas State Historical Association* 15 (July 1911): 75; Newcomb, *Indians of Texas*, 226. For a more recent sketch of Jumanos, see William B. Griffen, "Southern Periphery: East," in *Handbook of North American Indians*, ed. William C. Sturtevant, vol. 10, *Southwest*, ed. Alfonso Ortiz, 329–342. Jumanos were also known variously as Patarabueyes and Sumas. Indians identified as Jumanos have been placed along the Red River by some writers, but this appears to be the result of confusing Jumanos with Taovayas, a tribe of the Wichitas.

34. Robert S. Weddle, "Edge of Empire: Texas as a Spanish Frontier"; Charles W. Hackett, ed., *Historical Documents Relating to New Mexico, Nueva Vizcaya, and Approaches Thereto, to 1773*, 2:268–278.

35. Newcomb, *Indians of Texas*, 233; Walter P. Webb, H. Bailey Carroll, and Eldon S. Branda, *Handbook of Texas*, 1:933.

36. Frank D. Reeve, "The Apache Indians in Texas," *Southwestern Historical Quarterly* 50 (October 1946): 189; Newcomb, *Indians of Texas*, 104–105; Sandra L. Myers, "The Lipan Apaches," in Winfrey et al., *Indian Tribes of Texas*, 130.

37. George P. Winship, trans. and ed., *The Journey of Coronado, 1540–1542*, 111–112.

38. Webb, Carroll, and Branda, *Handbook of Texas*, 1:54–55.

39. Rupert N. Richardson, Ernest Wallace, and Adrian Anderson, *Texas: The Lone Star State*, 45; Myers, "Lipan Apaches," 140. The suggestion for rounding up and deporting the Lipan Apaches came from Colonel Jacobo Ugarte y Loyola, governor (1769–1777) of Coahuila. See Gary B. Starnes, "Juan de Ugalde (1729–1816) and the Provincias Internas of Coahuila and Texas," 32.

40. The Wichitas were linguistically related to both the Caddoes and Pawnees.

41. W. W. Newcomb, Jr., *The People Called Wichita*, 21, quotation.

42. Ibid., 21–22.

43. For commercial ties of La Harpe and Claude du Tisne with Wichitas, see Elizabeth A. H. John, *Storms Brewed in Other Men's Worlds: The Confrontation of Indians, Spanish, and French in the Southwest, 1540–1795*, 213–218.

44. John G. Varner and Jeannette J. Varner, trans. and eds., *The Florida of the Inca*, 498–504; Rex W. Strickland, "Moscoso's Journey through Texas," *Southwestern Historical Quarterly* 46 (October 1942): 115–116.

45. Newcomb, *Indians of Texas*, 22. For a speculative work on the origins of the Kichais, see Charles L. Rohrbaugh, "An Hypothesis for the Origin of the Kichai," in *Pathways to Plains Prehistory: Anthropological Perspectives of Plains Natives and Their Past*, ed. Don G. Wyckoff and Jack L. Hofman, 51–63. This group spoke a branch of the Caddoan language, also known as Kichai.

46. John R. Swanton, *Source Material on the History and Ethnology of the Caddo Indians*, 12. Swanton raised doubts about the Nazonis and Nabedaches

as original confederation members. The third and smallest confederacy was the Natchitoches, situated downstream on the Red River from the Kadohadachos.

47. Newcomb, *Indians of Texas*, 284–285; John, *Storms*, 166.

48. John, *Storms*, 166–167.

49. Ibid., 167.

50. Newcomb, *Indians of Texas*, 303; W. C. Nunn, "The Caddoes," in Winfrey et al., *Indian Tribes of Texas*, 26.

51. John, *Storms*, 167.

52. Ibid., 167–168.

53. Newcomb, *Indians of Texas*, 292; Nunn, "Caddoes," 23–24.

54. Newcomb, *Indians of Texas*, 289–290.

55. Swanton, *Source Material*, 140.

56. Ibid., 161; Newcomb, *Indians of Texas*, 300–301.

57. Newcomb, *Indians of Texas*, 290–291; Nunn, "Caddoes," 32. Cabeza de Vaca also recorded ceremonial weeping among the Indians of Malhado. See Covey, *Adventures*, 57–58.

58. John, *Storms*, 168–169.

59. Several bands often identified as Tonkawas were the Tonkawa proper, Mayeyes, Yerbipiames, and Yojaunes. The Yojaunes were in reality Wichitas who lost their identity when absorbed by Tonkawas in the second half of the eighteenth century.

60. W. W. Newcomb, Jr., and T. N. Campbell, "Southern Plains Ethnohistory: A Re-examination of the Escanjaques, Ahijados, and Cuitoas," in *Pathways to Plains Prehistory: Anthropological Perspectives of Plains Natives and Their Past*, ed. Don G. Wyckoff and Jack L. Hofman, 35–36, quotations; Albert S. Gatschet, *The Karankawa Indians, the Coast People of Texas*, 36–37.

61. For traditional treatment of the Tonkawas, see Newcomb, *Indians of Texas*, 133–153.

62. Marvin C. Burch, "The Indigenous Indians of the Lower Trinity River in Texas," *Southwestern Historical Quarterly* 60 (July 1956): 37.

63. Newcomb, *Indians of Texas*, 316.

64. Ibid., 320–326.

65. David G. McComb, *Texas: A Modern History*, 22; Webb, Carroll, and Branda, *Handbook of Texas*, 1:19–20, 3:1009–1010. Texas does have two Indian reservations—a small one for Alabama-Coushattas in the east and a minuscule one for Tiguas in the west—containing lands set aside for Indians who were relative latecomers.

2. Explorers and Conquistadors, 1519–1543

1. John F. Bannon, *The Spanish Borderlands Frontier, 1513–1821*, 8–9.

2. William W. Johnson, *Cortés*, 23–24; Michael C. Meyer and William L. Sherman, *The Course of Mexican History*, 99–101.

3. Donald E. Chipman, *Nuño de Guzmán and the Province of Pánuco in New Spain, 1518–1533*, 46–47; Robert S. Weddle, *Spanish Sea: The Gulf of*

Mexico in North American Discovery, 1500–1685, 97–99, 107. Spelled properly, the surname of the first European explorer of the Texas coast is Alvarez de Pineda, not Piñeda.

4. Weddle, *Spanish Sea,* 99–100. The Pineda sketch map is reproduced in Figure 4. In 1974 a stone tablet, allegedly carved by a member of the Pineda expedition, was found at Boca Chica near Brownsville, Texas. The authenticity of the stone is extremely questionable. It remains on display in the Rio Grande Valley Museum of Harlingen, Texas. See Figure 5.

5. For correction of a long-standing misidentification of the Río Grande with the Río de las Palmas (the Soto la Marina of colonial times), see Chipman, *Nuño de Guzmán,* 49–52, and Weddle, *Spanish Sea,* 100–105.

6. Meyer and Sherman, *Course of Mexican History,* 117–120; William H. Prescott, *History of the Conquest of Mexico, and History of the Conquest of Peru,* 393–397.

7. Ibid., 627–629.

8. Chipman, *Nuño de Guzmán,* 56–65. The patent to settle Amichel, originally awarded to Garay, was later bestowed on Narváez.

9. Ibid., 65–68.

10. Ibid., 68–73.

11. J. Benedict Warren, *The Conquest of Michoacán: The Spanish Domination of the Tarascan Kingdom in Western Mexico, 1521–1530,* xi.

12. Bannon, *Spanish Borderlands,* 22–23.

13. Covey, *Adventures,* 27–29.

14. Ibid., 30–35.

15. Ibid., 45–46.

16. Chipman, "Cabeza de Vaca's Route," 128.

17. Covey, *Adventures,* 59–60.

18. Ibid., 64–67.

19. Ibid., 68–69.

20. Ibid., 78–85.

21. *La relación y comentarios del gouernador Aluar núñez cabeça de vaca, de lo acaescido en las dos jornadas que hizo a las Indias, con priuilegio . . . ;* Campbell and Campbell, *Historic Indian Groups,* 65.

22. Campbell and Campbell, *Historic Indian Groups,* 10–11, 64–65.

23. Chipman, "Cabeza de Vaca's Route," 130–148.

24. Ibid., 129–132.

25. Ibid., 130.

26. Alex D. Krieger, "The Travels of Alvar Núñez Cabeza de Vaca in Texas and Mexico, 1534–1536," in *Homenaje a Pablo Martínez del Río en el vigésimoquinto aniversario de la primera edición de "Los Orígenes Americanos,"* 462–464; Covey, *Adventures,* 117, quotation.

27. Jesse E. Thompson, "Sagittectomy—First Recorded Surgical Procedure in the American Southwest, 1535: The Journey and Ministrations of Alvar Núñez Cabeza de Vaca," *New England Journal of Medicine* 289 (December 27, 1973): 1403–1407.

28. Krieger, "Travels of Cabeza de Vaca," 467–470; Newcomb, *Indians of Texas,* 225–229.

29. This part of the narrative, when recounted in Mexico City in the summer of 1536, did much to kindle interest in the north country.

30. Krieger, "Travels of Cabeza de Vaca," 470–472.

31. Covey, *Adventures,* 122.

32. Ibid., 125.

33. Ibid., 128.

34. Ibid., 122–125; Bolton, *Coronado,* 12.

35. Covey, *Adventures,* 124. The Seven Cities were allegedly founded in a distant land by seven Catholic bishops who fled the Iberian Peninsula during the Moorish conquest.

36. Chipman, *Nuño de Guzmán,* 249–250.

37. Hubert H. Bancroft, *History of Mexico,* 2:464–465.

38. Cleve Hallenbeck, *The Journey of Fray Marcos de Niza,* 6–7.

39. Ibid.

40. Bannon, *Spanish Borderlands,* 15.

41. For an excellent discussion of the controversy surrounding the extent of Marcos de Niza's travels, see David J. Weber's introduction to Hallenbeck, *Journey of Fray Marcos de Niza,* xix–xxvii.

42. Bolton, *Coronado,* 40–48.

43. Henry R. Wagner, *Spanish Voyages to the Northwest Coast of America in the Sixteenth Century,* 51–58. The partnership dissolved with Alvarado's death in the early stages of the Mixtón War (1541–1542).

44. Bolton, *Coronado,* 40–43.

45. Bannon, *Spanish Borderlands,* 17; Bolton, *Coronado,* 63–69.

46. Bannon, *Spanish Borderlands,* 18–19.

47. Bolton, *Coronado,* 183–188. The second Indian was named "the Turk, because he looked like one."

48. Ibid., 190.

49. Ibid., 192–231.

50. Ibid., 238–243. The name was applied to distant rimrock on the horizon, which gave the appearance of a stone fortification.

51. Winship, *Journey of Coronado,* 112.

52. Bolton, *Coronado,* 253–268.

53. Ibid., 269–287.

54. Newcomb, *Indians of Texas,* 247; Bolton, *Coronado,* 287–293.

55. Bolton, *Coronado,* 299–308. Bolton believed that Coronado passed near the modern Texas settlements of Texhoma, Stratford, Conlen, Dalhart, Middlewater, and Romero. As in the case of other early explorers and conquistadors, the route followed by Coronado is by no means agreed upon. The Panhandle-Plains Historical Museum (Canyon, Texas) and Coronado Quivira Museum (Lyons, Kansas) hosted major conferences, respectively, in 1990 and 1991 that were devoted to route interpretations.

56. Angélico Chávez, *Coronado's Friars,* 58–61.

57. A. Grove Day, *Coronado's Quest: The Discovery of the Southwestern States,* 299–319.

58. Carl O. Sauer, *Sixteenth-Century North America: The Land and the People as Seen by the Europeans,* 158.

59. Ibid., 168–172.

60. Varner and Varner, *Florida of the Inca,* 498–504; Strickland, "Moscoso's Journey through Texas," 115–116.

61. The route interpretation of Rex Strickland seems most plausible. For alternate interpretations, see, for example, J. W. Williams, "Moscoso's Trail in Texas," *Southwestern Historical Quarterly* 46 (October 1942): 138–157, and Stephens and Holmes, *Atlas of Texas,* 10.

62. Strickland, "Moscoso's Journey through Texas," 121–135; Newcomb, *Indians of Texas,* 285.

63. Day, *Coronado's Quest,* 257–258; Bolton, *Coronado,* 356, quotation.

64. Bolton, *Coronado,* 356–357.

65. Ibid., 357–358. For a recent study of the route followed by the de Soto expedition, see *De Soto Trail: National Historic Trail Study, Draft Report.*

66. Ibid., 330.

67. Henry R. Wagner, *Spanish Voyages,* 90–93.

68. Ibid. There is lack of agreement on whether Cabrillo broke an arm or a leg.

69. Bannon, *Spanish Borderlands,* 27.

3. The Northward Advance toward Texas, 1543–1680

1. Bolton, *Coronado,* 400.

2. Marcus Dods, trans., *The City of God by Saint Augustine,* 530–532; Lewis Hanke, *Aristotle and the American Indians: A Study in Race Prejudice in the Modern World,* 2–4.

3. Herbert E. Bolton, "The Spanish Occupation of Texas, 1519–1690," *Southwestern Historical Quarterly* 16 (July 1912): 1–2.

4. Carl O. Sauer, *The Road to Cíbola,* 9–10; Donald E. Chipman, "Nuño de Guzmán and His 'Grand Design' in New Spain," in *Homenaje a Don José María de la Peña y Cámara,* 217.

5. Chipman, "Grand Design," 217.

6. Ibid., 218–219.

7. Philip W. Powell, *Soldiers, Indians, and Silver: The Northward Advance of New Spain, 1550–1600,* 3–4.

8. Philip W. Powell, "Presidios and Towns on the Silver Frontier of New Spain, 1550–1580," *Hispanic American Historical Review* 24 (May 1944): 179–180; Powell, *Soldiers, Indians, and Silver,* 33, 39–40, 43, 48, quotation.

9. Bancroft, *History of Mexico,* 2:554; Powell, *Soldiers, Indians, and Silver,* 10–11.

10. Powell, *Soldiers, Indians, and Silver,* 11–12.

11. Visitation by Alonso de Santacruz (April 16, 1550), AGI, Guadalajara 5; Powell, *Soldiers, Indians, and Silver,* 12.

12. Donald E. Chipman, "The Oñate-Moctezuma-Zaldívar Families of Northern New Spain," *New Mexico Historical Review* 52 (October 1977): 302–306; Marc Simmons, *The Last Conquistador: Juan de Oñate and the Settling of the Far Southwest,* 30–47.

13. Powell, *Soldiers, Indians, and Silver,* 28–29.

14. J. Barto Arnold III and Robert S. Weddle, *The Nautical Archeology of Padre Island: The Spanish Shipwrecks of 1554,* 35–40; Carlos E. Castañeda, *Our Catholic Heritage in Texas,* 1:140–145; Weddle, *Spanish Sea,* 246–247.

15. Arnold and Weddle, *Nautical Archeology,* 40–48. Castañeda, *Catholic Heritage,* 1:145–156; Weddle, *Spanish Sea,* 247–248. It seems more likely that reports from survivors in the small craft launched the salvage operation. Castañeda maintained that a second survivor, Francisco Vásquez, was rescued by the salvage crews. The remains of the *Santa María de Yciar,* which had eluded archaeologists, were discovered in dredging operations in early 1990. Recent salvage is on permanent display at the Corpus Christi Museum of Science and History.

16. Weddle, *Spanish Sea,* 251–262.

17. Ibid., 265–281.

18. Lewis Hanke, *The Spanish Struggle for Justice in the Conquest of America,* 91, as quoted.

19. Clarence H. Haring, *The Spanish Empire in America,* 56–59.

20. Powell, *Soldiers, Indians, and Silver,* 105–126; Peter J. Bakewell, *Silver Mining and Society in Colonial Mexico: Zacatecas, 1546–1700,* 31–33.

21. Powell, *Soldiers, Indians, and Silver,* 141–148; Bakewell, *Silver Mining,* 32.

22. Stafford Poole, "'War by Fire and Blood': The Church and the Chichimecas, 1585," *The Americas* 22 (October 1965): 115–137; Powell, *Soldiers, Indians, and Silver,* 181–187.

23. Powell, *Soldiers, Indians, and Silver,* 186–203.

24. J. Lloyd Mecham, *Francisco de Ibarra and Nueva Vizcaya,* 59.

25. Oakah L. Jones, Jr., *Nueva Vizcaya: Heartland of the Spanish Frontier,* 19–20.

26. Weddle, *Spanish Sea,* 314–329.

27. Thomas W. Cutrer, *The English Texans,* 7–10.

28. Weddle, *Spanish Sea,* 333–337.

29. Vito Alessio Robles, *Coahuila y Tejas en la época colonial,* 89–90.

30. Weddle, *Spanish Sea,* 341–343, 350–351. For a discussion of the royal ordinances of 1573, see below in this chapter.

31. Ibid., 343–347.

32. Donald D. Brand, "The Early History of the Range Cattle Industry in Northern Mexico," *Agricultural History* 35 (July 1961): 132.

33. Richard J. Morissey, "The Northward Expansion of Cattle Ranching in New Spain, 1550–1600," *Agricultural History* 25 (July 1951): 115–117.

34. Brand, "Early History," 132–139.

35. Morissey, "Northward Expansion," 121.

36. *Colección de documentos inéditos relativos al descubrimiento, conquista,*

y organización de las antiguas posesiones españolas en América y Oceanía,
16:142–187; Hanke, *Aristotle and the American Indians,* 86–89.

37. Peter M. Dunne, *Pioneer Jesuits in Northern Mexico,* 17–19.

38. George P. Hammond and Agapito Rey, *The Rediscovery of New Mexico,*
1580–1594, 9–11; Herbert E. Bolton, ed., *Spanish Exploration in the South-*
west, 1542–1706, 137–138.

39. Simmons, *Last Conquistador,* 51; Castañeda, *Catholic Heritage,* 1:163–
170; Hammond and Rey, *Rediscovery of New Mexico,* 13–14.

40. Castañeda, *Catholic Heritage,* 1:169–170.

41. J. Lloyd Mecham, "Antonio de Espejo and His Journey to New Mexico,"
Southwestern Historical Quarterly 30 (October 1926): 114–122.

42. Krieger, "Travels of Cabeza de Vaca," 468; George P. Hammond and
Agapito Rey, trans. and eds., *Expedition into New Mexico Made by Antonio de*
Espejo, 1582–1583: As Revealed in the Journal of Diego Pérez de Luxán, a
Member of the Party, 105–108; Mecham, "Antonio de Espejo," 122–135;
W. H. Timmons, *El Paso: A Borderlands History,* 9–10.

43. Hammond and Rey, *Expedition into New Mexico,* 124; Castañeda,
Catholic Heritage, 1:178–179.

44. Mecham "Antonio de Espejo," 135–138.

45. George P. Hammond, *Don Juan de Oñate and the Founding of New*
Mexico, 10–12.

46. Hammond and Rey, *Rediscovery of New Mexico,* 39–48.

47. George P. Hammond and Agapito Rey, *Don Juan de Oñate: Colonizer of*
New Mexico, 1595–1628, 1:4–5; Hammond and Rey, *Rediscovery of New*
Mexico, 28–50; Castañeda, *Catholic Heritage,* 1:181–184.

48. Hammond, *Juan de Oñate,* 10–18; Hammond and Rey, *Juan de Oñate,*
1:7.

49. Hammond, *Juan de Oñate,* passim, 13–90.

50. Simmons, *Last Conquistador,* 91–101; Hammond and Rey, *Juan de*
Oñate, 1:15–16.

51. Simmons, *Last Conquistador,* 140–148; Hammond and Rey, *Juan de*
Oñate, 1:19–24. After Juan de Zaldívar's death, Oñate selected Vicente de Zaldívar as his *maestre de campo.*

52. Hammond and Rey, *Juan de Oñate,* 1:24–26. Oñate misidentified the
unfriendly Indians of south-central Kansas as Escanjaques. They were in fact
natives collectively known as Aguacanes. See Newcomb and Campbell, "Southern Plains Ethnohistory," 32, 38.

53. Hammond and Rey, *Juan de Oñate,* 1:26; Bannon, *Spanish Border-*
lands, 40.

54. Bannon, *Spanish Borderlands,* 38–42. For evidence of Santa Fe's origins,
dating from about 1608, as well as Juan de Oñate's larger than heretofore acknowledged role in its founding, see Simmons, *Last Conquistador,* 182–183.

55. Carlos E. Castañeda, "The Woman in Blue," *Age of Mary: An Exclu-*
sively Marian Magazine, Mystical City of God Issue (January–February 1958):
22–24; Castañeda, *Catholic Heritage,* 1:196–197.

56. Castañeda, "Woman in Blue," 22–24.

57. Ibid., 25; France V. Scholes and H. P. Mera, "Some Aspects of the Jumano Problem," in *Contributions to American Anthropology and History,* 6:287–288.

58. Frederick W. Hodge, George P. Hammond, and Agapito Rey, eds., *Fray Alonso Benavides' Revised Memorial of 1634,* 138; Castañeda, *Catholic Heritage,* 1:197–200. For a more detailed discussion of the Lady in Blue, see Charles W. Hackett, ed. and trans., *Pichardo's Treatise on the Limits of Louisiana and Texas,* 2:465–499.

59. Scholes and Mera, "Some Aspects," 287–288.

4. Río Grande Settlement and the French Challenge, 1656–1689

1. Charles W. Hackett, "The Revolt of the Pueblo Indians of New Mexico in 1680," *Quarterly of the Texas State Historical Association* 15 (October 1911): 98–100; Charles W. Hackett, ed., and Charmion C. Shelby, trans., *Revolt of the Pueblo Indians and Otermín's Attempted Reconquest, 1680–1682,* 1:xx.

2. Hackett and Shelby, *Revolt of the Pueblo Indians,* 1:xxi–xxiii.

3. France V. Scholes, *Troublous Times in New Mexico, 1659–1670,* 252–258. For a discussion of the administrations of López and Peñalosa, see idem, 34–87; 107–148.

4. Hackett and Shelby, *Revolt of the Pueblo Indians,* 1:xxii–xxviii.

5. Ibid., 1:liv–lxx

6. Ibid., 1:lxxii–lxxvii, cii–cvi. Loss of life among Spaniards had been heavy. More than 380 men, women, and children died in the Pueblo Revolt, but that number did not include the martyrdom of 21 religious. See idem, 1:liii.

7. Anne E. Hughes, *The Beginnings of Spanish Settlement in the El Paso District,* 315–320; Hackett and Shelby, *Revolt of the Pueblo Indians,* 1:cx–cxvii.

8. Charles W. Hackett, "The Retreat of the Spaniards from New Mexico in 1680, and the Beginnings of El Paso," *Southwestern Historical Quarterly,* Part II, 16 (January 1913): 275–276; Hackett and Shelby, *Revolt of the Pueblo Indians,* 1:cxix, quotation. Three Spanish settlements included San Lorenzo, San Pedro de Alcántara, and Presidio San José. Five missions consisted of Guadalupe, Santísimo Sacramento de la Ysleta, Senecú, Santa Getrudis de los Sumas, and San Francisco de los Sumas. See Timmons, *El Paso,* 19.

9. Scholes, *Troublous Times,* 9; Scholes and Mera, "Some Aspects," 286; Vina E. Walz, "A History of the El Paso Area, 1680–1692." Two additional missions in the El Paso district were San Francisco de los Sumas and La Soledad de los Janos, but both were located well beyond the confines of Texas. See Castañeda, *Catholic Heritage,* 1:250.

10. Hughes, *Beginnings of Spanish Settlement,* 313–314.

11. Castañeda, *Catholic Heritage,* 1:211–212.

12. Ibid., 213–214.

13. Ibid., 1:217. Castañeda attributed the request for missionaries to the continued influence of the Woman in Blue.

14. Francis B. Steck, "Forerunners of Captain de León's Expedition to Texas,

1670–1675," *Southwestern Historical Quarterly* 36 (July 1932): 2–15; Castañeda, *Catholic Heritage*, 1:217–222.

15. Steck, "Forerunners," 5–15.

16. Ibid., 20–22; Robert S. Weddle, *San Juan Bautista: Gateway to Spanish
Texas*, 7–9.

17. Steck, "Forerunners," 25–26. The diary of Fernando del Bosque is translated in Bolton, *Spanish Exploration*, 291–309.

18. Steck, "Forerunners," 26–27.

19. Webb, Carroll, and Branda, *Handbook of Texas*, 1:415; Castañeda,
Catholic Heritage, 1:255; Walz, "History of the El Paso Area," 117–118. Castañeda speculated that the mission and pueblo were founded in 1681.

20. Bolton, *Spanish Exploration*, 314–315; Scholes, "Some Aspects," 288;
Walz, "History of the El Paso Area," 127–129.

21. Bolton, *Spanish Exploration*, 315–316. The total number of missions or
mission pueblos is uncertain. Four of them were initially established on the Texas
side of the Río Grande, but they were abandoned within a year.

22. Scholes, *Troublous Times*, 7–8, 17, 247; Hackett and Shelby, *Revolt of
the Pueblo Indians*, 1:cxli–clxvii; Bolton, *Spanish Exploration*, 316.

23. Bolton, *Spanish Exploration*, 316–317. Mendoza's itinerary is reproduced on pages 320–343. The precise location of his encampment in west-central
Texas has not been determined.

24. Hughes, *Beginnings of Spanish Settlement*, 327, 388–391.

25. Letter from Ambassador Pedro Ronquillo to the King (August 9, 1686),
AGI, México 616; Francis Parkman, *La Salle and the Discovery of the Great
West*, 1–6.

26. Bannon, *Spanish Borderlands*, 92–94.

27. Parkman, *La Salle*, 286.

28. Bannon, *Spanish Borderlands*, 94–95; Weddle, Morkovsky, and Galloway, *Three Primary Documents*, 3.

29. Charles W. Hackett, "New Light on don Diego de Peñalosa: Proof That
He Never Made an Expedition from Santa Fe to Quivira and the Mississippi
River in 1662," *Mississippi Valley Historical Review* 6 (December 1919): 313–
323; Scholes, *Troublous Times*, 239–243.

30. Royal Cedula (December 10, 1678), AGI, México 616; Bannon, *Spanish
Borderlands*, 95.

31. Bannon, *Spanish Borderlands*, 95; Robert S. Weddle, *Wilderness Manhunt: The Spanish Search for La Salle*, 16–23. A negotiated peace did in fact
come about some three weeks after La Salle sailed from France.

32. Weddle, *Wilderness Manhunt*, 1–2.

33. Ibid., 2–3, 23.

34. Peter H. Wood, "La Salle: Discovery of a Lost Explorer," *American Historical Review* 89 (April 1984): 318.

35. Ibid., 300.

36. Ibid., 299, 301, 304–306.

37. Jean Delanglez, trans., *The Journal of Jean Cavelier: The Account of a*

Survivor of La Salle's Texas Expedition, 1684–1688, 57; Wood, "La Salle," 313–314.

38. Wood, "La Salle," 318.

39. Weddle, *Wilderness Manhunt,* 3–4.

40. Testimony of French Pirates (November 9–11, 1685), AGI, México 616; Weddle, *Wilderness Manhunt,* 5–14. The Armada de Barlovento (Windward Squadron) was a fleet charged with providing security for Spanish vessels in the Caribbean. See Bibiano Torres Ramírez, *La Armada de Barlovento,* 35–47.

41. Robert S. Weddle, "Spanish Search for French: A Path to Danger and Discovery," *American West* 20 (January-February 1983): 26.

42. Weddle, *Wilderness Manhunt,* 33, 54–55. Alonso de León's name was submitted to the viceroy on June 16, 1686.

43. Ibid., 59–64.

44. Ibid., 64–65.

45. Account of Two Piraguas Built in Veracruz (December 30, 1686), AGI, México 616; Weddle, "Spanish Search," 30.

46. Weddle, "Spanish Search," 28–34.

47. Letter from Viceroy Conde de Monclova to the King (June 20, 1687), AGI, México 616; Weddle, *Wilderness Manhunt,* 101–102.

48. Letter from Ambassador Pedro Ronquillo to the King (August 9, 1686), AGI, México 616, quotation; Weddle, *Wilderness Manhunt,* 102–107.

49. Weddle, *Wilderness Manhunt,* 133–148. It seems probable that Jean Géry had been a member of La Salle's colony.

50. Ibid., 160–172.

51. Letter from Viceroy Conde de Monclova to the King (March 20, 1688), AGI, México 616; Weddle, *Wilderness Manhunt,* 118–131.

52. Weddle, *Wilderness Manhunt,* 149–151.

53. Ibid., 152–158. Viceroy Monclova's name was applied to the seat of government in Coahuila.

54. Ibid., 174–176.

55. Ibid., 177–184. The location of La Salle's Fort St. Louis has been identified beyond reasonable doubt. It is at the Keeran Site on Garcitas Creek, Victoria County, precisely at the place indicated by Herbert E. Bolton in 1915. See Kathleen Gilmore, "La Salle's Fort St. Louis in Texas," *Bulletin of the Texas Archeological Society* 55 (1984): 61–72

56. Weddle, *Wilderness Manhunt,* 184–187.

57. Ibid., 189–202.

58. Ibid., 34. Ascent of the Río Grande is based on the testimony of Cíbolo and Jumano Indians.

59. Parkman, *La Salle,* 381–391; Weddle, *Wilderness Manhunt,* 66, 76.

60. Parkman, *La Salle,* 392–405; Delanglez, *Journal of Jean Cavelier,* 109, quotation.

61. For a discussion of "La Salle's Remnants," see Weddle, *Wilderness Manhunt,* 249–266. If Jean Géry was a member of the colony, the number was sixteen. The sixth child was named Eustache Bréman.

62. Wood, "La Salle," 314–315.
63. Weddle, *Wilderness Manhunt,* 205.

5. International Rivalry and the East Texas Missions, 1689–1714

1. John Lynch, *Spain under the Habsburgs,* 2:229, 254; John Langdon-Davies, *Carlos: The King Who Would Not Die,* 29; Carla R. Phillips, "Local History and Imperial Spain," *Locus: An Historical Journal of Regional Perspectives on National Topics* 2 (Spring 1990): 120.

2. The conflicts were the War of Devolution, 1667–1668; Dutch War, 1672–1678; and War of the League of Augsburg, 1688–1697.

3. Lino Gómez Canedo, *Primeras exploraciones y poblamiento de Texas (1686–1694),* 113; William E. Dunn, *Spanish and French Rivalry in the Gulf Region of the United States, 1678–1702: The Beginnings of Texas and Pensacola,* 110–111, quotation.

4. Report of the Fiscal de Hacienda to the Viceroy (November 30, 1716), AMH Tomo XVII; Gómez Canedo, *Primeras exploraciones,* 114–115.

5. Dunn, *Spanish and French Rivalry,* 111.

6. Gómez Canedo, *Primeras exploraciones,* 124–125; de León referred to the Frio River as the Río Zarco.

7. Weddle, *Wilderness Manhunt,* 207.

8. Report of the Fiscal de Hacienda to the Viceroy (November 30, 1716), AMH, Tomo XXVII, quotation; Dunn, *Spanish and French Rivalry,* 116–117; Weddle, *Wilderness Manhunt,* 208–209.

9. Gómez Canedo, *Primeras exploraciones,* xvi–xvii.

10. Diary of Alonso de León (1690), AGI, México 617; Gómez Canedo, *Primeras exploraciones,* xvii.

11. Diary of Alonso de León (1690), AGI, México 617; Weddle, *Wilderness Manhunt,* 209. In his diary de León recorded only that "we burned the fort."

12. Diary of Alonso de León (1690), AGI, México 617. De León indicated that five days (May 27–May 31) were spent constructing the first church in East Texas. The commemorative site established in 1936 near Weches, Texas, has not been confirmed by archaeological evidence.

13. Weddle, *Wilderness Manhunt,* 210–211.

14. Gómez Canedo, *Primeras exploraciones,* xviii–xix. The three priests left in East Texas were Miguel Fontcuberta, Francisco Casañas de Jesús María, and Antonio Bordoy.

15. Diary of Alonso de León (1690), AGI, México 617; Weddle, *Wilderness Manhunt,* 209–212.

16. Gómez Canedo, *Primeras exploraciones,* 153–157; Weddle, *Wilderness Manhunt,* 209–213.

17. Gómez Canedo, *Primeras exploraciones,* 159–161. See idem, n. 3, for statement on unidentified Indians.

18. Ibid., 161–165. It is presumed that Massanet meant Indian children who would serve as auxiliaries or examples of Hispanization, a concept used on the frontier of New Spain.

19. Castañeda, *Catholic Heritage*, 1:360–361.

20. Report of the Fiscal de Hacienda to the Viceroy (November 30, 1716), AMH, Tomo XXVII; Castañeda, *Catholic Heritage*, 1:357–358.

21. Testimony of Efforts to Remove Buoys (January 24, 1691), AGI, México 617. Discovery of the Cárdenas map allowed Bolton to establish the site of Fort St. Louis. See Herbert E. Bolton, "The Location of La Salle's Colony on the Gulf of Mexico," *Mississippi Valley Historical Review* 2 (September 1915): 165–182.

22. Castañeda, *Catholic Heritage*, 1:362–363.

23. Diary of Domingo Terán de los Ríos (1691), AGI, México 617; Castañeda, *Catholic Heritage*, 1:364.

24. Gómez Canedo, *Primeras exploraciones*, 173, 178, 240–241.

25. Diary of Domingo Terán de los Ríos (1691), AGI, México 617; Weddle, *Wilderness Manhunt*, 227–228. Martínez was able to recover two more French children, Eustache Bréman and Jean-Baptiste Talon, from the Karankawas.

26. Castañeda, *Catholic Heritage*, 1:366–367; Gómez Canedo, *Primeras exploraciones*, 182–184. After the service, Terán renamed the country Nuevo Reyno de la Montaña de Santander y Santillana.

27. Gómez Canedo, *Primeras exploraciones*, 185; Castañeda, *Catholic Heritage*, 1:368, quotation.

28. Castañeda, *Catholic Heritage*, 1:368–369.

29. Diary of Domingo Terán de los Ríos (1691), AGI, México 617. This satellite mission was later destroyed by a flood and abandoned in January 1692. See Webb, Carroll, and Branda, *Handbook of Texas*, 1:572.

30. Diary of Domingo Terán de los Ríos (1692), AGI, México 617.

31. Interrogatory of Domingo Terán de los Ríos (March 17–April 24, 1692), AGI, México 617.

32. Castañeda, *Catholic Heritage*, 1:371–372.

33. Letter from Viceroy Conde de Galve to the King (April 7, 1691), AGI, México 617; Castañeda, *Catholic Heritage*, 1:372–373; Gómez Canedo, *Primeras exploraciones*, 309.

34. Report of the Fiscal de Hacienda to the Viceroy (November 30, 1716), AMH, Tomo XXVII. Congregating Indians had been an aspect of Spanish policy in New Spain since the 1590s.

35. Castañeda, *Catholic Heritage*, 1:374–376. One of the deserters, José de Urrutia, figured importantly in subsequent events in Texas.

36. Robert C. Clark, *The Beginnings of Texas, 1684–1718*, 25–26; Dunn, *Spanish and French Rivalry*, 144–145.

37. Dunn, *Spanish and French Rivalry*, 146–147.

38. Account Made by Carlos de Sigüenza y Góngora (May 5, 1693), AGI, México 617; Instructions to Andrés de Arriola (September 16, 1698), AGI, México 617.

39. Account of Andrés de Arriola (December 1, 1698), AGI, México 617; John A. Caruso, *The Mississippi Valley Frontier: The Age of French Exploration and Settlement*, 225–226.

40. Nellis M. Crouse, *Lemoyne d'Iberville: Soldier of New France*, 1–154 passim, 155–158, 166–190.

41. Dunn, *Spanish and French Rivalry,* 204–205.

42. Ibid., 205–206.

43. Ibid., 206–215. The French occupied Mobile Bay in 1702, arguing that it was a preemptive move against the English.

44. Ross Phares, *Cavalier in the Wilderness: The Story of the Explorer and Trader Louis Juchereau de St. Denis,* 1–2, 27–34.

45. Ibid., 35–38.

46. Ibid., 38–39.

47. Translation of Patent to Luis de St. Denis (September 12, 1713), AMH, Tomo XXVII; Phares, *Cavalier in the Wilderness,* 41–48.

6. *The Permanent Occupation of Texas, 1714–1722*

1. For a discussion of the parentage and surname of Manuela, see Jack Jackson, Robert S. Weddle, and Winston De Ville, *Mapping Texas and the Gulf Coast: The Contributions of Saint-Denis, Oliván, and Le Maire,* 71–72, n. 22. The authors suggest that Manuela's mother was a daughter of Captain Ramón and that Manuela did not bear the name Ramón.

2. Eduardo E. Ríos, *Life of Fray Antonio Margil, O.F.M.,* 61; Weddle, *San Juan Bautista,* 18–19, quotation.

3. The second San Juan Bautista was founded at the site of modern Guerrero, Coahuila.

4. Weddle, *San Juan Bautista,* 18–28. The river crossings were named Paso Pacuache and Paso de Francia.

5. The latter mission and presidio were known collectively as San Juan Bautista del Río Grande.

6. Weddle, *San Juan Bautista,* 29–30.

7. Ibid., 73–86. Father Espinosa was a young, recently ordained priest (1703) assigned to mission San Juan Bautista.

8. Castañeda, *Catholic Heritage,* 2:21–23.

9. Weddle, *San Juan Bautista,* 90–92.

10. Ibid., 92–93. The Yojaunes have long been misidentified as a Tonkawan group. They were in fact Wichita-speaking Indians. See "Espinosa, Olivares, and the Colorado Indians, 1709," in T. N. Campbell, *The Indians of Southern Texas and Northeastern Mexico: Selected Writings of Thomas Nolan Campbell,* 63–64.

11. Weddle, *San Juan Bautista,* 93–97; John, *Storms,* 196–198.

12. John, *Storms,* 203–205.

13. Report of the Fiscal to the Viceroy (August 15, 1715), AMH, Tomo XXVII, quotation.

14. John, *Storms,* 205; Weddle, *San Juan Bautista,* 140–141. Likewise in the summer of 1715, attempts were made to reestablish missions at La Junta de los Ríos. Juan de Trasviña y Retis headed an entrada that included Fathers Gregorio Osorio and Juan Antonio García. Missionary activities in the region were later suspended from time to time because of Indian revolts. In 1719, for example,

only two priests were active in the vicinity. See Testimony of Proceedings on the Missions of La Junta de los Ríos (1719), AGI, Guadalajara 169.

15. Phares, *Cavalier in the Wilderness*, 98–99; Lester G. Bugbee, "The Real Saint-Denis," *Quarterly of the Texas State Historical Association* 1 (April 1898): 277–278. Shortly after his return from Texas, St. Denis was made a Knight of St. Louis.

16. Phares, *Cavalier in the Wilderness*, 81–92.

17. Course for the Missions [of Texas] from the Internal Presidios (February 16–July 11, 1716), AMH, Tomo XXVII. The first Spanish women in Texas were (1) married—María Antonia Longoria, Antonia de la Cerda, Antonia Vidales, Ana María Ximénez de Valdez, María Antonia Ximénez, Juana de San Miguel, and Josefa Sánchez; (2) single—Ana Guerra. The college of Nuestra Señora de Guadalupe de Zacatecas was first established in 1702 under the auspices of the college of Santa Cruz de Querétaro. A royal decree approving the college arrived in Mexico in 1706, and in January 1707 Father Antonio Margil de Jesús assumed the presidency of it. See Isidro Félix de Espinosa, *Crónica de los colegios de propaganda fide de la Nueva España*, 806–807, and Webb, Carroll, and Branda, *Handbook of Texas*, 2:294.

18. Castañeda's statement that Margil joined the Ramón expedition before it reached its destination is in error. See Castañeda, *Catholic Heritage*, 2:45–46; see also Marion A. Habig, "Mission San José y San Miguel de Aguayo, 1720–1824," *Southwestern Historical Quarterly* 71 (April 1968): 498, n. 10, and Ríos, *Life of Fray Antonio Margil*, 116. Margil's first letter from Texas was dated July 20, 1716.

19. Course for the Missions [of Texas] from the Internal Presidios (February 16–July 11, 1716), AMH, Tomo XXVII. Bolton placed the mission site on the east bank of the Neches River. See Herbert E. Bolton, "Native Tribes about the East Texas Missions," *Quarterly of the Texas State Historical Association* 11 (April 1908): 261–262. The precise location of this mission and several others has not been confirmed by archaeological evidence.

20. Castañeda, *Catholic Heritage*, 2:59–61; Bolton, "Native Tribes," 258–268.

21. Representation of Domingo Ramón to the Viceroy (July 22, 1716), AMH, Tomo XXVII; William E. Dunn, "Apache Relations in Texas, 1718–1750," *Quarterly of the Texas State Historical Association* 14 (January 1911): 201, quotation.

22. Phares, *Cavalier in the Wilderness*, 111–113. The value of the merchandise has been placed between 43,200 and 89,214 livres.

23. Castañeda, *Catholic Heritage*, 2:63–69.

24. I have accepted Father Espinosa's chronology and order of founding for these two missions, which are at variance with those of Castañeda. See Espinosa, *Crónica*, 724, and Castañeda, *Catholic Heritage*, 2:66–67. The Ais (Eyeish) and Adais were both independent Caddo tribes. See Newcomb, *Indians of Texas*, 282.

25. Phares, *Cavalier in the Wilderness*, 114.

26. Ibid., 114–118.

27. Letter from Antonio Olivares to the Viceroy [1716], AMH, Tomo XXVII.

28. Merits and Services of Martín de Alarcón (January 18, 1721), AGI, Guadalajara 117; Castañeda, *Catholic Heritage,* 2:70–81.

29. Castañeda, *Catholic Heritage,* 2:81–91.

30. Weddle, *San Juan Bautista,* 133–140. For an account of St. Denis in Mexico City, see Charmion C. Shelby, "St. Denis's Second Expedition to the Río Grande, 1716–1719," *Southwestern Historical Quarterly* 27 (January 1924): 210–214. St. Denis was back at his trading post at Natchitoches by February 1719 but was not joined by his wife until 1721. By then he had been named commandant at Natchitoches.

31. Weddle, *San Juan Bautista,* 145–147, 151–152; Letter from Félix de Espinosa to the Viceroy (February 28, 1718), AMH, Tomo XXVII, quotation.

32. Letter from Viceroy Marqués de Valero to the King (November 7, 1718), AGI, Guadalajara 117; Oakah L. Jones, Jr., *Los Paisanos: Spanish Settlers on the Northern Frontier of New Spain,* 41.

33. Castañeda, *Catholic Heritage,* 2:93–94.

34. Ibid., 2:93–94; Weddle, *San Juan Bautista,* 173. The indigenous population recruited for San Antonio de Valero were members of the Jarame, Pamaya, and Payaya tribes; at the time of the "transfer," San Francisco Solano had been moved twice and renamed San José; San Antonio de Valero, itself, was moved about 1719 and again in 1724.

35. Gilbert R. Cruz, *Let There Be Towns: Spanish Municipal Origins in the American Southwest, 1610–1810,* 58; Fray Francisco Céliz, *Diary of the Alarcón Expedition into Texas, 1718–1719,* 49. The Céliz diary contains no entries for April 26–May 4.

36. Castañeda, *Catholic Heritage,* 2:100–103. See Weddle, *San Juan Bautista,* 149–152, for details of recovering the cached merchandise and its delivery to mission Concepción.

37. Letter from Viceroy Marqués de Valero to the King (July 31, 1719), AGI, Guadalajara 117; Castañeda, *Catholic Heritage,* 2:102–107, 110, quotation.

38. Castañeda, *Catholic Heritage,* 2:107–109. Despite resigning the office, Alarcón continued to serve as governor for several more months.

39. Stanley G. Payne, *A History of Spain and Portugal,* 357–358; Weddle, *San Juan Bautista,* 156.

40. Weddle, *San Juan Bautista,* 156–157; Eleanor C. Buckley, "The Aguayo Expedition into Texas and Louisiana, 1719–1722," *Quarterly of the Texas State Historical Association* 15 (July 1911): 19–20. In Europe the "Chicken War" was known as the War of the Quadruple Alliance.

41. Castañeda, *Catholic Heritage,* 2:119–120.

42. Letter from the Marqués de San Miguel de Aguayo to the King (June 26, 1720), AGI, Guadalajara 117.

43. Letter from the Marqués de San Miguel de Aguayo to the Viceroy (January 12, 1715), AMH, Tomo XXVII; Proposal Made by the Marqués de San Miguel de Aguayo (November 9, 1715), AMH, Tomo XXVII.

44. Charles W. Hackett, "The Marquis of San Miguel de Aguayo and His

Recovery of Texas from the French, 1719–1723," *Southwestern Historical Quarterly* 49 (October 1945): 199–202, as quoted.

45. Castañeda, *Catholic Heritage*, 2:130–133.

46. Ibid., 2:124–130; Habig, "Mission San José," 479–499. Habig noted that when the Marqués de Aguayo visited mission San José in 1721 he found 227 Indians congregated there. The original site of San José was on the opposite (east) side of the river from its present location. Opposition from Father Olivares centered on congregating the Pampopas and Pastias at the proposed mission, for they were enemies of the Indians then living at San Antonio de Valero.

47. Course of the Aguayo Expedition in the Province of Texas (1722), AGI, Indiferente General 108, Tomo V.

48. Ibid.; Jack Jackson, *Los Mesteños: Spanish Ranching in Texas, 1721–1821*, 10–11. Jackson took note of livestock already in Texas by 1721 but began his prize-winning study of ranching with the Aguayo expedition.

49. Hackett, "Marquis of San Miguel," 204–205.

50. Course of the Aguayo Expedition in the Province of Texas (1722), AGI, Indiferente General 108, Tomo V; Weddle, *San Juan Bautista*, 164; Hackett, *Pichardo's Treatise*, 1:xi.

51. Testimony of the Possession of Missions (1721), AGI, Guadalajara 117. Mass was celebrated by Father Margil de Jesús on August 18, 1721, at Nuestra Señora de los Nacogdoches, the first of the reestablished missions.

52. Letter from the Marqués de San Miguel de Aguayo to the Viceroy (April 8, 1722), AGI, Guadalajara 117; Jackson, *Los Mesteños*, 11–12; Castañeda, *Catholic Heritage*, 2:147, 159–167. This small mission was merged with Valero in 1726.

53. Letter from the Marqués de San Miguel de Aguayo to the Viceroy (May 1, 1722), AGI, Guadalajara 117.

54. Letter from the Marqués de San Miguel de Aguayo to the Viceroy (June 13, 1722), AGI, Guadalajara 117; Castañeda, *Catholic Heritage*, 2:147–148.

55. Buckley, "Aguayo Expedition," 60–61, quotation; Charles W. Hackett, "Visitador Rivera's Criticisms of Aguayo's Work in Texas," *Hispanic American Historical Review* 16 (May 1936): 162–172, quotation. Hackett placed Aguayo's expenditures at more than 130,000 pesos.

7. *Retrenchment, Islanders, and Indians, 1722−1746*

1. Herbert E. Bolton, *Texas in the Middle Eighteenth Century: Studies in Spanish Colonial History and Administration*, 14.

2. Weddle, *San Juan Bautista*, 165–166; Ríos, *Life of Fray Antonio Margil*, 123–124.

3. Weddle, *San Juan Bautista*, 166–171. Hidalgo was sixty-seven years of age when he died, fifty-two of which had been spent as a religious. See Juan Domingo Arricivita, *Crónica seráfica y apostólica del Colegio de la Santa Cruz de Querétaro en la Nueva España*, 226.

4. Weddle, *San Juan Bautista,* 156, 171–172.

5. Retta Murphy, "The Journey of Pedro de Rivera, 1724–1728," *Southwestern Historical Quarterly* 41 (October 1937): 125–128; Castañeda, *Catholic Heritage,* 2:211–212.

6. Weddle, *San Juan Bautista,* 172.

7. Letter from the Marqués de Casafuerte to the King (March 2, 1730), AGI, Guadalajara 144.

8. Testimony of the Rivera Project (June 2, 1730), AGI, Guadalajara 144. Karankawa intransigence and an unhealthful location had forced the removal of presidio and mission La Bahía to the Guadalupe River in 1726.

9. Thomas H. Naylor and Charles W. Polzer, comps. and eds., *Pedro de Rivera and the Military Regulations for Northern New Spain, 1724–1729: A Documentary History of His Frontier Inspection and the "Reglamento de 1729,"* 160–161.

10. Weddle, *San Juan Bautista,* 171–174.

11. Ibid., 174. San Antonio de Valero served the Xarames, Payayas, Yerbipiames, Muruabes, and the Pacuaches at the time of Sevillano's inspection.

12. Ibid., 174–185.

13. Testimony of the Rivera Project (June 2, 1730), AGI, Guadalajara 144; Regulations for the Presidios of the Internal Provinces (1729), AGI, Guadalajara 144. Reductions in troop strength coupled with lower pay for the soldiers who remained in Texas resulted in a savings of over forty-five thousand pesos per year for the royal treasury.

14. Castañeda, *Catholic Heritage,* 2:237–238.

15. Ibid., 2:237–240.

16. Ibid. The missions were renamed La Purísima Concepción de Acuña, San Francisco de Espada, and San Juan Capistrano; the latter was changed from San José because of the existence of the older mission, San José y San Miguel de Aguayo.

17. Weddle, *San Juan Bautista,* 188.

18. Ibid., 188–189.

19. Dunn, "Apache Relations," 203–207.

20. Ibid.; Reeve, "Apache Indians in Texas," 194. The stock was thought to have been stolen from San Antonio. Also recovered were saddles, bridles, knives, spears, and the like, from Spanish sources. See John, *Storms,* 259.

21. Dunn, "Apache Relations," 209–216.

22. Ibid., 216–219, 223–225; Reeve, "Apache Indians in Texas," 194.

23. Copy of the Diary of Joseph Berroterán (1729), AGI, Guadalajara 513, quotation.

24. John, *Storms,* 263.

25. Newcomb, *Indians of Texas,* 156; Ernest Wallace and E. Adamson Hoebel, *The Comanches: Lords of the South Plains,* 6–8, 14, quotation.

26. The number of Islanders is often given as fifty-six, the total that departed Quauhtitlán near Mexico City on November 15, 1530, but a young girl died at San Juan Bautista. See Weddle, *San Juan Bautista,* 191–192; Castañeda, *Catholic Heritage,* 2:301.

27. Extract of Events Related to 400 Canary Island Families [1731], AGI, Guadalajara 178.

28. Castañeda, *Catholic Heritage*, 2:268–279. Matagorda Bay was no longer defended by a presidio after 1726.

29. Letter from the Marqués de Casafuerte to the King (September 1, 1731), AGI, Guadalajara 178; Testimony of Proceedings in 400 Families to Populate Texas (1731), AGI, Guadalajara 178. The royal decree applying to four hundred families was issued on February 4, 1729.

30. Jesús F. de la Teja, "Forgotten Founders: The Military Settlers of Eighteenth-Century San Antonio de Béxar," in *Tejano Origins in Eighteenth-Century San Antonio,* ed. Gerald E. Poyo and Gilberto M. Hinojosa, 36; Castañeda, *Catholic Heritage,* 2:301–302.

31. Gerald E. Poyo, "The Canary Islands Immigrants of San Antonio: From Ethnic Exclusivity to Community in Eighteenth-Century Béxar," in Poyo and Hinojosa, *Tejano Origins,* 42; Castañeda, *Catholic Heritage,* 2:302–310. The Canary Islanders' town, actually the second *villa* founded at Béxar, was named in honor of the viceroy's brother, the Duke of Béjar.

32. Castañeda, *Catholic Heritage,* 2:283–284.

33. T. R. Fehrenbach, *Lone Star: A History of Texas and the Texans,* 55.

34. Jesús F. de la Teja, "Indians, Soldiers, and Canary Islanders: The Making of a Texas Frontier Community," *Locus: An Historical Journal of Regional Perspectives on National Topics* 3 (Fall 1990): 83–84, quotation; Bolton, *Texas,* 22.

35. Castañeda, *Catholic Heritage,* 3:37–38. Fourteen soldiers were absent on an outing to the Río Grande.

36. Dunn, "Apache Relations," 233–238.

37. Ibid., 238–239, 248.

38. Ibid., 248–250.

39. F. de la Teja, "Indians, Soldiers, and Canary Islanders," 84–85.

40. Ibid., 87–88.

41. Jackson, *Los Mesteños,* 13–14.

42. Ibid., 12–13.

43. Ibid., 16.

44. Ibid., 16–17.

45. Ibid., 18.

46. Ibid., 17–18.

47. Bolton, *Texas,* 14–15.

48. Castañeda, *Catholic Heritage,* 3:49.

49. Complaints against Carlos Franquis de Lugo (1737), AGI, Guadalajara 103. The words were *"alcahuetes cornudos cabrones."*

50. Castañeda, *Catholic Heritage,* 3:49–58.

51. Ibid. Lugo's intransigence, incidentally, did not prevent his later advancement to a military post at Veracruz. See idem, 64–65.

52. Ibid., 3:67–71.

53. Ibid., 3:71. The Indian population in the five missions at the end of 1740 was as follows: Valero, 238; Concepción, 210; San Francisco, 121; San Juan,

169; and San José, 149. The total is 887, not 987 as calculated by Castañeda, see idem, 3:72.

54. Benedict Leutenegger, trans., "Memorial of Father Benito Fernández concerning the Canary Islanders, 1741," *Southwestern Historical Quarterly* 82 (October 1978): 266–267.

55. Ibid., 268–269. "Community" in this context is used to imply shared attitudes, experiences, and cultural similarities.

56. Russell M. Magnaghi, ed. and trans., "Texas as Seen by Governor Winthuysen, 1741–1744," *Southwestern Historical Quarterly* 88 (October 1984): 169. Although technically Los Adaes was the capital of Spanish Texas, the governors had not customarily resided there, and it had been overshadowed by the growth and size of San Antonio.

57. Phares, *Cavalier in the Wilderness*, 221; Magnaghi, "Texas as Seen," 170–171.

58. Magnaghi, "Texas as Seen," 175–176, as quoted.

59. Ibid., 174–176, as quoted.

60. F. de la Teja, "Indians, Soldiers, and Canary Islanders," 88–90; Affirmation of Agreement between the Isleños and the Missions (August 14, 1745), UTA, Transcripts, quotation.

61. Dunn, "Apache Relations," 248–252.

8. Mission, Presidio, and Settlement Expansion, 1746–1762

1. Bolton, *Texas*, 140–141.

2. Gary B. Starnes, *The San Gabriel Missions, 1746–1756*, 13. The locale was approximately 135 miles northeast of San Antonio near present Rockdale, Texas.

3. Ibid., 13–14; Letter from Mariano de los Dolores to Alonso Giraldo de Terreros (July 26, 1745), Transcripts, UTA.

4. Letter from Mariano Dolores to José de Urrutia [1745], AGI, Guadalajara 197; Starnes, *San Gabriel Missions*, 14–15.

5. Starnes, 13–14.

6. Ibid., 14–15; Letter from Fray Mariano de los Dolores to Benito Fernández de Santa Ana, (January 19, 1746), Transcripts, UTA.

7. Memorial of Francisco Xavier Marqués (March 14, 1746), AGI, Guadalajara 197; Starnes, *San Gabriel Missions*, 16–17, quotation.

8. Viceregal Decree of the Conde de Revilla Gigedo (February 14, 1747), Transcripts, UTA; Starnes, *San Gabriel Missions*, 19. Additional delays were occasioned by priority given to José de Escandón's plan (September 1746) to settle the Costa del Seno Mexicano.

9. Starnes, *San Gabriel Missions*, 19; Bolton, *Texas*, 173–174.

10. Proceedings of Governor Pedro del Barrio (July 25, 1748), AGI, México 1933B; Bolton, *Texas*, 187–188.

11. Bolton, *Texas*, 188–189.

12. Ibid., 189.

13. Letter from Pedro del Barrio to the Viceroy (June 25, 1748), AGI, Guadalajara 197; Starnes, *San Gabriel Missions,* 20–21.

14. Starnes, *San Gabriel Missions,* 21–22. Domingo de Arricivita became a noted historian of the Franciscans in Texas.

15. Ibid., 22, n. 12. No figures are available for Candelaria.

16. Bolton, *Texas,* 219–220.

17. Proceedings of Pedro del Barrio (July 1749), AGI, Guadalajara 197; Starnes, *San Gabriel Missions,* 24–25.

18. Starnes, *San Gabriel Missions,* 25–26.

19. Viceregal Decree (April 7, 1750) AGI, Guadalajara 197.

20. Inspection of José de Eca y Múzquiz (1750), AGI, Guadalajara 197; Starnes, *San Gabriel Missions,* 28–29. Totals for neophytes at the mission were as follows: Xavier, 161; Ildefonso, 176; Candelaria, 102.

21. Castañeda, *Catholic Heritage,* 3:303.

22. Memorial of the Conde de Revilla Gigedo (March 30, 1751), AGI, Guadalajara 197; Juan Agustín Morfi, *History of Texas, 1673–1779,* 2:330, quotation.

23. Starnes, *San Gabriel Missions,* 32; Castañeda, *Catholic Heritage,* 3:318–319.

24. Starnes, *San Gabriel Missions,* 33.

25. Ibid., 33–34.

26. Ibid., 34–37.

27. Castañeda, *Catholic Heritage,* 3:324–325.

28. Starnes, *San Gabriel Missions,* 39–43.

29. Robert S. Weddle, *The San Sabá Mission: Spanish Pivot in Texas,* 13–15. The campaigns of 1732 and 1739 were carried out, respectively, by Governor Juan Antonio Bustillo y Ceballos and Captain José de Urrutia.

30. Ibid., 16; Dunn, "Apache Relations," 251–252, quotation.

31. Bolton, *Texas,* 80.

32. Testimony of Toribio de Urrutia in San Antonio (November 25, 1749), AGI, México 1933A, quotation; William E. Dunn, "The Apache Mission on the San Saba River: Its Founding and Failure," *Southwestern Historical Quarterly* 17 (April 1914): 380–381; Weddle, *San Sabá Mission,* 23–25.

33. Castañeda, *Catholic Heritage,* 3:360–361.

34. Weddle, *San Sabá Mission,* 25–26.

35. Ibid., 26–27.

36. Course of the Bernardo de Miranda Expedition (1756), AGI, México 1933B; Castañeda, *Catholic Heritage,* 3:379–381. The later settlement of miners located south of the Llano River was named Los Almagres.

37. Merits and Services of Diego Ortiz Parrilla (May 3, 1770), AGI, Guadalajara 515; Weddle, *San Sabá Mission,* 37–38.

38. Correspondence of the Viceroy with Diego Ortiz Parrilla (1752), Guadalajara 301; Weddle, *San Sabá Mission,* 38–39.

39. Dunn, "Apache Mission," 382.

40. Dictum of the Auditor de Guerra (July 8, 1756), AGI, Guadalajara 197;

Weddle, *San Sabá Mission,* 38. The jurisdictional anomaly continued until 1765, when it was finally settled in Texas's favor.

41. Information for the Fiscal (February 21, 1758), AGI, Guadalajara 197; Weddle, *San Sabá Mission,* 41.

42. Dunn, "Apache Mission," 386–391. A royal cedula approving the transfer of missions from San Gabriel to San Sabá and the financial arrangements with Pedro Romero de Terreos came well after the fact. See Royal Cedula (October 15, 1758), AGI, México 1933B.

43. Castañeda, *Catholic Heritage,* 3:395.

44. Dunn, "Apache Mission," 394–395.

45. Weddle, *San Sabá Mission,* 45–46, as quoted.

46. Castañeda, *Catholic Heritage,* 3:396–397.

47. Weddle, *San Sabá Mission,* 53–54.

48. Ibid., 55–60.

49. Ibid., 64–69; Dunn, "Apache Mission," 413.

50. Weddle, *San Sabá Mission,* 64–69; Dunn, "Apache Mission," 413.

51. Weddle, *San Sabá Mission,* 72–82; Morfi, *History of Texas,* 2:381–383. Since there were no witnesses, the circumstances of Father José de Santiesteban's death are conjectural. At some point his body was decapitated.

52. Lesley B. Simpson, ed., *The San Sabá Papers: A Documentary Account of the Founding and Destruction of the San Sabá Mission,* 55–56; Weddle, *San Sabá Mission,* 87–89.

53. Henry E. Allen, "The Parrilla Expedition to the Red River in 1759," *Southwestern Historical Quarterly* 43 (July 1939): 54–55.

54. Ibid., 56–57.

55. Ibid., 58–60.

56. Muster of Soldiers Assigned to Diego Ortiz Parrilla (1759), AGI, México 1933A; Allen, "Parrilla Expedition," 60–61, quotation.

57. Statement of Diego Ortiz Parrilla (March 30, 1759), AGI, México 1933A, 1st quotation; Letter from Diego Ortiz Parrilla to the Viceroy (March 30, 1759), México 1933A, 2d quotation.

58. Allen, "Parrilla Expedition," 65.

59. Weddle, *San Sabá Mission,* 120; Allen, "Parrilla Expedition," 66–67. The fortification was located north of present Nocona, Texas, near Spanish Fort.

60. Weddle, *San Sabá Mission,* 123; Allen, "Parrilla Expedition," 68–71; Merits and Services of Diego Ortiz Parrilla (May 3, 1770), AGI, Guadalajara 515, quotation.

61. Allen, "Parrilla Expedition," 71. Treatment of Presidio San Luis de las Amarillas in the 1760s will be found in the following chapter.

62. Bolton, *Texas,* 327–328.

63. Ibid., 327–328.

64. Ibid., 330–332.

65. Castañeda, *Catholic Heritage,* 4:52–53.

66. Testimony of the Capture of Frenchmen and Negroes (February 1755), AGI, Guadalajara 329; Bolton, *Texas,* 337–342.

67. Copy of Patent in Expediente of Jacinto del Barrios (October 22, 1756), AGI, Guadalajara 329.

68. Testimony of the Capture of Frenchmen and Negroes (February 1755), AGI, Guadalajara 329; Bolton, *Texas,* 342–344.

69. Decree of the Marqués de las Amarillas (January 12, 1756), AGI, Guadalajara 329; Bolton, *Texas,* 340–347.

70. John V. Clay, *Spain, Mexico, and the Lower Trinity: An Early History of the Gulf Coast,* 55–56, as quoted.

71. Bolton, *Texas,* 374.

72. Robert S. Weddle, *The French Thorn: Rival Explorers in the Spanish Sea, 1682–1762,* 258–259.

73. Lawrence F. Hill, *José de Escandón and the Founding of Nuevo Santander: A Study in Spanish Colonization,* 56–57.

74. Weddle, *French Thorn,* 260.

75. Ibid., 264.

76. Ibid.

77. Hill, *José de Escandón,* 58.

78. Bolton, *Texas,* 293; Hill, *José de Escandón,* 66–67.

79. Hill, *José de Escandón,* 67–68.

80. Ibid., 59–63.

81. Castañeda, *Catholic Heritage,* 3 : 143; Hill, *José de Escandón,* 59–63.

82. Hill, *José de Escandón,* 65–66.

83. Weddle, *French Thorn,* 282–283; Gilberto M. Hinojosa, *A Borderlands Town in Transition: Laredo, 1755–1870,* 4–5, 91; Jackson, *Los Mesteños,* 23.

84. Bolton, *Texas,* 59–60, 316–317.

85. Hill, *José de Escandón,* 106–107.

86. Ibid.

87. For treatment of the El Paso communities—consisting of El Paso del Norte (modern Ciudad Juárez), San Lorenzo de Real, Senecú, Ysleta, and Socorro—in the middle decades of the seventeenth century, see Timmons, *El Paso,* 34–46.

88. Bolton, *Texas,* 96–97; F. de la Teja, "Indians, Soldiers, and Canary Islanders," 88.

89. Bolton, *Texas,* 95, 100–101.

9. *Texas and the Changing International Scene, 1762–1783*

1. Arthur S. Aiton, "The Diplomacy of the Louisiana Cession," *American Historical Review* 36 (July 1931): 712–720.

2. Orders of His Majesty the King (August 7, 1775), AGI, Guadalajara 274.

3. John, *Storms,* 376; Luis Navarro García, *Don José de Gálvez y la Comandancia General de las Provincias Internas del Norte de Nueva España,* 158.

4. Navarro García, *José de Gálvez,* 135.

5. Weddle, *San Sabá Mission,* 167. See Lawrence Kinnaird, ed. and trans., *The Frontiers of New Spain: Nicolás de Lafora's Description.*

6. Weddle, *San Sabá Mission,* 167–173.

7. Declarations of Soldiers at Presidio San Sabá (1771), AGI, Guadalajara 274.

8. Weddle, *San Sabá Mission*, 135–136. Norteños or northern nations consisted of Caddoan, Wichita, and Tonkawan affiliates of the Comanches.

9. Ibid., 133–135.

10. Ibid., 136–138.

11. Ibid.

12. Ibid., 140–142.

13. Proceedings of the Fiscal (April 20, 1761), AGI, Guadalajara 368, quotations; Papers Relating to Diego Ortiz Parrilla [1760], AGI, Guadalajara 368.

14. Proceedings on the Delivery of Command at Presidio San Sabá to Rábago y Terán (October 31, 1760), UTA, Transcripts.

15. Weddle, *San Sabá Mission*, 151; Castañeda, *Catholic Heritage*, 4:153–155.

16. Weddle, *San Sabá Mission*, 153–154.

17. Ibid., 154–155.

18. Morfi, *History of Texas*, 2:394.

19. Curtis D. Tunnell and W. W. Newcomb, Jr., *A Lipan Apache Mission: San Lorenzo de la Santa Cruz, 1762–1771*, 3; Weddle, *San Sabá Mission*, 156–157. See also Hons C. Richards, "The Establishment of the Candelaria and San Lorenzo Missions on the Upper Nueces."

20. Letter from Father Diego Jiménez to the Viceroy (January 27, 1763), AGI, México 1933B; Richards, "Establishment," 26. Founded in late 1762, mission Candelaria was located at the site of present Montell in northwestern Uvalde County.

21. Several of Rábago's letters written to the viceroy in 1763 to defend his actions are present in Testimony on the Founding of Two Missions in the Valley of San Joseph (1763), AGI, México 1933B.

22. Richards, "Establishment," 49–50; Morfi, *History of Texas*, 2:394–395.

23. Weddle, *San Sabá Mission*, 162–166.

24. Pat I. Nixon, *The Medical Story of Early Texas, 1528–1853*, 45–46; Weddle, *San Sabá Mission*, 167–170; Castañeda, *Catholic Heritage*, 4:192, as quoted.

25. Ernest Wallace and David M. Vigness, eds., *Documents of Texas History, Volume I (1528–1546)*, 22.

26. Appointment of Manuel de Oca as Commander at San Sabá (January 23, 1769) AGI, Guadalajara 515; Merits and Services of Manuel de Oca (November 5, 1763), AGI, Guadalajara 515; Richards, "Establishment," 69–70; Weddle, *San Sabá Mission*, 176–182.

27. Declarations of Soldiers at Presidio San Antonio de Béxar (1771), AGI, Guadalajara 274; Kinnaird, *Frontiers of New Spain*, 160–161.

28. Declaration of Soldiers at Presidio Nuestra Señora del Pilar (1771), AGI, Guadalajara 274, quotation; John, *Storms*, 435.

29. Letter from Angel de Martos to the Viceroy (March 17, 1766), AGI, Guadalajara 333; Bolton, *Texas*, 365–371. Martínez Pacheco escaped the inferno

and later stood trial in Mexico City, where he was exonerated. He subsequently served as governor of Texas.

30. Declarations of Soldiers at Presidio La Bahía del Espíritu Santo (1771), AGI, Guadalajara 274; John, *Storms*, 438.

31. John, *Storms*, 438–439.

32. Ibid., 439, quotation; Weddle, *San Sabá Mission*, 172–173.

33. Weddle, *San Sabá Mission*, 173; John, *Storms*, 439.

34. Weddle, *San Sabá Mission*, 174.

35. John, *Storms*, 377–378.

36. Herbert E. Bolton, ed. and trans., *Athanase de Mézières and the Louisiana-Texas Frontier, 1768–1780*, 1:66.

37. Ibid.

38. Ibid., 1:379–380.

39. Ibid., 1:70–71.

40. Ibid., 1:72–73.

41. Ibid., 1:67–69.

42. Ibid., 1:92–93.

43. Appointment of Barón de Ripperdá as Governor of Texas (March 24, 1768), AGI, Guadalajara 302; Webb, Carroll, and Branda, *Handbook of Texas*, 2:478.

44. Letter from Barón de Ripperdá to the Viceroy (February 15, 1770), AGI, Guadalajara 302, quotation; Morfi, *History of Texas*, 2:417–419.

45. Letter from Barón de Ripperdá to José de Gálvez (November 15, 1776), AGI, Guadalajara 302; Robert S. Weddle and Robert H. Thonhoff, *Drama and Conflict: The Texas Saga of 1776*, 10. Fuerte del Cíbolo remained in existence until 1782, when it was ordered closed by Commandant General Teodoro de Croix.

46. Richardson, Wallace, and Anderson, *Texas: The Lone Star State*, 45; Webb, Carroll, and Branda, *Handbook of Texas*, 2:301. The "New Regulations" were first published in Mexico in January 1772. For a translation, see Sidney B. Brinckerhoff and Odie B. Faulk, *Lancers for the King: A Study of the Frontier Military System of Northern New Spain, with a Translation of the Royal Regulations of 1772*, 12–67.

47. Herbert E. Bolton, "The Spanish Abandonment and Re-Occupation of East Texas, 1773–1779," *Quarterly of the Texas State Historical Association* 9 (October 1905): 81–83.

48. Ibid., 86–88.

49. Ibid., 89–98, as quoted.

50. Ibid., 99–123.

51. Report of Teodoro de Croix to José de Gálvez (August 27, 1781), AGI, Guadalajara 267.

52. Jesús F. de la Teja, "Land and Society in Eighteenth-Century San Antonio de Béxar: A Community on New Spain's Northern Frontier," 80–83.

53. Ibid., 83–86. The displaced persons from East Texas remained extremely unhappy with their circumstances at San Antonio. In 1778 they unsuccessfully petitioned for the right to found a new town on the San Marcos River.

54. Ibid., 86; Alicia V. Tjarks, "Comparative Demographic Analysis of Texas, 1777–1793," *Southwestern Historical Quarterly* 77 (January 1974): 294. Including mission Indians, the total population for Spanish settlements in 1777 was 3,103.

55. Patricia Seed, "Social Dimensions of Race: Mexico City, 1753," *Hispanic American Historical Review* 62 (November 1982): 569, 574.

56. Peter Gerhard, *The Northern Frontier of New Spain*, 27.

57. Navarro García, *José de Gálvez*, 158.

58. Webb, Carroll, and Branda, *Handbook of Texas*, 2:416–417. See Appendix 2.

59. Alfred B. Thomas, trans. and ed., *Teodoro de Croix and the Northern Frontier of New Spain, 1776–1783*, 17–18.

60. Ibid., 18–25. For a more favorable view of Bucareli's motives in denying Croix's request, see Bernard E. Bobb, *The Viceregency of Antonio María Bucareli in New Spain, 1771–1779*, 149–152.

61. Letter from Teodoro de Croix to José de Gálvez (July 17, 1777), AGI, Guadalajara 267; Wallace and Vigness, *Documents of Texas History*, 23. A third council held at Chihuahua essentially endorsed the recommendations of the first two.

62. Wallace and Vigness, *Documents of Texas History*, 24–25.

63. Thomas, *Teodoro de Croix*, 31.

64. Morfi, *History of Texas*, 2:429–430.

65. Athanase de Mézières to the Commandant General (February 20, 1778), AMH, Tomo XXVIII; Morfi, *History of Texas*, 2:430–432.

66. Morfi, *History of Texas*, 2:432–438.

67. Letter from Teodoro de Croix to José de Gálvez (March 29, 1779), AGI, Guadalajara 302.

68. Appointment of Felipe de Neve as Commandant Inspector of Presidios (April 13, 1782), AGI, Guadalajara 267; Morfi, *History of Texas*, 2:439–440.

69. Report of Teodoro de Croix to José de Gálvez (April 23, 1782), AGI, Guadalajara 253; Thomas, *Teodoro de Croix*, 43–45; Resume of Deaths and Robberies Perpetrated by Indians (July 30, 1781), AGI, Guadalajara 267.

70. Thomas, *Teodoro de Croix*, 45; Odie B. Faulk, *The Last Years of Spanish Texas, 1778–1821*, 62.

71. Report of Teodoro de Croix to José de Gálvez (October 30, 1781), AGI, Guadalajara 253. Almost as an afterthought, Croix praised Texas for its rich land, abundant rivers, and mineral deposits.

72. Thomas, *Teodoro de Croix*, 53–67.

73. Ibid., 65, 1st quotation; Report of Teodoro de Croix to José de Gálvez (January 23, 1780), AGI, Guadalajara 253, 2d quotation.

74. Castañeda, *Catholic Heritage*, 4:262–267. The transfer of the Coahuila missions near the Río Grande came about in late 1772.

10. *Anglo-American Concerns and the Decline of Missions,*
1783–1803

1. Castañeda, *Catholic Heritage,* 5 : 10–11, as quoted.
2. Ibid., 5 : 11, as quoted.
3. Robert H. Ferrell, *American Diplomacy: A History,* 56, as quoted.
4. Ibid., 59–60.
5. Ibid., 60.
6. Roberto M. Salmón, "A Thankless Job: Mexican Soldiers in the Spanish Borderlands," *Military History of the Southwest* 21 (Spring 1991): 10–11; Faulk, *Last Years,* 62.
7. Diary of the Anza Expedition against the Comanche Nation (August 15– September 10, 1779), AGI, Guadalajara 300.
8. Faulk, *Last Years,* 63–64.
9. Letter from Felipe de Neve to Domingo Cabello (October 1, 1783), BAM, Roll 15.
10. Faulk, *Last Years,* 64–65.
11. Ibid., 65–66.
12. Castañeda, *Catholic Heritage,* 5 : 7–8.
13. Ibid., 5 : 13, as quoted. In the first year of Gálvez's brief tenure, the Spanish pilot José de Evía carried out an extensive reconnaissance by sea of the Gulf Coast from the Mississippi River to Matagorda Bay. See Hackett, *Pichardo's Treatise,* 1 : 349–391.
14. Castañeda, *Catholic Heritage,* 5 : 13–14.
15. Ibid., 5 : 20–23. For Ugalde's campaigns in 1787–1788, see Al B. Nelson, "Campaigning in the Big Bend of the Río Grande in 1787," *Southwestern Historical Quarterly* 39 (January 1936): 200–227, and Al B. Nelson, "Juan de Ugalde and Picax-Andé Ins-Tinsle, 1787–1788," *Southwestern Historical Quarterly* 43 (April 1940): 438–464
16. Odie B. Faulk, *A Successful Failure,* 138–139; Report of Mariano Reyes to the Viceroy (May 1, 1790), BAM, Roll 20. Other coastal tribes mentioned in documentation relating to the founding of mission Rosario were Copanes, Cojanes, Guapites, and Karankawas. The two missions associated with Goliad were secularized in 1830 and 1831.
17. Benedict Leutenegger, ed. and trans., "New Documents on Father José Mariano Reyes," *Southwestern Historical Quarterly* 71 (April 1968), 585–586; Faulk, *Successful Failure,* 139–140.
18. Faulk, *Successful Failure,* 140.
19. Letter from Conde de Revilla Gigedo to Manuel de Silva (January 4, 1792), AGI, Guadalajara 363; Summary of Letters Received by the Commandant General (January 26, 1795), AGI, Guadalajara 363.
20. Letter from Manuel de Silva to the Conde de Revilla Gigedo (1791), AGI, Guadalajara 363; Faulk, *Successful Failure,* 140–142. Refugio continued to serve as a mission until 1830.
21. Benedict Leutenegger, trans., "Report on the San Antonio Missions in 1792," *Southwestern Historical Quarterly* 77 (April 1974): 488.

22. Ibid.

23. Faulk, *Last Years,* 78–79; Leutenegger, "Report," 488. Full secularization was not achieved at San Antonio until 1824. Upon completion of secularization, former missions were converted into parishes and placed under the control of parish priests.

24. Decree of Domingo Cabello (July 13, 1783), BA; Faulk, *Last Years,* 85.

25. Faulk, *Last Years,* 86–89.

26. Jackson, *Los Mesteños,* 341–342.

27. Ibid., 321–328. Private ranchers included Simón de Arocha, Luis Mariano Menchaca, Joaquín Leal, and Joaquín Flores.

28. Ibid., 349–350.

29. Ibid., 358.

30. Letter from Teodoro de Croix to Domingo Cabello (November 24, 1779), BAM, Roll 13; Faulk, *Last Years,* 89–91.

31. Faulk, *Last Years,* 94.

32. Tjarks, "Comparative Demographic Analysis," 296–303.

33. Ibid., 302.

34. Ibid.

35. Ibid., 326–328; Campbell, *Empire for Slavery,* 10–11, quotation.

36. Tjarks, "Comparative Demographic Analysis," 326–328, quotation; Campbell, *Empire for Slavery,* 10–11.

37. Castañeda, *Catholic Heritage,* 5:145.

38. Ibid., 5:149, as quoted.

39. Ibid., 5:150–155. The diary of the journey may be found in Noel M. Loomis and Abraham P. Nasatir, *Pedro Vial and the Roads to Santa Fe,* 268–285.

40. Castañeda, *Catholic Heritage,* 5:155–158.

41. Loomis and Nasatir, *Pedro Vial,* 288–315.

42. Ibid., 316–368; Webb, Carroll, and Branda, *Handbook of Texas,* 2:838–839.

43. Loomis and Nasatir, *Pedro Vial,* xvii–xviii; Webb, Carroll, and Branda, *Handbook of Texas,* 2:134.

44. Mattie A. Hatcher, "The Louisiana Background of the Colonization of Texas, 1763–1803," *Southwestern Historical Quarterly* 24 (January 1921): 169–178.

45. Letter from Pedro de Nava to Manuel Muñoz (August 27, 1796), BA.

46. Letter from Pedro de Nava to Manuel Muñoz (May 29, 1798), BA; Mattie A. Hatcher, "Conditions in Texas Affecting the Colonization Problem, 1795–1801," *Southwestern Historical Quarterly* 25 (October 1921): 86–90.

47. Hatcher, "Conditions in Texas," 88–89.

48. Ibid., 93–94.

49. Samuel F. Bemis, *Pinckney's Treaty: America's Advantage from Europe's Distress, 1783–1800,* 109–144, passim.

50. Faulk, *Last Years,* 114–115.

51. Ibid., 115, as quoted; Letter from Pedro de Nava to Manuel Muñoz (July 30, 1795), BA.

52. Maurine T. Wilson and Jack Jackson, *Philip Nolan and Texas: Expeditions to the Unknown Land,* 1–2.

53. Ibid., 2, as quoted. Nolan may have followed Wilkinson to Kentucky when the latter moved there in 1784.

54. James R. Jacobs, *Tarnished Warrior: Major-General James Wilkinson,* x, 92.

55. Wilson and Jackson, *Philip Nolan,* 7–9.

56. Ibid., 13, as quoted.

57. Ibid., 13–15.

58. Letter from Manuel Muñoz to Pedro de Nava (October 4, 1797), BA. See also Letter from Pedro de Nava to Felipe Nolan (October 31, 1797), BAM, Roll 27, in which the commandant general thanked Nolan for the gift of a gun and discussed Nolan's plans to drive horses to Louisiana.

59. Wilson and Jackson, *Philip Nolan,* 35–36.

60. Ibid., 47–64.

61. Ibid., 65–67.

62. Ibid., 68–73, 101. Seven of Nolan's men did manage to avoid capture. See Dan L. Flores, ed., *Journal of an Indian Trader: Anthony Glass and the Texas Trading Frontier, 1790–1810,* 15.

11. *The Twilight of Spanish Texas, 1803–1821*

1. Julia K. Garrett, *Green Flag over Texas: A Story of the Last Years of Spain in Texas,* 10, 5, 1st and 2d quotations; Richardson, Wallace, and Anderson, *Texas: The Lone Star State,* 48, 3d quotation.

2. Timothy E. Anna, *The Fall of the Royal Government in Mexico City,* 37; Luis Castillo Ledón, *Hidalgo: La vida del héroe,* 1:104–106.

3. Meyer and Sherman, *Course of Mexican History,* 281.

4. Castillo Ledón, *Hidalgo,* 1:111–114.

5. Hugh M. Hamill, Jr., *The Hidalgo Revolt: Prelude to Mexican Independence,* 55–64; Meyer and Sherman, *Course of Mexican History,* 285. Hidalgo's degree was conferred in Mexico City. See Castillo Ledón, *Hidalgo,* 1:25–26.

6. Meyer and Sherman, *Course of Mexican History,* 285–286; Hamill, *Hidalgo Revolt,* 69; Castillo Ledón, *Hidalgo,* 1:70.

7. Meyer and Sherman, *Course of Mexican History,* 286.

8. Hamill, *Hidalgo Revolt,* 109–117. San Juan de los Lagos is located in the present Mexican state of Jalisco. By late summer, the date of the uprising had been advanced to October 2, 1810.

9. Hamill, *Hidalgo Revolt,* 88.

10. Meyer and Sherman, *Course of Mexican History,* 288–289. For a discussion of the impact of violence on the class structure of Mexico, see Luis Villoro, *La revolución de independencia: Ensayo de interpretación histórica,* 70–87.

11. Meyer and Sherman, *Course of Mexican History,* 289–290.

12. Hamill, *Hidalgo Revolt,* 184–202.

13. Wilbert H. Timmons, *Morelos: Priest, Soldier, Statesman of Mexico,* 116–117.

14. Payne, *History of Spain and Portugal*, 2:424–425.

15. Ibid., 2:425–428.

16. Ibid., 2:428.

17. Raymond Carr, *Spain, 1808–1939*, 120–128.

18. Timmons, *Morelos*, 155–165; William S. Robertson, *Iturbide of Mexico*, 70–75; *Diccionario Porrúa de historia, biografía y geografía de México*, 1:519. For an excellent, revisionist interpretation of Mexican independence, see Anna, *Fall of the Royal Government*, especially xiii–xix, 204–209.

19. William M. Maloy, comp., *Treaties, Conventions, International Acts, Protocols, and Agreements between the United States of America and Other Powers, 1776–1909*, 1:506.

20. Richard Sternberg, "The Western Boundary of Louisiana, 1762–1803," *Southwestern Historical Quarterly* 35 (October 1931): 104, as quoted. Barbé-Marbois was a signatory of the treaty for the cession of Louisiana; see Maloy, *Treaties*, 511. Spain's position with regard to the limits of Louisiana was always unequivocal. In the words of the first Spanish commissioner: "The poor United States! If only there had passed to them rights other than the original ones of France over Louisiana! France had no other right than that of the possession permitted by Spain, and this possession was a fact limited in itself, it also left the limits of Louisiana fixed." Hackett, *Pichardo's Treatise*, 4:356, as quoted.

21. Sternberg, "Western Boundary," 105; Webb, Carroll, and Branda, *Handbook of Texas*, 2:374. See Hackett, *Pichardo's Treatise*, 1:xvii–xviii. Pichardo succeeded Fray Melchor Talamantes y Baeza, who had initially headed the commission.

22. Ray A. Billington, *Westward Expansion: A History of the American Frontier*, 450.

23. Flores, *Journal of an Indian Trader*, 22; Billington, *Westward Expansion*, 450. For the Thomas Freeman and Peter Custis accounts of this expedition, which contain rich material on the biota of the region, see Dan L. Flores, ed., *Jefferson and Southwest Exploration: The Freeman and Custis Accounts of the Red River Expedition of 1806*.

24. Faulk, *Last Years*, 124.

25. Ibid. Antonio Cordero was governor of Coahuila and acting governor of Texas.

26. Ibid., 125.

27. Ibid.; Merrill D. Peterson, *Thomas Jefferson and the New Nation: A Biography*, 849.

28. For a succinct treatment of the conspiracy, see Peterson, *Thomas Jefferson*, 841–855.

29. Billington, *Westward Expansion*, 451, as quoted.

30. W. Eugene Hollon, *The Lost Pathfinder: Zebulon Montgomery Pike*, 119–157, as quoted.

31. Ibid., 176–178; Stephens and Holmes, *Atlas of Texas*, 16.

32. Diary of the Amangual Expedition from Texas to New Mexico (March 30–December 23, 1808), BA; Faulk, *Last Years*, 127–128, quotation. Despite the expeditions of Francisco Amangual and the prior trailblazing of José Mares, the

direct route between San Antonio and Santa Fe was seldom used. Distance and the difficulty of travel through undeveloped lands as well as the threat of Indian attacks militated against both commerce and travel.

33. Flores, *Journal of an Indian Trader,* 18–24.

34. Ibid., 24–25.

35. Ibid., 38–82.

36. J. Villasana Haggard, "The House of Barr and Davenport," *Southwestern Historical Quarterly* 44 (July 1945): 70–73. Two additional owners were Luther Smith and Edward Murphy.

37. Wilson and Jackson, *Philip Nolan,* 73–74, as quoted.

38. Haggard, "House of Barr and Davenport," 73–74. Haggard erroneously attributed these decisions of the commandant general to Pedro de Nava, but Nava was relieved of office on November 4, 1802.

39. Ibid., 76–78, quotation; Letter from Davenport to Salcedo (February 6, 1812), BA.

40. Appointment of Manuel de Salcedo as Governor of Texas (March 13, 1807), AGI, Guadalajara 302. Selected at the age of thirty-one, Manuel de Salcedo remains Texas's youngest chief executive.

41. Félix D. Almaráz, Jr., *Tragic Cavalier: Governor Manuel Salcedo of Texas, 1808–1813,* 23; Nettie L. Benson, "A Governor's Report on Texas in 1809," *Southwestern Historical Quarterly* 71 (April 1968): 603–606.

42. Benson, "Governor's Report," 605–606.

43. Almaráz, *Tragic Cavalier,* 24–32.

44. Nettie L. Benson, "Texas Failure to Send a Deputy to the Spanish Cortes, 1810–1812," *Southwestern Historical Quarterly* 64 (July 1960): 14.

45. Benson, "Governor's Report," 610–612.

46. Ibid., 611.

47. Ibid., 612–613.

48. Ibid., 614–615.

49. Almaráz, *Tragic Cavalier,* 53.

50. Ibid., 55–59.

51. Ibid., 96.

52. Ibid., 118–120.

53. J. Villasana Haggard, "The Counter-Revolution of Béxar, 1811," *Southwestern Historical Quarterly* 43 (October 1939): 226–230.

54. Hamill, *Hidalgo Revolt,* 209–210.

55. Ibid., 213–216, quotation; Castillo Ledón, *Hidalgo,* 2:218.

56. The granary, known as the Alhóndiga, had been the scene of a bloody massacre of *peninsulares* on September 28, 1810. For details, see Lesley B. Simpson, *Many Mexicos,* 212–213.

57. Haggard, "Counter-Revolution of Béxar," 224, n. 9. The execution was carried out on August 3, 1811. See Frederic C. Chabot, ed., *Texas in 1811: The Las Casas and Sambrano Revolutions,* 102–103.

58. Harris G. Warren, *The Sword Was Their Passport, a History of American Filibustering in the Mexican Revolution,* 5. Revilla was a small village near the confluence of the Río Salado and Río Grande.

59. Ibid., 5–8.

60. Ibid., 20–24.

61. Almaráz, *Tragic Cavalier,* 123–125.

62. Warren, *Sword,* 24. Other capable U.S. citizens who joined Gutiérrez were Reuben Ross, Samuel Kemper, Henry Perry, and James B. Wilkinson, son of the infamous general.

63. Richard W. Gronet, "The United States and the Invasion of Texas," *The Americas* 25 (January 1969): 281.

64. Ibid., 293–294.

65. Ibid., 284, as quoted.

66. Harry M. Henderson, "The Magee-Gutiérrez Expedition," *Southwestern Historical Quarterly* 55 (July 1951): 46.

67. Ibid., 48–49.

68. Almaráz, *Tragic Cavalier,* 168. San Antonio had been elevated from a *villa* to a *ciudad* by Commandant General Salcedo in reward for its citizens' role in overturning the Las Casas regime.

69. Ibid., 169.

70. Ibid., 171

71. Warren, *Sword,* 50; Almaráz, *Tragic Cavalier,* 171. General Calleja became viceroy of New Spain in 1813.

72. For a discussion of the constitution, see Kathryn Garrett, "First Constitution of Texas, April 17, 1813," *Southwestern Historical Quarterly* 40 (April 1937): 290–308.

73. Webb, Carroll, and Branda, *Handbook of Texas,* 2:785.

74. For estimates of the size of the two armies, see Henderson, "Magee-Gutiérrez Expedition," 55–56; Garrett, *Green Flag over Texas,* 224; Mattie A. Hatcher, trans., "Joaquín de Arredondo's Report of the Battle of the Medina, August 18, 1813," *Quarterly of the Texas State Historical Association* 11 (January 1908): 225–226, quotation. Arredondo placed the size of Toledo's army at thirty-two hundred.

75. Hatcher, "Joaquín de Arredondo's Report," 220–227.

76. Almaráz, *Tragic Cavalier,* 180, quotation; Richardson, Wallace, and Anderson, *Texas: The Lone Star State,* 53, quotation.

77. For the names of the interim governors, see Appendix 1.

78. Webb, Carroll, and Branda, *Handbook of Texas,* 1:78–79.

79. Warren, *Sword,* 146–157. Toledo became a career Spanish diplomat. See Webb, Carroll, and Branda, *Handbook of Texas,* 2:786.

80. Warren, *Sword,* 169–171; Fane Downs, "Governor Antonio Martínez and the Defense of Texas from Foreign Invasion, 1817–1822," *Texas Military History* 7 (Spring 1968): 30–31. Aury's departure from Galveston created an opening for Jean Laffite to dominate the affairs of Galveston Island. For Laffite's slaving ventures, see Campbell, *Empire for Slavery,* 12.

81. Martín L. Guzmán, *Javier Mina, héroe de España y de México,* 234–236.

82. Campbell, *Empire for Slavery,* 12–13. For a discussion of the Red River settlements, see Rex W. Strickland, "Miller County, Arkansas Territory, the Frontier That Men Forgot," *Chronicles of Oklahoma* 18 (1940): 12–34, and Rex W.

Strickland, "Anglo-American Activities in Northeast Texas, 1803–1845," 64–94. The right of Anglo-Americans to settle legally in Texas would be granted to Moses Austin by Governor Antonio Martínez in late 1820. Even Arredondo, who had consistently opposed the presence of Anglo-Americans, gave his endorsement in early 1821 with the hope "that the said province will receive important augmentation, in agriculture, industry, and arts, by the new emigrants." See David B. Gracy II, *Moses Austin: His Life,* 200–207, as quoted.

83. Miriam Partlow, *Liberty, Liberty County, and the Atascosito District,* 53–60; Warren, *Sword,* 210–232.

84. For the text of the "Treaty of Friendship, Cession of the Floridas, and Boundaries, 1819," see Maloy, *Treaties,* 2:1651–1658. Ratifications were exchanged on February 22, 1821.

85. Warren, *Sword,* 233–236; Webb, Carroll, and Branda, *Handbook of Texas,* 2:77–78.

86. Warren, *Sword,* 239–254; Webb, Carroll, and Branda, *Handbook of Texas,* 2:78; Anne A. Brindley, "Jane Long," *Southwestern Historical Quarterly* 56 (October 1952): 226.

87. David J. Weber, *The Mexican Frontier, 1821–1846: The American Southwest under Mexico,* 4, 10, quotations; Joseph C. McElhannon, "Imperial Mexico and Texas," *Southwestern Historical Quarterly* 53 (October 1949): 120. Weber estimated the non-Indian population in 1821 at about twenty-five hundred. For a firsthand appraisal of Texas during Martínez's governorship, see Virginia H. Taylor, trans. and ed., *The Letters of Antonio Martínez, Last Governor of Texas, 1817–1822.*

12. The Legacies of Spanish Texas

1. President James K. Polk signed the Texas Admission Act on December 29, 1845, but the state government did not assume its functions until February 1846.

2. The Sabine River is an anglicized form of "Sabina," meaning cypress or juniper, while the Trinity River derives from Río de la Trinidad.

3. A subsequent edition of *Los Naufragios* was published in 1555 with only slight alterations. For the best translation of the *Joint Report,* see Basil C. Hedrick and Carroll L. Riley, *The Journey of the Vaca Party: The Account of the Narváez Expedition, 1528–1536, as Related by Gonzalo Fernández de Oviedo y Valdés.*

4. Campbell and Campbell, *Historic Indian Groups,* 64–65; Bandelier, *Journey of Cabeza de Vaca,* 65–66. Customs among the Karankawas such as marital arrangements and burial practices also come to light in the Cabeza de Vaca narrative.

5. Bandelier, *Journey of Cabeza de Vaca,* 88, 108–109, 126.

6. Winship, *Journey of Coronado,* 67, 74.

7. Swanton, *Source Material,* 30–31, as quoted. Luis Hernández de Biedma and Garcilaso de la Vega were also chroniclers of the expedition, although the latter was not a participant.

8. See, for example, Mattie A. Hatcher, trans. and ed., "Descriptions of the

Tejas or Asinai Indians, 1691–1722," *Southwestern Historical Quarterly* 30 (January 1927): 206–218; 30 (April 1927): 283–304; 31 (July 1927): 50–62; 31 (October 1927): 150–180.

9. John H. Jenkins, *Basic Texas Books: An Annotated Bibliography of Selected Works for a Research Library,* 157, as quoted.

10. Ibid., 156–157, as quoted.

11. Ibid., 387.

12. Phares, *Cavalier in the Wilderness,* 45.

13. Technically, the missions could not own land, rather they held it in trust for the Indians who "theoretically owned the temporalities." See Félix D. Almaráz, Jr., *The San Antonio Missions and Their System of Land Tenure,* 9–10, 53.

14. Robert H. Thonhoff, "The First Ranch in Texas," *West Texas Historical Association Year Book* 40 (October 1964): 90–91; Jackson, *Los Mesteños,* 23–24. Private ranches were probably not founded until after 1749, when peace with the Apaches was arranged at San Antonio.

15. Terry G. Jordan, *Trails to Texas: Southern Roots of Western Cattle Ranching,* 25–26, 98–102; Jackson, *Los Mesteños,* 593–594.

16. For reports on the presence of mesquite on the uplands of the Río Grande Valley in early Spanish Texas, see Inglis, *History of Vegetation,* 16–84 passim, 95.

17. Weddle, "Edge of Empire."

18. Cruz, *Let There Be Towns,* 56, quotation; Weddle, "Edge of Empire." Other viable communities dating from the colonial era are Nacogdoches, Goliad, and Laredo.

19. See Brinckerhoff and Faulk, *Lancers for the King;* Max L. Moorhead, *The Presidio: Bastion of the Borderlands;* and Thomas H. Naylor and Charles W. Polzer, comps. and eds., *The Presidio and Militia on the Northern Frontier of New Spain: A Documentary History, Volume One, 1570–1700.*

20. Mardith K. Schuetz, "The Indians of the San Antonio Missions," 2–3.

21. Ibid., 5.

22. Gerald E. Poyo and Gilberto M. Hinojosa, "Spanish Texas and Borderlands Historiography in Transition: Implications for United States History," *Journal of American History* 75 (September 1988): 411; Robert A. Calvert and Arnoldo De León, *The History of Texas,* 33, quotation.

23. John, *Storms,* xiii.

24. Jackson, *Los Mesteños,* 604. For an excellent discussion of Anglo-American attitudes toward persons of multicultural origins in Mexican Texas, see Arnoldo De León, *They Called Them Greasers: Anglo Attitudes toward Mexicans in Texas, 1821–1900,* 1–13.

25. Joseph W. McKnight, "The Spanish Influence on the Texas Law of Civil Procedure," *Texas Law Review* 38 (November 1959): 31–34.

26. Joseph W. McKnight, *The Spanish Elements in Modern Texas Law,* 3–4. McKnight has noted that exceptions over the years have been added until the basic rule is often obscured.

27. McKnight, "Spanish Influence," 46–48; McKnight, *Spanish Elements,* 4–5, quotations.

28. Betty E. Dobkins, *The Spanish Element in Texas Water Law,* ix. Dobkins

maintained that 26,280,000 acres of Texas's 170,000,000 acres originated under grants made by the crown of Spain or the Republic of Mexico.

29. William G. Winters, Jr., "The Shoreline for Spanish and Mexican Grants in Texas," *Texas Law Review* 38 (May 1960): 525–529, 537; McKnight, *Spanish Elements*, 5, quotation. Spanish law uses the mean highest high tide to determine the line belonging to the sovereign, while English law uses the mean high tide. Because it takes 18.6 years for the sun, moon, and earth to complete a cycle, a shoreline determined by taking the mean of all high tides is slightly different from a mean of the highest high tides within that span of time.

30. Ira G. Clark, *Water in New Mexico: A History of Its Management and Use*, 41.

31. McKnight, *Spanish Elements*, 6.

32. Hans W. Baade, "The Form of Marriage in Spanish North America," *Cornell Law Review* 61 (November 1975): 1–5; McKnight, *Spanish Elements*, 6–7; H. P. N. Gammel, comp., *The Laws of Texas, 1822–1897*, 2:678.

33. McKnight, *Spanish Elements*, 7, quotation; Gammel, *Laws of Texas*, 3:474. For examples of authorizations for individual adoption, see Gammel, 2:693, 2:1060. Mississippi approved an adoption statute in 1846.

34. Gammel, *Laws of Texas*, 2:341–345, 3:474, 4:423; McKnight, *Spanish Elements*, 7.

35. William O. Huie, "The Texas Constitutional Definition of the Wife's Separate Property," *Texas Law Review* 35 (October 1957): 1054–1055; McKnight, *Spanish Elements*, 8.

36. Joseph W. McKnight, "Spanish Law for the Protection of Surviving Spouses in North America," *Anuario de historia del derecho español* 57 (1987): 366–367; McKnight, *Spanish Elements*, 8.

37. Baade, "Form of Marriage," 2–4; McKnight, *Spanish Elements*, 8; Lawrence M. Friedman, *A History of American Law*, 342.

38. McKnight, *Spanish Elements*, 8.

39. Ibid., 8–9; Webb, Carroll, and Branda, *Handbook of Texas*, 1:830–831.

40. McKnight, *Spanish Elements*, 9.

41. Sam D. Ratcliffe, "'Escenas de Martiro': Notes on *The Destruction of Mission San Sabá*," *Southwestern Historical Quarterly* 94 (April 1991): 509–517. *The Destruction of Mission San Sabá in the Province of Texas and the Martyrdom of the Fathers Alonso Giraldo de Terreros, Joseph Santiesteban* is 83" (211 centimeters) in height and 115" (292 centimeters) in width. See Ratcliffe (517–521) for speculations concerning the identity of the painter. The status of this historic painting is currently being disputed by the United States Customs Service. In 1990 it was placed on temporary display at the Museum of Fine Arts, Houston.

42. The painting is a part of the F. Carrington Weems Collection, Houston. A description of *Les Costes aux Environs de la Riviere de Misisipi* . . . may be found in Robert S. Martin and James C. Martin, *Contours of Discovery: Printed Maps Delineating the Texas and Southwestern Chapters in the Cartographic History of North America, 1513–1930: A User's Guide*, 38–39. For a reproduction of

the cartouche, see Jim B. Pearson, Ben Procter, and William B. Conroy, *Texas: The Land and the People,* 124. This textbook also contains many excellent reproductions of art dating from the late colonial period.

43. Robert M. Quinn, "The Architectural Origins of the Southwestern Missions," *American West* 3 (Summer 1966): 93–94, quotations; Gilbert R. Cruz, ed., *Proceedings of the 1984 and 1985 San Antonio Missions Research Conferences,* 1, quotation. San Antonio de Valero, now known as the Alamo, is not a part of the National Historical Park. For a brief discussion of the architectural styles employed in the five missions at San Antonio, see Trent E. Sanford, *The Architecture of the Southwest: Indian, Spanish, American,* 161–171. Excellent photographs and architectural plans of the San Antonio missions may be found in David G. De Long, ed., *Historic American Buildings: Texas,* 1:3–51.

44. Max Berger, "Education in Texas during the Spanish and Mexican Periods," *Southwestern Historical Quarterly* 51 (July 1947): 42–43.

45. Ibid., 43.

46. I. J. Cox, "Educational Efforts in San Fernando de Béxar," *Quarterly of the Texas State Historical Association* 6 (July 1902): 35.

47. Arthur L. Campa, *Hispanic Culture in the Southwest,* 234–242.

48. Ibid., 226–230; Adel Speiser, "The Story of the Theatre in San Antonio," 1–3. For an excellent treatment of Hispanic theater in San Antonio during the late nineteenth and early twentieth centuries, see Nicolás Kanellos, *A History of Hispanic Theatre in the United States, Origins to 1940,* 71–103.

49. Nixon, *Medical History,* 68–78.

50. *Texas Almanac,* 67. Catholic adherents include Hispanics and other ethnic groups.

51. Poyo and Hinojosa, "Spanish Borderlands," 394.

Bibliography

Archival Materials

Archival materials utilized in the preparation of this book are preserved in the collections listed below. Individual reports, letters, proceedings, and the like are appropriately cited in the notes with their titles translated into English.

Archivo General de Indias, Seville (cited as AGI)
Archivo del Ministerio de Hacienda, Madrid (cited as AMH)
Béxar Archives, Austin (cited as BA)
Béxar Archives Microfilm, University of North Texas (cited as BAM)
University of Texas Archives, Austin (cited as UTA)

Published Documents and Guides

Barnes, Thomas C., Thomas H. Naylor, and Charles W. Polzer. *Northern New Spain: A Research Guide.* Tucson: University of Arizona Press, 1981.

Beers, Henry P. *Spanish and Mexican Records of the American Southwest: A Bibliographical Guide to Archive and Manuscript Sources.* Tucson: University of Arizona Press, 1979.

Benavides, Adán, Jr. *The Béxar Archives (1717–1836): A Name Guide.* Austin: University of Texas Press, 1989.

Bolton, Herbert E., ed. and trans. *Athanase de Mézières and the Louisiana-Texas Frontier, 1768–1780.* 2 vols. Cleveland: Arthur H. Clark, 1914.

Colección de documentos inéditos relativos al descubrimiento, conquista, y organización de las antiguas posesiones españolas en América y Oceanía. 42 vols. Vaduz: Kraus Reprint, 1964–1966.

Colección de documentos inéditos relativos al descubrimiento, conquista, y organización de las antiguas posesiones españolas de Ultramar. 25 vols. Vaduz: Kraus Reprint, 1967.

Cruz, Gilberto R., and James A. Irby, eds. and comps. *Texas Bibliography: A Manual on History Research Materials.* Austin: Eakin Press, 1982.

Cummins, Light T., and Alvin R. Bailey, Jr., eds. *A Guide to the History of Texas.* New York: Greenwood Press, 1988.

Gálvez, Bernardo de. *Instructions for Governing the Interior Provinces of New Spain, 1786.* Trans. and ed. by Donald E. Worcester. Berkeley: Quivira Society, 1951.

Gómez Canedo, Lino. *Los archivos de la historia de América: Período colonial español.* 2 vols. Mexico City: Instituto Panamericano de Geografía e Historia, 1961.

———, ed. *Primeras exploraciones y poblamiento de Texas (1686–1694).* Monterrey: Publicaciones del Instituto Tecnológico y de Estudios Superiores de Monterrey, 1968.

Hackett, Charles W., ed. *Historical Documents Relating to New Mexico, Nueva Vizcaya, and Approaches Thereto, to 1773.* 3 vols. Washington, D.C.: Carnegie Institution, 1923–1937.

———, ed. and trans. *Pichardo's Treatise on the Limits of Louisiana and Texas.* 4 vols. Austin: University of Texas Press, 1931–1946.

Jenkins, John H. *Basic Texas Books: An Annotated Bibliography of Selected Works for a Research Library.* Rev. ed. Austin: Texas State Historical Association, 1983.

Kinnaird, Lawrence, ed. *Spain in the Mississippi Valley, 1765–1794: Translations of Materials from the Spanish Archives in the Bancroft Library.* 3 vols. Washington, D.C.: U.S. Government Printing Office, 1946–1949.

Leal, Carmela, comp. and ed. "Translations of Statistical and Census Reports of Texas, 1782–1836, and Sources Relating to the Black in Texas, 1603–1803." Microfilm Publication. San Antonio: University of Texas Institute of Texan Cultures, 1979.

Revilla Gigedo, Conde de. *Informe sobre las misiones—1793—e instrucción reservada al Marqués de Branciforte—1794.* Ed. by José Bravo Ugarte. Mexico City: Editorial Jus, 1966.

Santos, Richard G. *Aguayo Expedition into Texas, 1721: An Annotated Translation of the Five Versions of the Diary Kept by Br. Juan Antonio de la Peña.* Austin: Jenkins Publishing, 1981.

Scurlock, Dan. *Spain in North America: Selected Sources on Spanish Colonial History, Archeology, Architecture and Art, and Material Culture.* [Austin]: Texas Historical Commission, 1973.

Stoddard, Ellwyn, Richard L. Nostrand, and Jonathan P. West. *Borderlands Sourcebook: A Guide to the Literature on Northern Mexico and the American Southwest.* Norman: University of Oklahoma Press, 1983.

Taylor, Virginia H., trans. and ed. *The Letters of Antonio Martínez, Last Governor of Texas, 1817–1822.* Austin: Texas State Library, 1957.

Tate, Michael L., ed. *The Indians of Texas: An Annotated Research Bibliography.* Metuchen, N.J.: Scarecrow Press, 1986.

Torres Lanzas, Pedro. *Catálogo de Mapas y Planos de México.* Reprint. 2 vols. Madrid: Ministerio de Cultura, 1985.

Wallace, Ernest, and David M. Vigness, eds. *Documents of Texas History, Volume I (1528–1546).* Lubbock: Library, Texas Technological College, 1960.

Weddle, Robert S., ed., Mary C. Morkovsky, and Patricia Galloway, assoc. eds.

Three Primary Documents: La Salle, the Mississippi, and the Gulf. College Station: Texas A&M University Press, 1987.

Winegarten, Ruthe, ed. *Finder's Guide to the Texas Woman: A Celebration of History Exhibit Archive.* Denton: Texas Woman's University Library, 1984.

Winship, George P., trans. and ed. *The Journey of Coronado, 1540–1542.* New York: Allerton, 1922.

Books

Alcocer, José A. *Bosque de la historia del Colegio de Nuestra Señora de Guadalupe y sus misiones, año de 1788.* Mexico City: Editorial Porrúa, 1958.

Alessio Robles, Vito. *Coahuila y Tejas en la época colonial.* Mexico City: Editorial Cultura, 1938.

Almaráz, Félix D., Jr. *The San Antonio Missions and Their System of Land Tenure.* Austin: University of Texas Press, 1989.

———. *Tragic Cavalier: Governor Manuel Salcedo of Texas, 1808–1813.* Austin: University of Texas Press, 1971.

An Exploration of a Common Legacy: A Conference on Border Architecture. [Austin]: Texas Historical Commission, [1978].

Anna, Timothy E. *The Fall of the Royal Government in Mexico City.* Lincoln: University of Nebraska Press, 1978.

———. *The Mexican Empire of Iturbide.* Lincoln: University of Nebraska Press, 1990.

Applegate, Howard G., and C. Wayne Hanselka. *La Junta de los Ríos del Norte y Conchos.* El Paso: Texas Western Press, 1974.

Arbingast, Stanley A., et al. *Atlas of Texas.* Austin: Bureau of Business Research, 1976.

Arnold, J. Barto, III, and Robert S. Weddle. *The Nautical Archeology of Padre Island: The Spanish Shipwrecks of 1554.* New York: Academic Press, 1978.

Arricivita, Juan Domingo. *Crónica seráfica y apostólica del Colegio de la Santa Cruz de Querétaro en la Nueva España.* Mexico City: Don Felipe de Zúñiga y Ontiveros, 1792.

Ashford, Gerald. *Spanish Texas: Yesterday and Today.* Austin: Jenkins Publishing, 1971.

Avellaneda, Ignacio. *Los sobrevivientes de la Florida: The Survivors of the De Soto Expedition.* Gainesville: P. K. Yonge Library of Florida History, 1990.

Bakewell, Peter J. *Silver Mining and Society in Colonial Mexico: Zacatecas, 1546–1700.* Cambridge: Cambridge University Press, 1971.

Bancroft, Hubert H. *History of Mexico.* 6 vols. San Francisco: A. L. Bancroft, 1883–1888.

———. *History of the North Mexican States and Texas.* 2 vols. San Francisco: A. L. Bancroft, 1884, 1889.

Bandelier, Fanny, trans. *The Journey of Alvar Núñez Cabeza de Vaca and His Companions from Florida to the Pacific, 1528–1536.* New York: Allerton, 1922.

Bannon, John F. *The Spanish Borderlands Frontier, 1513–1821.* New York: Holt, Rinehart and Winston, 1970.

Beck, Warren A., and Ynez D. Haase. *Historical Atlas of New Mexico.* Norman: University of Oklahoma Press, 1969.

Bemis, Samuel F. *Pinckney's Treaty: America's Advantage from Europe's Distress, 1783–1800.* New Haven: Yale University Press, 1960.

Billington, Ray A. *Westward Expansion: A History of the American Frontier.* 2d ed. New York: Macmillan, 1964.

Bobb, Bernard E. *The Viceregency of Antonio María Bucareli in New Spain, 1771–1779.* Austin: University of Texas Press, 1962.

Bolton, Herbert E. *Coronado: Knight of Pueblos and Plains.* Albuquerque: University of New Mexico Press, 1964.

———. *The Hasinais: Southern Caddoans as Seen by the First Europeans.* Norman: University of Oklahoma Press, 1987.

———. *The Mission as a Frontier Institution in the Spanish-American Colonies.* El Paso: Academic Reprints, 1962.

———. *The Spanish Borderlands: A Chronicle of Old Florida and the Southwest.* New Haven: Yale University Press, 1921.

———, ed. *Spanish Exploration in the Southwest, 1542–1706.* Reprint. New York: Barnes and Noble, 1963.

———. *Texas in the Middle Eighteenth Century: Studies in Spanish Colonial History and Administration.* Austin: University of Texas Press, 1970.

Bolton, Herbert E., and Thomas M. Marshall. *The Colonization of North America, 1492–1783.* New York: Macmillan, 1960.

Brinckerhoff, Sidney B., and Odie B. Faulk. *Lancers for the King: A Study of the Frontier Military System of Northern New Spain, with a Translation of the Royal Regulations of 1772.* Phoenix: Arizona Historical Foundation, 1965.

Brooks, Charles M., Jr. *Texas Missions: Their Romance and Architecture.* Dallas: Dealey and Lowe, 1936.

Buck, Samuel M. *Yanaguana's Successors: The Story of the Canary Islanders' Immigration into Texas in the Eighteenth Century.* San Antonio: Naylor, 1949.

Calvert, Robert A., and Arnoldo De León. *The History of Texas.* Arlington Heights, Ill.: Harlan Davidson, 1990.

Campa, Arthur L. *Hispanic Culture in the Southwest.* Norman: University of Oklahoma Press, 1979.

Campbell, Randolph B. *An Empire for Slavery: The Peculiar Institution in Texas, 1821–1865.* Baton Rouge: Louisiana State University Press, 1989.

Campbell, T. N. *The Indians of Southern Texas and Northeastern Mexico: Selected Writings of Thomas Nolan Campbell.* Austin: Texas Archeological Research Library, 1988.

Campbell, T. N., and T. J. Campbell. *Historic Indian Groups of the Choke Canyon Reservoir and Surrounding Area, Southern Texas.* Choke Canyon Series. San Antonio: Center for Archaeological Research, University of Texas, 1981.

———. *Indian Groups Associated with Spanish Missions of the San Antonio*

Missions National Historical Park. San Antonio: Center for Archaeological Research, University of Texas, 1985.

Carr, Raymond. *Spain, 1808–1939*. Oxford: Clarendon Press, 1966.

Carter, Hodding. *Doomed Road of Empire: The Spanish Trail of Conquest*. New York: McGraw-Hill, 1963.

Caruso, John A. *The Mississippi Valley Frontier: The Age of French Exploration and Settlement*. Indianapolis: Bobbs-Merrill, 1966.

Castañeda, Carlos E. *Our Catholic Heritage in Texas*. 7 vols. Austin: Von Boeck-mann–Jones, 1936–1958.

Castillo Ledón, Luis. *Hidalgo: La vida del héroe*. 2 vols. Mexico City: Talleres Gráficos de la Nación, 1948–1949.

Céliz, Francisco. *Diary of the Alarcón Expedition into Texas, 1718–1719*. Trans. by Fritz Leo Hoffmann. Los Angeles: Quivira Society, 1935.

Chabot, Frederick C. *The Alamo, Altar of Texas Liberty*. San Antonio: Naylor, 1931.

———. *San Antonio and Its Beginnings*. San Antonio: Artes Gráficas, 1936.

———, ed. *Texas in 1811: The Las Casas and Sambrano Revolutions*. San Antonio: Yanaguana Society, 1941.

Chávez, Angélico. *Coronado's Friars*. Washington, D.C.: Academy of American Franciscan History, 1968.

Chipman, Donald E. *Nuño de Guzmán and the Province of Pánuco in New Spain, 1518–1533*. Glendale, Calif.: Arthur H. Clark, 1967.

Clark, Ira G. *Water in New Mexico: A History of Its Management and Use*. Albuquerque: University of New Mexico Press, 1987.

Clark, Robert C. *The Beginnings of Texas, 1684–1718*. Bulletin 98. Austin: University of Texas, 1907.

Clay, John V. *Spain, Mexico, and the Lower Trinity: An Early History of the Gulf Coast*. Baltimore: Gateway Press, 1987.

Connor, Seymour V. *Texas: A History*. Arlington Heights, Ill.: AHM Publishing, 1971.

Covey, Cyclone, trans. *Cabeza de Vaca's Adventures in the Unknown Interior of America*. Reprint. Albuquerque: University of New Mexico Press, 1984.

Crouse, Nellis M. *Lemoyne d'Iberville: Soldier of New France*. Ithaca: Cornell University Press, 1954.

Cruz, Gilbert R. *Let There Be Towns: Spanish Municipal Origins in the American Southwest, 1610–1810*. College Station: Texas A&M University Press, 1988.

———, ed. *Proceedings of the 1984 and 1985 San Antonio Missions Research Conferences*. San Antonio: LEBCO Graphics, 1986.

Cutrer, Thomas W. *The English Texans*. San Antonio: University of Texas Institute of Texan Cultures, 1985.

Day, A. Grove. *Coronado's Quest: The Discovery of the Southwestern States*. Berkeley: University of California Press, 1940.

Delanglez, Jean, trans. *The Journal of Jean Cavelier: The Account of a Survivor of La Salle's Texas Expedition, 1684–1688*. Chicago: Institute of Jesuit History, 1938.

De León, Arnoldo. *The Tejano Community, 1836–1900*. Albuquerque: University of New Mexico Press, 1982.

———. *They Called Them Greasers: Anglo Attitudes toward Mexicans in Texas, 1821–1900*. Austin: University of Texas Press, 1983.

De Long, David G., ed. *Historic American Buildings: Texas*. 2 vols. New York: Garland Publishing, 1979.

De Soto Trail: National Historic Trail Study, Draft Report. N.p.: National Park Service, 1989.

Diccionario Porrúa de historia, biografía y geografía de México. 3d ed. 2 vols. Mexico City: Editorial Porrúa, 1970.

Dobkins, Betty E. *The Spanish Element in Texas Water Law*. Austin: University of Texas Press, 1959.

Dods, Marcus, trans. *The City of God by Saint Augustine*. New York: Modern Library, 1950.

Domínguez, María Ester. *San Antonio, Tejas, en la época colonial (1718–1821)*. Madrid: Ediciones de Cultura Hispánica, 1989.

Dunn, William E. *Spanish and French Rivalry in the Gulf Region of the United States, 1678–1702: The Beginnings of Texas and Pensacola*. Studies in History 1. Austin: University of Texas, 1917.

Dunne, Peter M. *Pioneer Jesuits in Northern Mexico*. Berkeley: University of California Press, 1944.

Espinosa, Isidro Félix de. *Crónica de los colegios de propaganda fide de la Nueva España*. Washington, D.C.: Academy of American Franciscan History, 1964.

Faulk, Odie B. *The Last Years of Spanish Texas, 1778–1821*. The Hague: Mouton, 1964.

———. *A Successful Failure*. Austin: Steck-Vaughn, 1965.

Fehrenbach, T. R. *Lone Star: A History of Texas and the Texans*. New York: Collier Books, 1980.

Ferrell, Robert H. *American Diplomacy: A History*. Rev. ed. New York: Norton, 1969.

Flores, Dan L., ed. *Jefferson and Southwestern Exploration: The Freeman and Custis Accounts of the Red River Expedition of 1806*. Norman: University of Oklahoma Press, 1984.

———. *Journal of an Indian Trader: Anthony Glass and the Texas Trading Frontier, 1790–1810*. College Station: Texas A&M University Press, 1985.

Friedman, Lawrence M. *A History of American Law*. New York: Simon and Schuster, 1973.

Gammel, H. P. N., comp. *The Laws of Texas, 1822–1897*. 10 vols. Austin: Gammel, 1898.

García, Clotilde P. *Captain Alonso Alvarez de Pineda and the Exploration of the Texas Coast and the Gulf of Mexico*. Austin: Jenkins Publishing, 1982.

Garrett, Julia K. *Green Flag over Texas: A Story of the Last Years of Spain in Texas*. New York: Cordova Press, 1939.

Gatschet, Albert S. *The Karankawa Indians, the Coast People of Texas*. Reprint. Millwood, N.Y.: Kraus Reprint, 1974.

Gerhard, Peter. *The Northern Frontier of New Spain*. Princeton: Princeton University Press, 1982.

Glick, Thomas F. *The Old World Background of the Irrigation System of San Antonio, Texas*. Southwestern Studies 35. [El Paso]: Texas Western Press, 1972.

Gracy, David B., II. *Moses Austin: His Life*. San Antonio: Trinity University Press, 1987.

Griffin, Charles C. *The United States and the Disruption of the Spanish Empire, 1810–1822: A Study of the Relations of the United States with Spain and with the Rebel Spanish Colonies*. New York: Columbia University Press, 1937.

Grizzard, Mary. *Spanish Colonial Art and Architecture of Mexico and the U.S. Southwest*. Lanham, Md.: University Press of America, 1986.

Guzmán, Martín L. *Javier Mina, héroe de España y de México*. Mexico City: Compañía General de Ediciones, 1966.

Habig, Marion A. *The Alamo Chain of Missions: A History of San Antonio's Five Old Missions*. Chicago: Franciscan Herald Press, 1969.

————. *The Alamo Mission: San Antonio de Valero, 1718–1793*. Chicago: Franciscan Herald Press, 1977.

Hackett, Charles W., ed., and Charmion C. Shelby, trans. *Revolt of the Pueblo Indians and Otermín's Attempted Reconquest, 1680–1682*. 2 vols. Albuquerque: University of New Mexico Press, 1942.

Hallenbeck, Cleve. *The Journey of Fray Marcos de Niza*. Dallas: Southern Methodist University Press, 1987.

Hamill, Hugh M., Jr. *The Hidalgo Revolt: Prelude to Mexican Independence*. Gainesville: University of Florida Press, 1970.

Hammond, George P. *Don Juan de Oñate and the Founding of New Mexico*. Santa Fe: El Palacio Press, 1927.

Hammond, George P., and Agapito Rey. *Don Juan de Oñate: Colonizer of New Mexico, 1595–1628*. 2 vols. Albuquerque: University of New Mexico Press, 1953.

————, trans. and eds. *Expedition into New Mexico Made by Antonio de Espejo, 1582–1583: As Revealed in the Journal of Diego Pérez de Luxán, a Member of the Party*. Reprint. New York: Arno Press, 1967.

————. *Narratives of the Coronado Expedition, 1540–1542*. Albuquerque, University of New Mexico Press, 1940.

————. *The Rediscovery of New Mexico, 1580–1594*. Albuquerque: University of New Mexico Press, 1966.

The Handbook of Victoria County. Edited by Penny Anderson et al. Austin: Texas State Historical Association, 1990.

Hanke, Lewis. *Aristotle and the American Indians: A Study in Race Prejudice in the Modern World*. Chicago: Henry Regnery, 1959.

————. *The Spanish Struggle for Justice in the Conquest of America*. Philadelphia: University of Pennsylvania Press, 1949.

Haring, Clarence H. *The Spanish Empire in America*. New York: Oxford University Press, 1947.

Hedrick, Basil C., and Carroll L. Riley. *The Journey of the Vaca Party: The Account of the Narváez Expedition, 1528–1536, as Related by Gonzalo Fernández de Oviedo y Valdés.* University Museum Studies. Carbondale: University of Southern Illinois, 1974.

Hill, Lawrence F. *José de Escandón and the Founding of Nuevo Santander: A Study in Spanish Colonization.* Columbus: Ohio State University Press, [1926].

Hinojosa, Gilberto M. *A Borderlands Town in Transition: Laredo, 1755–1870.* College Station: Texas A&M University Press, 1983.

Hodge, Frederick W., George P. Hammond, and Agapito Rey, eds. *Fray Alonso Benavides' Revised Memorial of 1634.* Albuquerque: University of New Mexico Press, 1945.

Hodge, Frederick W., and Theodore H. Lewis, eds. *Spanish Explorers in the Southern United States, 1528–1543.* Reprint. Austin: Texas State Historical Association, 1990.

Hollon, W. Eugene. *The Lost Pathfinder: Zebulon Montgomery Pike.* Norman: University of Oklahoma Press, 1949.

Hughes, Anne E. *The Beginnings of Spanish Settlement in the El Paso District.* Reprint. [Berkeley]: University of California Press, 1914.

Inglis, Jack M. *A History of Vegetation on the Rio Grande Plain.* Bulletin 45. Austin: Texas Parks and Wildlife Department, [1964].

Jackson, Jack. *Los Mesteños: Spanish Ranching in Texas, 1721–1821.* College Station: Texas A&M University Press, 1986.

Jackson, Jack, Robert S. Weddle, and Winston De Ville. *Mapping Texas and the Gulf Coast: The Contributions of Saint-Denis, Oliván, and Le Maire.* College Station: Texas A&M University Press, 1990.

Jacobs, James R. *Tarnished Warrior: Major-General James Wilkinson.* New York: Macmillan, 1938.

Jarrat, Rie. *Gutiérrez de Lara, Mexican-Texan: The Story of a Creole Hero.* Austin: Creole Texana, 1949.

John, Elizabeth A. H. *Storms Brewed in Other Men's Worlds: The Confrontation of Indians, Spanish, and French in the Southwest, 1540–1795.* College Station: Texas A&M University Press, 1975.

Johnson, William W. *Cortés.* Boston: Little, Brown, 1975.

Jones, Oakah L., Jr. *Los Paisanos: Spanish Settlers on the Northern Frontier of New Spain.* Norman: University of Oklahoma Press, 1979.

———. *Nueva Vizcaya: Heartland of the Spanish Frontier.* Albuquerque: University of New Mexico Press, 1988.

Jordan, Terry G. *Trails to Texas: Southern Roots of Western Cattle Ranching.* Lincoln: University of Nebraska Press, 1981.

Jordan, Terry G., John L. Bean, Jr., and William M. Holmes. *Texas: A Geography.* Boulder, Colo.: Westview Press, 1984.

Kanellos, Nicolás, *A History of Hispanic Theatre in the United States, Origins to 1940.* Austin: University of Texas Press, 1990.

Kelemen, Pál. *Art of the Americas: Ancient and Modern, with a Comparative Chapter on the Philippines.* New York: Thomas Y. Crowell, 1969.

Kinnaird, Lawrence, ed. and trans. *The Frontiers of New Spain: Nicolás de La-fora's Description.* Berkeley: Quivira Society, 1958.

Kubler, George, and Martin Soria. *Art and Architecture in Spain and Portugal and Their American Dominions, 1500–1800.* Baltimore: Penguin Books, 1959.

Lamb, Hubert H. *Weather, Climate, and Human Affairs: A Book of Essays and Other Papers.* New York: Routledge, 1988.

Langdon-Davies, John. *Carlos: The King Who Would Not Die.* Englewood Cliffs, N.J.: Prentice-Hall, 1962.

La relación y comentarios del gouernador Aluar núñez cabeça de vaca, de lo acaescido en las dos jornadas que hizo a las Indias, con priuilegio . . . Valladolid: Francisco fernández de Córdoua, 1555.

Leutenegger, Benedict. *Apostle of America, Fray Antonio Margil.* Chicago: Franciscan Herald Press, 1966.

————, trans. and ed. *Inventory of the Mission San Antonio de Valero, 1772.* Austin: Office of the State Archeologist, Texas Historical Commission, 1977.

Leutenegger, Benedict, trans., and Marion A. Habig, ed. *Nothingness Itself: Selected Writings of Ven. Fr. Antonio Margil, 1690–1724.* Chicago: Franciscan Herald Press, 1976.

Lister, Florence C., and Robert H. Lister. *Chihuahua: Storehouse of Storms.* Albuquerque: University of New Mexico Press, 1966.

Loomis, Noel M., and Abraham P. Nasatir. *Pedro Vial and the Roads to Santa Fe.* Norman: University of Oklahoma Press, 1967.

Lynch, John. *Spain under the Habsburgs.* 2 vols. New York: Oxford University Press, 1964, 1969.

McCloskey, Michael B. *The Formative Years of the Missionary College of Santa Cruz of Querétaro, 1683–1733.* Washington, D.C.: Academy of American Franciscan History, 1955.

McComb, David G. *Texas: A Modern History.* Austin: University of Texas Press, 1989.

McKnight, Joseph W. *The Spanish Elements in Modern Texas Law.* Dallas: N.p., 1979.

Maloy, William M., comp. *Treaties, Conventions, International Acts, Protocols, and Agreements between the United States of America and Other Powers, 1776–1909.* 2 vols. Washington, D.C.: U.S. Government Printing Office, 1910.

Martin, Robert S., and James C. Martin. *Contours of Discovery: Printed Maps Delineating the Texas and Southwestern Chapters in the Cartographic History of North America, 1513–1930, A User's Guide.* Austin: Texas State Historical Association, 1982.

Mecham, J. Lloyd. *Francisco de Ibarra and Nueva Vizcaya.* Durham: Duke University Press, 1927.

Meinig, D. W. *Imperial Texas: An Interpretive Essay in Cultural Geography.* Austin: University of Texas Press, 1969.

Meyer, Michael C. *Water in the Hispanic Southwest: A Social and Legal History, 1550–1850.* Tucson: University of Arizona Press, 1984.

Meyer, Michael C., and William L. Sherman. *The Course of Mexican History.* 3d ed. New York: Oxford University Press, 1987.

Moorhead, Max L. *The Apache Frontier: Jacobo Ugarte and Spanish-Indian Relations in Northern New Spain, 1769–1791.* Norman: University of Oklahoma Press, 1968.

———. *The Presidio: Bastion of the Borderlands.* Norman: University of Oklahoma Press, 1975.

Morfi, Juan Agustín. *History of Texas, 1673–1779.* Trans. and ed. by Carlos E. Castañeda. 2 vols. Albuquerque: Quivira Society, 1935.

Myers, Sandra L. *The Ranch in Spanish Texas.* El Paso: Texas Western Press, 1969.

Navarro García, Luis. *Don José de Gálvez y la Comandancia General de las Provincias Internas del Norte de Nueva España.* Seville: Escuela de Estudios Hispano-Americanos de Sevilla, 1964.

———. *Las Provincias Internas en el siglo XIX.* Seville: Escuela de Estudios Hispano-Americanos de Sevilla, 1965.

Naylor, Thomas H., and Charles W. Polzer, comps. and eds. *Pedro de Rivera and the Military Regulations for Northern New Spain, 1724–1729: A Documentary History of His Frontier Inspection and the "Reglamento de 1729."* Tucson: University of Arizona Press, 1988.

———. *The Presidio and Militia on the Northern Frontier of New Spain: A Documentary History, Volume One: 1570–1700.* Tucson: University of Arizona Press, 1986.

Newcomb, W. W., Jr. *The Indians of Texas: From Prehistoric to Modern Times.* Austin: University of Texas Press, 1961.

———. *The People Called Wichita.* Phoenix: Indian Tribal Series, 1976.

Nixon, Pat I. *The Medical Story of Early Texas, 1528–1853.* [Lancaster, Pa.: Lancaster Press], 1946.

Oberste, William H. *History of the Refugio Mission.* Refugio, Tex.: Refugio Timely Remarks, 1942.

———. *The Restless Friar: Venerable Fray Antonio Margil de Jesús, Missionary to the Americas—Apostle of Texas.* Austin: Von Boeckmann-Jones, 1970.

O'Connor, Kathryn S. *The Presidio La Bahía del Espíritu Santo de Zúñiga, 1721 to 1846.* Austin: Von Boeckmann-Jones, 1966.

Parkman, Francis. *La Salle and the Discovery of the Great West.* Boston: Little, Brown, 1901.

Partlow, Miriam. *Liberty, Liberty County, and the Atascosito District.* Austin: Pemberton Press, 1974.

Payne, Stanley G. *A History of Spain and Portugal.* 2 vols. Madison: University of Wisconsin Press, 1973.

Pearson, Jim B., Ben Procter, and William B. Conroy. *Texas: The Land and the People.* 3d ed. Dallas: Hendrick-Long Publishing, 1987.

Pérez de Luxán, Diego. *Expedition into Mexico Made by Antonio de Espejo, 1582–1583.* Los Angeles: Quivira Society, 1929.

Peterson, Merrill D. *Thomas Jefferson and the New Nation: A Biography.* New York: Oxford University Press, 1970.

Phares, Ross. *Cavalier in the Wilderness: The Story of the Explorer and Trader Louis Juchereau de St. Denis*. Baton Rouge: Louisiana State University Press, 1952.

Powell, Philip W. *Soldiers, Indians, and Silver: The Northward Advance of New Spain, 1550–1600*. Berkeley: University of California Press, 1952.

Poyo, Gerald E., and Gilberto M. Hinojosa, eds. *Tejano Origins in Eighteenth-Century San Antonio*. Austin: University of Texas Press, 1991.

Prescott, William H. *History of the Conquest of Mexico, and History of the Conquest of Peru*. New York: Modern Library, n.d.

Priestley, Herbert I. *José de Gálvez, Visitor-General of New Spain, 1765–1771*. Berkeley: University of California Press, 1916.

Ratchford, Fannie E., ed. *The Story of Champ d'Asile as Told by Two of the Colonists*. Trans. by Donald Joseph. Dallas: Book Club of Texas, 1937.

Reeves, Jesse S. *The Napoleonic Exiles in America: A Study in American Diplomatic History, 1815–1819*. Baltimore: Johns Hopkins University Press, 1905.

Richardson, Rupert N., Ernest Wallace, and Adrian Anderson. *Texas: The Lone Star State*. 5th ed. Englewood Cliffs, N.J.: Prentice-Hall, 1988.

Ríos, Eduardo E. *Life of Fray Antonio Margil, O.F.M.* Trans. and revised by Benedict Leutenegger. Washington, D.C.: Academy of American Franciscan History, 1959.

Robb, John D. *Hispanic Folk Music of New Mexico and the Southwest: A Self-Portrait of a People*. Norman: University of Oklahoma Press, 1980.

Robertson, William S. *Iturbide of Mexico*. Durham: Duke University Press, 1952.

Salinas, Martín. *Indians of the Rio Grande Delta: Their Role in the History of Southern Texas and Northeastern Mexico*. Austin: University of Texas Press, 1990.

Sanford, Trent E. *The Architecture of the Southwest: Indian, Spanish, American*. New York: Norton, 1950.

Sauer, Carl O. *The Road to Cíbola*. Berkeley: University of California Press, 1932.

———. *Sixteenth-Century North America: The Land the People as Seen by the Europeans*. Berkeley: University of California Press, 1971.

Scholes, France V. *Troublous Times in New Mexico, 1659–1670*. Albuquerque: University of New Mexico Press, 1942.

Schwartz, Ted. *Forgotten Battlefield of the First Texas Revolution: The Battle of the Medina, August 18, 1813*. Ed. by Robert H. Thonhoff. Austin: Eakin Press, 1985.

Simmons, Marc. *The Last Conquistador: Juan de Oñate and the Settling of the Far Southwest*. Norman: University of Oklahoma Press, 1991.

Simpson, Lesley B. *Many Mexicos*. 4th ed. Berkeley: University of California Press, 1967.

———, ed. *The San Sabá Papers: A Documentary Account of the Founding and Destruction of the San Sabá Mission*. San Francisco: John Howell-Books, 1959.

Sonnichsen, C. L. *Pass of the North: Four Centuries on the Rio Grande*. El Paso: Texas Western Press, 1968.

Spell, Lota M. *Pioneer Printer: Samuel Bangs in Mexico and Texas*. Austin: University of Texas Press, 1963.

Starnes, Gary B. *The San Gabriel Missions, 1746–1756*. Madrid: Ministry of Foreign Affairs, Government of Spain, 1969.

Stephens, A. Ray, and William M. Holmes. *Historical Atlas of Texas*. Norman: University of Oklahoma Press, 1989.

Swanton, John R. *The Indian Tribes of North America*. Bulletin 145. Washington, D.C.: Bureau of American Ethnology, 1952.

———. *The Indians of the Southeastern United States*. Bulletin 137. Washington, D.C.: Bureau of American Ethnology, 1946.

———. *Source Material of the History and Ethnology of the Caddo Indians*. Washington, D.C.: U.S. Government Printing Office, 1942.

Texas Almanac and State Industrial Guide, 1988–1989. Dallas: Dallas Morning News, 1987.

Thomas, Alfred B., trans. and ed. *Teodoro de Croix and the Northern Frontier of New Spain, 1776–1783*. Norman: University of Oklahoma Press, 1941.

Timmons, Wilbert H. *El Paso: A Borderlands History*. El Paso: Texas Western Press, 1990.

———. *Morelos: Priest, Soldier, Statesman of Mexico*. El Paso: Texas Western Press, 1963.

Torres Ramírez, Bibiano. *La Armada de Barlovento*. Seville: Escuela de Estudios Hispano-Americanos, 1981.

Tunnell, Curtis D., and W. W. Newcomb, Jr. *A Lipan Apache Mission: San Lorenzo de la Santa Cruz, 1762–1771*. Bulletin 14. Austin: Texas Memorial Museum, 1969.

Varner, John G., and Jeannette J. Varner, trans. and eds. *The Florida of the Inca*. Austin: University of Texas Press, 1951.

Velásquez, María del Carmen. *Establecimiento y pérdida del septentrión de Nueva España*. Mexico City: El Colegio de México, 1974.

Vigness, David M. *The Revolutionary Decades*. Austin: Steck-Vaughn, 1965.

———. *Spanish Texas, 1519–1810*. Boston: American Press, 1983.

Villoro, Luis. *La revolución de independencia: Ensayo de interpretación histórica*. Mexico City: Universidad Nacional Autónoma de México, 1953.

Wagner, Henry R. *The Spanish Southwest, 1542–1794*. Albuquerque: Quivira Society, 1937.

———. *Spanish Voyages to the Northwest Coast of America in the Sixteenth Century*. Amsterdam: N. Israel, 1966.

Wallace, Ernest, and E. Adamson Hoebel. *The Comanches: Lords of the South Plains*. Norman: University of Oklahoma Press, 1952.

Warren, Harris G. *The Sword Was Their Passport, a History of American Filibustering in the Mexican Revolution*. Baton Rouge: Louisiana State University Press, 1943.

Warren, J. Benedict. *The Conquest of Michoacán: The Spanish Domination of the Tarascan Kingdom in Western Mexico, 1521–1530.* Norman: University of Oklahoma Press, 1985.

Webb, Walter P. *The Great Plains.* New York: Grosset and Dunlap, 1931.

Webb, Walter P., H. Bailey Carroll, and Eldon S. Branda, eds. *The Handbook of Texas.* 3 vols. Austin: Texas State Historical Association, 1952, 1976.

Weber, David J. *The Mexican Frontier, 1821–1846: The American Southwest under Mexico.* Albuquerque: University of New Mexico Press, 1982.

———, ed. *New Spain's Far Northern Frontier: Essays on Spain in the American Southwest, 1540–1821.* Reprint. Dallas: Southern Methodist University Press, 1988.

Weddle, Robert S. *The French Thorn: Rival Explorers in the Spanish Sea, 1682–1762.* College Station: Texas A&M University Press, 1991.

———. *San Juan Bautista: Gateway to Spanish Texas.* Austin: University of Texas Press, 1968.

———. *The San Sabá Mission: Spanish Pivot in Texas.* Austin: University of Texas Press, 1964.

———. *Spanish Sea: The Gulf of Mexico in North American Discovery, 1500–1685.* College Station: Texas A&M University Press, 1985.

———. *Wilderness Manhunt: The Spanish Search for La Salle.* Austin: University of Texas Press, 1973.

Weddle, Robert S., and Robert H. Thonhoff. *Drama and Conflict: The Texas Saga of 1776.* Austin: Madrona Press, 1976.

Wilson, Maurine T., and Jack Jackson. *Philip Nolan and Texas: Expeditions to the Unknown Land.* Waco: Texian Press, 1987.

Winfrey, Dorman H., et al. *Indian Tribes of Texas.* Waco: Texian Press, 1971.

Worcester, Donald E., ed. and trans. *Instructions for Governing the Interior Provinces of Spain, 1786, by Bernardo de Gálvez.* Berkeley: Quivira Society, 1951.

Yoakum, Henderson. *History of Texas from Its First Settlement in 1685 to Its Annexation to the United States in 1846.* 2 vols. New York: Redfield, 1855–1856.

Articles and Chapters in Books

Aiton, Arthur S. "The Diplomacy of the Louisiana Cession." *American Historical Review* 36 (July 1931): 701–720.

Allen, Henry E. "The Parrilla Expedition to the Red River in 1759." *Southwestern Historical Quarterly* 43 (July 1939): 53–71.

Andrew, Bunyan H. "Some Queries concerning the Texas-Louisiana Sabine Boundary." *Southwestern Historical Quarterly* 53 (July 1949): 1–18.

Arneson, Edwin P. "Early Irrigation in Texas." *Southwestern Historical Quarterly* 25 (October 1921): 121–130.

Baade, Hans W. "The Form of Marriage in Spanish North America." *Cornell Law Review* 61 (November 1975): 1–89.

———. "Marriage Contracts in French and Spanish Louisiana: A Study in 'Notarial' Jurisprudence." *Tulane Law Review* 53 (December 1979): 3–92.

Barker, Eugene C. "The African Slave Trade in Texas." *Quarterly of the Texas State Historical Association* 6 (October 1902): 145–158.

Benson, Nettie L. "Bishop Marín de Porras and Texas." *Southwestern Historical Quarterly* 51 (July 1947): 16–40.

———, ed and trans. "A Governor's Report on Texas in 1809." *Southwestern Historical Quarterly* 71 (April 1968): 603–615.

———. "Texas Failure to Send a Deputy to the Spanish Cortes, 1810–1812." *Southwestern Historical Quarterly* 64 (July 1960): 14–35.

Berger, Max. "Education in Texas during the Spanish and Mexican Periods." *Southwestern Historical Quarterly* 51 (July 1947): 41–53.

Bolton, Herbert E. "The Beginnings of Mission Nuestra Señora del Refugio: *Southwestern Historical Quarterly* 19 (April 1916): 400–404.

———. "The Founding of Mission Rosario: A Chapter in the History of the Gulf Coast." *Quarterly of the Texas State Historical Association* 10 (October 1906): 113–139.

———. "The Founding of the Missions on the San Gabriel River, 1745–1749." *Southwestern Historical Quarterly* 17 (April 1914): 323–378.

———. "The Jumano Indians in Texas, 1650–1771." *Quarterly of the Texas State Historical Association* 15 (July 1911): 66–84.

———. "The Location of La Salle's Colony on the Gulf of Mexico." *Mississippi Valley Historical Review* 2 (September 1915): 165–182.

———. "Native Tribes about the East Texas Missions." *Quarterly of the Texas State Historical Association* 11 (April 1908): 249–276.

———. "The Spanish Abandonment and Re-Occupation of East Texas, 1773–1779." *Quarterly of the Texas State Historical Association* 9 (October 1905): 67–137.

———. "Spanish Activities on the Lower Trinity River, 1746–1771." *Southwestern Historical Quarterly* 16 (April 1913): 339–377.

———. "The Spanish Occupation of Texas, 1519–1690." *Southwestern Historical Quarterly* 16 (July 1912): 1–26.

———. "Tienda de Cuervo's *Ynspección* of Laredo, 1757." *Quarterly of the Texas State Historical Association* 6 (January 1903): 187–203.

Brand, Donald D. "The Early History of the Range Cattle Industry in Northern Mexico." *Agricultural History* 35 (July 1961): 132–139.

Brindley, Anne A., "Jane Long." *Southwestern Historical Quarterly* 56 (October 1952): 211–238.

Bronitsky, Gordon. "Indian Assimilation in the El Paso Area." *New Mexico Historical Review* 62 (April 1987): 151–161.

Brooks, Philip C. "Spain's Farewell to Louisiana, 1803–1821." *Mississippi Valley Historical Review* 27 (June 1940): 29–40.

Buckley, Eleanor C. "The Aguayo Expedition into Texas and Louisiana, 1719–1722." *Quarterly of the Texas State Historical Association* 15 (July 1911): 1–65.

Bugbee, Lester G. "The Real Saint-Denis." *Quarterly of the Texas State Historical Association* 1 (April 1898): 266–281.

Burch, Marvin C. "The Indigenous Indians of the Lower Trinity River of Texas." *Southwestern Historical Quarterly* 60 (July 1956): 36–52.

Campbell, T. N. "Coahuiltecans and Their Neighbors." In *Handbook of North American Indians,* ed. William C. Sturtevant, vol. 10, *Southwest,* ed. Alfonso Ortiz. 343–358. Washington, D.C.: Smithsonian Institution, 1983.

Castañeda, Carlos E. "The Woman in Blue." *The Age of Mary: An Exclusively Marian Magazine,* Mystical City of God Issue (January–February 1958): 22–29.

Chipman, Donald E. "In Search of Cabeza de Vaca's Route across Texas: An Historiographical Survey." *Southwestern Historical Quarterly* 91 (October 1987): 127–148.

———. "Nuño de Guzmán and His 'Grand Design' in New Spain." In *Homenaje a Don José María de la Peña y Cámara.* Madrid: Ediciones José Porrúa Turanzas, 1969.

———. "The Oñate-Moctezuma-Zaldívar Families of Northern New Spain." *New Mexico Historical Review* 52 (October 1977): 297–310.

———. "Spanish Texas." In *Texas through Time: Evolving Interpretations,* ed. Walter L. Buenger and Robert A. Calvert. College Station: Texas A&M University Press, 1991.

Collins, Gladys. "Spanish West Texas, 1535–1769." *West Texas Historical Association Year Book* 7 (June 1931): 95–114.

Cox, I. J. "Educational Efforts in San Fernando de Béxar." *Quarterly of the Texas State Historical Association* 6 (July 1902): 27–63.

———. "The Louisiana-Texas Frontier during the Burr Conspiracy." *Mississippi Valley Historical Review* 10 (December 1923): 274–284.

Crimmins, M. L. "Augustus William Magee, the Second Advance Courier of American Expansion to Texas." *West Texas Historical Association Year Book* 20 (October 1944): 92–99.

Dabbs, Jack A., trans. and ed. "Additional Notes on the Champ-d'Asile." *Southwestern Historical Quarterly* 54 (January 1951): 347–358.

Davenport, Harbert, and Joseph K. Wells. "The First Europeans in Texas, 1528–1536." *Southwestern Historical Quarterly,* Part I, 22 (October 1918): 111–142; Part II, 22 (January 1919): 205–259.

Day, James M. "The Karankawas." In Dorman H. Winfrey et al., *Indian Tribes of Texas.* Waco: Texian Press, 1971.

Din, Gilbert C. "Spain's Immigration Policy in Louisiana and the American Penetration, 1792–1803." *Southwestern Historical Quarterly* 76 (January 1973): 255–276.

Downs, Fane. "Governor Antonio Martínez and the Defense of Texas from Foreign Invasion, 1817–1822." *Texas Military History* 7 (Spring 1968): 27–43.

Dunn, William E. "The Apache Mission on the San Saba River: Its Founding and Failure." *Southwestern Historical Quarterly* 17 (April 1914): 379–414.

———. "Apache Relations in Texas, 1718–1750." *Quarterly of the Texas State Historical Association* 14 (January 1911): 198–274.

———. "The Founding of Nuestra Señora del Refugio, the Last Spanish Mission in Texas." *Southwestern Historical Quarterly* 25 (January 1922): 174–184.

———. "Missionary Activities among the Eastern Apaches Previous to the Founding of the San Sabá Mission." *Quarterly of the Texas State Historical Association* 15 (January 1912): 186–200.

———. "The Spanish Search for La Salle's Colony on the Bay of Espíritu Santo, 1685–1689." *Southwestern Historical Quarterly* 19 (April 1916): 323–369.

F. de la Teja, Jesús. "Forgotten Founders: The Military Settlers of Eighteenth-Century San Antonio de Béxar." In *Tejano Origins in Eighteenth-Century San Antonio,* ed. Gerald E. Poyo and Gilberto Hinojosa. Austin: University of Texas Press, 1991.

———. "Indians, Soldiers, and Canary Islanders: The Making of a Texas Frontier Community." *Locus: An Historical Journal of Regional Perspectives on National Topics* 3 (Fall 1990): 81–96.

Faulk, Odie, trans. and ed. "A Description of Texas in 1803." *Southwestern Historical Quarterly* 66 (April 1963): 513–515.

———. "The Penetration of Foreigners and Foreign Ideas into Spanish East Texas, 1793–1810." *East Texas Historical Journal* 2 (October 1964): 87–98.

———. "Ranching in Spanish Texas." *Hispanic American Historical Review* 45 (May 1965): 257–266.

Flores, Dan L. "The Ecology of the Red River in 1806: Peter Custis and Early Southwestern Natural History." *Southwestern Historical Quarterly* 88 (July 1984): 1–42.

Forrestal, Peter P., trans. "Peña's Diary of the Aguayo Expedition." *Preliminary Studies of the Texas Catholic Historical Society* 2 (January 1935): 3–68.

———. "The Venerable Padre Fray Antonio Margil de Jesús." *Preliminary Studies of the Texas Catholic Historical Society* 2 (April 1932): 5–34.

Garrett, Kathryn. "The First Constitution of Texas, April 17, 1813." *Southwestern Historical Quarterly* 40 (April 1937): 290–308.

———. "The First Newspaper of Texas: Gaceta de Texas." *Southwestern Historical Quarterly* 40 (January 1937): 200–215.

Gilmore, Kathleen. "La Salle's Fort St. Louis in Texas." *Bulletin of the Texas Archeological Society* 55 (1984): 61–72.

Griffen, William B. "Southern Periphery: East." In *Handbook of North American Indians,* ed. William C. Sturtevant, vol. 10, *Southwest,* ed. Alfonso Ortiz. 329–342. Washington, D.C.: Smithsonian Institution, 1983.

Gronet, Richard W. "The United States and the Invasion of Texas." *Americas* 25 (January 1969): 281–306.

Habig, Marion A. "Mission San José y San Miguel de Aguayo, 1720–1824." *Southwestern Historical Quarterly* 71 (April 1969): 496–516.

Hackett, Charles W. "The Marquis of San Miguel de Aguayo and His Recovery of Texas from the French, 1719–1723." *Southwestern Historical Quarterly* 49 (October 1945): 193–214.

———. "New Light on don Diego de Peñalosa: Proof That He Never Made an Expedition from Santa Fe to Quivira and the Mississippi River in 1662." *Mississippi Valley Historical Review* 6 (December 1919): 313–335.

———. "The Retreat of the Spaniards from New Mexico in 1680, and the Beginnings of El Paso." *Southwestern Historical Quarterly*, Part I, 16 (October 1912): 137–168; Part II, 16 (January 1913): 259–276.

———. The Revolt of the Pueblo Indians of New Mexico in 1680." *Quarterly of the Texas State Historical Association* 15 (October 1911): 93–147.

———. "Visitador Rivera's Criticisms of Aguayo's Work in Texas." *Hispanic American Historical Review* 16 (May 1936): 162–172.

Haggard, J. Villasana. "The Counter-Revolution of Béxar, 1811." *Southwestern Historical Quarterly* 43 (October 1939): 222–235.

———. "The House of Barr and Davenport." *Southwestern Historical Quarterly* 44 (July 1945): 66–88.

———. "The Neutral Ground between Louisiana and Texas, 1806–1821." *Louisiana Historical Quarterly* 28 (October 1945): 1001–1128.

Hatcher, Mattie A. "Conditions in Texas Affecting the Colonization Problem, 1795–1801." *Southwestern Historical Quarterly* 25 (October 1921): 81–97.

———, trans. and ed. "Descriptions of the Tejas or Asinai Indians, 1691–1722." *Southwestern Historical Quarterly*, Part I, 30 (January 1925): 206–218; Part II, 30 (April 1927): 283–304; Part III, 31 (July 1927): 50–62; Part IV, 31 (October 1927): 150–180.

———, trans. "The Expedition of Don Domingo Terán de los Ríos into Texas." *Preliminary Studies of the Texas Catholic Historical Society* 2 (January 1932): 3–67.

———. "Joaquín de Arredondo's Report on the Battle of the Medina, August 18, 1813." *Quarterly of the Texas State Historical Association* 11 (January 1908): 220–236.

———. "The Louisiana Background of the Colonization of Texas, 1763–1803." *Southwestern Historical Quarterly* 24 (January 1921): 169–194.

———. "The Municipal Government of San Fernando de Béxar, 1730–1800." *Quarterly of the Texas State Historical Association* 8 (April 1905): 277–352.

———, trans. "Texas in 1820." *Southwestern Historical Quarterly* 23 (July 1919): 47–68.

Henderson, Harry M. "The Magee-Gutiérrez Expedition." *Southwestern Historical Quarterly* 55 (July 1951): 43–61.

Hoese, H. Dickson. "On the Correct Landfall of La Salle in Texas, 1685." *Louisiana History* 19 (Winter 1978): 5–32.

Hoffmann, Fritz L., trans. "The Mezquía Diary of the Alarcón Expedition into Texas, 1718." *Southwestern Historical Quarterly* 41 (April 1938): 312–323.

Holmes, Jack D. L. "The Marqués de Casa-Calvo, Nicolás deFiniels, and the 1805 Spanish Expedition through East Texas and Louisiana." *Southwestern Historical Quarterly* 69 (January 1966): 324–339.

Huie, William O. "The Texas Constitutional Definition of the Wife's Separate Property." *Texas Law Review* 35 (October 1957): 1054–1070.

Hutchins, Wells A. "The Community Acequia: Its Origins and Development." *Southwestern Historical Quarterly* 31 (January 1928): 261–284.

Jackson, Donald. "Zebulon Pike 'Tours' Mexico." *American West* 3 (Summer 1966): 67–71, 89–93.

Jordan, Terry G. "Pioneer Evaluation of Vegetation in Frontier Texas." *Southwestern Historical Quarterly* 76 (January 1973): 233–254.

Kelley, Dayton, "The Tonkawas." In Dorman H. Winfrey et al., *Indian Tribes of Texas*. Waco: Texian Press, 1971.

Kilgore, Dan. "Texas Cattle Origins." *Cattleman* 69 (January 1983), 110–120.

Krieger, Alex D. "The Travels of Alvar Núñez Cabeza de Vaca in Texas and Mexico, 1534–1536." In *Homenaje a Pablo Martínez de Río en el vigésimoquinto aniversario de la primera edición de 'Los Orígenes Americanos.'* Mexico City: Instituto Nacional de Antropología e Historia, 1961.

Leutenegger, Benedict, trans. "Memorial of Father Benito Fernández concerning the Canary Islanders, 1741." *Southwestern Historical Quarterly* 82 (October 1978): 265–296.

———, ed. and trans. "New Documents on Father José Mariano Reyes." *Southwestern Historical Quarterly* 71 (April 1968): 583–602.

———, trans. "Report on the San Antonio Missions in 1792." Intro. and notes by Marion A. Habig. *Southwestern Historical Quarterly* 77 (April 1974): 487–498.

———. "Two Franciscan Documents on Early San Antonio, Texas." *Americas* 25 (October 1968): 191–206.

McCaleb, Walter F. "The First Period of the Gutiérrez-Magee Expedition." *Quarterly of the Texas State Historical Association* 4 (January 1901): 218–229.

McElhannon, Joseph C. "Imperial Mexico and Texas." *Southwestern Historical Quarterly* 53 (October 1949): 117–150.

McKnight, Joseph. "Legitimation and Adoption on the Anglo-Hispanic Frontier of the United States." *Legal History Review* 53 (1985): 135–150.

———. "The Spanish Influence on the Texas Law of Civil Procedure." *Texas Law Review* 38 (November 1959): 24–54.

———. "Spanish Law for the Protection of Surviving Spouses in North America." *Anuario de historia del derecho español* 57 (1987): 365–406.

Magnaghi, Russell M., ed. and trans. "Texas as Seen by Governor Winthuysen, 1714–1744." *Southwestern Historical Quarterly* 88 (October 1984): 167–180.

Mecham, J. Lloyd. "Antonio de Espejo and His Journey to New Mexico." *Southwestern Historical Quarterly* 30 (October 1926): 114–138.

Moore, Mary L., and Delmar L. Beene, trans. and eds. "The Interior Provinces of New Spain: The Report of Hugo O'Conor." *Arizona and the West* 13 (Autumn 1971): 265–282.

Morrisey, Richard J. "The Northward Expansion of Cattle Ranching in New Spain, 1550–1600." *Agricultural History* 25 (July 1951): 115–121.

Murphy, Retta. "The Journey of Pedro de Rivera, 1724–1728." *Southwestern Historical Quarterly* 41 (October 1937): 125–141.

Myers, Sandra L. "The Lipan Apaches." In Dorman H. Winfrey et al., *Indian Tribes of Texas*. Waco: Texian Press, 1971.

Nelson, Al B. "Campaigning in the Big Bend of the Río Grande in 1787." *Southwestern Historical Quarterly* 39 (January 1936): 200–227.

———. "Juan de Ugalde and Picax-Andé Ins-Tinsle, 1787–1788." *Southwestern Historical Quarterly* 43 (April 1940): 438–464.

Newcomb, W. W., Jr. "Karankawa." In *Handbook of North American Indians,* ed. William C. Sturtevant, vol. 10, *Southwest,* ed. Alfonso Ortiz. 359–367. Washington, D.C.: Smithsonian Institution, 1983.

Newcomb, W. W., Jr., and T. N. Campbell. "Southern Plains Ethnohistory: A Re-examination of the Escanjaques, Ahijados, and Cuitoas." In *Pathways to Plains Prehistory: Anthropological Perspectives of Plains Natives and Their Past,* ed. Don G. Wyckoff and Jack L. Hofman. Duncan, Okla.: Cross Timbers Press, 1982.

Nixon, Pat I. "Liotot and Jalot, Two French Surgeons of Early Texas." *Southwestern Historical Quarterly* 43 (July 1939): 42–52.

Nunn, W. C. "The Caddoes." In Dorman H. Winfrey et al., *Indian Tribes of Texas.* Waco: Texian Press, 1971.

Patten, Roderick B., trans. and ed. "Miranda's Inspection of Los Almagres: His Journal, Report, and Petition." *Southwestern Historical Quarterly* 74 (October 1970): 223–252.

Phillips, Carla R. "Local History and Imperial Spain." *Locus: An Historical Journal of Regional Perspectives on National Topics* 2 (Spring 1990): 119–129.

Poole, Stafford, "'War by Fire and Blood': The Church and the Chichimecas, 1585." *Americas* 22 (October 1965): 115–137.

Powell, Philip W. "Presidios and Towns on the Silver Frontier of New Spain, 1550–1580." *Hispanic American Historical Review* 24 (May 1944): 179–200.

Poyo, Gerald E. "The Canary Islands Immigrants of San Antonio: From Ethnic Exclusivity to Community in Eighteenth-Century Béxar." In *Tejano Origins in Eighteenth-Century San Antonio,* ed. Gerald E. Poyo and Gilberto Hinojosa. Austin: University of Texas Press, 1991.

Poyo, Gerald E., and Gilberto M. Hinojosa. "Spanish Texas and Borderlands Historiography in Transition: Implications for United States History." *Journal of American History* 75 (September 1988): 393–416.

Quinn, Robert M. "The Architectural Origins of the Southwest Missions." *American West* 3 (Summer 1966): 57–66, 93–94.

Ratcliffe, Sam D. "'Escenas de Martiro': Notes on *The Destruction of Mission San Sabá*." *Southwestern Historical Quarterly* 94 (April 1991): 507–534.

Rathjen, Fred. "The Physiography of the Texas Panhandle." *Southwestern Historical Quarterly* 64 (January 1961): 315–332.

Reeve, Frank D. "The Apache Indians in Texas." *Southwestern Historical Quarterly* 50 (October 1946): 189–219.

Reindorp, Reginald C., trans. "The Founding of Missions at La Junta de los Ríos." *Supplementary Studies of the Catholic Historical Society* 1 (April 1938): 5–28.

Rohrbaugh, Charles L. "An Hypothesis for the Origin of Kichai." In *Pathways to Plains Prehistory: Anthropological Perspectives of Plains Natives and Their Past,* ed. Don G. Wyckoff and Jack L. Hofman. Duncan, Okla.: Cross Timbers Press, 1982.

Salmón, Roberto M. "A Thankless Job: Mexican Soldiers in the Spanish Border-lands." *Military History of the Southwest* 21 (Spring 1991): 1–19.

Scholes, France V., and H. P. Mera. "Some Aspects of the Jumano Problem." In *Contributions to American Anthropology and History*, vol. 6. Washington, D.C.: Carnegie Institution, 1940.

Seed, Patricia. "Social Dimensions of Race: Mexico City, 1753." *Hispanic American Historical Review* 62 (November 1982): 569–606.

Shelby, Charmion C. "St. Denis's Second Expedition to the Río Grande, 1716–1719." *Southwestern Historical Quarterly* 27 (January 1924): 190–216.

Sibley, Marilyn M., ed. "Across Texas in 1767: The Travels of Captain Pagès." *Southwestern Historical Quarterly* 70 (April 1967): 593–622.

Spell, Lota M. "The First Text Book Used in Texas." *Southwestern Historical Quarterly* 29 (April 1926): 289–295.

———. "Samuel Bangs: The First Printer in Texas." *Southwestern Historical Quarterly* 35 (April 1932): 267–278.

Steck, Francis B. "Forerunners of Captain de León's Expedition to Texas, 1670–1675." *Southwestern Historical Quarterly* 36 (July 1932): 1–28.

Sternberg, Richard. "The Western Boundary of Louisiana, 1762–1803." *Southwestern Historical Quarterly* 35 (October 1931): 95–108.

Strickland, Rex W. "Miller County, Arkansas Territory, the Frontier That Men Forgot." *Chronicles of Oklahoma* 18 (1940): 12–34; 19 (1941): 37–54.

———. "Moscoso's Journey through Texas." *Southwestern Historical Quarterly* 46 (October 1942): 109–137.

Thompson, Jesse E. "Sagittectomy—First Recorded Surgical Procedure in the American Southwest, 1535: The Journey and Ministrations of Alvar Núñez Cabeza de Vaca." *New England Journal of Medicine* 289 (December 27, 1973): 1403–1407.

Thonhoff, Robert H. "The First Ranch in Texas." *West Texas Historical Association Year Book* 40 (October 1964): 90–97.

Timmons, Wilbert H. "The Population of the El Paso Area—a Census of 1784." *New Mexico Historical Review* 52 (October 1977): 311–316.

———. "Tadeo Ortiz and Texas." *Southwestern Historical Quarterly* 72 (July 1968): 21–33.

Tjarks, Alicia V. "Comparative Demographic Analysis of Texas, 1777–1793." *Southwestern Historical Quarterly* 77 (January 1974): 291–338.

Trigger, Bruce G. "Early Native North American Responses to European Contact: Romantic versus Rationalistic Interpretations." *Journal of American History* 77 (March 1991), 1195–1215.

Vigness, David M. "Don Hugo Oconor and New Spain's Northeastern Frontier, 1764–1776." *Journal of the West* 6 (January 1967): 27–40.

Walters, Paul H. "Secularization of the La Bahía Mission." *Southwestern Historical Quarterly* 54 (January 1951): 287–300.

Warren, Harris G. "José Alvarez de Toledo's Initiation as a Filibuster, 1811–1813." *Hispanic American Historical Review* 20 (February 1940): 58–82.

———. "The Origin of General Minas's Invasion of Mexico." *Southwestern Historical Quarterly* 42 (July 1938): 1–20.

Weddle, Robert S. "La Salle's Survivors." *Southwestern Historical Quarterly* 75 (April 1972): 413–433.

———. "San Juan Bautista: Mother of Texas Missions." *Southwestern Historical Quarterly* 71 (April 1968): 542–563.

———. "Spanish Search for French Fort: A Path to Danger and Discovery." *American West* 20 (January-February 1983): 26–34.

Wedel, Waldo R. "Coronado, Quivira, and Kansas: An Archeologist's View." *Great Plains Quarterly* 10 (Summer 1990): 139–151.

West, Elizabeth H., trans. "Bonilla's Brief Compendium of the History of Texas, 1772." *Quarterly of the Texas State Historical Association* 8 (July 1904): 3–78.

———. "De León's Expedition of 1689." *Quarterly of the Texas State Historical Association* 8 (January 1905): 199–224.

———, ed. and trans. "Diary of José Bernardo Gutiérrez de Lara, 1811–1812." *American Historical Review* 34 (October 1928): 55–77; 34 (January 1929): 281–294.

Williams, J. W. "Moscoso's Trail in Texas." *Southwestern Historical Quarterly* 46 (October 1942): 138–157.

Winters, William G., Jr. "The Shoreline for Spanish and Mexican Grants in Texas." *Texas Law Review* 38 (May 1960): 523–537.

Wood, Peter H. "La Salle: Discovery of a Lost Explorer." *American Historical Review* 89 (April 1984): 294–323.

Theses, Dissertations, and Unpublished Works

F. de la Teja, Jesús. "Land and Society in Eighteenth-Century San Antonio de Béxar: A Community on New Spain's Northern Frontier." Ph.D. diss., University of Texas at Austin, 1988.

Krieger, Alex D. "Un nuevo estudio de la ruta seguida por Cabeza de Vaca a través de Norte América." Ph.D. diss., Universidad Nacional Autónoma de México, 1955.

Richards, Hons C. "The Establishment of the Candelaria and San Lorenzo Missions on the Upper Nueces." M.A. thesis, University of Texas, 1936.

Schuetz, Mardith K. "The Indians of the San Antonio Missions." Ph.D. diss., University of Texas, 1980.

Shields, Carla S. "Spanish Influence on East Texas Place Names and Vocabulary." M.A. thesis, East Texas State University, 1966.

Speiser, Adel. "The Story of the Theatre in San Antonio." M.A. thesis, St. Mary's University of San Antonio, 1948.

Starnes, Gary B. "Juan de Ugalde (1729–1816) and the Provincias Internas of Coahuila and Texas." Ph.D. diss., Texas Christian University, 1971.

Strickland, Rex W. "Anglo-American Activities in Northeastern Texas, 1803–1845." Ph.D. diss., University of Texas, 1936.

Walz, Vina E. "A History of the El Paso Area, 1680–1692." Ph.D. diss., University of New Mexico, 1951.

Weddle, Robert S. "Edge of Empire: Texas as a Spanish Frontier, 1519–1821." Manuscript, 1986.

Index

Acevedo, Fr. Antonio, 69, 70
Acoma, Pueblo, 37, 56, 59
Acubadao Indians, 12
Adaesaños, 187, 290n.53
Adais Indians, 114, 280n.24
Adams, John Quincy, 239
Agreda, María de Jesús de, 61–62
agriculture, 6, 7; among Caddoes, 19,
    21, 87, 91; in economy, 205, 207;
    at San Antonio, 136, 140. *See also*
    farming
Aguacane Indians, 273n.52
Aguayo, Joseph de Azlor y Virto de
    Vera, Marqués de San Miguel de,
    8, 119; accomplishments, 126–
    128, 133, 136, 147, 246; becomes
    governor, 120; reestablishes Texas
    missions, 121, 123; resigns as gov-
    ernor, 126; at San Antonio, 124
Aguirre, Pedro de, 110
Ais Indians, 114, 280n.24
Alabama-Coushatta Indians, 210
Alarcón, Martín de, 8, 115–119, 245
Aldama, Ignacio, 232
Aldama, Juan de, 219, 233
Allen, Henry E., 163
Allende, Ignacio, 219, 233
Almaráz, Félix D., Jr., xii, 232, 237
Alvarado, Hernando de, 37
Alvarado, Pedro de, 26, 35, 36; death
    of, 41
Alvarez Barreiro, Juan, 9
Alvarez de Pineda, Alonso, xi, 22, 27;
    maps Gulf Coast, 243; at Pánuco

River, 26; spelling of name, 268–
    269n.3; voyage of, 24
Alvarez Travieso, Vicente, 143
Amangual, Francisco, 227, 295n.32
Amarillas, Marqués de las (Agustín de
    Ahumada y Villalón), 158, 165,
    169
American Revolution, 192, 193, 194,
    195, 196
American Southwest. *See* Spanish
    Borderlands
Amerindians, 22
Amichel, 24
Anadarko Indians, 18
Andalucia (Spain), 22
Anegado Indians, 12
Angelina River, 40, 123
Anglo-Americans, xi, 6, 8, 195–197,
    210–216, 237, 259; as filibusters,
    235; at Pecan Point, 239; Salcedo's
    views of, 231; settlement patterns
    of, 8; views on Texas, 240
animals (indigenous), 6, 8, 11, 13, 14,
    19, 21; bison, 37–38, 87, 154
Anza, Juan Bautista de, 198
Apache Indians, 13; campaigns against,
    156–157, 160–161, 178, 181,
    184, 190–191, 197, 199; raids on
    San Antonio, 133–135, 138–139,
    145; use of horses, 15–17, 60, 62,
    64, 67, 69, 107, 130
Apachería, 146, 156
Apatzingán, Mex., 221
Aranda, Count of, 196

Xaviera de Echeverz, Ignacia, 119
Ximénez, María Antonia, 280n.17
Ximénez de Valdez, Ana María, 280n.17

Ybarbo, Gil Antonio, 186, 187
Yguaze Indians, 12, 13, 30
Yojaune Indians, 268n.59, 279n.10
Ysleta, Tex., 69
Yucatán, 23, 24, 77, 106

Zacatecas (town), 51, 53, 54, 112
Zacateco Indians, 46, 47
Zaldívar, Juan de (the elder), 47
Zaldívar, Juan de, 40, 47, 59
Zaldívar, Vicente de (the elder), 47, 59
Zaldívar, Vicente de, 59, 273n.51
Zambrano, Juan Manuel, 233, 234
Zárate, Fr. Ascencio de, 61
Zavaleta, Fr. Juan, 69, 70
Zumárraga, Fr. Juan de (bishop of Mexico), 34, 35
Zuñi Pueblos, 35, 36